Cases in Communications Law

From the Wadsworth Series in Mass Communication and Journalism

General Mass Communication

Biagi, *Media/Impact: An Introduction to Mass Media*, Ninth Edition
Hilmes, *Connections: A Broadcast History Reader*
Hilmes, *Only Connect: A Cultural History of Broadcasting in the United States*, Third Edition
Lester, *Visual Communication: Images with Messages*, Fifth Edition
Overbeck, *Major Principles of Media Law,* 2011 Edition
Straubhaar/LaRose, *Media Now: Understanding Media, Culture, and Technology*, Sixth Edition
Zelezny, *Cases in Communications Law*, Sixth Edition
Zelezny, *Communications Law: Liberties, Restraints, and the Modern Media*, Sixth Edition

Journalism

Bowles/Borden, *Creative Editing*, Sixth Edition
Hilliard, *Writing for Television, Radio, and New Media*, Tenth Edition
Kessler/McDonald, *When Words Collide: A Media Writer's Guide to Grammar and Style*, Seventh Edition
Rich, *Writing and Reporting News: A Coaching Method*, Sixth Edition

Public Relations and Advertising

Diggs-Brown, *The PR Styleguide: Formats for Public Relations Practice*, Second Edition
Drewniany/Jewler, *Creative Strategy in Advertising*, Tenth Edition
Hendrix, *Public Relations Cases*, Eighth Edition
Newsom/Haynes, *Public Relations Writing: Form and Style*, Ninth Edition
Newsom/Turk/Kruckeberg, *This Is PR: The Realities of Public Relations*, Tenth Edition

Research and Theory

Baran and Davis, *Mass Communication Theory: Foundations, Ferment, and Future*, Fifth Edition
Sparks, *Media Effects Research: A Basic Overview*, Third Edition
Wimmer and Dominick, *Mass Media Research: An Introduction*, Ninth Edition

CASES IN
COMMUNICATIONS LAW

Liberties, Restraints, and
the Modern Media

Sixth Edition

John D. Zelezny

Attorney at Law

WADSWORTH
CENGAGE Learning

Australia • Brazil • Japan • Korea • Mexico • Singapore • Spain • United Kingdom • United States

WADSWORTH
CENGAGE Learning

*Cases in Communications Law:
Liberties, Restraints, and the Modern
Media*, Sixth Edition
John D. Zelezny

Publisher: Michael Rosenberg

Development Editor: David Estrin

Assistant Editor: Jillian D'Urso

Editorial Assistant: Erin Pass

Media Editor: Jessica Badiner

Marketing Manager: Bryant Chrzan

Marketing Coordinator: Diane Macanan

Marketing Communications Manager:
Christine Dobberpuhl

Content Project Manager: Rosemary
Winfield

Art Director: Linda Helcher

Print Buyer: Justin Palmeiro

Production Service: Pre-Press PMG, Pradhiba
Kannaiyan

Compositor: Pre-Press PMG

For product information and technology assistance, contact us at
Cengage Learning Customer & Sales Support, 1-800-354-9706.

For permission to use material from this text or product,
submit all requests online at **www.cengage.com/permissions**.
Further permissions questions can be emailed to
permissionrequest@cengage.com.

Library of Congress Control Number: 2009942309

ISBN-13: 978-0-495-90297-3
ISBN-10: 0-495-90297-7

Wadsworth
20 Channel Center Street
Boston, MA 02210
USA

Cengage Learning is a leading provider of customized learning
solutions with office locations around the globe, including Singapore,
the United Kingdom, Australia, Mexico, Brazil, and Japan. Locate your
local office at: **international.cengage.com/region**.

Cengage Learning products are represented in Canada by
Nelson Education Ltd.

For your course and learning solutions, visit **www.cengage.com**

Purchase any of our products at your local college store or at our
preferred online store **www.CengageBrain.com**.

Printed in the United States of America
1 2 3 4 5 6 7 13 12 11 10 9

CONTENTS

PREFACE

In this book, I have aimed to present a wide range of cases that will familiarize students with judicial reasoning on key principles and controversies of communications law. Most of the cases are from the Supreme Court of the United States, and these cases stand as precedent that all other courts in the nation must follow. The Supreme Court, however, has not rendered decisions on all important aspects of communications law. Furthermore, trends in the law sometimes are fueled by the rulings of lower courts long before those trends are validated by the Supreme Court, if ever. Therefore, this book also contains cases from the state courts and lower federal courts in order to provide a more complete and up-to-date picture of communications law.

Some of the cases are classics from decades past; others are very recent. Several new cases in this edition represent key communications-law battlegrounds in such areas as social networking sites, access to public officials' emails, the melding of commercial and noncommercial speech, government caps on the size of media companies, and the latest wave of broadcast indecency complaints.

Because this book is intended for students in journalism, public relations, telecommunications, and other communications fields—not law school students—the judicial opinions have been thoroughly edited to focus only on substantive points of communications law. Most judicial discussion pertaining to technical issues of legal procedure has been eliminated. As a result, the edited cases in this book typically are only half the length of the original versions that are found in a law library.

Furthermore, in order to improve readability, most of the formal legal citations have been summarily omitted from these cases. Only those citations pertaining to other highly instructive or "landmark" cases have been retained. For the same reason, judicial footnotes also have been summarily edited out of the cases.

This book is intended as a companion to a narrative textbook or outline on communications law. The organization of sections follows the chapter arrangement in the textbook published by Wadsworth / Cengage Learning—*Communications Law: Liberties, Restraints, and the Modern Media,* 6th edition. But most of the cases in this book would be referred to by name, in one order or another, in virtually any textbook on communications law.

John D. Zelezny

Chapter One
INTRODUCTION

WHY STUDY CASES?

The heart and soul of American law is found in court decisions—the decisions rendered on a case-by-case basis to resolve real-life legal disputes. Other sources of law are more readily recognized, such as the U.S. Constitution. And the laws enacted by legislative and administrative bodies are organized more neatly, codified, and typically arranged by subject. But ultimately the law boils down to case decisions.

Constitutional provisions, statutes, and regulations—all these combine to make up the skeletal framework of American law. Court decisions give the framework life. The case-by-case rulings of judges ultimately determine how the other forms of law will be interpreted and applied. Even the U.S. Constitution—ingenious and eloquent document that it is—is only as powerful as the judicial interpretations of its provisions.

Court decisions influence the future because of the "doctrine of precedent." In appellate courts and some trial courts the judges' rulings are routinely embodied in written opinions that are published in sets of bound volumes. These published rulings serve as precedent that must be followed by that court and all lower courts in the same jurisdiction. If a future case presents the same legal problem, the doctrine of precedent dictates that the later case be decided in the same manner as the earlier case. Rulings of the U.S. Supreme Court are particularly significant because they serve as precedent for all other courts, state and federal. But Supreme Court cases aren't the only ones worth reading. The Supreme Court decides only a handful of communications law cases each year. Therefore, lower court decisions can add valuable insights to key trends and principles in the law.

In this book you will find a selection of case opinions from the U.S. Supreme Court, lower federal courts, and a few state courts. The cases in this volume have been selected to add depth to the principles of law discussed in a communications law textbook. These cases will help bring some of the principles to life and make them more memorable. Reading these cases also will provide scholarly insights into judicial reasoning and legal history.

HOW TO FIND CASES

More than 50,000 cases are published each year in the United States, most of them by appellate courts. The case opinions are published in sets of bound volumes called *court reports*, sometimes also referred to as *reporters*. Some of these publications are directly sanctioned by courts, in which case they are called *official* reports. But most of the court reports in the United States are published by private, commercial publishers.

Sets of case reports are published for decisions of particular courts, for all state-court decisions within a particular state, and for state-court decisions within designated regions of the country. Also available are some specialized reporters that publish only cases within broad categories of law. One of these is the *Media Law Reporter*, which contains cases pertaining to the mass communications media. Sometimes a single judicial opinion may be found in several different sets of court reports.

1

Published cases are easy to find if you have a formal citation. Every published case has at least one citation, or *cite*, indicating where the case may be located within a set of court reports. For example, the following is a citation for a U.S. Supreme Court case:

Hustler Magazine v. Falwell, 485 U.S. 46 (1988).

The first part of the citation is the name of the case. It reflects the names of the principal parties involved in the dispute, separated by the abbreviation *v.* for *versus*. At the trial level the name of the suing party, the plaintiff, is always listed first. But at the appellate level some courts will alter the original case name, if necessary, so that the appealing party is listed first—even though the appealing party might have been the defendant. In the foregoing example, defendant *Hustler Magazine* brought the appeal to the Supreme Court. The first number in the cite, *485*, is the volume number of the court reporter. The *U.S.* abbreviation refers to the title of the reporter, in this case the *United States Reports*. The number *46* is the page number. And finally, *1988* is the year in which the case was decided.

Decisions of the U.S. Supreme Court are reported in several publications. Libraries are most likely to subscribe to one of the following: the *United States Reports* (cited *U.S.*), which is the official publication; the *Supreme Court Reporter* (*S. Ct.*); and the *United States Supreme Court Reports, Lawyers' Edition* (*L. Ed.*).

Sometimes you will see a case name followed by two or more *parallel citations*. For example, the full *Hustler Magazine* citation might look like this:

Hustler Magazine v. Falwell, 485 U.S. 46, 108 S. Ct. 876, 99 L. Ed. 2d 41 (1988).

Decisions of the intermediate federal courts, the U.S. courts of appeals, are published in the *Federal Reporter* (cited *F. F.2d,* or *F.3d,* depending on the series).

Decisions of the federal district courts, when written opinions are issued, are published in the *Federal Supplement* (*F. Supp.*).

Most states have their own bound sets of reports for the opinions of state court judges. In some states separate reports are published for different levels of courts. For example, decisions of the Illinois Supreme Court are published in *Illinois Reports*, and decisions of the intermediate appellate courts are contained in *Illinois Appellate Court Reports*. However, rather than subscribe to all of these state reporters, particularly from distant states, libraries are more likely to house the regional reporters published by West Publishing Co. The regional reporters contain decisions by the states' highest courts and most states' intermediate courts of appeal for a particular multi-state geographical area. All of the regional reporters have a first and second series. In a second series, volumes are numbered beginning again at 1. The reporters and their second-series cite abbreviations are as follows:

Southern Reporter (*So.2d*)
South Eastern Reporter (*S.E.2d*)
South Western Reporter (*S.W.2d*)
North Eastern Reporter (*N.E.2d*)
North Western Reporter (*N.W.2d*)

Atlantic Reporter (*A.2d*)
Pacific Reporter (*P.2d*)

It's easy to look up a case for which you have a citation and access to the proper set of case reports. However, suppose you have no case citations but you want to locate some court cases that have addressed a particular problem in communications law. This process is more complicated and time-consuming because cases are arranged in the reporters chronologically, not by subject.

One way to find cases is to consult a legal digest. A digest is a topical compilation of case references—essentially a giant index to cases. Digests, like court reports, are published for particular jurisdictions and sometimes for individual courts within a jurisdiction. For example, if you wanted to find U.S. Supreme Court decisions on a given topic, you might consult the *U.S. Supreme Court Digest.*

Another way to find cases is by consulting a legal encyclopedia. Unlike digests, which are simply topical compilations of case citations, legal encyclopedias summarize entire fields of law in narrative form. The narrative is extensively footnoted with references to cases, and the encyclopedias are updated with periodic supplements. The two main encyclopedias are *Corpus Juris Secundum* and *American Jurisprudence 2d.* Each contains about 100 volumes, with the textual content organized alphabetically under hundreds of broad topics, such as "libel and slander" or "copyrights." Within each of these topics may be dozens or even hundreds of headings for particular legal principles or problems. One of the difficulties of finding cases through legal encyclopedias or digests is that you must first learn the organizational nomenclature used by the publishers.

Still another way to locate cases on particular issues of law is to conduct a computer database search. Legal research has become increasingly computerized, and widely used computer research services include WESTLAW, LEXIS, and FindLaw. These services offer hundreds of different databases, such as databases for U.S. Supreme Court decisions, for court decisions of a particular state, or for court decisions relating to copyright law, trademarks, or interstate commerce. An advantage of this research method is that the computer quickly retrieves cases by searching for whatever words or phrases you specify. For example, you might ask the computer to find all Supreme Court cases in which *New York Times* appears in the case name. Or, you might retrieve all cases in which the words *hidden* and *camera* appear together in a court opinion. Professional users of some legal database services pay substantial hourly search fees. However, these computer services are available on some college campuses, without hourly fees, for academic research.

LEGAL TERMS

Considerable legal terminology is necessarily encountered when reading court cases. Following is a guide to some common and important legal terms. A glossary with additional terms appears at the end of this book.

Trial courts / appellate courts. A *trial court* is the first court to handle a legal dispute. In this court evidence is presented to determine the facts of the case, and the trial judge applies the law to those facts. In an *appellate court* a panel of judges determines whether the court below made any errors in its application of the law and whether those errors warrant a different result.

Plaintiff / defendant. The *plaintiff* is the party who initiates a civil lawsuit. The party against whom a legal remedy is sought is the *defendant*.

Complaint / answer. A *complaint* is the initial court document filed by a plaintiff. It identifies the alleged legal violation and formally requests a legal remedy, such as monetary compensation. An *answer* is a defendant's formal legal response to a complaint. The answer might deny facts alleged by the plaintiff, or it might claim certain legal defenses or privileges.

Cause of action. A *cause of action* is a particular factual occurrence or circumstance that entitles a person to sue. Some cases involve multiple causes of action. For example, in the *Falwell* case, the plaintiff alleged causes of action for libel, invasion of privacy, and intentional infliction of mental distress.

Summary judgment. *Summary judgment* is a common procedure for ending a lawsuit prior to trial. A party to a lawsuit is entitled to summary judgment in his favor if there is no disputable issue of fact and established legal rules clearly dictate that he would prevail at trial.

Appellant / respondent. The party that appeals a court judgment to a higher court is the *appellant*, sometimes also called the **petitioner**. The party against whom the appeal is made is the *respondent*, sometimes also called the **appellee**.

Damages / injunction. The most common form of legal relief sought by plaintiffs is *damages*—an award of money. Another common legal remedy is an *injunction*—a court order that a defendant act, or refrain from acting, in a particular manner.

Judgment of the court. A *judgment* is the final decree of a court—the disposition of the case, the determination of which side "wins." At the appellate level, the judgment of the court usually is to **affirm** (uphold) or **reverse** (overturn) the judgment of the court below.

Opinion of the court. An *opinion* is an official, written explanation of the reasons behind the court's judgment. Opinions are generally issued for publication only by appellate courts, though some trial courts also issue written opinions. When a panel of appellate judges cannot reach agreement in a particular case, then the prevailing view is stated in a **majority opinion**. The judges who agree with the final disposition of a case, but for different reasons, may write **concurring opinions**. Judges who disagree with the final outcome of the case may write **dissenting opinions**.

U.S. District Court. The main trial court in the federal judicial system is *U.S. District Court*. At least one of these courts is located in every state.

U.S. Court of Appeals. The *Court of Appeals* is the intermediate appellate court in the federal judicial system—the next step up from district court. The nation is divided into twelve geographic *circuits*, each with one of these intermediate courts.

U.S. Supreme Court. The *Supreme Court*, with its nine justices in Washington, D.C., is the top court in the federal judicial system and the final authority on the meaning of the U.S. Constitution.

Writ of certiorari. A *writ of certiorari* is a kind of discretionary order commonly used by the U.S. Supreme Court to indicate which cases the Court will hear on appeal. If the writ is denied, this means the Court refused to hear an appeal, and the judgment of the lower court therefore stands as the final word. If the writ is granted, this means the Supreme Court has decided to hear the appeal, and the court below is ordered to send the case record up to the high court. This is also referred to as granting "cert."

HOW TO READ AND BRIEF CASES

To enhance your understanding of communications law it is important to read cases critically. This means reading carefully and analyzing each paragraph a court has written until you're sure you understand the rationale behind it. Speed-reading and skimming are techniques of relatively little benefit when it comes to reading cases. Rather, it is methodical, thoughtful reading that pays the greatest dividends.

To help make sure that you truly understand the cases you are assigned to read, and that you're prepared to discuss them in class, you may want to prepare a written "brief" of each case. A case brief is a concise summary, usually no longer than a single page, in which a judicial decision is broken into its key elements. In order to effectively brief a case, you must organize your thoughts and hone in on the facts and legal principles that were most determinative of the court's decision.

There are many methods for briefing cases. Here is a streamlined format that should prove useful for class preparation and review purposes:

Heading:	First, write the case name, the court that issued the decision, and the year of the decision.
Facts:	Summarize in your own words the essential facts that initially led to the legal conflict. Also state, in an additional sentence or two, how the case was decided in the court(s) below.
Issue:	State the legal issue or issues raised on appeal. For example, in the *Hustler* case noted earlier the issue might be stated as follows: "Whether public figure Jerry Falwell may recover damages for emotional harm allegedly caused by the publication of an offensive parody about him."
Decision:	State the disposition of the case on appeal and summarize the Court's rationale for its ruling. This is the heart of your brief; you must accurately and concisely explain *why* the court arrived at its decision.
Rule of law:	In one final sentence, state the legal rule or principle that can be derived from the case to guide future conduct. For example, the rule from the *Hustler* case might be stated as follows: "The First Amendment prohibits public persons from recovering damages for intentional infliction of mental distress via publication unless the plaintiff can show that the publication contained false statements of fact that were made with actual malice."

Chapter Two
THE FIRST AMENDMENT

This chapter contains cases that speak to important, general principles of First Amendment law. By no means do these cases illustrate all the guidelines that courts use in applying the First Amendment. However, from the standpoint of modern communicators, these selected cases do illustrate some of the judicial precepts that are employed over and over again to resolve First Amendment conflicts.

Near v. Minnesota, the first case presented, is a landmark U.S. Supreme Court case from 1931. The case established the doctrine against prior restraints on speech.

Miami Herald v. Tornillo posed the interesting question of whether it is constitutionally permissible for government to require that newspapers carry certain kinds of speech in the interest of balance and fairness. Does such a requirement further First Amendment ideals, or abridge them?

Simon & Schuster v. Crime Victims Board is a 1992 case in which the Supreme Court made it clear that financial burdens may amount to abridgments of speech, within the meaning of the Constitution.

Heffron v. Int. Soc. for Krishna Consciousness is one of the leading precedents concerning "time, place, and manner" restrictions and the extent to which they are more likely to be upheld than restrictions on the content of speech.

Cincinnati v. Discovery Network, Inc. is a 1993 case that is instructive to compare with *Heffron*. This case illustrates why most regulations on speech cannot qualify as "time, place, and manner" restrictions.

First National Bank v. Bellotti established that business corporations, just like individuals or media organizations, have wide latitude to speak out on public issues. This is distinguished from supporting particular *candidates*, where the danger of corruption justifies restrictions.

McIntyre v. Ohio Elections Commission is a leading decision concerning the right of individuals or organizations to engage in anonymous political speech–an American tradition.

Kincaid v. Gibson is a relatively recent case that's instructive on the "public forum" concept and the free-speech rights of the collegiate press.

And *Morse v. Frederick*, though not exactly a mass media case, shows how the Supreme Court under Chief Justice Roberts is divided over the extent of students' speech rights and the deference that should be accorded school officials.

NEAR V. MINNESOTA
Supreme Court of the United States, 1931
283 U.S. 697

Chief Justice HUGHES delivered the opinion of the Court.

Chapter 285 of the Session Laws of Minnesota for the year 1925 provides for the abatement, as a public nuisance, of a "malicious, scandalous, and defamatory newspaper, magazine, or other periodical." Section one of the Act is as follows:

> "Section 1. Any person who, as an individual, or as a member or employee of a firm, or association or organization, or as an officer, director, member, or employee of a corporation, shall be engaged in the business of regularly or customarily producing, publishing, or circulating, having in possession, selling, or giving away
> (a) an obscene, lewd, and lascivious newspaper, magazine, or other periodical, or
> (b) a malicious, scandalous, and defamatory newspaper, magazine, or other periodical, is guilty of a nuisance, and all persons guilty of such nuisance may be enjoined, as hereinafter provided...."

Under this statute, clause (b), the County Attorney of Hennepin County brought this action to enjoin the publication of what was described as a "malicious, scandalous, and defamatory newspaper, magazine, and periodical," known as *The Saturday Press,* published by the defendants in the city of Minneapolis. The complaint alleged that the defendants, on September 24, 1927, and on eight subsequent dates in October and November, 1927, published and circulated editions of that periodical which were "largely devoted to malicious, scandalous, and defamatory articles." ...

Without attempting to summarize the contents of the voluminous exhibits attached to the complaint, we deem it sufficient to say that the articles charged in substance that a Jewish gangster was in control of gambling, bootlegging, and racketeering in Minneapolis, and that law-enforcing officers and agencies were not energetically performing their duties. Most of the charges were directed against the Chief of Police; he was charged with gross neglect of duty, illicit relations with gangsters, and with participation in graft. The County Attorney was charged with knowing the existing conditions and with failure to take adequate measures to remedy them. The Mayor was accused of inefficiency and dereliction. One member of the grand jury was stated to be in sympathy with the gangsters....

The District Court made findings of fact, which followed the allegations of the complaint and found in general terms that the editions in question were "chiefly devoted to malicious, scandalous, and defamatory articles," concerning the individuals named. The court further found that the defendants through these publications "did engage in the business of regularly and customarily producing, publishing, and circulating a malicious, scandalous, and defamatory newspaper," and that "the said publication" "under said name of *The Saturday Press,* or any other name, constitutes a public nuisance under the laws of the State." Judgment was thereupon entered adjudging that "the newspaper, magazine, and periodical known as *The Saturday Press,*" as a public nuisance, "be and is hereby abated." The judgment perpetually enjoined the defendants "from producing, editing, publishing, circulating, having in their possession, selling, or giving away any publication whatsoever which is a malicious, scandalous, or defamatory newspaper, as defined by law," and also "from further conducting said nuisance under the name and title of said *The Saturday Press* or any other name or title."...

From the judgment as thus affirmed, the defendant Near appeals to this Court.

This statute, for the suppression as a public nuisance of a newspaper or periodical, is unusual, if not unique, and raises questions of grave importance transcending the local interests involved in the particular action. It is no longer open to doubt that the liberty of the press, and of speech, is within the liberty safeguarded by the due process clause of the Fourteenth Amendment from invasion by state action. It was found impossible to conclude that this essential personal liberty of the citizen was left unprotected by the general guaranty of fundamental rights of person and property. *Gitlow v. New York,* 268 U.S. 652, 666.... Liberty, in each of its phases, has its history and connotation and, in the present instance, the inquiry is as to the historic conception of the liberty of the press and whether the statute under review violates the essential attributes of that liberty....

.... The object of the statute is not punishment, in the ordinary sense, but suppression of the offending newspaper or periodical. The reason for the enactment, as the state court has said, is that prosecutions to enforce penal statutes for libel do not result in "efficient repression or suppression of the evils of scandal." Describing the business of publication as a public nuisance does not obscure the substance of the proceeding that the statute authorizes. It is the continued publication of scandalous and defamatory matter that constitutes the business and the declared nuisance. In the case of public officers, it is the reiteration of charges of official misconduct, and the fact that the newspaper or periodical is principally devoted to that purpose, that exposes it to suppression. In the present instance, the proof was that nine editions of the newspaper or periodical in question were published on successive dates, and that they were chiefly devoted to charges against public officers and in relation to the prevalence and protection of crime. In such a case, these officers are not left to their ordinary remedy in a suit for libel, or the authorities to a prosecution for criminal libel. Under this statute, a publisher of a newspaper or periodical, undertaking to conduct a campaign to expose and to censure official derelictions, and devoting his publication principally to that purpose, must face not simply the possibility of a verdict against him in a suit or prosecution for libel, but a determination that his newspaper or periodical is a public nuisance to be abated, and that this abatement and suppression will follow unless he is prepared with legal evidence to prove the truth of the charges and also to satisfy the court that, in addition to being true, the matter was published with good motives and for justifiable ends.

This suppression is accomplished by enjoining publication and that restraint is the object and effect of the statute.

.... The statute not only operates to suppress the offending newspaper or periodical but to put the publisher under an effective censorship. When a newspaper or periodical is found to be "malicious, scandalous, and defamatory," and is suppressed as such, resumption of publication is punishable as a contempt of court by fine or imprisonment. Thus, where a newspaper or periodical has been suppressed because of the circulation of charges against public officers of official misconduct, it would seem to be clear that the renewal of the publication of such charges would constitute a contempt and that the judgment would lay a permanent restraint upon the publisher, to escape which he must satisfy the court as to the character of a new publication. Whether he would be permitted again to publish matter deemed to be derogatory to the same or other public officers would depend upon the court's ruling. In the present instance the judgment restrained the defendants from "publishing, circulating, having in their possession, selling, or giving away any publication whatsoever which is a malicious, scandalous, or defamatory newspaper, as defined by law." The law gives no definition except that covered by the words "scandalous and defamatory," and publications charging official misconduct are of that class....

If we cut through mere details of procedure, the operation and effect of the statute in substance is that public authorities may bring the owner or publisher of a newspaper or periodical before a judge upon a charge of conducting a business of publishing scandalous and defamatory matter—in particular that the matter consists of charges against public officers of official dereliction—and unless the owner or publisher is able and disposed to bring competent evidence to satisfy the judge that the charges are true and are published with good motives and for justifiable ends, his newspaper or periodical is suppressed and further publication is made punishable as a contempt. This is of the essence of censorship.

The question is whether a statute authorizing such proceedings in restraint of publication is consistent with the conception of the liberty of the press as historically conceived and guaranteed. In determining the extent of the constitutional protection, it has been generally, if not universally, considered that it is the chief purpose of the guaranty to prevent previous restraints upon publication. The struggle in England, directed against the legislative power of the licenser, resulted in renunciation of the censorship of the press. The liberty deemed to be established was thus described by Blackstone: "The liberty of the press is indeed essential to the nature of a free state; but this consists in laying no previous restraints upon publications, and not in freedom from censure for criminal matter when published. Every freeman has an undoubted right to lay what sentiments he pleases before the public; to forbid this, is to destroy the freedom of the press; but if he publishes what is improper, mischievous, or illegal, he must take the consequence of his own temerity."

The criticism upon Blackstone's statement has not been because immunity from previous restraint upon publication has not been regarded as deserving of special emphasis, but chiefly because that immunity cannot be deemed to exhaust the conception of the liberty guaranteed by [*715] state and federal constitutions. The point of criticism has been "that the mere exemption from previous restraints cannot be all that is secured by the constitutional provisions"; and that "the liberty of the press might be rendered a mockery and a delusion, and the phrase itself a by-word, if, while every man was at liberty to publish what he pleased, the public authorities might nevertheless punish him for harmless publications." But it is recognized that punishment for the abuse of the liberty accorded to the press is essential to the protection of the public, and that the common law rules that subject the libeler to responsibility for the public offense, as well as for the private injury, are not abolished by the protection extended in our constitutions....

The objection has also been made that the principle as to immunity from previous restraint is stated too broadly, if every such restraint is deemed to be prohibited. That is undoubtedly true; the protection even as to previous restraint is not absolutely unlimited. But the limitation has been recognized only in exceptional cases: "When a nation is at war many things that might be said in time of peace are such a hindrance to its effort that their utterance will not be endured so long as men fight and that no Court could regard them as protected by any constitutional right." *Schenck v. United States,* 249 U.S. 47, 52. No one would question but that a government might prevent actual obstruction to its recruiting service or the publication of the sailing dates of transports or the number and location of troops. On similar grounds, the primary requirements of decency may be enforced against obscene publications. The security of the community life may be protected against incitements to acts of violence and the overthrow by force of orderly government. The constitutional guaranty of free speech does not "protect a man from an injunction against uttering words that may have all the effect of force." *Gompers v. Buck Stove & Range Co.,* 221 U.S. 418, 439. These limitations are not applicable here....

The exceptional nature of its limitations places in a strong light the general conception that liberty of the press, historically considered and taken up by the Federal Constitution, has meant, principally although not exclusively, immunity from previous restraints or censorship. The conception of the liberty of the press in this country had broadened with the exigencies of the colonial period and with the efforts to secure freedom from oppressive administration. That liberty was especially cherished for the immunity it afforded from previous restraint of the publication of censure of public officers and charges of official misconduct....

.... Some degree of abuse is inseparable from the proper use of everything, and in no instance is this more true than in that of the press. It has accordingly been decided by the practice of the States, that it is better to leave a few of its noxious branches to their luxuriant growth, than, by pruning them away, to injure the vigor of those yielding the proper fruits. And can the wisdom of this policy be doubted by any who reflect that to the press alone, checkered as it is with abuses, the world is indebted for all the triumphs which have been gained by reason and humanity over error and oppression; who reflect that to the same beneficient source the United States owe much of the rights which conducted them to the ranks of a free and independent nation, and which have improved their political system into a shape so auspicious to their happiness? Had 'Sedition Acts,' forbidding every publication that might bring the constituted agents into contempt or disrepute, or that might excite the hatred of the people against the authors of unjust or pernicious measures, been uniformly enforced against the press, might not the United States have been languishing at this day under the infirmities of a sickly Confederation? Might they not, possibly, be miserable colonies, groaning under a foreign yoke?"

The fact that for approximately one hundred and fifty years there has been almost an entire absence of attempts to impose previous restraints upon publications relating to the malfeasance of public officers is significant of the deep-seated conviction that such restraints would violate constitutional right. Public officers, whose character and conduct remain open to debate and free discussion in the press, find their remedies for false accusations in actions under libel laws providing for redress and punishment, and not in proceedings to restrain the publication of newspapers and periodicals....

The importance of this immunity has not lessened. While reckless assaults upon public men, and efforts to bring obloquy upon those who are endeavoring faithfully to discharge official duties, exert a baleful influence and deserve the severest condemnation in public opinion, it cannot be said that this abuse is greater, and it is believed to be less, than that which characterized the period in which our institutions took shape. Meanwhile, the administration of government has become more complex, the opportunities for malfeasance and corruption have multiplied, crime has grown to most serious proportions, and the danger of its protection by unfaithful officials and of the impairment of the fundamental security of life and property by criminal alliances and official neglect, emphasizes the primary need of a vigilant and courageous press, especially in great cities. The fact that the liberty of the press may be abused by miscreant purveyors of scandal does not make any the less necessary the immunity of the press from previous restraint in dealing with official misconduct. Subsequent punishment for such abuses as may exist is the appropriate remedy, consistent with constitutional privilege....

The statute in question cannot be justified by reason of the fact that the publisher is permitted to show, before injunction issues, that the matter published is true and is published with good motives and for justifiable ends. If such a statute, authorizing suppression and injunction on such a basis, is constitutionally valid, it would be equally permissible for the legislature to provide that at any time the publisher of any newspaper could be brought before a court, or even an administrative officer (as the constitutional protection may not be regarded as resting on mere procedural details) and required to produce proof of the truth of his publication, or of what he intended to publish, and of his motives, or stand enjoined. If this can be done, the legislature may provide machinery for determining in the complete exercise of its discretion what are justifiable ends and restrain publication accordingly. And it would be but a step to a complete system of censorship. The recognition of authority to impose previous restraint upon publication in order to protect the community against the circulation of charges of misconduct, and especially of official misconduct, necessarily would carry with it the admission of the authority of the censor against which the constitutional barrier was erected. The preliminary freedom, by virtue of the very reason for its existence, does not depend, as this Court has said, on proof of truth.

Equally unavailing is the insistence that the statute is designed to prevent the circulation of scandal, which tends to disturb the public peace and to provoke assaults and the commission of crime. Charges of reprehensible conduct, and in particular of official malfeasance, unquestionably create a public scandal, but the theory of the constitutional guaranty is that even a more serious public evil would be caused by authority to prevent publication....

For these reasons we hold the statute, so far as it authorized the proceedings in this action under clause (b) of section one, to be an infringement of the liberty of the press guaranteed by the Fourteenth Amendment. We should add that this decision rests upon the operation and effect of the statute, without regard to the question of the truth of the charges contained in the particular periodical. The fact that the public officers named in this case, and those associated with the charges of official dereliction, may be deemed to be impeccable, cannot affect the conclusion that the statute imposes an unconstitutional restraint upon publication.

Judgment reversed.

MIAMI HERALD PUBLISHING CO. V. TORNILLO

Supreme Court of the United States, 1974
418 U.S. 241

Chief Justice BURGER delivered the opinion of the Court.

The issue in this case is whether a state statute granting a political candidate a right to equal space to reply to criticism and attacks on his record by a newspaper violates the guarantees of a free press.

I

In the fall of 1972, appellee, Executive Director of the Classroom Teachers Association ... was a candidate for the Florida House of Representatives. On September 20, 1972, and again on September 29, 1972, appellant printed editorials critical of appellee's candidacy. In response to these editorials appellee demanded that appellant print verbatim his replies, defending the role of the Classroom Teachers Association and the organization's accomplishments for the citizens of Dade County. Appellant declined to print the appellee's replies, and appellee brought suit in Circuit Court, Dade County, seeking declaratory and injunctive relief and actual and punitive damages in excess of $ 5,000. The action was premised on Florida Statute § 104.38 (1973), a "right of reply" statute which provides that if a candidate for nomination or election is assailed regarding his personal character or official record by any newspaper, the candidate has the right to demand that the newspaper print, free of cost to the candidate, any reply the candidate may make to the newspaper's charges. The reply must appear in as conspicuous a place and in the same kind of type as the charges which prompted the reply, provided it does not take up more space than the charges. Failure to comply with the statute constitutes a first-degree misdemeanor.

Appellant sought a declaration that §104.38 was unconstitutional. After an emergency hearing requested by appellee, the Circuit Court denied injunctive relief because, absent special circumstances, no injunction could properly issue against the commission of a crime, and held that § 104.38 was unconstitutional as an infringement on the freedom of the press under the First and Fourteenth Amendments to the Constitution. The Circuit Court concluded that dictating what a newspaper must print was no different from dictating what it must not print. The Circuit Judge viewed the statute's vagueness as serving "to restrict and stifle protected expression." Appellee's cause was dismissed with prejudice.

... [T]he Florida Supreme Court [held] that § 104.38 did not violate constitutional guarantees. It held that free speech was enhanced and not abridged by the Florida right-of-reply statute, which in that court's view, furthered the "broad societal interest in the free flow of information to the public." It also held that the statute is not impermissibly vague; the statute informs "those who are subject to it as to what conduct on their part will render them liable to its penalties."...

III

A

The challenged statute creates a right to reply to press criticism of a candidate for nomination or election. The statute was enacted in 1913, and this is only the second recorded case decided under its provisions.

Appellant contends the statute is void on its face because it purports to regulate the content of a newspaper in violation of the First Amendment. Alternatively it is urged that the statute is void for vagueness since no editor could know exactly what words would call the statute into operation. It is also contended that the statute fails to distinguish between critical comment which is and which is not defamatory.

B

The appellee and supporting advocates of an enforceable right of access to the press vigorously argue that government has an obligation to ensure that a wide variety of views reach the public…. It is urged that at the time the First Amendment to the Constitution was ratified in 1791 as part of our Bill of Rights, the press was broadly representative of the people it was serving. While many of the newspapers were intensely partisan and narrow in their views, the press collectively presented a broad range of opinions to readers. Entry into publishing was inexpensive; pamphlets and books provided meaningful alternatives to the organized press for the expression of unpopular ideas and often treated events and expressed views not covered by conventional newspapers. A true marketplace of ideas existed in which there was relatively easy access to the channels of communication.

Access advocates submit that although newspapers of the present are superficially similar to those of 1791 the press of today is in reality very different from that known in the early years of our national existence. In the past half century a communications revolution has seen the introduction of radio and television into our lives, the promise of a global community through the use of communications satellites, and the specter of a "wired" nation by means of an expanding cable television network with two-way capabilities.

The printed press, it is said, has not escaped the effects of this revolution. Newspapers have become big business and there are far fewer of them to serve a larger literate population. Chains of newspapers, national newspapers, national wire and news services, and one-newspaper towns, are the dominant features of a press that has become noncompetitive and enormously powerful and influential in its capacity to manipulate popular opinion and change the course of events. Major metropolitan newspapers have collaborated to establish news services national in scope. Such national news organizations provide syndicated "interpretive reporting" as well as syndicated features and commentary, all of which can serve as part of the new school of "advocacy journalism."

The elimination of competing newspapers in most of our large cities, and the concentration of control of media that results from the only newspapers being owned by the same interests which own a television station and a radio station, are important components of this trend toward concentration of control of outlets to inform the public.

The result of these vast changes has been to place in a few hands the power to inform the American people and shape public opinion. Much of the editorial opinion and commentary that is printed is that of syndicated columnists distributed nationwide and, as a result, we are told, on national and world issues there tends to be a homogeneity of editorial opinion, commentary, and interpretive analysis. The abuses of bias and manipulative reportage are, likewise, said to be the result of the vast accumulations of unreviewable power in the modern media empires. In effect, it is claimed, the public has lost any ability to respond or to contribute in a meaningful way to the debate on issues. The monopoly of the means of communication allows for little or no critical analysis of the media except in professional journals of very limited readership....

Appellee cites the report of the Commission on Freedom of the Press, chaired by Robert M. Hutchins, in which it was stated, as long ago as 1947, that "[the] right of free public expression has ... lost its earlier reality."

The obvious solution, which was available to dissidents at an earlier time when entry into publishing was relatively inexpensive, today would be to have additional newspapers. But the same economic factors that have caused the disappearance of vast numbers of metropolitan newspapers, have made entry into the marketplace of ideas served by the print media almost impossible. It is urged that the claim of newspapers to be "surrogates for the public" carries with it a concomitant fiduciary obligation to account for that stewardship. From this premise it is reasoned that the only effective way to insure fairness and accuracy and to provide for some accountability is for government to take affirmative action. The First Amendment interest of the public in being informed is said to be in peril because the "marketplace of ideas" is today a monopoly controlled by the owners of the market....

IV

However much validity may be found in these arguments, at each point the implementation of a remedy such as an enforceable right of access necessarily calls for some mechanism, either governmental or consensual. If it is governmental coercion, this at once brings about a confrontation with the express provisions of the First Amendment and the judicial gloss on that Amendment developed over the years.

... A responsible press is an undoubtedly desirable goal, but press responsibility is not mandated by the Constitution and like many other virtues it cannot be legislated.

Appellee's argument that the Florida statute does not amount to a restriction of appellant's right to speak because "the statute in question here has not prevented the *Miami Herald* from saying anything it wished" begs the core question. Compelling editors or publishers to publish that which "'reason' tells them should not be published" is what is at issue in this case. The Florida statute operates as a command in the same sense as a statute or regulation forbidding appellant to publish specified matter. Governmental restraint on publishing need not fall into familiar or traditional patterns to be subject to constitutional limitations on governmental powers. The Florida statute exacts a penalty on the basis of the content of a newspaper. The first phase of the penalty resulting from the compelled printing of a reply is exacted in terms of the cost in printing and composing time and materials and in taking up space that could be devoted to other material the newspaper may have preferred to print. It is correct, as appellee contends, that a newspaper is not subject to the finite technological limitations of time that confront a broadcaster but it is not correct to say that, as an economic reality, a newspaper can proceed to infinite expansion of its column space to accommodate the replies that a government agency determines or a statute commands the readers should have available.

Faced with the penalties that would accrue to any newspaper that published news or commentary arguably within the reach of the right-of-access statute, editors might well conclude that the safe course is to avoid controversy. Therefore, under the operation of the Florida statute, political and electoral coverage would be blunted or reduced. Government-enforced right of access inescapably "dampens the vigor and limits the variety of public debate."...

Even if a newspaper would face no additional costs to comply with a compulsory access law and would not be forced to forgo publication of news or opinion by the inclusion of a reply, the Florida statute fails to clear the barriers of the First Amendment because of its intrusion into the function of editors. A newspaper is more than a passive receptacle or conduit for news, comment, and advertising. The choice of material to go into a newspaper, the decisions made as to limitations on the size and content of the paper, and treatment of public issues and public officials—whether fair or unfair—constitute the exercise of editorial control and judgment. It has yet to be demonstrated how governmental regulation of this crucial process can be exercised consistent with First Amendment guarantees of a free press as they have evolved to this time. Accordingly, the judgment of the Supreme Court of Florida is reversed.

SIMON & SCHUSTER V. CRIME VICTIMS BOARD
Supreme Court of the United States, 1991
502 U.S. 105

Justice O'CONNOR delivered the opinion of the Court.

New York's "Son of Sam" law requires that an accused or convicted criminal's income from works describing his crime be deposited in an escrow account. These funds are then made available to the victims of the crime and the criminal's other creditors. We consider whether this statute is consistent with the First Amendment.

I

A

In the summer of 1977, New York was terrorized by a serial killer popularly known as the Son of Sam. The hunt for the Son of Sam received considerable publicity, and by the time David Berkowitz was identified as the killer and apprehended, the rights to his story were worth a substantial amount. Berkowitz's chance to profit from his notoriety while his victims and their families remained uncompensated did not escape the notice of New York's Legislature. The State quickly enacted the statute as issue, NY Exec Law § 632-a.

The statute was intended to "ensure that monies received by the criminal under such circumstances shall first be made available to recompense the victims of that crime for their loss and suffering." As the author of the statute explained, "It is abhorrent to one's sense of justice and decency that an individual ... can expect to receive large sums of money—while five people are dead, [and] other people were injured as a result of his conduct."

The Son of Sam law, as later amended, requires any entity contracting with an accused or convicted person for a depiction of the crime to submit a copy of the contract to respondent Crime Victims Board, and to turn over any income under that contract to the Board. This requirement applies to all such contracts in any medium of communication....

Subsection (10) broadly defines "person convicted of a crime" to include "any person convicted of a crime in this state either by entry of a plea of guilty or by conviction after trial *and any person who has voluntarily and intelligently admitted the commission of a crime for which such person is not prosecuted.*" (emphasis added). Thus a person who has never been accused or convicted of a crime in the ordinary sense, but who admits in a book or other work to having committed a crime, is within the statute's coverage.

Since its enactment in 1977, the Son of Sam law has been invoked only a handful of times. As might be expected, the individuals whose profits the Board has sought to escrow have all become well known for having committed highly publicized crime….

This case began in 1986, when the Board first became aware of the contract between petitioner Simon & Schuster and admitted organized crime figure Henry Hill.

B

Looking back from the safety of the Federal Witness Protection Program, Henry Hill recalled: "At the age of twelve my ambition was to be a gangster. To be a wiseguy. To me being a wiseguy was better than being president of the United States." Whatever one might think of Hill, at the very least it can be said that he realized his dreams. After a career spanning twenty-five years, Hill admitted engineering some of the most daring crimes of his day, including the 1978-79 Boston College basketball point-shaving scandal, and the theft of $6 million from Lufthansa Airlines in 1978, the largest successful cash robbery in American history….

Hill was arrested in 1980. In exchange for immunity from prosecution, he testified against many of his former colleagues….

In August 1981, Hill entered into a contract with author Nicholas Pileggi for the production of a book about Hill's life. The following month, Hill and Pileggi signed a publishing agreement with Simon & Schuster. Under the agreement, Simon & Schuster agreed to make payments to both Hill and Pileggi….

The result of Hill and Pileggi's collaboration was *Wiseguy,* which was published in January 1986. The book depicts, in colorful detail, the day-to-day existence of organized crime, primarily in Hill's first-person narrative. Throughout *Wiseguy,* Hill frankly admits to having participated in an astonishing variety of crimes….

Wiseguy was reviewed favorably: *The Washington Post* called it an "amply detailed and entirely fascinating book that amounts to a piece of revisionist history," while *New York Daily News* columnist Jimmy Breslin named it "the best book on crime in America ever written." The book was also a commercial success: Within nineteen months of its publication, more than a million copies were in print….

C

… The [Crime Victims] Board determined that *Wiseguy* was covered by § 632-a of the Executive Law, that Simon & Schuster had violated the law by failing to turn over its contract with Hill to the Board and by making payments to Hill, and that all money owed to Hill under the contract had to be turned over to the Board to be held in escrow for the victims of Hill's crimes….

Simon & Schuster brought suit … seeking a declaration that the Son of Sam law violates the First Amendment and an injunction barring the statute's enforcement….

II

A

A statute is presumptively inconsistent with the First Amendment if it imposes a financial burden on speakers because of the content of their speech. As we emphasized in invalidating a content-based magazine tax, "official scrutiny of the content of publications as the basis for imposing a tax is entirely incompatible with the First Amendment's guarantee of freedom of the press." *Arkansas Writers' Project, Inc. v. Ragland,* 481 U.S. 221 (1987).

... It is but one manifestation of a far broader principle: "Regulations which permit the Government to discriminate on the basis of the content of the message cannot be tolerated under the First Amendment." ...

The Son of Sam law is such a content-based statute. It singles out income derived from expressive activity for a burden the State places on no other income, and it is directed only at works with a specified content. Whether the First Amendment "speaker" is considered to be Henry Hill, whose income the statute places in escrow because of the story he has told, or Simon & Schuster, which can publish books about crime with the assistance of only those criminals willing to forgo renumeration for at least five years, the statute plainly imposes a financial disincentive only on speech of a particular content....

... In order to justify such differential treatment, "the State must show that its regulation is necessary to serve a compelling state interest and is narrowly drawn to achieve that end."

B

The Board disclaims, as it must, any state interest in suppressing descriptions of crime out of solicitude for the sensibilities of readers. As we have often had occasion to repeat, "'[T]he fact that society may find speech offensive is not a sufficient reason for suppressing it. Indeed, if it is the speaker's opinion that gives offense, that consequence is a reason for according it constitutional protection.'" *Hustler Magazine, Inc. v. Falwell,* 485 U.S. 46 (1988). "If there is a bedrock principle underlying the First Amendment, it is that the Government may not prohibit the expression of an idea simply because society finds the idea itself offensive or disagreeable.'" [quoting *Texas v. Johnson,* 491 U.S. 397 (1989), in which the Court overturned the conviction of a man who had conveyed his political view by burning an American flag]....

There can belittle doubt, on the other hand, that the State has a compelling interest in ensuring that victims of crime are compensated by those who harm them....

The State likewise has an undisputed compelling interest in ensuring that criminals do not profit from their crimes....

The Board attempts to define the State's interest more narrowly, as "ensuring that criminals do not profit from storytelling about their crimes before their victims have a meaningful opportunity to be compensated for their injuries." Here the Board is on far shakier ground. The Board cannot explain why the State should have any greater interest in compensating victims from the proceeds of such "storytelling" than from any of the criminal's other assets. Nor can the Board offer any justification for a distinction between this expressive activity and any other activity in connection with its interest in transferring the fruits of crime from criminals to their victims. Thus even if the State can be said to have an interest in classifying a criminal's assets in this manner, that interest is hardly compelling....

In short, the State has a compelling interest in compensating victims from the fruits of the crime, but little in any interest in limiting such compensation to the proceeds of the wrongdoer's speech about the crime....

III

The Federal Government and many of the States have enacted statutes designed to serve purposes similar to that served by the Son of Sam law. Some of these statutes may be quite different from New York's, and we have no occasion to determine the constitutionality of these other laws. We conclude simply that in the Son of Sam law, New York has singled our speech on a particular subject for a financial burden that it places on no other speech and no other income. The State's interest in compensating victims from the fruits of crime is a compelling one, but the Son of Sam law is not narrowly tailored to advance that objective. As a result, the statute is inconsistent with the First Amendment.

The judgment of the Court of Appeals is accordingly reversed.

HEFFRON V. INT. SOC. FOR KRISHNA CONSCIOUSNESS
Supreme Court of the United States, 1981
452 U.S. 640

Justice WHITE delivered the opinion of the Court.

The question presented for review is whether a State, consistent with the First and Fourteenth Amendments, may require a religious organization desiring to distribute and sell religious literature and to solicit donations at a state fair to conduct those activities only at an assigned location within the fairgrounds even though application of the rule limits the religious practices of the organization.

I

Each year, the Minnesota Agricultural Society (Society), a public corporation organized under the laws of Minnesota, operates a State Fair on a 125-acre state-owned tract located in St. Paul, Minn.... During the past five years, the average total attendance for the twelve-day Fair has been 1,320,000 persons. The average daily attendance on weekdays has been 115,000 persons and on Saturdays and Sundays 160,000.

... [T]he Society promulgated Minnesota State Fair Rule 6.05 which provides in relevant part that

> "[s]ale or distribution of any merchandise, including printed or written material except under license issued [by] the Society and/or from a duly-licensed location, shall be a misdemeanor."

As Rule 6.05 is construed and applied by the Society, "all persons, groups, or firms which desire to sell, exhibit, or distribute materials during the annual State Fair must do so only from fixed locations on the fairgrounds." Although the Rule does not prevent organizational representatives from walking about the fairgrounds and communicating in face-to-face discussions, it does require that any exhibitor conduct its sales, distribution, and fund solicitation operations from a booth rented from the Society. Space in the fairgrounds is rented to all comers in a nondiscriminatory fashion on a first-come, first-served basis with the rental charge based on the size and location of the booth. The Rule applies alike to nonprofit, charitable, and commercial enterprises.

One day prior to the opening of the 1977 Minnesota State Fair, respondents International Society for Krishna Consciousness, Inc. (ISKCON), an international religious society espousing the views of the Krishna religion … filed suit against numerous state officials seeking a declaration that Rule 6.05, both on its face and as applied, violated respondents' rights under the First Amendment, and seeking injunctive relief prohibiting enforcement of the Rule against ISKCON and its members…. [T]he trial court granted the state officials' motion for summary judgment, upholding the constitutionality of Rule 6.05….

On appeal, the Minnesota Supreme Court reversed ….

II

The State does not dispute that the oral and written dissemination of the Krishnas' religious views and doctrines is protected by the First Amendment….

It is also common ground, however, that the First Amendment does not guarantee the right to communicate one's views at all times and places or in any manner that may be desired…. As the Minnesota Supreme Court recognized, the activities of ISKCON, like those of others protected by the First Amendment, are subject to reasonable time, place, and manner restrictions…. The issue here … is whether Rule 6.05 is a permissible restriction on the place and manner of communicating the views of the Krishna religion…

A major criterion for a valid time, place, and manner restriction is that the restriction "may not be based upon either the content or subject matter of speech." Rule 6.05 qualifies in this respect, since … the Rule applies evenhandedly to all who wish to distribute and sell written materials or to solicit funds. No person or organization, whether commercial or charitable, is permitted to engage in such activities except from a booth rented for those purposes.

Nor does Rule 6.05 suffer from the more covert forms of discrimination that may result when arbitrary discretion is vested in some governmental authority. The method of allocating space is a straightforward first-come, first-served system. The Rule is not open to the kind of arbitrary application that this Court has condemned as inherently inconsistent with a valid time, place, and manner regulation because such discretion has the potential for becoming a means of suppressing a particular point of view.

A valid time, place, and manner regulation must also "serve a significant governmental interest." Here, the principal justification asserted by the State in support of Rule 6.05 is the need to maintain the orderly movement of the crowd given the large number of exhibitors and persons attending the Fair.

The fairgrounds comprise a relatively small area of 125 acres, the bulk of which is covered by permanent buildings, temporary structures, parking lots, and connecting thoroughfares…. Because the Fair attracts large crowds, it is apparent that the State's interest in the orderly movement and control of such an assembly of persons is a substantial consideration.

As a general matter, it is clear that a State's interest in protecting the "safety and convenience" of persons using a public forum is a valid governmental objective. Furthermore, consideration of a forum's special attributes is relevant to the constitutionality of a regulation since the significance of the governmental interest must be assessed in light of the characteristic nature and function of the particular forum involved. This observation bears particular import in the present case since respondents make a number of analogies between the fairgrounds and city streets which have "immemorially been held in trust for the use of the public and … have been used for purposes of assembly, communicating thoughts between citizens, and discussing public questions." But it is clear that there are significant differences between a street and the fairgrounds. A street is continually open, often uncongested, and constitutes not only a necessary conduit in the daily affairs of a locality's citizens, but also a place where people may enjoy the open air or the company of friends and neighbors in a relaxed environment. The Minnesota Fair, as described above, is a temporary event attracting great numbers of visitors who come to the event for a short period to see and experience the host of exhibits and attractions at the Fair. The flow of the crowd and demands of safety are more pressing in the context of the Fair….

The Minnesota Supreme Court recognized that the State's interest in the orderly movement of a large crowd and in avoiding congestion was substantial and that Rule 6.05 furthered that interest significantly. Nevertheless, the Minnesota Supreme Court declared that the case did not turn on the "importance of the state's undeniable interest in preventing the widespread disorder that would surely exist if no regulation such as Rule 6.05 were in effect" but upon the significance of the State's interest in avoiding whatever disorder would likely result from granting members of ISKCON an exemption from the Rule. Approaching the case in this way, the court concluded that although some disruption would occur from such an exemption, it was not of sufficient concern to warrant confining the Krishnas to a booth….

As we see it, the Minnesota Supreme Court took too narrow a view of the State's interest in avoiding congestion and maintaining the orderly movement of fair patrons on the fairgrounds. The justification for the Rule should not be measured by the disorder that would result from granting an exemption solely to ISKCON….

… The court recognized that some disorder would inevitably result from exempting the Krishnas from the Rule. Obviously, there would be a much larger threat to the State's interest in crowd control if all other religious, nonreligious, and noncommercial organizations could likewise move freely about the fairgrounds distributing and selling literature and soliciting funds at will.

Given these considerations, we hold that the State's interest in confining distribution, selling, and fund solicitation activities to fixed locations is sufficient to satisfy the requirement that a place or manner restriction must serve a substantial state interest….

For Rule 6.05 to be valid as a place and manner restriction, it must also be sufficiently clear that alternative forums for the expression of respondents' protected speech exist despite the effects of the Rule. Rule 6.05 is not vulnerable on this ground. First, the Rule does not prevent ISKCON from [giving gifts and seeking contributions] anywhere outside the fairgrounds. More importantly, the Rule has not been shown to deny access within the forum in question. Here, the Rule does not exclude ISKCON from the fairgrounds, nor does it deny that organization the right to conduct any desired activity at some point within the forum. Its members may mingle with the crowd and orally propagate their views. The organization may also arrange for a booth and distribute and sell literature and solicit funds from that location on the fairgrounds itself....

The judgment of the Supreme Court of Minnesota is reversed ....

CINCINNATI V. DISCOVERY NETWORK, INC.
Supreme Court of the United States, 1993
507 U.S. 410

Justice STEVENS delivered the opinion of the Court.

Motivated by its interest in the safety and attractive appearance of its streets and sidewalks, the city of Cincinnati has refused to allow respondents to distribute their commercial publications through freestanding news racks located on public property. The question presented is whether this refusal is consistent with the First Amendment....

I

Respondent, Discovery Network, Inc., is engaged in the business of providing adult educational, recreational, and social programs to individuals in the Cincinnati area. It advertised those programs in a free magazine that it publishes nine times a year.... Approximately one third of these magazines are distributed through the thirty-eight newsracks that the city authorized Discovery to place on public property in 1989.

Respondent, Harmon Publishing Company, Inc., publishes and distributes a free magazine that advertises real estate for sale.... In 1989 Harmon received the city's permission to install twenty-four newsracks at approved locations. About fifteen percent of its distribution in the Cincinnati area is through those devices.

In March 1990, the city's Director of Public Works notified each of the respondents that its permit to use dispensing devices on public property was revoked, and ordered the newsracks removed within thirty days. Each notice explained that respondent's publication was a "commercial handbill" within the meaning of § 714-1-C of the Municipal Code and therefore § 714-23 of the Code prohibited its distribution on public property....

IV

The Court has held that government may impose reasonable restrictions on the time, place, or manner of engaging in protected speech provided that they are adequately justified without reference to the content of the regulated speech.... The city contends that its regulation of newsracks qualifies as such a restriction because the interests in safety and esthetics that it serves are entirely unrelated to the content of respondents' publications. Thus, the argument goes, the *justification* for the regulation is content neutral.

The argument is unpersuasive because the very basis for the regulation is the difference in content between ordinary newspapers and commercial speech. True, there is no evidence that the city has acted with animus toward the ideas contained within respondents' publications, but just last Term we expressly rejected the argument that "discriminatory ... treatment is suspect under the First Amendment only when the legislature intends to suppress certain ideas." *Simon & Schuster v. Members of New York State Crime Victims Bd.* Regardless of the [purpose] of the city, it has enacted a sweeping ban on the use of newsracks that distribute "commercial handbills," but not "newspapers." Under the city's newsrack policy, whether any particular newsrack falls within the ban is determined by the content of the publication resting inside that newsrack. Thus, by any commonsense understanding of the term, the ban in this case is "content-based."

.... We agree with the city that its desire to limit the total number of newsracks is "justified" by its interest in safety and esthetics. The city has not, however, limited the number of newsracks; it has limited (to zero) the number of newsracks *distributing commercial publications....* [T]here is no justification for that particular regulation other than the city's naked assertion that commercial speech has "low value." It is the absence of a neutral justification for its selective ban on newsracks that prevents the city from defending its newsrack policy as content-neutral....

Cincinnati has enacted a sweeping ban that bars from its sidewalks a whole class of constitutionally protected speech. As did the District Court and the Court of Appeals, we conclude that Cincinnati has failed to justify that policy.... Cincinnati's categorical ban on the distribution, via newsrack, of "commercial handbills" cannot be squared with the dictates of the First Amendment.

FIRST NATIONAL BANK OF BOSTON V. BELLOTTI
Supreme Court of the United States, 1978
435 U.S. 765

[The appellants, several national banking associations and business corporations, wanted to spend money to publicize their opposition to a Massachusetts referendum proposal authorizing the legislature to enact a graduated personal income tax. They brought this lawsuit to challenge the constitutionality of a state criminal statute (§ 8) that prohibited them and other business corporations from making contributions or expenditures "for the purpose of ... influencing or affecting the vote on any question submitted to the voters, other than one materially affecting any of the property, business, or assets of the corporation." The statute specified that corporations found in violation could receive a maximum fine of $50,000, and individual officers who violate the section could be fined up to $10,000 and imprisoned for a year. The appellants filed a lawsuit seeking to have § 8 declared unconstitutional, but the Supreme Judicial Court of Massachusetts upheld the statute.]

Justice POWELL delivered the opinion of the Court.

....

III

The court below framed the principal question in this case as whether and to what extent corporations have First Amendment rights. We believe that the court posed the wrong question. The Constitution often protects interests broader than those of the party seeking their vindication. The First Amendment, in particular, serves significant societal interests. The proper question therefore is not whether corporations "have" First Amendment rights and, if so, whether they are coextensive with those of natural persons. Instead, the question must be whether § 8 abridges expression that the First Amendment was meant to protect. We hold that it does.

A

The speech proposed by appellants is at the heart of the First Amendment's protection.

"The freedom of speech and of the press guaranteed by the Constitution embraces at the least the liberty to discuss publicly and truthfully all matters of public concern without previous restraint or fear of subsequent punishment…. Freedom of discussion, if it would fulfill its historic function in this nation, must embrace all issues about which information is needed or appropriate to enable the members of society to cope with the exigencies of their period." *Thornhill v. Alabama*, 310 U.S. 88, 101-102 (1940).

The referendum issue that appellants wish to address falls squarely within this description. In appellants' view, the enactment of a graduated personal income tax, as proposed to be authorized by constitutional amendment, would have a seriously adverse effect on the economy of the State. The importance of the referendum issue to the people and government of Massachusetts is not disputed. Its merits, however, are the subject of sharp disagreement….

… The question in this case, simply put, is whether the corporate identity of the speaker deprives this proposed speech of what otherwise would be its clear entitlement to protection. We turn now to that question.

B

…

The press cases emphasize the special and constitutionally recognized role of that institution in informing and educating the public, offering criticism, and providing a forum for discussion and debate. But the press does not have a monopoly on either the First Amendment or the ability to enlighten…. [T]he Court's decisions involving corporations in the business of communication or entertainment are based not only on the role of the First Amendment in fostering individual self-expression but also on its role in affording the public access to discussion, debate, and the dissemination of information and ideas. Even decisions seemingly based exclusively on the individual's right to express himself acknowledge that the expression may contribute to society's edification….

C

We thus find no support in the First or Fourteenth Amendment, or in the decisions of this Court, for the proposition that speech that otherwise would be within the protection of the First Amendment loses that protection simply because its source is a corporation that cannot prove, to the satisfaction of a court, a material effect on its business or property. The "materially affecting" requirement is not an identification of the boundaries of corporate speech etched by the Constitution itself. Rather, it amounts to an impermissible legislative prohibition of speech based on the identity of the interests that spokesmen may represent in public debate over controversial issues and a requirement that the speaker have a sufficiently great interest in the subject to justify communication….

In the realm of protected speech, the legislature is constitutionally disqualified from dictating the subjects about which persons may speak and the speakers who may address a public issue…. Especially where, as here, the legislature's suppression of speech suggests an attempt to give one side of a debatable public question an advantage in expressing its views to the people, the First Amendment is plainly offended. Yet the State contends that its action is necessitated by governmental interests of the highest order. We next consider these asserted interests.

V

The constitutionality of § 8's prohibition of the "exposition of ideas" by corporations turns on whether it can survive the exacting scrutiny necessitated by a state-imposed restriction of freedom of speech. Especially where, as here, a prohibition is directed at speech itself, and the speech is intimately related to the process of governing, "the State may prevail only upon showing a subordinating interest which is compelling, and the burden is on the Government to show the existence of such an interest." ...

A

Preserving the integrity of the electoral process, preventing corruption, and "sustaining the active, alert responsibility of the individual citizen in a democracy for the wise conduct of government" are interests of the highest importance. Preservation of the individual citizen's confidence in government is equally important.

[The State] advances a number of arguments in support of its view that these interests are endangered by corporate participation in discussion of a referendum issue. They hinge upon the assumption that such participation would exert an undue influence on the outcome of a referendum vote, and—in the end—destroy the confidence of the people in the democratic process and the integrity of government. According to appellee, corporations are wealthy and powerful and their views may drown out other points of view. If appellee's arguments were supported by record or legislative findings that corporate advocacy threatened imminently to undermine democratic processes, thereby denigrating rather than serving First Amendment interests, these arguments would merit our consideration. But there has been no showing that the relative voice of corporations has been overwhelming or even significant in influencing referenda in Massachusetts, or that there has been any threat to the confidence of the citizenry in government.

Nor are appellee's arguments inherently persuasive or supported by the precedents of this Court. Referenda are held on issues, not candidates for public office. The risk of corruption perceived in cases involving candidate elections simply is not present in a popular vote on a public issue. To be sure, corporate advertising may influence the outcome of the vote; this would be its purpose. But the fact that advocacy may persuade the electorate is hardly a reason to suppress it: The Constitution "protects expression which is eloquent no less than that which is unconvincing." We noted only recently that "the concept that government may restrict the speech of some elements of our society in order to enhance the relative voice of others is wholly foreign to the First Amendment." Moreover, the people in our democracy are entrusted with the responsibility for judging and evaluating the relative merits of conflicting arguments. They may consider, in making their judgment, the source and credibility of the advocate....

Because that portion of § 8 challenged by appellants prohibits protected speech in a manner unjustified by a compelling state interest, it must be invalidated. The judgment of the Supreme Judicial Court is reversed.

McIntyre v. Ohio Elections Commission

Supreme Court of the United States, 1995
514 U.S. 334

Justice STEVENS delivered the opinion of the Court.

The question presented is whether an Ohio statute that prohibits the distribution of anonymous campaign literature is a "law . . . abridging the freedom of speech" within the meaning of the First Amendment.

I

On April 27, 1988, Margaret McIntyre distributed leaflets to persons attending a public meeting at the Blendon Middle School in Westerville, Ohio. At this meeting, the superintendent of schools planned to discuss an imminent referendum on a proposed school tax levy. The leaflets expressed Mrs. McIntyre's opposition to the levy. There is no suggestion that the text of her message was false, misleading, or libelous. She had composed and printed it on her home computer and had paid a professional printer to make additional copies. Some of the handbills identified her as the author; others merely purported to express the views of "CONCERNED PARENTS AND TAX PAYERS." Except for the help provided by her son and a friend, who placed some of the leaflets on car windshields in the school parking lot, Mrs. McIntyre acted independently.

While Mrs. McIntyre distributed her handbills, an official of the school district, who supported the tax proposal, advised her that the unsigned leaflets did not conform to the Ohio election laws. Undeterred, Mrs. McIntyre appeared at another meeting on the next evening and handed out more of the handbills.

The proposed school levy was defeated at the next two elections, but it finally passed on its third try in November 1988. Five months later, the same school official filed a complaint with the Ohio Elections Commission charging that Mrs. McIntyre's distribution of unsigned leaflets violated § 3599.09(A) of the Ohio Code. The commission agreed and imposed a fine of $100.

[The law stated in part that "No person shall write, print, post, or distribute … a notice, placard, dodger, advertisement, sample ballot, or any other form of general publication which is designed to promote the nomination or election or defeat of a candidate, or to promote the adoption or defeat of any issue, or to influence the voters in any election, or make an expenditure for the purpose of financing political communications through newspapers, magazines, outdoor advertising facilities, direct mailings, or other similar types of general public political advertising, or through flyers, handbills, or other nonperiodical printed matter, unless there appears on such form of publication in a conspicuous place or is contained within said statement the name and residence or business address of the chairman, treasurer, or secretary of the organization issuing the same, or the person who issues, makes, or is responsible therefor.]

Mrs. McIntyre passed away during the pendency of this litigation. Even though the amount in controversy is only $ 100, petitioner, as the executor of her estate, has pursued her claim in this Court. Our grant of certiorari reflects our agreement with his appraisal of the importance of the question presented.

II

Ohio maintains that the statute under review is a reasonable regulation of the electoral process. The State does not suggest that all anonymous publications are pernicious or that a statute totally excluding them from the marketplace of ideas would be valid. This is a wise (albeit implicit) concession, for the anonymity of an author is not ordinarily a sufficient reason to exclude her work product from the protections of the First Amendment.

"Anonymous pamphlets, leaflets, brochures, and even books have played an important role in the progress of mankind." *Talley v. California,* 362 U.S. at 64. Great works of literature have frequently been produced by authors writing under assumed names. Despite readers' curiosity and the public's interest in identifying the creator of a work of art, an author generally is free to decide whether or not to disclose his or her true identity. The decision in favor of anonymity may be motivated by fear of economic or official retaliation, by concern about social ostracism, or merely by a desire to preserve as much of one's privacy as possible. Whatever the motivation may be, at least in the field of literary endeavor, the interest in having anonymous works enter the marketplace of ideas unquestionably outweighs any public interest in requiring disclosure as a condition of entry. Accordingly, an author's decision to remain anonymous, like other decisions concerning omissions or additions to the content of a publication, is an aspect of the freedom of speech protected by the First Amendment.

The freedom to publish anonymously extends beyond the literary realm. In *Talley,* the Court held that the First Amendment protects the distribution of unsigned handbills urging readers to boycott certain Los Angeles merchants who were allegedly engaging in discriminatory employment practices. 362 U.S. 60. Writing for the Court, Justice Black noted that "persecuted groups and sects from time to time throughout history have been able to criticize oppressive practices and laws either anonymously or not at all." Id., at 64. Justice Black recalled England's abusive press licensing laws and seditious libel prosecutions, and he reminded us that even the arguments favoring the ratification of the Constitution advanced in the Federalist Papers were published under fictitious names....

III

California had defended the Los Angeles ordinance at issue in *Talley* as a law "aimed at providing a way to identify those responsible for fraud, false advertising, and libel." We rejected that argument because nothing in the text or legislative history of the ordinance limited its application to those evils.... The Ohio statute likewise contains no language limiting its application to fraudulent, false, or libelous statements; to the extent, therefore, that Ohio seeks to justify § 3599.09(A) as a means to prevent the dissemination of untruths, its defense must fail for the same reason given in *Talley.* As the facts of this case demonstrate, the ordinance plainly applies even when there is no hint of falsity or libel.

Ohio's statute does, however, contain a different limitation: It applies only to unsigned documents designed to influence voters in an election. In contrast, the Los Angeles ordinance prohibited all anonymous handbilling "in any place under any circumstances." For that reason, Ohio correctly argues that *Talley* does not necessarily control the disposition of this case. We must, therefore, decide whether and to what extent the First Amendment's protection of anonymity encompasses documents intended to influence the electoral process....

… [A]s we have explained on many prior occasions, the category of speech regulated by the Ohio statute occupies the core of the protection afforded by the First Amendment:

> "Discussion of public issues and debate on the qualifications of candidates are integral to the operation of the system of government established by our Constitution. The First Amendment affords the broadest protection to such political expression in order 'to assure [the] unfettered inter change of ideas for the bringing about of political and social changes desired by the people.' *Roth v. United States,* 354 U.S. 476, 484 (1957)…."

…. No form of speech is entitled to greater constitutional protection than Mrs. McIntyre's. When a law burdens core political speech, we apply "exacting scrutiny," and we uphold the restriction only if it is narrowly tailored to serve an overriding state interest….

IV

Nevertheless, the State argues that, even under the strictest standard of review, the disclosure requirement in § 3599.09(A) is justified by two important and legitimate state interests. Ohio judges its interest in preventing fraudulent and libelous statements and its interest in providing the electorate with relevant information to be sufficiently compelling to justify the anonymous speech ban…. Insofar as the interest in informing the electorate means nothing more than the provision of additional information that may either buttress or undermine the argument in a document, we think the identity of the speaker is no different from other components of the document's content that the author is free to include or exclude…. Thus, Ohio's informational interest is plainly insufficient to support the constitutionality of its disclosure requirement.

The state interest in preventing fraud and libel stands on a different footing. We agree with Ohio's submission that this interest carries special weight during election campaigns when false statements, if credited, may have serious adverse consequences for the public at large. Ohio does not, however, rely solely on § 3599.09(A) to protect that interest. Its Election Code includes detailed and specific prohibitions against making or disseminating false statements during political campaigns. These regulations apply both to candidate elections and to issue-driven ballot measures. Thus, Ohio's prohibition of anonymous leaflets plainly is not its principal weapon against fraud. Rather, it serves as an aid to enforcement of the specific prohibitions and as a deterrent to the making of false statements by unscrupulous prevaricators. Although these ancillary benefits are assuredly legitimate, we are not persuaded that they justify § 3599.09(A)'s extremely broad prohibition.

As this case demonstrates, the prohibition encompasses documents that are not even arguably false or misleading…. Moreover, as this case also demonstrates, the absence of the author's name on a document does not necessarily protect either that person or a distributor of a forbidden document from being held responsible for compliance with the Election Code. Nor has the State explained why it can more easily enforce the direct bans on disseminating false documents against anonymous authors and distributors than against wrongdoers who might use false names and addresses in an attempt to avoid detection. We recognize that a State's enforcement interest might justify a more limited identification requirement, but Ohio has shown scant cause for inhibiting the leafletting at issue here.

VI

Under our Constitution, anonymous pamphleteering is not a pernicious, fraudulent practice, but an honorable tradition of advocacy and of dissent. Anonymity is a shield from the tyranny of the majority…. The State may, and does, punish fraud directly. But it cannot seek to punish fraud indirectly by indiscriminately outlawing a category of speech, based on its content, with no necessary relationship to the danger sought to be prevented. One would be hard pressed to think of a better example of the pitfalls of Ohio's blunderbuss approach than the facts of the case before us.

The judgment of the Ohio Supreme Court is reversed.

It is so ordered.

Justice SCALIA, with whom The Chief Justice joins, dissenting.

At a time when both political branches of Government and both political parties reflect a popular desire to leave more decision-making authority to the States, today's decision moves in the opposite direction, adding to the legacy of inflexible central mandates (irrevocable even by Congress) imposed by this Court's constitutional jurisprudence. In an opinion which reads as though it is addressing some peculiar law like the Los Angeles municipal ordinance at issue in *Talley v. California*, 362 U.S. 60 (1960), the Court invalidates a species of protection for the election process that exists, in a variety of forms, in every State except California, and that has a pedigree dating back to the end of the 19th century. Preferring the views of the English utilitarian philosopher John Stuart Mill to the considered judgment of the American people's elected representatives from coast to coast, the Court discovers a hitherto unknown right-to-be-unknown while engaging in electoral politics. I dissent from this imposition of free-speech imperatives that are demonstrably not those of the American people today, and that there is inadequate reason to believe were those of the society that begat the First Amendment ….

KINCAID V. GIBSON

U.S. Court of Appeals for the Sixth Circuit, 2001
236 F.3d 342

R. GUY COLE, JR., Circuit Judge.

Plaintiffs-Appellants Charles Kincaid and Capri Coffer appeal the district court's grant of summary judgment upholding Defendants-Appellees' confiscation and ban on distribution of a college yearbook edited by Coffer. Upon en banc review, we determine that the KSU officials violated the First Amendment rights of Kincaid and Coffer. Accordingly, we REVERSE the order of the district court and REMAND the case with instructions to enter judgment in favor of Kincaid and Coffer and to determine the relief to which they are entitled.

I. BACKGROUND

A. Factual Background

At the times relevant to this case, both Kincaid and Coffer were registered students at Kentucky State University ("KSU"), a public, state-funded university. Betty Gibson was KSU's Vice President for Student Affairs. KSU funded production and distribution of The Thorobred, the student yearbook. KSU students composed and produced The Thorobred, with limited advice from the university's student publications advisor....

Coffer served as the editor of the yearbook during the 1993-94 academic year. Although a student-photographer and at least one other student assisted her at one point, Coffer organized and put together the yearbook herself after her staff members lost interest in the project. Coffer endeavored to "do something different" with the yearbook in order to "bring Kentucky State University into the nineties"; she also sought to "present a yearbook to the student population that was what they [had] never seen before." To these ends, Coffer created a purple cover using a material known as "rain shower foil stamp," and, for the first time, gave the yearbook a theme. The theme, "destination unknown," described the atmosphere of "uncertainty" that Coffer believed characterized the time; Coffer found evidence of this uncertainty in students wondering "where are we going in our lives," in high unemployment rates, and in a current controversy regarding whether KSU was going to become a community college. Coffer included pictures in the yearbook depicting events at KSU and in its surrounding community, and political and current events in the nation and world at large. The yearbook covered both the 1992-93 and 1993-94 academic years because the students working on the 1992-93 yearbook had fallen behind schedule. Although the yearbook was originally projected to contain 224 pages, Coffer testified that the final product contained only 128 pages, because she did not have enough pictures to fill 224 pages and because the university administration took no interest in the publication. Coffer completed the yearbook several thousand dollars under budget, and sent the yearbook to the printer in May or June of 1994.

When the yearbook came back from the printer in November 1994, Gibson objected to several aspects of it, finding the publication to be of poor quality and "inappropriate." In particular, Gibson objected to the yearbook's purple cover (KSU's school colors are green and gold), its "destination unknown" theme, the lack of captions under many of the photos, and the inclusion of current events ostensibly unrelated to KSU. After consulting with KSU President Mary Smith and other unnamed university officials, Gibson and Smith decided to confiscate the yearbooks and to withhold them from the KSU community. Gibson contacted Leslie Thomas, KSU's Director of Student Life, and instructed her to secure the yearbooks so that they would not be distributed....

B. Procedural Background

In November 1995, Kincaid and Coffer sued Gibson, Smith, and individual members of the KSU Board of Regents ... alleging that the university's confiscation of and failure to distribute the 1992-94 KSU student yearbook violated their rights under the First and Fourteenth Amendments to the United States Constitution. Kincaid and Coffer sought damages and injunctive relief.

II.

Both parties moved for summary judgment on the yearbook claim. The district court applied a forum analysis to the students' First Amendment claim, and found that the KSU yearbook was a nonpublic forum. The district court reasoned that Kincaid and Coffer had "put forth no evidence that The Thorobred was intended to reach or communicate with anybody but KSU students," and held that "the yearbook was not intended to be a journal of expression and communication in a public forum sense, but instead was intended to be a journal of the 'goings on' in [a] particular year at KSU." Having found that the yearbook was not a public forum, the court held that the university officials' refusal to distribute the yearbook "on the grounds that the yearbook was not of proper quality and did not represent the school a[s] it should," was reasonable. Accordingly, the court granted the KSU officials' motion for summary judgment and denied the students' motion. Both in finding that the KSU yearbook was a nonpublic forum and in finding that the KSU officials' actions were reasonable, the district court relied in part upon *Hazelwood Sch. Dist. v. Kuhlmeier*, 484 U.S. 260 (1988).

A divided panel of this court affirmed the district court's opinion. We granted en banc review to determine whether the panel and the district court erred in applying Hazelwood — a case that deals exclusively with the First Amendment rights of students in a high school setting—to the university setting, and to examine whether the district court erred in finding that the student-plaintiffs failed as a matter of law to submit sufficient evidence to prove that the KSU yearbook is a limited public forum rather than a nonpublic forum….

III. DISCUSSION

The issue before us is whether the university officials violated the First Amendment rights of Kincaid and Coffer by confiscating and failing to distribute the KSU student yearbook. For the reasons that follow, we apply a forum analysis to the question and hold that the KSU yearbook constitutes a limited (or "designated") public forum. Accordingly, we analyze the actions taken by the university officials with respect to the yearbook under strict scrutiny, and conclude that the officials' confiscation of the yearbooks violated Kincaid's and Coffer's First Amendment rights.

A. Application of Public Forum Doctrine

We begin with the fundamental principle that there can be "no doubt that the First Amendment rights of speech and association extend to the campuses of state universities." *Widmar v. Vincent*, 454 U.S. 263, 268-69 (1981). KSU is a state-funded, public university. As such, the actions KSU officials take in their official capacities constitute state actions for purposes of First Amendment analysis. Further, the funds and materials that KSU allocates toward production of The Thorobred constitute state property. By confiscating the yearbooks at issue in this case, the KSU officials have restricted access to state property used for expressive purposes. "The Supreme Court has adopted a forum analysis for use in determining whether a state-imposed restriction on access to public property is constitutionally permissible." Accordingly, we find that forum analysis is appropriate in this case….

B. Type of Forum

There is no real dispute in this case that the forum in question is The Thorobred itself. The parties dispute strenuously, however, the appropriate characterization of The Thorobred under forum analysis. Kincaid and Coffer contend that the yearbook is a limited public forum, subject only to reasonable time, place, and manner regulations, and to only those content-based regulations that are narrowly crafted to serve a compelling state interest. The KSU officials respond that the yearbook is a nonpublic forum, subject to all reasonable regulations that preserve the yearbook's purpose.

The Supreme Court has recognized three types of fora. The first type is a traditional public forum. A traditional public forum is a place "which by long tradition or by government fiat ha[s] been devoted to assembly and debate," such as a street or park. In traditional public fora, "the rights of the state to limit expressive activity are sharply circumscribed": the government may enforce content-based restrictions only if they are narrowly drawn to serve a compelling interest, and may enforce content-neutral time, place, and manner regulations only if they are "narrowly tailored to serve a significant government interest, and leave open ample alternative channels of communication." The second type of forum has been alternatively described as a "limited public forum," and as a "designated public forum," see *Arkansas Educ. Television Comm'n v. Forbes*, 523 U.S. 666, 679 (1998). The government may open a limited public forum "for use by the public at large for assembly and speech, for use by certain speakers, or for the discussion of certain subjects." Although the government need not retain the open nature of a limited public forum, "as long as it does so it is bound by the same standards as apply in a traditional public forum." The third and final type of forum is a nonpublic forum. The government may control access to a nonpublic forum "based on subject matter and speaker identity so long as the distinctions drawn are reasonable in light of the purpose served by the forum and are viewpoint neutral."

The parties agree that The Thorobred is not a traditional public forum. To determine whether the yearbook is a limited public forum, the touchstone of our analysis is whether the government intended to open the forum at issue....

1. Policy

KSU's written policy toward The Thorobred is found in a section of the student handbook entitled "Student Publications." In addition to stating KSU's policy toward the yearbook, the handbook describes the university's structure for oversight of the publication. The yearbook (along with the student newspaper) is "under the management of the Student Publications Board." The Student Publications Board ("SPB"), in turn, is composed of students, faculty members, and university officials. Both the university's written policy and the structure it created to oversee the yearbook evidence KSU's intention that the yearbook serve as a limited public forum.

First and foremost, the policy places editorial control of the yearbook in the hands of a student editor or editors. Although the policy provides for the establishment of minimum qualifications for student editors, once a student is appointed editor, editorial control of the yearbook's content belongs to her. This is made clear by the policy's description of the Student Publications Advisor, a university employee. The policy directs that the SPB "shall require the use of an experienced advisor," but limits the advisor's role to "assur[ing] that the . . . yearbook is not overwhelmed by ineptitude and inexperience." Indeed, the policy expressly limits the types of changes that the advisor may make to the yearbook:

> In order to meet the responsible standards of journalism, an advisor may require changes in the form of materials submitted by students, but such changes must deal only with the form or the time and manner of expressions rather than alteration of content.

This language is revealing: not only does it direct the university's chosen advisor to refrain from editing the content of the yearbook, it also tracks the Supreme Court's description of the limitations on government regulation of expressive activity in a limited public forum. KSU's intent to limit its own oversight to time, place, and manner aspects of the yearbook is also seen in the policy's treatment of the SPB. The policy declares that one of the duties of the SPB is to "[a]pprove the written publications policy of each student publication, including such items as purpose, size, quantity controls, and time, place, and manner of distribution." This language reiterates the university's intent to limit its oversight of the yearbook to general and administrative matters, and to cede authority over the yearbook's content to the students who published it. Finally, the publications policy opens with language that indicates that the expressive activity contained in student publications is to be largely unrestrained: "The Board of Regents respects the integrity of student publications and the press, and the rights to exist in an atmosphere of free and responsible discussion and of intellectual exploration." Such self-imposed restraint is strong evidence of KSU's intent to create a limited public forum, rather than to reserve to itself the right to edit or determine The Thorobred's content....

2. Practice

In addition to examining KSU's stated policy, we must examine the university's actual practice to determine whether it truly intended to create a limited public forum in The Thorobred. Indeed, we have noted that "'actual practice speaks louder than words'" in determining whether the government intended to create a limited public forum. The record before us contains substantial evidence from varied sources that the SPB followed its stated "hands off" policy in actual practice. Coffer testified without contradiction that Vice President Gibson—who Coffer described as a "friend" with whom she was "on excellent terms"—"never expressed any concern about what the content might be in the yearbook" prior to its publication, but rather limited her concerns to the yearbook's release date. Nor did the SPB exercise oversight of the yearbook's content. Laura Jo Cullen, the university's publications advisor to the yearbook and an ex officio member of the SPB, testified that the SPB limited its oversight of the yearbook to issues such as advertising rates and selection of editors, and that in the time during which she had been associated with the yearbook, the Board had never attempted to control the content of the yearbook....

3. Nature of the Property and Compatibility with Expressive Activity

In addition to the university's policy and practice, an examination of the nature of the forum at issue and its compatibility with expressive activity further indicates that KSU intended to open The Thorobred to the student editors as a limited public forum. The KSU yearbook is a student publication that, by its very nature, exists for the purpose of expressive activity.... As a creative publication, the yearbook is easily distinguished from other government for a whose natures are not so compatible with free expression. Nor is The Thorobred a closely monitored classroom activity in which an instructor assigns student editors a grade, or in which a university official edits content....

4. Context

We are also persuaded that the context within which this case arises indicates that The Thorobred constitutes a limited public forum. The university is a special place for purposes of First Amendment jurisprudence. The danger of "chilling . . . individual thought and expression . . . is especially real in the University setting, where the State acts against a background and tradition of thought and experiment that is at the center of our intellectual and philosophic tradition." The university environment is the quintessential "marketplace of ideas," which merits full, or indeed heightened, First Amendment protection. In addition to the nature of the university setting, we find it relevant that the editors of The Thorobred and its readers are likely to be young adults— Kincaid himself was thirty-seven at the time of his March 1997 deposition. Thus, there can be no justification for suppressing the yearbook on the grounds that it might be "unsuitable for immature audiences." Compare *Hazelwood,* 484 U.S. at 271, with *Widmar,* 454 U.S. at 274 n.14 ("University students are, of course, young adults. They are less impressionable than younger students "). Accordingly, we find that the fact that the forum at issue arises in the university context mitigates in favor of finding that the yearbook is a limited public forum.

5. KSU Officials' Arguments

The KSU officials dispute this substantial evidence of the university's intent to create a limited public forum in the student yearbook. They argue that a limited public forum cannot exist unless the government has opened the forum at issue for "indiscriminate use by the general public." … This reasoning badly distorts a basic tenet of public forum law. It is true that one of the ways in which the government may create or designate a public forum is by opening the forum "for indiscriminate use by the general public." But the government may create a limited public forum in other ways as well: "a public forum may be created by government designation of a place or channel of communication for use by the public at large for assembly and speech, for use by certain speakers, or for the discussion of certain subjects." Thus, the proposition put forth by the university officials and relied upon by the district court—i.e., that the government must open a forum for indiscriminate use by the general public in order to create a designated public forum—is erroneous....

In sum, our review of KSU's policy and practice with regard to The Thorobred, the nature of the yearbook and its compatibility with expressive activity, and the university context in which the yearbook is created and distributed, all provide strong evidence of the university's intent to designate the yearbook as a limited public forum. Accordingly, we must determine whether the university officials' actions with respect to the yearbook were constitutional.

C. Constitutionality of University Officials' Actions

As discussed, the government may impose only reasonable time, place, and manner regulations, and content-based regulations that are narrowly drawn to effectuate a compelling state interest, on expressive activity in a limited public forum....

Upon their return from the printer, the 1992-94 yearbooks were delivered to the office of Laura Cullen, the student publications advisor. Before they could be distributed to Kincaid and other KSU students, Gibson ordered Leslie Thomas to have them secured; Thomas complied, and, without any notification or explanation to Cullen, the yearbooks were spirited away. To this day—nearly six years after the yearbooks returned from the printer—the university refuses to distribute them. This is not a reasonable time, place, or manner regulation of expressive activity. Nor is it a narrowly crafted regulation designed to preserve a compelling state interest. Rather, wholesale confiscation of printed materials, which the state feels reflect poorly on its institutions, is as broadly sweeping a regulation as the state might muster. Further, the university officials' action leaves open no alternative grounds for similar expressive activity. The record contains no other student forum for recording words and pictures to reflect the experience of KSU students during the 1992 through 1994 school years. Indeed, the likelihood of the existence of any such alternative forum at this late date, when virtually all of the students who were at KSU in the early 1990s will have surely moved on, is extraordinarily slim. Accordingly, the KSU officials' confiscation of the yearbooks violates the First Amendment, and the university has no constitutionally valid reason to withhold distribution of the 1992-94 Thorobred from KSU students from that era.

The KSU officials argue that withholding the yearbooks is excusable because they were regulating the style and form of the yearbooks rather than their content. At oral argument, counsel for the officials argued that the record contains no evidence that the officials withheld distribution of the yearbooks based on content, or that they altered the content of the yearbooks. This argument is simply not credible. First, the record makes clear that Gibson sought to regulate the content of the 1992-94 yearbook: in addition to complaining about the yearbook's color, lack of captions, and overall quality, Gibson withheld the yearbooks because she found the yearbook theme of "destination unknown" inappropriate. Gibson also disapproved of the inclusion of pictures of current events, and testified that "[t]here were a lot of pictures in the back of the book that . . . to me, looked like a *Life* magazine." Gibson further stated that the inclusion of pictures of current events "was not exactly what I thought it should have been, and it wasn't what other people who viewed it thought it should have been." And after the yearbooks came back from the printer, Gibson complained to Cullen that "[s]everal persons have received the book, and are thoroughly disappointed at the quality and content." Thus, it is quite clear that Gibson attempted to regulate the content of The Thorobred once it was printed.

The officials' argument also fails because they have, in effect, altered The Thorobred. Confiscation ranks with forced government speech as amongst the purest forms of content alteration. There is little if any difference between hiding from public view the words and pictures students use to portray their college experience, and forcing students to publish a state-sponsored script. In either case, the government alters student expression by obliterating it....

Even were we to assume, as the KSU officials argue, that the yearbook was a nonpublic forum, confiscation of the yearbook would still violate Kincaid's and Coffer's free speech rights. Although the government may act to preserve a nonpublic forum for its intended purposes, its regulation of speech must nonetheless be reasonable, and it must not attempt to suppress expression based on the speaker's viewpoint. The actions taken by the KSU officials fail under even this relaxed standard....

... [T]he KSU officials' actions were not reasonable because they were arbitrary and conflicted with the university's own stated policy. The university's publications policy states that "the Thorobred yearbook shall be under the management of the Student Publications Board." Yet Thomas testified that neither Gibson nor any other KSU administrators discussed with the SPB the drastic act of confiscating the yearbooks. Further, the university's policy gave Cullen the power to "require changes in the form of materials submitted by students [that] . . . deal . . . with the form or the time and manner of expressions." Yet, the KSU officials never even consulted Cullen, the student publications advisor, before they seized the yearbooks....

IV. CONCLUSION

The district court erred by granting summary judgment to the university officials and denying it to Kincaid and Coffer because the record clearly shows KSU's intent to designate The Thorobred as a limited public forum. ... The university's confiscation of this journal of expression was arbitrary and unreasonable. As such, it violated Kincaid's and Coffer's First Amendment rights.

In light of the clearly established contours of the public forum doctrine and the substantially developed factual record in this case, the district court should have denied the KSU officials' motion for summary judgment and granted Kincaid's and Coffer's summary judgment motion. Accordingly, we REVERSE the judgment of the district court and REMAND the case with instructions to enter judgment in favor of Kincaid and Coffer, and to determine the relief to which they are entitled.

MORSE V. FREDERICK
Supreme Court of the United States, 2007
551 U.S. 393

Chief Justice ROBERTS delivered the opinion of the Court.

At a school-sanctioned and school-supervised event, a high school principal saw some of her students unfurl a large banner conveying a message she reasonably regarded as promoting illegal drug use. Consistent with established school policy prohibiting such messages at school events, the principal directed the students to take down the banner. One student—among those who had brought the banner to the event—refused to do so. The principal confiscated the banner and later suspended the student. The Ninth Circuit held that the principal's actions violated the First Amendment, and that the student could sue the principal for damages.

Our cases make clear that students do not "shed their constitutional rights to freedom of speech or expression at the schoolhouse gate." *Tinker v. Des Moines Independent Community School Dist.* At the same time, we have held that "the constitutional rights of students in public school are not automatically coextensive with the rights of adults in other settings," *Bethel School Dist. No. 403 v. Fraser,* and that the rights of students "must be 'applied in light of the special characteristics of the school environment.'" *Hazelwood School Dist. v. Kuhlmeier.* Consistent with these principles, we hold that schools may take steps to safeguard those entrusted to their care from speech that can reasonably be regarded as encouraging illegal drug use. We conclude that the school officials in this case did not violate the First Amendment by confiscating the pro-drug banner and suspending the student responsible for it.

I

On January 24, 2002, the Olympic Torch Relay passed through Juneau, Alaska, on its way to the winter games in Salt Lake City, Utah. The torchbearers were to proceed along a street in front of Juneau-Douglas High School (JDHS) while school was in session. Petitioner Deborah Morse, the school principal, decided to permit staff and students to participate in the Torch Relay as an approved social event or class trip. Students were allowed to leave class to observe the relay from either side of the street. Teachers and administrative officials monitored the students' actions. Respondent Joseph Frederick, a JDHS senior, was late to school that day. When he arrived, he joined his friends (all but one of whom were JDHS students) across the street from the school to watch the event. Not all the students waited patiently. Some became rambunctious, throwing plastic cola bottles and snowballs and scuffling with their classmates. As the torchbearers and camera crews passed by, Frederick and his friends unfurled a 14 foot banner bearing the phrase: "BONG HiTS 4 JESUS." The large banner was easily readable by the students on the other side of the street. Principal Morse immediately crossed the street and demanded that the banner be taken down. Everyone but Frederick complied. Morse confiscated the banner and told Frederick to report to her office, where she suspended him for 10 days. Morse later explained that she told Frederick to take the banner down because she thought it encouraged illegal drug use, in violation of established school policy....

Frederick administratively appealed his suspension, but the Juneau School District Superintendent upheld it, limiting it to time served (8 days). In a memorandum setting forth his reasons, the superintendent determined that Frederick had displayed his banner "in the midst of his fellow students, during school hours, at a school-sanctioned activity." He further explained that Frederick "was not disciplined because the principal of the school 'disagreed' with his message, but because his speech appeared to advocate the use of illegal drugs."

....

Frederick then filed suit ... alleging that the school board and Morse had violated his First Amendment rights. He sought declaratory and injunctive relief, unspecified compensatory damages, punitive damages, and attorney's fees. The District Court granted summary judgment for the school board and Morse, ruling that they were entitled to qualified immunity and that they had not infringed Frederick's First Amendment rights....

The Ninth Circuit reversed. Deciding that Frederick acted during a "school-authorized activit[y]," and "proceed[ing] on the basis that the banner expressed a positive sentiment about marijuana use," the court nonetheless found a violation of Frederick's First Amendment rights because the school punished Frederick without demonstrating that his speech gave rise to a "risk of substantial disruption." The court further concluded that Frederick's right to display his banner was so "clearly established" that a reasonable principal in Morse's position would have understood that her actions were unconstitutional ....

....

II

At the outset, we reject Frederick's argument that this is not a school speech case—as has every other authority to address the question. The event occurred during normal school hours. It was sanctioned by Principal Morse "as an approved social event or class trip," and the school district's rules expressly provide that pupils in "approved social events and class trips are subject to district rules for student conduct." Teachers and administrators were interspersed among the students and charged with supervising them. The high school band and cheerleaders performed. Frederick, standing among other JDHS students across the street from the school, directed his banner toward the school, making it plainly visible to most students. Under these circumstances, we agree with the superintendent that Frederick cannot "stand in the midst of his fellow students, during school hours, at a school-sanctioned activity and claim he is not at school." ....

III

The message on Frederick's banner is cryptic. It is no doubt offensive to some, perhaps amusing to others. To still others, it probably means nothing at all. Frederick himself claimed "that the words were just nonsense meant to attract television cameras." But Principal Morse thought the banner would be interpreted by those viewing it as promoting illegal drug use, and that interpretation is plainly a reasonable one. As Morse later explained in a declaration, when she saw the sign, she thought that "the reference to a 'bong hit' would be widely understood by high school students and others as referring to smoking marijuana." She further believed that "display of the banner would be construed by students, District personnel, parents and others witnessing the display of the banner, as advocating or promoting illegal drug use"—in violation of school policy....

We agree with Morse....

.... Gibberish is surely a possible interpretation of the words on the banner, but it is not the only one, and dismissing the banner as meaningless ignores its undeniable reference to illegal drugs.

IV

The question thus becomes whether a principal may, consistent with the First Amendment, restrict student speech at a school event, when that speech is reasonably viewed as promoting illegal drug use. We hold that she may....

....

Drawing on the principles applied in our student speech cases, we have held in the Fourth Amendment context that "while children assuredly do not 'shed their constitutional rights . . . at the schoolhouse gate,' . . . the nature of those rights is what is appropriate for children in school." ....

....

The "special characteristics of the school environment," and the governmental interest in stopping student drug abuse—reflected in the policies of Congress and myriad school boards, including JDHS—allow schools to restrict student expression that they reasonably regard as promoting illegal drug use....

....

School principals have a difficult job, and a vitally important one. When Frederick suddenly and unexpectedly unfurled his banner, Morse had to decide to act—or not act—on the spot. It was reasonable for her to conclude that the banner promoted illegal drug use—in violation of established school policy—and that failing to act would send a powerful message to the students in her charge, including Frederick, about how serious the school was about the dangers of illegal drug use. The First Amendment does not require schools to tolerate at school events student expression that contributes to those dangers. The judgment of the United States Court of Appeals for the Ninth Circuit is reversed, and the case is remanded for further proceedings consistent with this opinion.

Justice STEVENS, with whom Justice SOUTER and Justice GINSBURG join, dissenting.

....

I agree with the Court that the principal should not be held liable for pulling down Frederick's banner. I would hold, however, that the school's interest in protecting its students from exposure to speech "reasonably regarded as promoting illegal drug use," cannot justify disciplining Frederick for his attempt to make an ambiguous statement to a television audience simply because it contained an oblique reference to drugs. The First Amendment demands more, indeed, much more.

The Court holds otherwise only after laboring to establish two uncontroversial propositions: first, that the constitutional rights of students in school settings are not coextensive with the rights of adults; and second, that deterring drug use by schoolchildren is a valid and terribly important interest. As to the first, I take the Court's point that the message on Frederick's banner is not *necessarily* protected speech, even though it unquestionably would have been had the banner been unfurled elsewhere. As to the second, I am willing to assume that the Court is correct that the pressing need to deter drug use supports JDHS's rule prohibiting willful conduct that expressly "advocates the use of substances that are illegal to minors." But it is a gross non sequitur to draw from these two unremarkable propositions the remarkable conclusion that the school may suppress student speech that was never meant to persuade anyone to do anything.

In my judgment, the First Amendment protects student speech if the message itself neither violates a permissible rule nor expressly advocates conduct that is illegal and harmful to students. This nonsense banner does neither, and the Court does serious violence to the First Amendment in upholding—indeed, lauding—a school's decision to punish Frederick for expressing a view with which it disagreed.

....

To the extent the Court defers to the principal's ostensibly reasonable judgment, it abdicates its constitutional responsibility. The beliefs of third parties, reasonable or otherwise, have never dictated which messages amount to proscribable advocacy....

Even if advocacy could somehow be wedged into Frederick's obtuse reference to marijuana, that advocacy was at best subtle and ambiguous. There is abundant precedent ... for the proposition that when the "First Amendment is implicated, the tie goes to the speaker."

....

I respectfully dissent.

Chapter Three
RISKS TO PUBLIC SAFETY

If there is to be an exception to First Amendment protection, the most logical exception would be speech that is likely to provoke actual, physical harm to others. This section includes cases that deal with two different branches of this problem. The first concern is possible physical harm on the grandest of scales—threats to national security. The second concern is an area of law that is rapidly evolving—civil lawsuits by individuals who claim they were personally, physically injured because of material that appeared in the media.

New York Times Co. v. United States is commonly known as the Pentagon Papers case. Though the justices were widely split in their reasoning and did not produce a clear constitutional standard, the case is notable as a high-stakes confrontation between a government attempt to censor on national security grounds and leading newspapers' claims of political free speech.

United States v. The Progressive, Inc. is the only other conflict between publishing rights and national security censorship that has prompted an appellate court ruling.

Olivia N. v. National Broadcasting Co. was an early case in a long line that's sometimes referred to as "pied piper" cases, in which audience members imitate scenes observed on television and in the process injure themselves or someone else. Plaintiffs generally have not been successful in these lawsuits.

Winter v. G.P. Putnam's Sons represents a more difficult legal issue: whether the media should be liable for injuries when the media content was specifically *intended* to guide action. This case illustrates the various legal theories under which an injured plaintiff might sue.

Doe v. MySpace, Inc. looks at the special problems created by user-generated content on Web-based services – and the strong immunity from tort liability that those services enjoy under sec. 230 of the Communications Decency Act.

American Amusement Machine Ass'n v. Kendrick is a recent case with a different twist, a challenge to a local ordinance that attempted to protect children from the perceived harmful effects of violent video games.

NEW YORK TIMES CO. V. UNITED STATES
Supreme Court of the United States, 1971
403 U.S. 713

Opinion by: PER CURIAM

We granted certiorari in these cases in which the United States seeks to enjoin the *New York Times* and the *Washington Post* from publishing the contents of a classified study entitled "History of U.S. Decision-Making Process on Viet Nam Policy."

"Any system of prior restraints of expression comes to this Court bearing a heavy presumption against its constitutional validity." *Bantam Books, Inc. v. Sullivan,* 372 U.S. 58, 70 (1963); see also *Near v. Minnesota,* 283 U.S. 697 (1931). The Government "thus carries a heavy burden of showing justification for the imposition of such a restraint." The District Court for the Southern District of New York in the *New York Times* case and the District Court for the District of Columbia and the Court of Appeals for the District of Columbia Circuit in the *Washington Post* case held that the Government had not met that burden. We agree.

The judgment of the Court of Appeals for the District of Columbia Circuit is therefore affirmed. The order of the Court of Appeals for the Second Circuit is reversed and the case is remanded with directions to enter a judgment affirming the judgment of the District Court for the Southern District of New York. The stays entered June 25, 1971, by the Court are vacated. The judgments shall issue forthwith.

So ordered.

Justice BLACK, with whom Justice DOUGLAS joins, concurring.

… I believe that every moment's continuance of the injunctions against these newspapers amounts to a flagrant, indefensible, and continuing violation of the First Amendment. Furthermore, after oral argument, I agree completely that we must affirm the judgment of the Court of Appeals for the District of Columbia Circuit and reverse the judgment of the Court of Appeals for the Second Circuit for the reasons stated by my Brothers DOUGLAS and BRENNAN. In my view it is unfortunate that some of my Brethren are apparently willing to hold that the publication of news may sometimes be enjoined. Such a holding would make a shambles of the First Amendment.

Our Government was launched in 1789 with the adoption of the Constitution. The Bill of Rights, including the First Amendment, followed in 1791. Now, for the first time in the 182 years since the founding of the Republic, the federal courts are asked to hold that the First Amendment does not mean what it says, but rather means that the Government can halt the publication of current news of vital importance to the people of this country.

In seeking injunctions against these newspapers and in its presentation to the Court, the Executive Branch seems to have forgotten the essential purpose and history of the First Amendment…. Madison and the other Framers of the First Amendment, able men that they were, wrote in language they earnestly believed could never be misunderstood: "Congress shall make no law … abridging the freedom … of the press…." Both the history and language of the First Amendment support the view that the press must be left free to publish news, whatever the source, without censorship, injunctions, or prior restraints.

In the First Amendment the Founding Fathers gave the free press the protection it must have to fulfill its essential role in our democracy. The press was to serve the governed, not the governors. The Government's power to censor the press was abolished so that the press would remain forever free to censure the Government. The press was protected so that it could bare the secrets of government and inform the people. Only a free and unrestrained press can effectively expose deception in government. And paramount among the responsibilities of a free press is the duty to prevent any part of the government from deceiving the people and sending them off to distant lands to die of foreign fevers and foreign shot and shell. In my view, far from deserving condemnation for their courageous reporting, the *New York Times,* the *Washington Post,* and other newspapers should be commended for serving the purpose that the Founding Fathers saw so clearly. In revealing the workings of government that led to the Vietnam War, the newspapers nobly did precisely that which the Founders hoped and trusted they would do....

Justice DOUGLAS, with whom Justice BLACK joins, concurring.

While I join the opinion of the Court I believe it necessary to express my views more fully.

It should be noted at the outset that the First Amendment provides that "Congress shall make no law ... abridging the freedom of speech, or of the press." That leaves, in my view, no room for governmental restraint on the press.

There is, moreover, no statute barring the publication by the press of the material that the *Times* and the *Post* seek to use....

The Government says that it has inherent powers to go into court and obtain an injunction to protect the national interest, which in this case is alleged to be national security.

Near v. Minnesota, 283 U.S. 697, repudiated that expansive doctrine in no uncertain terms.

The dominant purpose of the First Amendment was to prohibit the widespread practice of governmental suppression of embarrassing information. It is common knowledge that the First Amendment was adopted against the widespread use of the common law of seditious libel to punish the dissemination of material that is embarrassing to the powers-that-be. The present cases will, I think, go down in history as the most dramatic illustration of that principle. A debate of large proportions goes on in the Nation over our posture in Vietnam. That debate antedated the disclosure of the contents of the present documents. The latter are highly relevant to the debate in progress.

Secrecy in government is fundamentally anti-democratic, perpetuating bureaucratic errors. Open debate and discussion of public issues are vital to our national health. On public questions there should be "uninhibited, robust, and wide-open" debate....

Justice BRENNAN, concurring.

I write separately in these cases only to emphasize what should be apparent: that our judgments in the present cases may not be taken to indicate the propriety, in the future, of issuing temporary stays and restraining orders to block the publication of material sought to be suppressed by the Government....

The error that has pervaded these cases from the outset was the granting of any injunctive relief whatsoever, interim or otherwise. The entire thrust of the Government's claim throughout these cases has been that publication of the material sought to be enjoined "could," or "might," or "may" prejudice the national interest in various ways. But the First Amendment tolerates absolutely no prior judicial restraints of the press predicated upon surmise or conjecture that untoward consequences may result. Our cases, it is true, have indicated that there is a single, extremely narrow class of cases in which the First Amendment's ban on prior judicial restraint may be overridden. Our cases have thus far indicated that such cases may arise only when the Nation "is at war," *Schenck v. United States,* 249 U.S. 47, 52 (1919), during which times "no one would question but that a government might prevent actual obstruction to its recruiting service or the publication of the sailing dates of transports or the number and location of troops." *Near v. Minnesota,* 283 U.S. 697, 716 (1931). Even if the present world situation were assumed to be tantamount to a time of war, or if the power of presently available armaments would justify even in peacetime the suppression of information that would set in motion a nuclear holocaust, in neither of these actions has the Government presented or even alleged that publication of items from or based upon the material at issue would cause the happening of an event of that nature. [O]nly governmental allegation and proof that publication must inevitably, directly, and immediately cause the occurrence of an event kindred to imperiling the safety of a transport already at sea can support even the issuance of an interim restraining order. In no event may mere conclusions be sufficient: for if the Executive Branch seeks judicial aid in preventing publication, it must inevitably submit the basis upon which that aid is sought to scrutiny by the judiciary. And therefore, every restraint issued in this case, whatever its form, has violated the First Amendment—and not less so because that restraint was justified as necessary to afford the courts an opportunity to examine the claim more thoroughly. Unless and until the Government has clearly made out its case, the First Amendment commands that no injunction may issue....

Justice STEWART, with whom Justice WHITE joins, concurring.

In the governmental structure created by our Constitution, the Executive is endowed with enormous power in the two related areas of national defense and international relations....

In the absence of the governmental checks and balances present in other areas of our national life, the only effective restraint upon executive policy and power in the areas of national defense and international affairs may lie in an enlightened citizenry—in an informed and critical public opinion which alone can here protect the values of democratic government. For this reason, it is perhaps here that a press that is alert, aware, and free most vitally serves the basic purpose of the First Amendment. For without an informed and free press there cannot be an enlightened people.

Yet it is elementary that the successful conduct of international diplomacy and the maintenance of an effective national defense require both confidentiality and secrecy....

I think there can be but one answer to this dilemma, if dilemma it be. The responsibility must be where the power is. If the Constitution gives the Executive a large degree of unshared power in the conduct of foreign affairs and the maintenance of our national defense, then under the Constitution the Executive must have the largely unshared duty to determine and preserve the degree of internal security necessary to exercise that power successfully....

This is not to say that Congress and the courts have no role to play. Undoubtedly Congress has the power to enact specific and appropriate criminal laws to protect government property and preserve government secrets. Congress has passed such laws, and several of them are of very colorable relevance to the apparent circumstances of these cases. And if a criminal prosecution is instituted, it will be the responsibility of the courts to decide the applicability of the criminal law under which the charge is brought. Moreover, if Congress should pass a specific law authorizing civil proceedings in this field, the courts would likewise have the duty to decide the constitutionality of such a law as well as its applicability to the facts proved.

But in the cases before us we are asked neither to construe specific regulations nor to apply specific laws. We are asked, instead, to perform a function that the Constitution gave to the Executive, not the Judiciary. We are asked, quite simply, to prevent the publication by two newspapers of material that the Executive Branch insists should not, in the national interest, be published. I am convinced that the Executive is correct with respect to some of the documents involved. But I cannot say that disclosure of any of them will surely result in direct, immediate, and irreparable damage to our Nation or its people. That being so, there can under the First Amendment be but one judicial resolution of the issues before us. I join the judgments of the Court.

Justice WHITE, with whom Justice STEWART joins, concurring.

I concur in today's judgments, but only because of the concededly extraordinary protection against prior restraints enjoyed by the press under our constitutional system. I do not say that in no circumstances would the First Amendment permit an injunction against publishing information about government plans or operations. Nor, after examining the materials the Government characterizes as the most sensitive and destructive, can I deny that revelation of these documents will do substantial damage to public interests. Indeed, I am confident that their disclosure will have that result. But I nevertheless agree that the United States has not satisfied the very heavy burden that it must meet to warrant an injunction against publication in these cases, at least in the absence of express and appropriately limited congressional authorization for prior restraints in circumstances such as these.

Justice MARSHALL, concurring.

The Government contends that the only issue in these cases is whether in a suit by the United States, "the First Amendment bars a court from prohibiting a newspaper from publishing material whose disclosure would pose a 'grave and immediate danger to the security of the United States.'" With all due respect, I believe the ultimate issue in these cases is even more basic than the one posed by the Solicitor General. The issue is whether this Court or the Congress has the power to make law.

In these cases there is no problem concerning the President's power to classify information as "secret" or "top secret." Congress has specifically recognized Presidential authority, which has been formally exercised in Exec. Order 10501 (1953), to classify documents and information. Nor is there any issue here regarding the President's power as Chief Executive and Commander in Chief to protect national security by disciplining employees who disclose information and by taking precautions to prevent leaks.

The problem here is whether in these particular cases the Executive Branch has authority to invoke the equity jurisdiction of the courts to protect what it believes to be the national interest. The Government argues that in addition to the inherent power of any government to protect itself, the President's power to conduct foreign affairs and his position as Commander in Chief give him authority to impose censorship on the press to protect his ability to deal effectively with foreign nations and to conduct the military affairs of the country. Of course, it is beyond cavil that the President has broad powers by virtue of his primary responsibility for the conduct of our foreign affairs and his position as Commander in Chief. And in some situations it may be that under whatever inherent powers the Government may have, as well as the implicit authority derived from the President's mandate to conduct foreign affairs and to act as Commander in Chief, there is a basis for the invocation of the equity jurisdiction of this Court as an aid to prevent the publication of material damaging to "national security," however that term may be defined.

It would, however, be utterly inconsistent with the concept of separation of powers for this Court to use its power of contempt to prevent behavior that Congress has specifically declined to prohibit. There would be a similar damage to the basic concept of these co-equal branches of Government if when the Executive Branch has adequate authority granted by Congress to protect "national security" it can choose instead to invoke the contempt power of a court to enjoin the threatened conduct. The Constitution provides that Congress shall make laws, the President executes laws, and courts interpret laws. It did not provide for government by injunction in which the courts and the Executive Branch can "make law" without regard to the action of Congress. It may be more convenient for the Executive Branch if it need only convince a judge to prohibit conduct rather than ask the Congress to pass a law, and it may be more convenient to enforce a contempt order than to seek a criminal conviction in a jury trial. Moreover, it may be considered politically wise to get a court to share the responsibility for arresting those who the Executive Branch has probable cause to believe are violating the law. But convenience and political considerations of the moment do not justify a basic departure from the principles of our system of government....

Chief Justice BURGER, dissenting.

So clear are the constitutional limitations on prior restraint against expression, that from the time of *Near v. Minnesota,* 283 U.S. 697 (1931), until recently in *Organization for a Better Austin v. Keefe,* 402 U.S. 415 (1971), we have had little occasion to be concerned with cases involving prior restraints against news reporting on matters of public interest. There is, therefore, little variation among the members of the Court in terms of resistance to prior restraints against publication. Adherence to this basic constitutional principle, however, does not make these cases simple. In these cases, the imperative of a free and unfettered press comes into collision with another imperative, the effective functioning of a complex modern government and specifically the effective exercise of certain constitutional powers of the Executive. Only those who view the First Amendment as an absolute in all circumstances—a view I respect, but reject—can find such cases as these to be simple or easy.

These cases are not simple for another and more immediate reason. We do not know the facts of the cases. No District Judge knew all the facts. No Court of Appeals judge knew all the facts. No member of this Court knows all the facts.

Why are we in this posture, in which only those judges to whom the First Amendment is absolute and permits of no restraint in any circumstances or for any reason, are really in a position to act?

I suggest we are in this posture because these cases have been conducted in unseemly haste....

Justice HARLAN, with whom The Chief Justice and Justice BLACKMUN join, dissenting.

These cases forcefully call to mind the wise admonition of Mr. Justice Holmes, dissenting in *Northern Securities Co. v. United States,* 193 U.S. 197, 400-401 (1904):

> "Great cases like hard cases make bad law. For great cases are called great, not by reason of their real importance in shaping the law of the future, but because of some accident of immediate overwhelming interest which appeals to the feelings and distorts the judgment. These immediate interests exercise a kind of hydraulic pressure which makes what previously was clear seem doubtful, and before which even well settled principles of law will bend."

With all respect, I consider that the Court has been almost irresponsibly feverish in dealing with these cases.

Both the Court of Appeals for the Second Circuit and the Court of Appeals for the District of Columbia Circuit rendered judgment on June 23. The *New York Times'* petition for certiorari, its motion for accelerated consideration thereof, and its application for interim relief were filed in this Court on June 24 at about 11 a.m. The application of the United States for interim relief in the *Post* case was also filed here on June 24 at about 7:15 p.m. This Court's order setting a hearing before us on June 26 at 11 a.m., a course that I joined only to avoid the possibility of even more peremptory action by the Court, was issued less than 24 hours before. The record in the *Post* case was filed with the Clerk shortly before 1 p.m. on June 25; the record in the *Times* case did not arrive until 7 or 8 p.m. that same night. The briefs of the parties were received less than two hours before argument on June 26.

This frenzied train of events took place in the name of the presumption against prior restraints created by the First Amendment. Due regard for the extraordinarily important and difficult questions involved in these litigations should have led the Court to shun such a precipitate timetable. In order to decide the merits of these cases properly, some or all of the following questions should have been faced:

1. Whether the Attorney General is authorized to bring these suits in the name of the United States. This question involves as well the construction and validity of a singularly opaque statute—the Espionage Act, 18 U. S. C. § 793 (e).
2. Whether the First Amendment permits the federal courts to enjoin publication of stories which would present a serious threat to national security. See *Near v. Minnesota,* 283 U.S. 697, 716 (1931) (dictum).
3. Whether the threat to publish highly secret documents is of itself a sufficient implication of national security to justify an injunction on the theory that regardless of the contents of the documents harm enough results simply from the demonstration of such a breach of secrecy.
4. Whether the unauthorized disclosure of any of these particular documents would seriously impair the national security.
5. What weight should be given to the opinion of high officers in the Executive Branch of the Government with respect to questions 3 and 4.
6. Whether the newspapers are entitled to retain and use the documents notwithstanding the seemingly uncontested facts that the documents, or the

originals of which they are duplicates, were purloined from the Government's possession and that the newspapers received them with knowledge that they had been feloniously acquired.

7. Whether the threatened harm to the national security or the Government's possessory interest in the documents justifies the issuance of an injunction against publication in light of—

a. The strong First Amendment policy against prior restraints on publication;

b. The doctrine against enjoining conduct in violation of criminal statutes; and

c. The extent to which the materials at issue have apparently already been otherwise disseminated.

These are difficult questions of fact, of law, and of judgment; the potential consequences of erroneous decision are enormous. The time that has been available to us, to the lower courts, and to the parties has been wholly inadequate for giving these cases the kind of consideration they deserve.

Justice BLACKMUN, dissenting.

....

At this point the focus is on only the comparatively few documents specified by the Government as critical. So far as the other material—vast in amount—is concerned, let it be published and published forthwith if the newspapers, once the strain is gone and the sensationalism is eased, still feel the urge so to do.

But we are concerned here with the few documents specified from the forty-seven volumes.

The *New York Times* clandestinely devoted a period of three months to examining the forty-seven volumes that came into its unauthorized possession. Once it had begun publication of material from those volumes, the New York case now before us emerged. It immediately assumed, and ever since has maintained, a frenetic pace and character. Seemingly, once publication started, the material could not be made public fast enough. Seemingly, from then on, every deferral or delay, by restraint or otherwise, was abhorrent and was to be deemed violative of the First Amendment and of the public's "right immediately to know." Yet that newspaper stood before us at oral argument and professed criticism of the Government for not lodging its protest earlier than by a Monday telegram following the initial Sunday publication....

Two federal district courts, two United States courts of appeals, and this Court— within a period of less than three weeks from inception until today—have been pressed into hurried decision of profound constitutional issues on inadequately developed and largely assumed facts without the careful deliberation that, one would hope, should characterize the American judicial process....

The First Amendment, after all, is only one part of an entire Constitution. Article II of the great document vests in the Executive Branch primary power over the conduct of foreign affairs and places in that branch the responsibility for the Nation's safety. Each provision of the Constitution is important, and I cannot subscribe to a doctrine of unlimited absolutism for the First Amendment at the cost of downgrading other provisions....

I therefore would remand these cases to be developed expeditiously, of course, but on a schedule permitting the orderly presentation of evidence from both sides, with the use of discovery, if necessary, as authorized by the rules, and with the preparation of briefs, oral argument, and court opinions of a quality better than has been seen to this point....

United States v. The Progressive, Inc.
United States District Court, Western District of Wisconsin, 1979
467 F. Supp. 990

Opinion: Memorandum and Order

[Free-lance writer Howard Morland, while on assignment for *The Progressive* magazine, prepared an article describing the operation of a hydrogen bomb. The article was entitled, "The H-Bomb Secret How We Got It, Why We're Telling It." On February 27, 1979, a copy of the Morland manuscript was delivered to the Department of Energy offices in Germantown, Maryland, with a request that the Department verify the technical accuracy of the material. Government officials determined that a significant portion of the article contained information that the Atomic Energy Act, 42 U.S.C. § 2014(y), required to be classified as Restricted Data. Government officials met with representatives of the magazine and told them that publication of the article would constitute a violation of the Atomic Energy Act and would give an advantage to foreign nations in the development of thermonuclear technology. The government asked the magazine to omit those portions of the article that contained Secret Restricted Data. After considering the request, the magazine responded that it intended to publish the entire article. The federal government then went to court for an injunction that would prohibit *The Progressive* from publishing any of the Restricted Data contained in the article.]

Under the facts here alleged, the question before this Court involves a clash between allegedly vital security interests of the United States and the competing constitutional doctrine against prior restraint in publication.

In its argument and briefs, plaintiff relies on national security, as enunciated by Congress in The Atomic Energy Act of 1954, as the basis for classification of certain documents. Plaintiff contends that, in certain areas, national preservation and self-interest permit the retention and classification of government secrets. The government argues that its national security interest also permits it to impress classification and censorship upon information originating in the public domain, if when drawn together, synthesized and collated, such information acquires the character of presenting immediate, direct, and irreparable harm to the interests of the United States.

Defendants argue that freedom of expression as embodied in the First Amendment is so central to the heart of liberty that prior restraint in any form becomes anathema. They contend that this is particularly true when a nation is not at war and where the prior restraint is based on surmise or conjecture. While acknowledging that freedom of the press is not absolute, they maintain that the publication of the projected article does not rise to the level of immediate, direct, and irreparable harm that could justify incursion into First Amendment freedoms....

Defendants contend that the projected article merely contains data already in the public domain and readily available to any diligent seeker. They say other nations already have the same information or the opportunity to obtain it. How then, they argue, can they be in violation of 42 U.S.C. §§ 2274(b) and 2280 which purport to authorize injunctive relief against one who would disclose restricted data "with reason to believe such data will be utilized to injure the United States or to secure an advantage to any foreign nation..."?

Although the government states that some of the information is in the public domain, it contends that much of the data is not, and that the Morland article contains a core of information that has never before been published.

Furthermore, the government's position is that whether or not specific information is "in the public domain" or has been "declassified" at some point is not determinative. The government states that a court must look at the nature and context of prior disclosures and analyze what the practical impact of the prior disclosures are as contrasted to that of the present revelation....

Does the article provide a "do-it yourself" guide for the hydrogen bomb? Probably not.... One does not build a hydrogen bomb in the basement. However, the article could possibly provide sufficient information to allow a medium-size nation to move faster in developing a hydrogen weapon. It could provide a ticket to by-pass blind alleys....

Defendants have stated that publication of the article will alert the people of this country to the false illusion of security created by the government's futile efforts at secrecy. They believe publication will provide the people with needed information to make informed decisions on an urgent issue of public concern.

However, this Court can find no plausible reason why the public needs to know the technical details about hydrogen bomb construction to carry on an informed debate on this issue. Furthermore, the Court believes that the defendants' position in favor of nuclear non-proliferation would be harmed, not aided, by the publication of this article.

The defendants have also relied on the decision in the *New York Times* case. In that case, the Supreme Court refused to enjoin the *New York Times* and the *Washington Post* from publishing the contents of a classified historical study of United States decision-making in Viet Nam, the so-called "Pentagon Papers."

This case is different in several important respects. In the first place, the study involved in the *New York Times* case contained historical data relating to events that occurred some three to twenty years previously. Secondly, the Supreme Court agreed with the lower court that no cogent reasons were advanced by the government as to why the article affected national security except that publication might cause some embarrassment to the United States.

A final and most vital difference between these two cases is the fact that a specific statute is involved here. Section 2274 of The Atomic Energy Act prohibits anyone from communicating, transmitting, or disclosing any restricted data to any person "with reason to believe such data will be utilized to injure the United States or to secure an advantage to any foreign nation."...

The Court is of the opinion that the government has shown that the defendants had reason to believe that the data in the article, if published, would injure the United States or give an advantage to a foreign nation. Extensive reading and studying of the documents on file lead to the conclusion that not all the data is available in the public realm in the same fashion, if it is available at all.

What is involved here is information dealing with the most destructive weapon in the history of mankind, information of sufficient destructive potential to nullify the right to free speech and to endanger the right to life itself.

Stripped to its essence then, the question before the Court is a basic confrontation between the First Amendment right to freedom of the press and national security.

Our Founding Fathers believed, as we do, that one is born with certain inalienable rights that, as the Declaration of Independence intones, include the right to life, liberty, and the pursuit of happiness. The Constitution, including the Bill of Rights, was enacted to make those rights operable in everyday life.

The Court believes that each of us is born seized of a panoply of basic rights, that we institute governments to secure these rights and that there is a hierarchy of values attached to these rights which is helpful in deciding the clash now before us.

… While it may be true in the long-run, as Patrick Henry instructs us, that one would prefer death to life without liberty, nonetheless, in the short-run, one cannot enjoy freedom of speech, freedom to worship, or freedom of the press unless one first enjoys the freedom to live.

Faced with a stark choice between upholding the right to continued life and the right to freedom of the press, most jurists would have no difficulty in opting for the chance to continue to breathe and function as they work to achieve perfect freedom of expression.

Is the choice here so stark? Only time can give us a definitive answer. But considering another aspect of this panoply of rights we all have is helpful in answering the question now before us. This aspect is the disparity of the risk involved.

The destruction of various human rights can come about in differing ways and at varying speeds. Freedom of the press can be obliterated overnight by some dictator's imposition of censorship or by the slow nibbling away at a free press through successive bits of repressive legislation enacted by a nation's lawmakers. Yet, even in the most drastic of such situations, it is always possible for a dictator to be overthrown, for a bad law to be repealed, or for a judge's error to be subsequently rectified. Only when human life is at stake are such corrections impossible.

The case at bar is so difficult precisely because the consequences of error involve human life itself and on such an awesome scale.

The Secretary of State states that publication will increase thermonuclear proliferation and that this would "irreparably impair the national security of the United States." The Secretary of Defense says that dissemination of the Morland paper will mean a substantial increase in the risk of thermonuclear proliferation and lead to use or threats that would "adversely affect the national security of the United States."

Howard Morland asserts that "if the information in my article were not in the public domain, it should be put there … so that ordinary citizens may have informed opinions about nuclear weapons."

Erwin Knoll, the editor of *The Progressive,* states he is "totally convinced that publication of the article will be of substantial benefit to the United States because it will demonstrate that this country's security does not lie in an oppressive and ineffective system of secrecy and classification but in open, honest, and informed public debate about issues which the people must decide."

The Court is faced with the difficult task of weighing and resolving these divergent views.

A mistake in ruling against *The Progressive* will seriously infringe cherished First Amendment rights. If a preliminary injunction is issued, it will constitute the first instance of prior restraint against a publication in this fashion in the history of this country, to this Court's knowledge. Such notoriety is not to be sought. It will curtail defendants' First Amendment rights in a drastic and substantial fashion. It will infringe upon our right to know and to be informed as well.

A mistake in ruling against the United States could pave the way for thermonuclear annihilation for us all. In that event, our right to life is extinguished and the right to publish becomes moot.

In [*Near v. Minnesota*], the Supreme Court recognized that publication of troop movements in time of war would threaten national security and could therefore be restrained. Times have changed significantly since 1931 when *Near* was decided. Now war by foot soldiers has been replaced in large part by war by machines and bombs. No longer need there be any advance warning or any preparation time before a nuclear war could be commenced.

In light of these factors, this Court concludes that publication of the technical information on the hydrogen bomb contained in the article is analogous to publication of troop movements or locations in time of war and falls within the extremely narrow exception to the rule against prior restraint.

Because of this "disparity of risk," because the government has met its heavy burden of showing justification for the imposition of a prior restraint on publication of the objected-to technical portions of the Morland article, and because the Court is unconvinced that suppression of the objected-to technical portions of the Morland article would in any plausible fashion impede the defendants in their laudable crusade to stimulate public knowledge of nuclear armament and bring about enlightened debate on national policy questions, the Court finds that the objected-to portions of the article fall within the narrow area recognized by the Court in *Near v. Minnesota* in which a prior restraint on publication is appropriate.

The government has met its burden under section 2274 of The Atomic Energy Act. In the Court's opinion, it has also met the test enunciated by two Justices in the *New York Times* case, namely grave, direct, immediate, and irreparable harm to the United States....

Plaintiff has proven all necessary prerequisites for issuance of a preliminary injunction restraining defendants from publishing or disclosing any Restricted Data contained in the Morland article until a final determination in this action has been made by the Court.

[The magazine appealed the preliminary injunction, and it looked as though this case would ultimately wind up in the U.S. Supreme Court. While the appeal was pending, however, a few newspapers published the information that the magazine had been enjoined from running. The government then decided to drop its complaint against The Progressive, *and the case was dismissed as moot.]*

OLIVIA N. v. NATIONAL BROADCASTING CO.
Court of Appeal of California, 1981
178 Cal. Rptr. 888

Opinion by: CHRISTIAN

Olivia N. appeals from a judgment of nonsuit terminating her action against the National Broadcasting Company and the Chronicle Broadcasting Company. Appellant sought damages for physical and emotional injury inflicted by assailants who had seen a television broadcast of a film drama....

.... [A]ppellant's counsel in his opening statement to the jury indicated that the evidence would establish negligence and recklessness on respondents' part, rather than incitement. At the conclusion of appellant's opening statement, respondents moved for a judgment of nonsuit on the grounds that appellant admittedly could not meet the test for incitement. (*Brandenburg v. Ohio* (1969) 395 U.S. 444, 447.) Appellant's counsel again acknowledged his inability to meet the incitement test; the trial court granted respondents' motion and rendered judgment dismissing the action....

At 8 p.m. on September 10, 1974, NBC telecast nationwide, and Chronicle Broadcasting Company broadcast locally, a film entitled "Born Innocent." "The subject matter of the television film was the harmful effect of a state-run home upon an adolescent girl who had become a ward of the state. In one scene of the film, the young girl enters the community bathroom of the facility to take a shower. She is then shown taking off her clothes and stepping into the shower, where she bathes for a few moments. Suddenly, the water stops and a look of fear comes across her face. Four adolescent girls are standing across from her in the shower room. One of the girls is carrying a 'plumber's helper,' waving it suggestively by her side. The four girls violently attack the younger girl, wrestling her to the floor. The young girl is shown naked from the waist up, struggling as the older girls force her legs apart. Then, the television film shows the girl with the plumber's helper making intense thrusting motions with the handle of the plunger until one of the four says, 'That's enough.' The young girl is left sobbing and naked on the floor." It is alleged that on September 14, 1974, appellant, aged nine, was attacked and forcibly "artificially raped" with a bottle by minors at a San Francisco beach. The assailants had viewed and discussed the "artificial rape" scene in "Born Innocent," and the film allegedly caused the assailants to decide to commit a similar act on appellant. Appellant offered to show that NBC had knowledge of studies on child violence and should have known that susceptible persons might imitate the crime enacted in the film. Appellant alleged that "Born Innocent" was particularly likely to cause imitation and that NBC televised the film without proper warning in an effort to obtain the largest possible viewing audience. Appellant alleged that as a proximate result of respondents' telecast, she suffered physical and psychological damage.

Appellant contends that where there is negligence liability could constitutionally be imposed despite the absence of proof of incitement as defined in Brandenburg v. Ohio. Appellant argues in the alternative that a different definition of "incitement" should be applied to the present circumstances....

Appellant does not seek to impose a prior restraint on speech; rather, she asserts civil liability premised on traditional negligence concepts. But the chilling effect of permitting negligence actions for a television broadcast is obvious. "The fear of damage awards … may be markedly more inhibiting than the fear of prosecution under a criminal statute." Realistically, television networks would become significantly more inhibited in the selection of controversial materials if liability were to be imposed on a simple negligence theory. "[The] pall of fear and timidity imposed upon those who would give voice to public criticism is an atmosphere in which the First Amendment freedoms cannot survive." (*New York Times Co. v. Sullivan,* 376 U.S. 254, 278.) The deterrent effect of subjecting the television networks to negligence liability because of their programming choices would lead to self-censorship that would dampen the vigor and limit the variety of public debate.

Although the First Amendment is not absolute, the television broadcast of "Born Innocent" does not, on the basis of the opening statement of appellant's attorney, fall within the scope of unprotected speech. Appellant concedes that the film did not advocate or encourage violent acts and did not constitute an "incitement" within the meaning of Brandenburg v. Ohio. Notwithstanding the pervasive effect of the broadcasting media and the unique access afforded children, the effect of the imposition of liability could reduce the U.S. adult population to viewing only what is fit for children. Incitement is the proper test here. In areas outside of obscenity the United States Supreme Court has "consistently held that the fact that protected speech may be offensive to some does not justify its suppression. See, e.g., *Cohen v. California,* 403 U.S. 15 (1971)." … [T]he television broadcast which is the subject of this action concededly did not fulfill the incitement requirements of Brandenburg. [The expression must be "directed to inciting or producing imminent lawless action and … likely to incite or produce such action."] Thus it is constitutionally protected.

Appellant would distinguish between the fictional presentation of "Born Innocent" and news programs and documentaries. But that distinction is too blurred to protect adequately First Amendment values. "Everyone is familiar with instances of propaganda through fiction. What is one man's amusement, teaches another's doctrine." If a negligence theory is recognized, a television network or local station could be liable when a child imitates activities portrayed in a news program or documentary. Thus, the distinction urged by appellant cannot be accepted…. The trial court's determination that the First Amendment bars appellant's claim where no incitement is alleged must be upheld.

Appellant argues from *Weirum v. RKO General, Inc.* (1975) 15 Cal.3d 40 [123 Cal.Rptr. 468, 539 P.2d 36], that the First Amendment should not bar a negligence action. In *Weirum,* the California Supreme Court upheld a jury finding that a Los Angeles rock radio station was liable for the wrongful death of a motorist killed by two teenagers participating in a contest sponsored by the station. The court emphasized that the youthful contestants' reckless conduct was stimulated by the radio station's broadcast. Limiting its ruling, the court indicated that "[the] giveaway contest was no commonplace invitation to an attraction available on a limited basis. It was a competitive scramble in which the thrill of the chase to be the one and only victor was intensified by the live broadcasts that accompanied the pursuit…. In [other] situations there [was] no attempt, as here, to generate a competitive pursuit on public streets, accelerated by repeated importuning by radio to be the very first to arrive at a particular destination." Disposing of the radio station's First Amendment claim, the court said: "Defendant's contention that the giveaway contest must be afforded the deference due society's interest in the First Amendment is clearly without merit. The issue here is civil accountability for the foreseeable results of a broadcast that created an undue risk of harm to decedent. The First Amendment does not sanction the infliction of physical injury merely because achieved by word, rather than act." Although the language utilized by the Supreme Court was broad, it must be understood in light of the particular facts of that case. The radio station's broadcast was designed to encourage its youthful listeners to be the first to arrive at a particular location in order to win a prize and gain momentary glory. The Weirum broadcasts actively and repeatedly encouraged listeners to speed to announced locations. Liability was imposed on the broadcaster for urging listeners to act in an inherently dangerous manner. No such urging can be imputed to respondents here. Appellant only alleges that the teenage viewers of "Born Innocent" acted on the stimulus of the broadcast rather than in response to encouragement of such conduct. Weirum does not control the present case....

The judgment is affirmed.

WINTER V. G.P. PUTNAM'S SONS
United States Court of Appeals for the Ninth Circuit, 1991
938 F.2d 1033

SNEED, Circuit Judge.

Plaintiffs are mushroom enthusiasts who became severely ill from picking and eating mushrooms after relying on information in *The Encyclopedia of Mushrooms,* a book published by the defendant. Plaintiffs sued the publisher and sought damages under various theories. The district court granted summary judgment for the defendant.

FACTS AND PROCEEDINGS BELOW

The Encyclopedia of Mushrooms is a reference guide containing information on the habitat, collection, and cooking of mushrooms. It was written by two British authors and originally published by a British publishing company. Defendant Putnam, an American book publisher, purchased copies of the book from the British publisher and distributed the finished product in the United States. Putnam neither wrote nor edited the book.

Plaintiffs purchased the book to help them collect and eat wild mushrooms. In 1988, plaintiffs went mushroom hunting and relied on the descriptions in the book in determining which mushrooms were safe to eat. After cooking and eating their harvest, plaintiffs became critically ill. Both have required liver transplants.

Plaintiffs allege that the book contained erroneous and misleading information concerning the identification of the most deadly species of mushrooms. In their suit against the book publisher, plaintiffs allege liability based on products liability, breach of warranty, negligence, negligent misrepresentation, and false representations. Defendant moved for summary judgment asserting that plaintiffs' claims failed as a matter of law because 1) the information contained in a book is not a product for the purposes of strict liability under products liability law; and 2) defendant is not liable under any remaining theories because a publisher does not have a duty to investigate the accuracy of the text it publishes. The district court granted summary judgment for the defendant. Plaintiffs appeal. We affirm.

DISCUSSION

A book containing Shakespeare's sonnets consists of two parts, the material and print therein, and the ideas and expression thereof. The first may be a product, but the second is not. The latter, were Shakespeare alive, would be governed by copyright laws; the laws of libel, to the extent consistent with the First Amendment; and the laws of misrepresentation, negligent misrepresentation, negligence, and mistake. These doctrines applicable to the second part are aimed at the delicate issues that arise with respect to intangibles such as ideas and expression. Products liability law is geared to the tangible world.

A. Products Liability

The language of products liability law reflects its focus on tangible items. In describing the scope of products liability law, the *Restatement (Second) of Torts* lists examples of items that are covered. All of these are tangible items, such as tires, automobiles, and insecticides. The American Law Institute clearly was concerned with including all physical items but gave no indication that the doctrine should be expanded beyond that area.

The purposes served by products liability law also are focused on the tangible world and do not take into consideration the unique characteristics of ideas and expression. Under products liability law, strict liability is imposed on the theory that "[t]he costs of damaging events due to defectively dangerous products can best be borne by the enterprisers who make and sell these products." Strict liability principles have been adopted to further the "cause of accident prevention ... [by] the elimination of the necessity of proving negligence." Additionally, because of the difficulty of establishing fault or negligence in products liability cases, strict liability is the appropriate legal theory to hold manufacturers liable for defective products. Thus, the seller is subject to liability "even though he has exercised all possible care in the preparation and sale of the product." It is not a question of fault but simply a determination of how society wishes to assess certain costs that arise from the creation and distribution of products in a complex technological society in which the consumer thereof is unable to protect himself against certain product defects.

Although there is always some appeal to the involuntary spreading of costs of injuries in any area, the costs in any comprehensive cost/benefit analysis would be quite different were strict liability concepts applied to words and ideas. We place a high priority on the unfettered exchange of ideas. We accept the risk that words and ideas have wings we cannot clip and which carry them we know not where. The threat of liability without fault (financial responsibility for our words and ideas in the absence of fault or a special undertaking or responsibility) could seriously inhibit those who wish to share thoughts and theories. As a New York court commented, with the specter of strict liability, "[w]ould any author wish to be exposed ... for writing on a topic which might result in physical injury? e.g. How to cut trees; How to keep bees?" Walter v. Bauer, 109 Misc. 2d 189, 191, 439 N.Y.S.2d 821, 823 (Sup. Ct. 1981) (student injured doing science project described in textbook; court held that the book was not a product for purposes of products liability law). One might add: "Would anyone undertake to guide by ideas expressed in words either a discrete group, a nation, or humanity in general?" ...

Plaintiffs suggest, however, that our fears would be groundless were strict liability rules applied only to books that give instruction on how to accomplish a physical activity and that are intended to be used as part of an activity that is inherently dangerous. We find such a limitation illusory. Ideas are often intimately linked with proposed action, and it would be difficult to draw such a bright line. While "How To" books are a special genre, we decline to attempt to draw a line that puts "How To Live A Good Life" books beyond the reach of strict liability while leaving "How To Exercise Properly" books within its reach.

Plaintiffs' argument is stronger when they assert that *The Encyclopedia of Mushrooms* should be analogized to aeronautical charts. Several jurisdictions have held that charts that graphically depict geographic features or instrument approach information for airplanes are "products" for the purpose of products liability law. Plaintiffs suggest that *The Encyclopedia of Mushrooms* can be compared to aeronautical charts because both items contain representations of natural features and both are intended to be used while engaging in a hazardous activity. We are not persuaded.

Aeronautical charts are highly technical tools. They are graphic depictions of technical, mechanical data. The best analogy to an aeronautical chart is a compass. Both may be used to guide an individual who is engaged in an activity requiring certain knowledge of natural features. Computer software that fails to yield the result for which it was designed may be another. In contrast, *The Encyclopedia of Mushrooms* is like a book on how to use a compass or an aeronautical chart. The chart itself is like a physical "product" while the "How to Use" book is pure thought and expression.

Given these considerations, we decline to expand products liability law to embrace the ideas and expression in a book. We know of no court that has chosen the path to which the plaintiffs point.

B. The Remaining Theories

As discussed above, plaintiffs must look to the doctrines of copyright, libel, misrepresentation, negligent misrepresentation, negligence, and mistake to form the basis of a claim against the defendant publisher. Unless it is assumed that the publisher is a guarantor of the accuracy of an author's statements of fact, plaintiffs have made no case under any of these theories other than possibly negligence. Guided by the First Amendment and the values embodied therein, we decline to extend liability under this theory to the ideas and expression contained in a book.

In order for negligence to be actionable, there must be a legal duty to exercise due care. The plaintiffs urge this court that the publisher had a duty to investigate the accuracy of *The Encyclopedia of Mushrooms'* contents. We conclude that the defendants have no duty to investigate the accuracy of the contents of the books it publishes. A publisher may of course assume such a burden, but there is nothing inherent in the role of publisher or the surrounding legal doctrines to suggest that such a duty should be imposed on publishers. Indeed the cases uniformly refuse to impose such a duty. Were we tempted to create this duty, the gentle tug of the First Amendment and the values embodied therein would remind us of the social costs....

For the reasons outlined above, the decision of the district court is AFFIRMED.

DOE v. MYSPACE, INC.
U.S. Court of Appeals for the Fifth Circuit
528 F.3d 413

EDITH BROWN CLEMENT, Circuit Judge:

Jane and Julie Doe ("the Does") appeal the district court's dismissal of their claims for negligence and gross negligence, and its finding that the claims were barred by the Communications Decency Act ("CDA"), 47 U.S.C § 230, and Texas common law. For the following reasons, we affirm the decision of the district court.

I. FACTS AND PROCEEDINGS

MySpace.com is a Web-based social network.... Members have complete discretion regarding the amount and type of information that is included in a personal profile. Members over the age of sixteen can choose the degree of privacy they desire regarding their profile; that is, they determine who among the MySpace.com membership is allowed to view their profile. Once a profile has been created, the member can use it to extend "invitations" to existing friends who are also MySpace.com users and to communicate with those friends online by linking to their profiles, or using e-mail, instant messaging, and blogs, all of which are hosted through the MySpace.com platform.

Members can also meet new people at MySpace.com through user groups focused on common interests such as film, travel, music, or politics. MySpace.com has a browser feature that allows members to search the Web site's membership using criteria such as geographic location or specific interests....

MySpace.com membership is free to all who agree to the Terms of Use. To establish a profile, users must represent that they are at least fourteen years of age. The profiles of members who are aged fourteen and fifteen are automatically set to "private" by default, in order to limit the amount of personal information that can be seen on the member's profile by MySpace.com users who are not in their existing friends network and to prevent younger teens from being contacted by users they do not know. Although MySpace.com employs a computer program designed to search for clues that underage members have lied about their age to create a profile on the Web site, no current technology is foolproof. All members are cautioned regarding the type of information they release to other users on the Web site, including a specific prohibition against posting personal information ....

In the summer of 2005, at age thirteen, Julie Doe ("Julie") lied about her age, represented that she was eighteen years old, and created a profile on MySpace.com. This action allowed her to circumvent all safety features of the Web site and resulted in her profile being made public; nineteen-year-old Pete Solis ("Solis") was able to initiate contact with Julie in April 2006 when she was fourteen. The two communicated offline on several occasions after Julie provided her telephone number. They met in person in May 2006, and, at this meeting, Solis sexually assaulted Julie.

Julie's mother, Jane Doe, first sued MySpace, Inc., its parent company, News Corporation (collectively "MySpace"), and Solis in a Texas state court on her own behalf and on behalf of her daughter, alleging that MySpace failed to implement basic safety measures to prevent sexual predators from communicating with minors on its Web site. The Does' original petition asserted claims for fraud, negligent misrepresentation, negligence, and gross negligence against MySpace, and claims for sexual assault and intentional infliction of emotional distress against Solis. MySpace answered the petition and filed special exceptions, asserting among other things, that the CDA and Texas common law barred the Does' claims....

.... In their complaint, the Does alleged:

8. To access the social network, one must create a MySpace account. In order to create a MySpace account, all one has to do is enter a name, email address, gender, country, and date of birth. . . . .

9. Once signed up, each MySpace user is given his or her own personal webpage to create. MySpace users are then prompted to post photographs and personal information on their webpage. Typically, a MySpace user's webpage is viewable by any other MySpace user. Further, any MySpace user can contact any other MySpace user through internal email and/or instant messaging on MySpace.

. . . .

11. The catalyst behind MySpace's amazing surge in popularity is their underage users demographic. According to MySpace, approximately 22 percent of MySpace visitors are minors, under the age of 18. MySpace actively and passively markets itself to minors.

. . . .

27. In the summer of 2005, 14-year-old Julie created a profile on MySpace. At the time, Julie was only 13-years-old. Despite MySpace's supposed safety precautions and protections prohibiting anyone under 14-years-old from using MySpace, Julie was easily able to create a profile.

. . . .

41. Defendants owed a legal duty to 14-year-old Julie to institute and enforce appropriate security measures and policies that would substantially decrease the likelihood of danger and harm that MySpace posed to her.

The district court in Texas dismissed with prejudice the Does' claims for negligence and gross negligence, finding that the claims were barred by the CDA and Texas common law.... The Does now appeal the district court's dismissal of their claims for negligence and gross negligence, arguing that § 230(c)(1) of the CDA is inapplicable here because their claims do not implicate MySpace as a "publisher" protected by the Act and because MySpace not only published but was also partially responsible for creating the content of the information that was exchanged between Julie and Solis. Doe next argues that § 230(c)(2) does not immunize MySpace's failure to take reasonable steps to ensure minors' safety.... We hold, however, that the Does' claims of negligence are barred by § 230(c)(1) of the CDA.

. . . .

III. DISCUSSION

In October 1998, Congress recognized the rapid development of the Internet and the benefits generated by Web-based service providers to the public.... In light of its findings, Congress enacted the CDA for several policy reasons, including "to remove disincentives for the development and utilization of blocking and filtering technologies that empower parents to restrict their children's access to objectionable or inappropriate online material." To achieve that policy goal, Congress provided broad immunity under the CDA to Web-based service providers for all claims stemming from their publication of information created by third parties, referred to as the "Good Samaritan" provision. ("No provider or user of an interactive computer service shall be treated as the publisher or speaker of any information provided by another information content provider."). Indeed, "[n]o cause of action may be brought and no liability may be imposed under any State or local law that is inconsistent with this section."

Courts have construed the immunity provisions in § 230 broadly in all cases arising from the publication of user-generated content. For example, the Ninth Circuit held that a Web-based dating-service provider was not liable when an unidentified party posted a false online personal profile for a popular actress, causing her to receive sexually explicit phone calls, letters, and faxes at her home....

....

Parties complaining that they were harmed by a Web site's publication of user-generated content have recourse; they may sue the third-party user who generated the content, but not the interactive computer service that enabled them to publish the content online.

The Does appear to agree with the consensus among courts regarding the liability provisions in § 230(c)(1). They argue, however, that their claims against MySpace do not attempt to treat it as a "publisher" of information; therefore, they argue that § 230 does not immunize MySpace from their claims and state tort law applies in full effect. The Does attempt to distinguish their case from ... contrary authority by claiming that this case is predicated solely on MySpace's failure to implement basic safety measures to protect minors. The district court rejected the Does' argument, stating:

> The Court, however, finds this artful pleading to be disingenuous. It is quite obvious the underlying basis of Plaintiffs' claims is that, through postings on MySpace, Pete Solis and Julie Doe met and exchanged personal information which eventually led to an in-person meeting and the sexual assault of Julie Doe. If MySpace had not published communications between Julie Doe and Solis, including personal contact information, Plaintiffs assert they never would have met and the sexual assault never would have occurred. No matter how artfully Plaintiffs seek to plead their claims, the Court views Plaintiffs' claims as directed toward MySpace in its publishing, editorial, and/or screening capacities.

....

[T]he Does' ... allegations are merely another way of claiming that MySpace was liable for publishing the communications and they speak to MySpace's role as a publisher of online third-party-generated content.

The Does further argue for the first time on appeal that MySpace is not immune under the CDA because it partially created the content at issue, alleging that it facilitates its members' creation of personal profiles and chooses the information they will share with the public through an online questionnaire. The Does also contend that MySpace's search features qualify it as an "information content provider," as defined in the CDA: "The term 'information content provider' means any person or entity that is responsible, in whole or in part, for the creation or development of information provided through the Internet or any other interactive computer service."

Nothing in the record, however, supports such a claim; indeed, Julie admitted that she lied about her age to create the profile and exchanged personal information with Solis. In the February 1, 2007 hearing before the district court, the Does admitted that Julie created the content, disclosing personal information that ultimately led to the sexual assault, but stressed that their cause of action was rooted in the fact that MySpace should have implemented safety technologies to prevent Julie and her attacker from meeting:

> THE COURT: I want to get this straight. You have a 13-year-old girl who lies, disobeys all of the instructions, later on disobeys the warning not to give personal information, obviously, [and] does not communicate with the parent. More important, the parent does not exercise the parental control over the minor. The minor gets sexually abused, and you want somebody else to pay for it? This is the lawsuit that you filed?

> MR. ITKIN [Counsel for the Does]: Yes, your Honor.

> . . . .

.... We [hold that] the Does' ... negligence and gross negligence claims are barred by the CDA, which prohibits claims against Web-based interactive computer services based on their publication of third-party content....

IV. CONCLUSION

The judgment of the district court is AFFIRMED.

AMERICAN AMUSEMENT MACHINE ASS'N V. KENDRICK
U.S. Court of Appeals for the Seventh Circuit, 2001
244 F.3d 572

POSNER, Circuit Judge.

The manufacturers of video games and their trade association seek to enjoin, as a violation of freedom of expression, the enforcement of an Indianapolis ordinance that seeks to limit the access of minors to video games that depict violence. Denial of a preliminary injunction has precipitated this appeal.

The ordinance defines the term "harmful to minors" to mean "an amusement machine that predominantly appeals to minors' morbid interest in violence or minors' prurient interest in sex, is patently offensive to prevailing standards in the adult community as a whole with respect to what is suitable material for persons under the age of eighteen (18) years, lacks serious literary, artistic, political or scientific value as a whole for persons under" that age, and contains either "graphic violence" or "strong sexual content." "Graphic violence," which is all that is involved in this case (so far as appears, the plaintiffs do not manufacture, at least for exhibition in game arcades and other public places, video games that have "strong sexual content"), is defined to mean "an amusement machine's visual depiction or representation of realistic serious injury to a human or human-like being where such serious injury includes amputation, decapitation, dismemberment, bloodshed, mutilation, maiming, or disfiguration [disfigurement]."

The ordinance forbids any operator of five or more video-game machines in one place to allow a minor unaccompanied by a parent, guardian, or other custodian to use "an amusement machine that is harmful to minors," requires appropriate warning signs, and requires that such machines be separated by a partition from the other machines in the location and that their viewing areas be concealed from persons who are on the other side of the partition. Operators of fewer than five games in one location are subject to all but the partitioning restriction. Monetary penalties, as well as suspension and revocation of the right to operate the machines, are specified as remedies for violations of the ordinance.

The ordinance was enacted in 2000, but has not yet gone into effect, in part because we stayed it pending the decision of the appeal. The legislative history indicates that the City believes that participation in violent video games engenders violence on the part of the players, at least when they are minors. The City placed in evidence videotapes of several of the games that it believes violate the ordinance.

Although the district judge agreed with the plaintiffs that video games, possibly including some that would violate the ordinance, are "speech" within the meaning of the First Amendment and that children have rights under the free-speech clause, he held that the ordinance would violate the amendment only if the City lacked "a reasonable basis for believing the Ordinance would protect children from harm." He found a reasonable basis in a pair of empirical studies by psychologists that found that playing a violent video game tends to make young persons more aggressive in their attitudes and behavior, and also in a larger literature finding that violence in the media engenders aggressive feelings. The judge also ruled that the ordinance's tracking of the conventional standard for obscenity eliminated any concern that the ordinance might be excessively vague....

The ordinance brackets violence with sex, and the City asks us to squeeze the provision on violence into a familiar legal pigeonhole, that of obscenity, which is normally concerned with sex and is not protected by the First Amendment, while the plaintiffs insist that since their games are not obscene in the conventional sense they must receive the full protection of the First Amendment. Neither position is compelling. Violence and obscenity are distinct categories of objectionable depiction, and so the fact that obscenity is excluded from the protection of the principle that government may not regulate the content of expressive activity (as distinct from the time, place, or manner of the activity) neither compels nor forecloses a like exclusion of violent imagery....

We shall discover some possible intersections between the concerns that animate obscenity laws and the concerns that animate the Indianapolis ordinance as we proceed, but in general the concerns are different. The main worry about obscenity, the main reason for its proscription, is not that it is harmful, which is the worry behind the Indianapolis ordinance, but that it is offensive. A work is classified as obscene not upon proof that it is likely to affect anyone's conduct, but upon proof that it violates community norms regarding the permissible scope of depictions of sexual or sex-related activity. Obscenity is to many people disgusting, embarrassing, degrading, disturbing, outrageous, and insulting, but it generally is not believed to inflict temporal (as distinct from spiritual) harm; or at least the evidence that it does is not generally considered as persuasive as the evidence that other speech that can be regulated on the basis of its content, such as threats of physical harm, conspiratorial communications, incitements, frauds, and libels and slanders, inflicts such harm....

One can imagine an ordinance directed at depictions of violence because they, too, were offensive. Maybe violent photographs of a person being drawn and quartered could be suppressed as disgusting, embarrassing, degrading, or disturbing without proof that they are likely to cause any of the viewers to commit a violent act. They might even be described as "obscene," in the same way that photographs of people defecating might be, and in many obscenity statutes are, included within the legal category of the obscene, even if they have nothing to do with sex. In common speech, indeed, "obscene" is often just a synonym for repulsive, with no sexual overtones at all.

But offensiveness is not the basis on which Indianapolis seeks to regulate violent video games. Nor could the ordinance be defended on that basis. The most violent game in the record, "The House of the Dead," depicts zombies being killed flamboyantly, with much severing of limbs and effusion of blood; but so stylized and patently fictitious is the cartoon-like depiction that no one would suppose it "obscene" in the sense in which a photograph of a person being decapitated might be described as "obscene." It will not turn anyone's stomach. The basis of the ordinance, rather, is a belief that violent video games cause temporal harm by engendering aggressive attitudes and behavior, which might lead to violence.

This is a different concern from that which animates the obscenity laws, though it does not follow from this that government is helpless to respond to the concern by regulating such games. Protecting people from violence is at least as hallowed a role for government as protecting people from graphic sexual imagery. *Chaplinsky v. New Hampshire* permits punishment of "fighting words," that is, words likely to cause a breach of the peace— violence. Such punishment is permissible "content based" regulation, and in effect Indianapolis is arguing that violent video games incite youthful players to breaches of the peace. But this is to use the word "incitement" metaphorically. As we'll see, no showing has been made that games of the sort found in the record of this case have such an effect. Nor can such a showing be dispensed with on the ground that preventing violence is as canonical a role of government as shielding people from graphic sexual imagery. The issue in this case is not violence as such, or directly; it is violent images; and here the symmetry with obscenity breaks down. Classic literature and art, and not merely today's popular culture, are saturated with graphic scenes of violence, whether narrated or pictorial. The notion of forbidding not violence itself, but pictures of violence, is a novelty, whereas concern with pictures of graphic sexual conduct is of the essence of the traditional concern with obscenity.

There is a hint, though, that the City is also concerned with the welfare of the game-playing children themselves, and not just the welfare of their potential victims. This concern is implicit in the City's citation of *Ginsberg v. New York,* 390 U.S. 629 (1968), which holds that potential harm to children's ethical and psychological development is a permissible ground for trying to shield them from forms of sexual expression that fall short of obscenity.... In the present setting, concern with the welfare of the child might take two forms. One is a concern with the potential psychological harm to children of being exposed to violent images, and would be unrelated to the broader societal concern with violence that was the primary motivation for the ordinance. Another, subtler concern would be with the consequences for the child incited or predisposed to commit violent acts by exposure to violent images....

If the community ceased to find obscenity offensive, yet sought to retain the prohibition of it on the ground that it incited its consumers to commit crimes or to engage in sexual discrimination, or that it interfered with the normal sexual development of its underage consumers, a state would have to present a compelling basis for believing that these were harms actually caused by obscenity and not pretexts for regulation on grounds not authorized by the First Amendment.... We must consider whether the City of Indianapolis has ... grounds for thinking that violent video games cause harm either to the game players or (the point the City stresses) the public at large.

The grounds must be compelling and not merely plausible. Children have First Amendment rights. This is not merely a matter of pressing the First Amendment to a dryly logical extreme. The murderous fanaticism displayed by young German soldiers in World War II, alumni of the Hitler Jugend, illustrates the danger of allowing government to control the access of children to information and opinion. Now that eighteen-year-olds have the right to vote, it is obvious that they must be allowed the freedom to form their political views on the basis of uncensored speech before they turn eighteen, so that their minds are not a blank when they first exercise the franchise. And since an eighteen-year-old's right to vote is a right personal to him rather than a right to be exercised on his behalf by his parents, the right of parents to enlist the aid of the state to shield their children from ideas of which the parents disapprove cannot be plenary either. People are unlikely to become well-functioning, independent-minded adults and responsible citizens if they are raised in an intellectual bubble.

No doubt the City would concede this point if the question were whether to forbid children to read without the presence of an adult *The Odyssey,* with its graphic descriptions of Odysseus's grinding out the eye of Polyphemus with a heated, sharpened stake, killing the suitors, and hanging the treacherous maidservants; or *The Divine Comedy* with its graphic descriptions of the tortures of the damned; or *War and Peace* with its graphic descriptions of execution by firing squad, death in childbirth, and death from war wounds. Or if the question were whether to ban the stories of Edgar Allen Poe, or the famous horror movies made from the classic novels of Mary Wollstonecraft Shelley (*Frankenstein*) and Bram Stoker (*Dracula*). Violence has always been and remains a central interest of humankind and a recurrent, even obsessive theme of culture both high and low. It engages the interest of children from an early age, as anyone familiar with the classic fairy tales collected by Grimm, Andersen, and Perrault are aware. To shield children right up to the age of eighteen from exposure to violent descriptions and images would not only be quixotic, but deforming; it would leave them unequipped to cope with the world as we know it.

Maybe video games are different. They are, after all, interactive. But this point is superficial, in fact, erroneous. All literature (here broadly defined to include movies, television, and the other photographic media, and popular as well as highbrow literature) is interactive; the better it is, the more interactive....

The City rightly does not rest on "what everyone knows" about the harm inflicted by violent video games.... The social science evidence on which the City relies consists primarily of [a] pair of psychological studies ... which are reported in Craig A. Anderson & Karen E. Dill, "Personality Processes and Individual Differences—Video Games and Aggressive Thoughts, Feelings, and Behavior in the Laboratory and in Life," 78 J. Personality & Soc. Psych. 772 (2000). Those studies do not support the ordinance. There is no indication that the games used in the studies are similar to those in the record of this case or to other games likely to be marketed in game arcades in Indianapolis. The studies do not find that video games have ever caused anyone to commit a violent act, as opposed to feeling aggressive, or have caused the average level of violence to increase anywhere....

... Common sense says that the City's claim of harm to its citizens from these games is implausible, at best wildly speculative. Common sense is sometimes another word for prejudice, and the common sense reaction to the Indianapolis ordinance could be overcome by social scientific evidence, but has not been. The ordinance curtails freedom of expression significantly and, on this record, without any offsetting justification, "compelling" or otherwise.

It is conceivable, though, unlikely, that in a plenary trial the City can establish the legality of the ordinance. We need not speculate on what evidence might be offered, or, if none is offered (in which event a permanent injunction should promptly be entered), what amendments might bring the ordinance into conformity with First Amendment principles. We have emphasized the "literary" character of the games in the record and the unrealistic appearance of their "graphic" violence. If the games used actors and simulated real death and mutilation convincingly, or if the games lacked any story line and were merely animated shooting galleries (as several of the games in the record appear to be), a more narrowly drawn ordinance might survive a constitutional challenge.

That we need not decide today. The plaintiffs are entitled to a preliminary injunction. Not only have they shown a strong likelihood of ultimate victory should the City persist with the case; they will suffer irreparable harm if the ordinance is permitted to go into effect, because compliance with it will impose costs on them of altering their facilities and will also cause them to lose revenue. And given the entirely conjectural nature of the benefits of the ordinance to the people of Indianapolis, the harm of a preliminary injunction to the City must be reckoned slight, and outweighed by the harm that denying the injunction would impose on the plaintiffs. The judgment is therefore reversed, and the case remanded with instructions to enter a preliminary injunction.

Reversed and Remanded, with Instructions.

Chapter Four
DAMAGE TO REPUTATION

Included in this section are seven cases from the modern era of libel law—an era in which the U.S. Supreme Court has intervened to place constitutional limits on the ability of disparaged plaintiffs to recover damages in court. Libel law is an area of law with ancient, common-law origins. By the mid 1900s in the United States libel had evolved into a very complex tort with specialized legal presumptions, privileges, and rules of evidence. The recent constitutionalization of libel law has assured that First Amendment rights weigh more heavily in the balance, but it has also produced even greater legal complexity.

New York Times Co. v. Sullivan, one of the most important First Amendment cases ever decided, marks the beginning of the modern era of libel law in 1964. In this case the Supreme Court established the "actual malice" standard.

Harte-Hanks Communications v. Connaughton is a more recent decision that illustrates exactly what the "actual malice" standard means and how it is applied to the facts of a case.

Gertz v. Robert Welch, Inc., perhaps the second most important libel case ever decided, halted the spread of the "actual malice" rule and established that that standard was not constitutionally required in all defamation cases.

Milkovich v. Lorain Journal Co. is the Supreme Court's ruling concerning the constitutional boundaries of libel law's most important "privilege"—the privilege to express personal opinions.

Kaelin v. Globe Communications Corp., a 1998 decision, illustrates how the lower courts apply Supreme Court precedent and how some courts handle the problem of headlines that don't match accompanying stories.

Zeran v. America Online was the first case to interpret an important federal statute as granting immunity to Internet service providers when they are sued over content posted by "third parties."

Grace v. eBay Inc. is a recent decision that disagrees with *Zeran's* statutory interpretation and would apply to Internet services the basic common-law rules of liability. This legal debate over the federal statute and the breadth of immunity is important because the Internet is a medium that's ripe for defamation.

NEW YORK TIMES CO. V. SULLIVAN
Supreme Court of the United States, 1964
376 U.S. 254

Justice BRENNAN delivered the opinion of the Court.

We are required in this case to determine for the first time the extend to which the constitutional protections for speech and press limit a State's power to award damages in a libel action brought by a public official against critics of his official conduct.

Respondent L. B. Sullivan is one of the three elected Commissioners of the City of Montgomery, Alabama. [As the commissioner of public affairs, one of his duties was to supervise the Police Department.] ....

Respondent's complaint alleged that he had been libeled by statements in a full-page advertisement that was carried in the *New York Times* on March 29, 1960. Entitled "Heed Their Rising Voices," the advertisement began by stating that "As the whole world knows by now, thousands of Southern Negro students are engaged in widespread nonviolent demonstrations in positive affirmation of the right to live in human dignity as guaranteed by the U.S. Constitution and the Bill of Rights." It went on to charge that "in their efforts to uphold these guarantees, they are being met by an unprecedented wave of terror by those who would deny and negate that document which the whole world looks upon as setting the pattern for modern freedom. * * *" Succeeding paragraphs purported to illustrate the "wave of terror" by describing certain alleged events. The text concluded with an appeal for funds for three purposes: support of the student movement, "the struggle for the right-to-vote," and the legal defense of Dr. Martin Luther King, Jr., leader of the movement, against a perjury indictment then pending in Montgomery.

The text appeared over the names of sixty-four persons, many widely known for their activities in public affairs, religion, trade unions, and the performing arts.... The advertisement was signed at the bottom of the page by the "Committee to Defend Martin Luther King and the Struggle for Freedom in the South," and the officers of the Committee were listed....

[Most of the allegations in the ad were accurate, but it did contain several statements that were not true. For example, the Alabama State College student dining hall was not "padlocked in an attempt to starve [students] into submission," as the ad alleged. Nor did police armed with shotguns at any time "ring" the campus. And Dr. King had been arrested only four times, not seven, as stated in the ad. Though the ad never referred to Sullivan by name, he sued the Times *for libel, claiming that the accusations in the ad would be seen as pertaining to him in his capacity as supervisor of the police. A jury awarded Sullivan $500,000, the full amount claimed, and the Supreme Court of Alabama affirmed.]*

II

Under Alabama law applied in this case, a publication is "libelous per se" if the words "tend to injure a person in his reputation" or to "bring [him] into public contempt".... The jury must find that the words were published "of and concerning" the plaintiff, but where the plaintiff is a public official his place in the governmental hierarchy is sufficient evidence to support a finding that his reputation has been affected by statements that reflect upon the agency of which he is in charge. Once "libel per se" has been established, the defendant has no defense as to stated facts unless he can persuade the jury that they were true in all their particulars.... Unless he can discharge the burden of proving truth, general damages are presumed, and may be awarded without proof of pecuniary injury....

The question before us is whether this rule of liability, as applied to an action brought by a public official against critics of his official conduct, abridges the freedom of speech and of the press that is guaranteed by the First and Fourteenth Amendments....

[W]e consider this case against the background of a profound national commitment to the principle that debate on public issues should be uninhibited, robust, and wide-open, and that it may well include vehement, caustic, and sometimes unpleasantly sharp attacks on government and public officials. The present advertisement, as an expression of grievance and protest on one of the major public issues of our time, would seem clearly to qualify for the constitutional protection. The question is whether it forfeits that protection by the falsity of some of its factual statements and by its alleged defamation of respondent....

A rule compelling the critic of official conduct to guarantee the truth of all his factual assertions—and to do so on pain of libel judgments virtually unlimited in amount—leads to ... "self-censorship." Allowance of the defense of truth, with the burden of proving it on the defendant, does not mean that only false speech will be deterred.... Under such a rule, would-be critics of official conduct may be deterred from voicing their criticism, even though it is believed to be true and even though it is in fact true, because of doubt whether it can be proved in court or fear of the expense of having to do so.... The rule thus dampens the vigor and limits the variety of public debate. It is inconsistent with the First and Fourteenth Amendments.

The constitutional guarantees require, we think, a federal rule that prohibits a public official from recovering damages for a defamatory falsehood relating to his official conduct unless he proves that the statement was made with "actual malice"—that is, with knowledge that it was false or with reckless disregard of whether it was false or not....

Such a privilege for criticism of official conduct is appropriately analogous to the protection accorded a public official when *he* is sued for libel by a private citizen....

We conclude that such a privilege is required by the First and Fourteenth Amendments.

III

....

... This Court's duty is not limited to the elaboration of constitutional principles; we must also in proper cases review the evidence to make certain that those principles have been constitutionally applied. This is such a case, particularly since the question is one of alleged trespass across "the line between speech unconditionally guaranteed and speech which may legitimately be regulated." ...

Applying these standards, we consider that the proof presented to show actual malice lacks the convincing clarity that the constitutional standard demands, and hence that it would not constitutionally sustain the judgment for respondent under the proper rule of law....

[T]here is evidence that the *Times* published the advertisement without checking its accuracy against the news stories in the *Times'* own files. The mere presence of the stories in the files does not, of course, establish that the *Times* "knew" the advertisement was false, since the state of mind required for actual malice would have to be brought home to the persons in the *Times'* organization having responsibility for the publication of the advertisement. With respect to the failure of those persons to make the check, the record shows that they relied upon their knowledge of the good reputation of many of those whose names were listed as sponsors of the advertisement, and upon the letter from A. Philip Randolph, known to them as a responsible individual, certifying that the use of the names was authorized. There was testimony that the persons handling the advertisement saw nothing in it that would render it unacceptable under the *Times'* policy of rejecting advertisements containing "attacks of a personal character"; their failure to reject it on this ground was not unreasonable. We think the evidence against the *Times* supports at most a finding of negligence in failing to discover the misstatements, and is constitutionally insufficient to show the recklessness that is required for a finding of actual malice....

The judgment of the Supreme Court of Alabama is reversed and the case is remanded to that court for further proceedings not inconsistent with this opinion.

HARTE-HANKS COMMUNICATIONS, INC. v. CONNAUGHTON
Supreme Court of the United States, 1989
491 U.S. 657

Justice STEVENS delivered the opinion of the Court.

I

Respondent, Daniel Connaughton, was the unsuccessful candidate for the Office of Municipal Judge of Hamilton, Ohio, in an election conducted on November 8, 1983. Petitioner is the publisher of the *Journal News,* a local newspaper that supported the reelection of the incumbent, James Dolan. A little over a month before the election, the incumbent's Director of Court Services resigned and was arrested on bribery charges. A grand jury investigation of those charges was in progress on November 1, 1983. On that date, the *Journal News* ran a front page story quoting Alice Thompson, a grand jury witness, as stating that Connaughton had used "dirty tricks" and offered her and her sister jobs and a trip to Florida "in appreciation" for their help in the investigation.

... Connaughton filed an action for damages, alleging that the article was false, that it had damaged his personal and professional reputation, and that it had been published with actual malice....

... [T]he jury awarded Connaughton $5,000 in compensatory damages and $195,000 in punitive damages....

The Court of Appeals affirmed....

II

Petitioner contends that the Court of Appeals made two basic errors. First, while correctly stating the actual malice standard announced in *New York Times Co. v. Sullivan,* the court actually applied a less severe standard that merely required a showing of "highly unreasonable conduct constituting an extreme departure from the standards of investigation and reporting ordinarily adhered to by responsible publishers." Second, the court failed to make an independent *de novo* review of the entire record and therefore incorrectly relied on subsidiary facts implicitly established by the jury's verdict instead of drawing its own inferences from the evidence.

... Petitioner is plainly correct in recognizing that a public figure plaintiff must prove more than an extreme departure from professional standards and that a newspaper's motive in publishing a story—whether to promote an opponent's candidacy or to increase its circulation—cannot provide a sufficient basis for finding actual malice....

... Nevertheless, when the opinion is read as a whole, it is clear that the conclusion concerning the newspaper's departure from accepted standards and the evidence of motive were merely supportive of the court's ultimate conclusion that the record "demonstrated a reckless disregard as to the truth or falsity of Thompson's allegations and thus provided clear and convincing proof of 'actual malice' as found by the jury." ...

III

The most important witness to the bribery charges against the Director of Court Services was Patsy Stephens, Alice Thompson's older sister. In a tape-recorded interview conducted in Connaughton's home between 12:30 and 4:30 a.m. on September 17, 1983, Stephens explained how, on forty or fifty occasions, she had visited with the court administrator, Billy Joe New, in his office and made cash payments to dispose of "DUI" and other minor criminal charges against her former husband and various other relatives and acquaintances. On September 22, pursuant to an arrangement made by Connaughton at the suggestion of the county prosecutor, Stephens took a lie detector test. After learning that she had passed the test, Connaughton filed a written complaint against New. In due course, New was arrested, indicted, and convicted.

Alice Thompson was one of the eight persons present at the tape-recorded interview on September 17....

Late in October, New's lawyer, Henry Masana, met with Jim Blount, the editorial director of the *Journal News,* and Joe Cocozzo, the newspaper's publisher, to arrange a meeting with Alice Thompson. Masana explained that Thompson wanted to be interviewed about the "dirty tricks" Connaughton was using in his campaign. Thereafter, on October 27, Blount and Pam Long, a *Journal News* reporter, met with Thompson in the lawyer's office and tape-recorded the first of the two statements that provided the basis for the story that Long wrote and the *Journal News* published on November 1.

The tape of Alice Thompson's interview is one hour and twenty minutes long. Significant portions of it are inaudible or incoherent. It is clear, however, that Thompson made these specific charges:

— that Connaughton had stated his purpose in taping the interview with Patsy Stephens was to get evidence with which he could confront New and Judge Dolan and "scare them into resigning" without making any public use of the tapes;
— that he would pay the expenses for a three-week vacation in Florida for the two sisters;
— that he would buy a restaurant for the two sisters' parents to operate;
— that he would provide jobs for both Patsy Stephens and Alice Thompson;
— that he would take them out to a victory dinner at an expensive French restaurant after the election; and
— that Connaughton would not allow knowledge of the sisters' involvement to become public.

During the course of the interview, Thompson indicated that she had told her story to the *Cincinnati Enquirer,* which declined to print it, and that the local police, likewise, were not interested....

On October 31, a reporter for the *Journal News* telephoned Connaughton and asked him to attend a meeting with Jim Blount, stating "that the endorsement may hang in the balance." Connaughton met with the reporter, Blount, and Cocozzo that afternoon....

... Connaughton acknowledged that the meetings that Thompson described had taken place and that there had been some speculative discussion about each of the subjects that Thompson mentioned. He stated, however, that Thompson's account of their meetings was "obviously shaded and bizarre," and that there was "absolutely" no "*quid pro quo* for information."

Thus, while categorically denying that he intended to confront New and Judge Dolan with tape of the Stephens interview to scare them into resigning, Connaughton admitted that he might well have speculated about what they would say or do if they heard the tapes. Similarly, while denying that he had promised Stephens and Thompson anonymity, he agreed that he had told them that he had hoped that they could remain anonymous. He also categorically denied that he had promised Stephens a job at the Municipal Court, or promised to set their parents up in a restaurant, although he did acknowledge a general conversation in which his wife had discussed the possibility that if her dream of opening "a gourmet ice cream shop" should materialize, the sisters might work there. There were similar acknowledgments of references to a possible Florida trip and post-election victory dinner, but denials of any promises....

The following day, the lead story in the *Journal News*—under the headline "Bribery case witness claims jobs, trip offered"—reported that "[a] woman called to testify before the ... Grand Jury in the Billy Joe New bribery case claims Dan Connaughton, candidate for Hamilton Municipal Judge, offered her and her sister jobs and a trip to Florida 'in appreciation' for their help." ... Each of Thompson's allegations was accurately reported, including her claims that Connaughton had promised to "protect her anonymity," that he had promised Stephens "a municipal court job" and Thompson some other sort of work, that he had invited both sisters on "a post-election trip to Florida," and that he had offered "to set up Thompson's parents ... in the restaurant business." ... Connaughton's contrary version of the events was also accurately reported....

The jury listened to the tape recordings of the two conflicting interviews and also observed the demeanor of the two witnesses as they testified in open court. They found that Connaughton was telling the truth and that Thompson's charges were false.... The jury's verdict in this case derived additional support from several critical pieces of information that strongly support the inference that the *Journal News* acted with actual malice in printing Thompson's false and defamatory statements.

IV

On October 27, after the interview with Alice Thompson, the managing editor of the *Journal News* assembled a group of reporters and instructed them to interview all of the witnesses to the conversation between Connaughton and Thompson with one exception—Patsy Stephens. No one was asked to interview her and no one made any attempt to do so. This omission ... is utterly bewildering in light of the fact that the *Journal News* committed substantial resources to investigating Thompson's claims, yet chose not to interview the one witness who was most likely to confirm Thompson's account of the events. However, if the *Journal News* had serious doubts concerning the truth of Thompson's remarks, but was committed to running the story, there was good reason not to interview Stephens—while denials coming from Connaughton's supporters might be explained as motivated by a desire to assist Connaughton, a denial coming from Stephens would quickly put an end to the story....

The newspaper's decision not to listen to the tapes of the Stephens interview in Connaughton's home also supports the finding of actual malice. During the Connaughton interview, Long and Blount asked if they could hear the tapes. Connaughton agreed, and later made the tapes available. Much of what Thompson had said about the interview could easily have been verified or disproved by listening to the tapes.... Although simply one piece of evidence in a much larger picture, one might reasonably infer in light of this broader context that the decision not to listen to the tapes was motivated by a concern that they would raise additional doubts concerning Thompson's veracity....

V

....

There is little doubt that "public discussion of the qualifications of a candidate for elective office presents what is probably the strongest possible case for application of the *New York Times* rule," and the strongest possible case for independent review....

We have not gone so far, however, as to accord the press absolute immunity in its coverage of public figures or elections. If a false and defamatory statement is published with knowledge of falsity or a reckless disregard for the truth, the public figure may prevail. A "reckless disregard" for the truth, however, requires more than a departure from reasonably prudent conduct. "There must be sufficient evidence to permit the conclusion that the defendant in fact entertained serious doubts as to the truth of his publication." ...

There is no dispute that Thompson's charges had been denied not only by Connaughton, but also by five other witnesses before the story was published. Thompson's most serious charge—that Connaughton intended to confront the incumbent judge with the tapes to scare him into resigning and otherwise not to disclose the existence of the tapes—was not only highly improbable, but inconsistent with the fact that Connaughton had actually arranged a lie detector test for Stephens and then delivered the tapes to the police. These facts were well known to the *Journal News* before the story was published. Moreover, because the newspaper's interviews of Thompson and Connaughton were captured on tape, there can be no dispute as to what was communicated, nor how it was said. The hesitant, inaudible, and sometimes unresponsive and improbable tone of Thompson's answers to various leading questions raise obvious doubts about her veracity....

It is also undisputed that Connaughton made the tapes of the Stephens interview available to the *Journal News* and that no one at the newspaper took the time to listen to them. Similarly, there is no question that the *Journal News* was aware that Patsy Stephens was a key witness and that they failed to make any effort to interview her....

There is a remarkable similarity between this case—and in particular, the newspaper's failure to interview Stephens and failure to listen to the tape recording of the September 17 interview at Connaughton's home—and the facts that supported the Court's judgment in *Curtis Publishing Co. v. Butts*, 388 U.S. 130 (1967). In *Butts* the evidence showed that the *Saturday Evening Post* had published an accurate account of an unreliable informant's false description of the Georgia athletic director's purported agreement to "fix" a college football game. Although there was reason to question the informant's veracity, just as there was reason to doubt Thompson's story, the editors did not interview a witness who had the same access to the facts as the informant and did not look at films that revealed what actually happened at the game in question....

As in *Butts*, the evidence in the record in this case, when reviewed in its entirety, is "unmistakably" sufficient to support a finding of actual malice. The judgment of the Court of Appeals is accordingly

Affirmed.

Gertz v. Robert Welch, Inc.
Supreme Court of the United States, 1974
418 U.S. 323

Justice POWELL delivered the opinion of the Court.

This Court has struggled for nearly a decade to define the proper accommodation between the law of defamation and the freedoms of speech and press protected by the First Amendment. With this decision we return to that effort. We granted certiorari to reconsider the extent of a publisher's constitutional privilege against liability for defamation of a private citizen.

I

In 1968 a Chicago policeman named Nuccio shot and killed a youth named Nelson. The state authorities prosecuted Nuccio for the homicide and ultimately obtained a conviction for murder in the second degree. The Nelson family retained petitioner Elmer Gertz, a reputable attorney, to represent them in civil litigation against Nuccio.

Respondent publishes *American Opinion,* a monthly outlet for the views of the John Birch Society. Early in the 1960s the magazine began to warn of a nationwide conspiracy to discredit local law enforcement agencies and create in their stead a national police force capable of supporting a Communist dictatorship. As part of the continuing effort to alert the public to this assumed danger, the managing editor of *American Opinion* commissioned an article on the murder trial of Officer Nuccio. For this purpose he engaged a regular contributor to the magazine. In March 1969, respondent published the resulting article under the title "FRAME-UP: Richard Nuccio And The War On Police." The article purports to demonstrate that the testimony against Nuccio at his criminal trial was false and that his prosecution was part of the Communist campaign against police.

In his capacity as counsel for the Nelson family in the civil litigation, petitioner attended the coroner's inquest into the boy's death and initiated actions for damages, but he neither discussed Officer Nuccio with the press nor played any part in the criminal proceeding. Notwithstanding petitioner's remote connection with the prosecution of Nuccio, respondent's magazine portrayed him as an architect of the "frame-up." According to the article, the police file on petitioner took "a big, Irish cop to lift." The article stated that petitioner had been an official of the "Marxist League for Industrial Democracy, originally known as the Intercollegiate Socialist Society, which has advocated the violent seizure of our government." It labeled Gertz a "Leninist" and a "Communist-fronter." ...

These statements contained serious inaccuracies…. There was no basis for the charge that petitioner was a "Leninist" or a "Communist-fronter." And he had never been a member of the "Marxist League for Industrial Democracy " or the "Intercollegiate Socialist Society."…

Petitioner … claimed that the falsehoods published by respondent injured his reputation as a lawyer and a citizen….

… [R]espondent filed a pretrial motion for summary judgment, claiming a constitutional privilege against liability for defamation. It asserted that petitioner was a public official or a public figure and that the article concerned an issue of public interest and concern. For these reasons, respondent argued, it was entitled to invoke the privilege enunciated in *New York Times Co. v. Sullivan.* Under this rule respondent would escape liability unless petitioner could prove publication of defamatory falsehood "with 'actual malice'—that is, with knowledge that it was false or with reckless disregard of whether it was false or not." …

… [T]he District Court concluded that the *New York Times* standard should govern this case even though petitioner was not a public official or public figure. It accepted respondent's contention that that privilege protected discussion of any public issue without regard to the status of a person defamed therein…. This conclusion anticipated the reasoning of a plurality of this Court in *Rosenbloom v. Metromedia, Inc.,* 403 U.S. 29 (1971)….

II

The principal issue in this case is whether a newspaper or broadcaster that publishes defamatory falsehoods about an individual who is neither a public official nor a public figure may claim a constitutional privilege against liability for the injury inflicted by those statements….

… The eight Justices who participated in *Rosenbloom* announced their views in five separate opinions, none of which commanded more than three votes. The several statements not only reveal disagreement about the appropriate result in that case, they also reflect divergent traditions of thought about the general problem of reconciling the law of defamation with the First Amendment. One approach has been to extend the *New York Times* test to an expanding variety of situations. Another has been to vary the level of constitutional privilege for defamatory falsehood with the status of the person defamed. And a third view would grant to the press and broadcast media absolute immunity from liability for defamation….

III

We begin with the common ground. Under the First Amendment there is no such thing as a false idea. However pernicious an opinion may seem, we depend for its correction not on the conscience of judges and juries but on the competition of other ideas. But there is no constitutional value in false statements of fact….

Although the erroneous statement of fact is not worthy of constitutional protection, it is nevertheless inevitable in free debate…. The First Amendment requires that we protect some falsehood in order to protect speech that matters….

The *New York Times* standard defines the level of constitutional protection appropriate to the context of defamation of a public person.... For the reasons stated below, we conclude that the state interest in compensating injury to the reputation of private individuals requires that a different rule should obtain with respect to them....

... The first remedy of any victim of defamation is self-help—using available opportunities to contradict the lie or correct the error and thereby to minimize its adverse impact on reputation. Public officials and public figures usually enjoy significantly greater access to the channels of effective communication and hence have a more realistic opportunity to counteract false statements then private individuals normally enjoy. Private individuals are therefore more vulnerable to injury, and the state interest in protecting them is correspondingly greater.

More important than the likelihood that private individuals will lack effective opportunities for rebuttal, there is a compelling normative consideration underlying the distinction between public and private defamation plaintiffs. An individual who decides to seek governmental office must accept certain necessary consequences of that involvement in public affairs. He runs the risk of closer public scrutiny than might otherwise be the case. And society's interest in the officers of government is not strictly limited to the formal discharge of official duties....

Those classified as public figures stand in a similar position. Hypothetically, it may be possible for someone to become a public figure through no purposeful action of his own, but the instances of truly involuntary public figures must be exceedingly rare. For the most part those who attain this status have assumed roles of especial prominence in the affairs of society. Some occupy positions of such persuasive power and influence that they are deemed public figures for all purposes. More commonly, those classed as public figures have thrust themselves to the forefront of particular public controversies in order to influence the resolution of the issues involved. In either event, they invite attention and comment.

Even if the foregoing generalities do not obtain in every instance, the communications media are entitled to act on the assumption that public officials and public figures have voluntarily exposed themselves to increased risk of injury from defamatory falsehood concerning them. No such assumption is justified with respect to a private individual. He has not accepted public office or assumed an "influential role in ordering society." He has relinquished no part of his interest in the protection of his own good name, and consequently he has a more compelling call on the courts for redress of injury inflicted by defamatory falsehood. Thus, private individuals are not only more vulnerable to injury than public officials and public figures; they are also more deserving of recovery.

For these reasons we conclude that the States should retain substantial latitude in their efforts to enforce a legal remedy for defamatory falsehood injurious to the reputation of a private individual....

We hold that, so long as they do not impose liability without fault, the States may define for themselves the appropriate standard of liability for a publisher or broadcaster of defamatory falsehood injurious to a private individual. This approach provides a more equitable boundary between the competing concerns involved here. It recognizes the strength of the legitimate state interest in compensating private individuals for wrongful injury to reputation, yet shields the press and broadcast media from the rigors of strict liability for defamation....

IV

Our accommodation of the competing values at stake in defamation suits by private individuals allows the States to impose liability on the publisher or broadcaster of defamatory falsehood on a less demanding showing than that required by *New York Times.*... [W]e endorse this approach in recognition of the strong and legitimate state interest in compensating private individuals for injury to reputation. But this countervailing state interest extends no further than compensation for actual injury. For the reasons stated below, we hold that the States may not permit recovery of presumed or punitive damages, at least when liability is not based on a showing of knowledge of falsity or reckless disregard for the truth.

The common law of defamation is an oddity of tort law, for it allows recovery of purportedly compensatory damages without evidence of actual loss. Under the traditional rules pertaining to actions for libel, the existence of injury is presumed from the fact of publication....

We would not, of course, invalidate state law simply because we doubt its wisdom, but here we are attempting to reconcile state law with a competing interest grounded in the constitutional command of the First Amendment. It is therefore appropriate to require that state remedies for defamatory falsehood reach no farther than is necessary to protect the legitimate interest involved. It is necessary to restrict defamation plaintiffs who do not prove knowledge of falsity or reckless disregard for the truth to compensation for actual injury.... [A]ll awards must be supported by competent evidence concerning the injury, although there need be no evidence which assigns an actual dollar value to the injury.

We also find no justification for allowing awards of punitive damages against publishers and broadcasters held liable under state-defined standards of liability for defamation. In most jurisdictions jury discretion over the amounts awarded is limited only by the gentle rule that they not be excessive. Consequently, juries assess punitive damages in wholly unpredictable amounts bearing no necessary relation to the actual harm caused. And they remain free to use their discretion selectively to punish expressions of unpopular views. Like the doctrine of presumed damages, jury discretion to award punitive damages unnecessarily exacerbates the danger of media self-censorship.... In short, the private defamation plaintiff who establishes liability under a less demanding standard than that stated by *New York Times* may recover only such damages as are sufficient to compensate him for actual injury.

V

Notwithstanding our refusal to extend the *New York Times* privilege to defamation of private individuals, respondent contends that we should affirm the judgment below on the ground that petitioner is either a public official or a public figure. There is little basis for the former assertion. Several years prior to the present incident, petitioner had served briefly on housing committees appointed by the mayor of Chicago, but at the time of publication he had never held any remunerative governmental position....

In this context it is [also] plain that petitioner was not a public figure. He played a minimal role at the coroner's inquest, and his participation related solely to his representation of a private client. He took no part in the criminal prosecution of Officer Nuccio. Moreover, he never discussed either the criminal or civil litigation with the press and was never quoted as having done so. He plainly did not thrust himself into the vortex of this public issue, nor did he engage the public's attention in an attempt to influence its outcome....

We therefore conclude that the *New York Times* standard is inapplicable to this case and that the trial court erred in entering judgment for respondent....

Reversed and remanded.

MILKOVICH V. LORAIN JOURNAL CO.

Supreme Court of the United States, 1990
497 U.S. 1

Chief Justice REHNQUIST delivered the opinion of the Court.

Respondent J. Theodore Diadiun authored an article in an Ohio newspaper implying that petitioner Michael Milkovich, a local high school wrestling coach, lied under oath in a judicial proceeding about an incident involving petitioner and his team which occurred at a wrestling match. Petitioner sued Diadiun and the newspaper for libel, and the Ohio Court of Appeals affirmed a lower court entry of summary judgment against petitioner. This judgment was based in part on the grounds that the article constituted an "opinion" protected from the reach of state defamation law by the First Amendment to the United States Constitution. We hold that the First Amendment does not prohibit the application of Ohio's libel laws to the alleged defamations contained in the article.

... Petitioner Milkovich, now retired, was the wrestling coach at Maple Heights High School in Maple Heights, Ohio. In 1974, his team was involved in an altercation at a home wrestling match with a team from Mentor High School. Several people were injured. In response to the incident, the Ohio High School Athletic Association (OHSAA) held a hearing at which Milkovich ... testified. Following the hearing, OHSAA placed the Maple Heights team on probation.... Thereafter, several parents and wrestlers sued OHSAA in the Court of Common Pleas of Franklin County, Ohio, seeking a restraining order against OHSAA's ruling on the grounds that they had been denied due process in the OHSAA proceeding. [Milkovich] testified in that proceeding. The court overturned OHSAA's probation and ineligibility orders on due process grounds.

The day after the court rendered its decision, respondent Diadiun's column appeared in the *News-Herald*.... The column bore the heading "Maple beat the law with the 'big lie,'" beneath which appeared Diadiun's photograph and the words "TD Says." The carryover page headline announced "... Diadiun says Maple told a lie." The column contained the following passages:

"... a lesson was learned (or relearned) yesterday by the student body of Maple Heights High School, and by anyone who attended the Maple-Mentor wrestling meet of last Feb. 8.

"A lesson which, sadly, in view of the events of the past year, is well they learned early.

"It is simply this: If you get in a jam, lie your way out.

"If you're successful enough, and powerful enough, and can sound sincere enough, you stand an excellent chance of making the lie stand up, regardless of what really happened.

"The teachers responsible were mainly Maple wrestling coach, Mike Milkovich, and former superintendent of schools, H. Donald Scott.

....

"Anyone who attended the meet, whether he be from Maple Heights, Mentor, or impartial observer, knows in his heart that Milkovich and Scott lied at the hearing after each having his solemn oath to tell the truth.

"But they got away with it.

"Is that the kind of lesson we want our young people learning from their high school administrators and coaches?

"I think not."

Petitioner commenced a defamation action against respondents ... alleging that the headline of Diadiun's article and the nine passages quoted above "accused plaintiff of committing the crime of perjury, an indictable offense in the State of Ohio, and damaged plaintiff directly in his life-time occupation of coach and teacher, and constituted libel per se." ...

Since the latter half of the 16th century, the common law has afforded a cause of action for damage to a person's reputation by the publication of false and defamatory statements.

... As the common law developed in this country, apart from the issue of damages, one usually needed only allege an unprivileged publication of false and defamatory matter to state a cause of action for defamation. The common law generally did not place any additional restrictions on the type of statement that could be actionable. Indeed, defamatory communications were deemed actionable regardless of whether they were deemed to be statements of fact or opinion....

However, due to concerns that unduly burdensome defamation laws could stifle valuable public debate, the privilege of "fair comment" was incorporated into the common law as an affirmative defense to an action for defamation. "The principle of 'fair comment' afforded legal immunity for the honest expression of opinion on matters of legitimate public interest when based upon a true or privileged statement of fact." As this statement implies, comment was generally privileged when it concerned a matter of public concern, was upon true or privileged facts, represented the actual opinion of the speaker, and was not made solely for the purpose of causing harm....

In 1964, we decided in *New York Times Co. v. Sullivan*, 376 U.S. 254, that the First Amendment ... placed limits on the application of the state law of defamation. There the Court recognized the need for "a federal rule that prohibits a public official from recovering damages for a defamatory falsehood relating to his official conduct unless he proves that the statement was made with 'actual malice.'"...

Three years later, in *Curtis Publishing Co v. Butts*, 388 U.S. 130 (1967), a majority of the Court determined that "the *New York Times* test should apply to criticism of 'public figures' as well as 'public officials.'"...

The next step in this constitutional evolution was the Court's consideration of a private individual's defamation actions involving statements of public concern. Although the issue was initially in doubt, the Court ultimately concluded that the *New York Times* malice standard was inappropriate for a private person attempting to prove he was defamed on matters of public interest. *Gertz v. Robert Welch, Inc.* 418 U.S. 323 (1974).... Nevertheless, the Court believed that certain significant constitutional protections were warranted in this area. First we held that the States could not impose liability without requiring some showing of fault. Second, we held that the States could not permit recovery of presumed or punitive damages on less than a showing of *New York Times* malice.

Still later, in *Philadelphia Newspapers, Inc. v. Hepps*, 475 U.S. 767 (1986), we held "that the common-law presumption that defamatory speech is false cannot stand when a plaintiff seeks damages against a media defendant for speech of public concern." In other words, the Court fashioned "a constitutional requirement that the plaintiff bear the burden of showing falsity, as well as fault, before recovering damages." ...

We have also recognized constitutional limits on the *type* of speech that may be the subject of state defamation actions. In *Greenbelt Cooperative Publishing Assn., Inc. v. Bresler*, 398 U.S. 6 (1970), a real estate developer had engaged in negotiations with a local city council for a zoning variance on certain of his land, while simultaneously negotiating with the city on other land the city wished to purchase from him. A local newspaper published certain articles stating that some people had characterized the developer's negotiating position as "blackmail," and the developer sued for libel. Rejecting a contention that liability could be premised on the notion that the word "blackmail" implied the developer had committed the actual crime of blackmail, we held that "the imposition of liability on such a basis was constitutionally impermissible—that as a matter of constitutional law, the word 'blackmail' in these circumstances was not slander when spoken, and not libel when reported in the *Greenbelt News Review*." Noting that the published reports "were accurate and full," the Court reasoned that "even the most careless reader must have perceived that the word was no more than rhetorical hyperbole, a vigorous epithet used by those who considered [the developer's] negotiating position extremely unreasonable." ...

Respondents would have us recognize, in addition to the established safeguards discussed above, still another First Amendment-based protection for defamatory statements which are categorized as "opinion" as opposed to "fact." For this proposition they rely principally on the following dictum from our opinion in *Gertz*:

"Under the First Amendment there is no such thing as a false idea. However pernicious an opinion may seem, we depend for its correction not on the conscience of judges and juries but on the competition of other ideas. But there is no constitutional value in false statements of fact."

... Read in context, though, the fair meaning of the passage is to equate the word "opinion" in the second sentence with the word "idea" in the first sentence....

Thus we do not think this passage from *Gertz* was intended to create a wholesale defamation exemption for anything that might be labeled "opinion." Not only would such an interpretation be contrary to the tenor and context of the passage, but it would also ignore the fact that expressions of "opinion" may often imply an assertion of objective fact.

If a speaker says, "In my opinion John Jones is a liar," he implies a knowledge of facts which lead to the conclusion that Jones told an untruth. Even if the speaker states the facts upon which he bases his opinion, if those facts are either incorrect or incomplete, or if his assessment of them is erroneous, the statement may still imply a false assertion of fact. Simply couching such statements in terms of opinion does not dispel these implications; and the statement, "In my opinion Jones is a liar," can cause as much damage to reputation as the statement, "Jones is a liar." ...

… [W]e think the "breathing space" which "freedoms of expression require in order to survive," is adequately secured by existing constitutional doctrine without the creation of an artificial dichotomy between "opinion" and fact.

Foremost, we think *Hepps* stands for the proposition that a statement on matters of public concern must be provable as false before there can be liability under state defamation law, at least in situations, like the present, where a media defendant is involved. Thus, unlike the statement, "In my opinion Mayor Jones is a liar," the statement, "In my opinion Mayor Jones shows his abysmal ignorance by accepting the teachings of Marx and Lenin," would not be actionable. *Hepps* ensures that a statement of opinion relating to matters of public concern that does not contain a provably false factual connotation will receive full constitutional protection….

We are not persuaded that, in addition to these protections, an additional separate constitutional privilege for "opinion" is required to ensure the freedom of expression guaranteed by the First Amendment. The dispositive question in the present case then becomes whether or not a reasonable fact finder could conclude that the statements in the Diadiun column imply an assertion that petitioner Milkovich perjured himself in a judicial proceeding. We think this question must be answered in the affirmative….

We also think the connotation that petitioner committed perjury is sufficiently factual to be susceptible of being proved true or false….

… The judgment of the Ohio Court of Appeals is reversed and the case remanded for further proceedings not inconsistent with this opinion.

KAELIN V. GLOBE COMMUNICATIONS CORP.
U.S. Court of Appeals for the Ninth Circuit, 1998
162 F.3d 1036

SILVERMAN, Circuit Judge:

One week after O.J. Simpson was acquitted of the murders of Nicole Brown Simpson and Ronald Goldman, the front page of the *National Examiner* proclaimed the following: COPS THINK KATO DID IT!

… he fears they want him for perjury, say pals.
The cops did not think that Kato Kaelin murdered Brown and Goldman. The publisher of the *National Examiner* did not believe that they did. Furthermore, its editor testified at deposition that he was concerned that the front-page headline did not accurately reflect the content of the article about Kaelin that appeared inside the publication at page seventeen. We hold that reasonable jurors could find that clear and convincing evidence established: (1) the front-page headline falsely insinuated that the police believed that Kaelin committed the murders; and (2) the false insinuation was not necessarily cured by the subheading or by the non-defamatory story about Kaelin that appeared seventeen pages away. We also hold that Kaelin produced sufficiently clear and convincing evidence of the newspaper's knowledge of falsity or reckless disregard for the truth of its headline to defeat a motion for summary judgment. We reverse the grant of summary judgment in favor of the publisher and remand for trial.

FACTUAL AND PROCEDURAL BACKGROUND

Brian "Kato" Kaelin became known to the public during the course of the criminal trial of O.J. Simpson as the houseguest at Simpson's estate. Kaelin testified to various events surrounding the killings of Nicole Brown Simpson and Ronald Goldman. Simpson was acquitted of the double murders on October 3, 1995. One week later, the *National Examiner,* a weekly newspaper published by Globe Communications Corporation, featured the [above] headline on its cover....

Inside the paper, on page seventeen, in large, boldface, capital letters, the following headline appeared over the text of the article:

KATO KAELIN ...

COPS THINK HE DID IT!

... he fears they want him for perjury, say pals.
The first four paragraphs of the article read as follows:

Kato Kaelin is still a suspect in the murder of Nicole Brown Simpson and Ron Goldman, friends fear.

They are worried that LAPD cops are desperately looking for a way to put Kato behind bars for perjury.

"We're sure the cops have been trying to prove that Kato didn't tell them everything he knows, that somehow he spoiled their case against O.J.," says one pal. "It's not true, but we think they're out to get even with Kato."

....

The remainder of the article contained other comments supposedly made by Kaelin's friends regarding the Simpson case. It also contained several references to a book about Kaelin by author Marc Eliot.

In a letter dated October 12, 1995, Kaelin demanded a retraction. Globe refused. Kaelin then filed this libel action against Globe in the Superior Court of California, and Globe removed it to federal court on the basis of diversity of citizenship.

During discovery, John Garton, the news editor of the *National Examiner* and Globe's designated representative, testified at deposition as follows:

Q. Okay. Did you have any concerns when you saw this headline of September 22nd [the deadline for the article] about the way this headline was framed?

A. I wasn't mad about it.

Q. What do you mean by that?

A. Journalistically I didn't think it was the best headline in the world.

Q. Were you concerned that it implied that Kato had committed the murders or played some role in them?

A. No, I just didn't think it was very accurate to the story. It could have been better.

Q. Other than what is actually written in Exhibit 2 [prior published articles], any of the things that are in those articles, did the *National Examiner* have in its possession on September 22, 1995, any information that a police officer anywhere thought that Kato Kaelin was involved in Nicole Brown Simpson's and Ronald Goldman's murders?

A. No.

Q....What did you think, on September 22, 1995, about what the words "Cops Think He Did It" meant? What is the "it" to which this statement—

A. Perjury.

Q. Perjury?

A. Mm-hmm.

Q. Did you have any concern that a reader might connect the "Cops Think He Did It" with the other information in the article that refers to allegations that Mr. Kaelin was involved in the murders themselves?

A. I was a bit concerned about it, yes, but in fact I thought the second part of the headline coped with that....

Globe filed a motion for summary judgment, claiming, in pertinent part, that Kaelin could not prove that Globe acted with actual malice.

Focusing its analysis on the text of the article rather than on the headline, which was the heart of Kaelin's claim, the district court ruled that Kaelin "...has not submitted any evidence which tends to show that Defendants actually doubted the truth of the story or acted in reckless disregard of the truth."...

STANDARD OF REVIEW

....

A public figure in a defamation case "cannot recover unless he proves by clear and convincing evidence that the defendant published the defamatory statement with actual malice, i.e., with 'knowledge that it was false or with reckless disregard of whether it was false or not.'" *Masison v. New Yorker Magazine, Inc.,* 501 U.S. 496 (1991) [quoting *New York Times Co. v. Sullivan,* 376 U.S. 254, 279-80 (1964)]. The parties do not dispute that Kaelin is a public figure.... The appropriate summary judgment question is whether a reasonable jury could find, by clear and convincing evidence, that Kaelin has shown actual malice....

DISCUSSION

I

Although Kaelin complains about the first sentence of the article on page seventeen, we assume for the purposes of this appeal that the text of the story is not defamatory. This case is about the headlines, especially the one appearing on the cover. The first issue is whether the headlines alone are susceptible of a false and defamatory meaning and, if so, whether they can be the basis of a libel action even though the accompanying story is not defamatory.

A

As already seen, the front-page headline consists of two sentences. The first— "COPS THINK KATO DID IT!"—states what the cops supposedly think. The second— "... he fears they want him for perjury, say pals"—is what Kato's pals supposedly said. These two sentences express two different thoughts and are not mutually exclusive.

California courts in libel cases have emphasized that "the publication is to be measured, not so much by its effect when subjected to the critical analysis of a mind trained in the law, but by the natural and probable effect upon the mind of the average reader."

Since the publication occurred just one week after O.J. Simpson's highly publicized acquittal for murder, we believe that a reasonable person, at that time, might well have concluded that the "it" in the first sentence of the cover and internal headlines referred to the murders. Such a reading of the first sentence is not negated by or inconsistent with the second sentence as a matter of logic, grammar, or otherwise. In our view, an ordinary reader reasonably could have read the headline to mean that the cops think that Kato committed the murders and that Kato fears that he is wanted for perjury.

Globe argues that the "it" refers to perjury. Even assuming that such a reading is reasonably possible, it is not the only reading that is reasonably possible as a matter of law. So long as the publication is reasonably susceptible of a defamatory meaning, a factual question for the jury exists.

B

Globe argues that even if the front-page headline could be found to be false and defamatory, the totality of the publication is not. Globe's position is that because the text of the accompanying story is not defamatory, the headline by itself cannot be the basis of a libel action under California law.

It is true that a defamatory meaning must be found, if at all, in a reading of the publication as a whole....

Although California courts have not had occasion to opine on whether a headline alone can be the basis of a libel action, it is certainly clear under California law that headlines are not irrelevant, extraneous, or liability-free zones. They are essential elements of a publication....

As we held in *Eastwood v. National Enquirer, Inc.,* 123 F.3d 1249, 1256 (9th Cir. 1997) ... a court must examine the totality of the circumstances of the publication. In Eastwood, we held that the publisher of the *National Enquirer* could be found to have defamed Clint Eastwood by falsely representing in a front-page headline and in more subtle ways that he had consented to an exclusive interview with the paper. Our conclusion was based not on any requirement that each part of the article be independently defamatory, but rather on the fact that the totality of the circumstances showed the editors' intent to mislead readers.

Globe argues that the entirety of the publication, including the story itself, clears up any false and defamatory meaning that could be found on the cover. Whether it does or not is a question of fact for the jury. The Kaelin story was located seventeen pages away from the cover. In this respect, the *National Examiner's* front-page headline is unlike a conventional headline that immediately precedes a newspaper story, and nowhere does the cover headline reference the internal page where readers could locate the article. A reasonable juror could conclude that the Kaelin article was too far removed from the cover headline to have the salutary effect that Globe claims.

II

To defeat a motion for summary judgment, Kaelin also must come forward with clear and convincing evidence that Globe published the defamatory statements with actual malice.

Kaelin has produced the following evidence from which we believe a reasonable juror could find actual malice:

First, Globe editor John Garton testified at his deposition that he saw the headline before it ran and did not think that it "was very accurate to the story." He stated that he was "a bit concerned" that readers might connect the "it" in the headline with the murders. This is direct evidence from which a reasonable juror could find that Globe knew that the headline was factually inaccurate or that Globe acted with reckless disregard for the truth. It is for a jury to decide whether, as Globe argues, it intended to clarify the sentence "COPS THINK KATO DID IT!" with the sentence that followed, "… he fears they want him for perjury, say pals." The editors' statements of their subjective intention are matters of credibility for a jury.

Second, it is undisputed that Globe ran the headline "COPS THINK KATO DID IT!" knowing that it had no reason to believe that Kaelin was a murder suspect. This is not a case where Globe relied in good faith on information that turned out to be false. It is undisputed that Globe never believed Kaelin to be a suspect in the murders. The fact that Globe ran the headlines anyway —"acting with a 'high degree of awareness of … probable falsity'"—is circumstantial evidence of actual malice.

Third, Garton testified at his deposition that "the front page of the tabloid paper is what we sell the paper on, not what's inside it." That testimony permits a reasonable juror to draw the inference that Globe had a pecuniary motive for running a headline that, in Garton's words, was not "very accurate to the story."

CONCLUSION

.... We hold today that a reasonable juror could find, by clear and convincing evidence, that the headlines are defamatory, and that Globe's editors acted with actual malice in their decision to run a headline from which a reasonable juror could conclude that Kaelin was a murder suspect. Since we conclude that Kaelin has come forward with evidence from which a jury could find clear and convincing proof of actual malice, Globe's motion for summary judgment should have been denied.

Reversed and Remanded.

ZERAN V. AMERICA ONLINE, INC.
U.S. Court of Appeals for the Fourth Circuit, 1997
129 F.3d 327

WILKINSON, Chief Judge:

Kenneth Zeran brought this action against America Online, Inc. ("AOL"), arguing that AOL unreasonably delayed in removing defamatory messages posted by an unidentified third party, refused to post retractions of those messages, and failed to screen for similar postings thereafter. The district court granted judgment for AOL on the grounds that the Communications Decency Act of 1996 ("CDA")—47 U.S.C. § 230— bars Zeran's claims. Zeran appeals, arguing that § 230 leaves intact liability for interactive computer service providers who possess notice of defamatory material posted through their services. He also contends that § 230 does not apply here because his claims arise from AOL's alleged negligence prior to the CDA's enactment. Section 230, however, plainly immunizes computer service providers like AOL from liability for information that originates with third parties. Furthermore, Congress clearly expressed its intent that § 230 apply to lawsuits, like Zeran's, instituted after the CDA's enactment. Accordingly, we affirm the judgment of the district court.

I.

"The Internet is an international network of interconnected computers," currently used by approximately forty million people worldwide. One of the many means by which individuals access the Internet is through an interactive computer service. These services offer not only a connection to the Internet as a whole, but also allow their subscribers to access information communicated and stored only on each computer service's individual proprietary network. AOL is just such an interactive computer service. Much of the information transmitted over its network originates with the company's millions of subscribers. They may transmit information privately via electronic mail, or they may communicate publicly by posting messages on AOL bulletin boards, where the messages may be read by any AOL subscriber.

.... On April 25, 1995, an unidentified person posted a message on an AOL bulletin board advertising "Naughty Oklahoma T-Shirts." The posting described the sale of shirts featuring offensive and tasteless slogans related to the April 19, 1995, bombing of the Alfred P. Murrah Federal Building in Oklahoma City. Those interested in purchasing the shirts were instructed to call "Ken" at Zeran's home phone number in Seattle, Washington. As a result of this anonymously perpetrated prank, Zeran received a high volume of calls, comprised primarily of angry and derogatory messages, but also including death threats. Zeran could not change his phone number because he relied on its availability to the public in running his business out of his home. Later that day, Zeran called AOL and informed a company representative of his predicament. The employee assured Zeran that the posting would be removed from AOL's bulletin board but explained that as a matter of policy AOL would not post a retraction. The parties dispute the date that AOL removed this original posting from its bulletin board.

On April 26, the next day, an unknown person posted another message advertising additional shirts with new tasteless slogans related to the Oklahoma City bombing. Again, interested buyers were told to call Zeran's phone number, to ask for "Ken," and to "please call back if busy" due to high demand. The angry, threatening phone calls intensified. Over the next four days, an unidentified party continued to post messages on AOL's bulletin board, advertising additional items including bumper stickers and key chains with still more offensive slogans. During this time period, Zeran called AOL repeatedly and was told by company representatives that the individual account from which the messages were posted would soon be closed. Zeran also reported his case to Seattle FBI agents. By April 30, Zeran was receiving an abusive phone call approximately every two minutes....

Zeran ... filed this suit against AOL.... AOL answered Zeran's complaint and interposed 47 U.S.C. § 230 as an affirmative defense. AOL then moved for judgment on the pleadings .... The district court granted AOL's motion, and Zeran filed this appeal.

II.

A.

.... Zeran seeks to hold AOL liable for defamatory speech initiated by a third party. He argued to the district court that once he notified AOL of the unidentified third party's hoax, AOL had a duty to remove the defamatory posting promptly, to notify its subscribers of the message's false nature, and to effectively screen future defamatory material. Section 230 entered this litigation as an affirmative defense pled by AOL. The company claimed that Congress immunized interactive computer service providers from claims based on information posted by a third party.

The relevant portion of § 230 states: "No provider or user of an interactive computer service shall be treated as the publisher or speaker of any information provided by another information content provider." 47 U.S.C. § 230(c)(1). By its plain language, § 230 creates a federal immunity to any cause of action that would make service providers liable for information originating with a third-party user of the service. Specifically, § 230 precludes courts from entertaining claims that would place a computer service provider in a publisher's role. Thus, lawsuits seeking to hold a service provider liable for its exercise of a publisher's traditional editorial functions—such as deciding whether to publish, withdraw, postpone, or alter content—are barred.

The purpose of this statutory immunity is not difficult to discern. Congress recognized the threat that tort-based lawsuits pose to freedom of speech in the new and burgeoning Internet medium. The imposition of tort liability on service providers for the communications of others represented, for Congress, simply another form of intrusive government regulation of speech. Section 230 was enacted, in part, to maintain the robust nature of Internet communication and, accordingly, to keep government interference in the medium to a minimum. In specific statutory findings, Congress recognized the Internet and interactive computer services as offering "a forum for a true diversity of political discourse, unique opportunities for cultural development, and myriad avenues for intellectual activity." It also found that the Internet and interactive computer services "have flourished, to the benefit of all Americans, with a minimum of government regulation." Congress further stated that it is "the policy of the United States ... to preserve the vibrant and competitive free market that presently exists for the Internet and other interactive computer services, unfettered by Federal or State regulation."

None of this means, of course, that the original culpable party who posts defamatory messages would escape accountability. While Congress acted to keep government regulation of the Internet to a minimum, it also found it to be the policy of the United States "to ensure vigorous enforcement of Federal criminal laws to deter and punish trafficking in obscenity, stalking, and harassment by means of computer." Id. § 230(b)(5). Congress made a policy choice, however, not to deter harmful online speech through the separate route of imposing tort liability on companies that serve as intermediaries for other parties' potentially injurious messages.

.... The specter of tort liability in an area of such prolific speech would have an obvious chilling effect. It would be impossible for service providers to screen each of their millions of postings for possible problems. Faced with potential liability for each message republished by their services, interactive computer service providers might choose to severely restrict the number and type of messages posted. Congress considered the weight of the speech interests implicated and chose to immunize service providers to avoid any such restrictive effect.

Another important purpose of § 230 was to encourage service providers to self-regulate the dissemination of offensive material over their services. In this respect, § 230 responded to a New York state court decision, *Stratton Oakmont, Inc. v. Prodigy Servs. Co.,* 1995 N.Y. Misc. LEXIS 229, 1995 WL 323710 (N.Y. Sup. Ct. May 24, 1995). There, the plaintiffs sued Prodigy—an interactive computer service like AOL—for defamatory comments made by an unidentified party on one of Prodigy's bulletin boards. The court held Prodigy to the strict liability standard normally applied to original publishers of defamatory statements, rejecting Prodigy's claims that it should be held only to the lower "knowledge" standard usually reserved for distributors. The court reasoned that Prodigy acted more like an original publisher than a distributor both because it advertised its practice of controlling content on its service and because it actively screened and edited messages posted on its bulletin boards.

Congress enacted § 230 to remove the disincentives to self-regulation created by the Stratton Oakmont decision. Under that court's holding, computer service providers who regulated the dissemination of offensive material on their services risked subjecting themselves to liability, because such regulation cast the service provider in the role of a publisher....

B.

Zeran argues, however, that the § 230 immunity eliminates only publisher liability, leaving distributor liability intact. Publishers can be held liable for defamatory statements contained in their works even absent proof that they had specific knowledge of the statement's inclusion. According to Zeran, interactive computer service providers like AOL are normally considered instead to be distributors, like traditional news vendors or book sellers. Distributors cannot be held liable for defamatory statements contained in the materials they distribute unless it is proven at a minimum that they have actual knowledge of the defamatory statements upon which liability is predicated.

Zeran contends that he provided AOL with sufficient notice of the defamatory statements appearing on the company's bulletin board. This notice is significant, says Zeran, because AOL could be held liable as a distributor only if it acquired knowledge of the defamatory statements' existence.

Because of the difference between these two forms of liability, Zeran contends that the term "distributor" carries a legally distinct meaning from the term "publisher." Accordingly, he asserts that Congress' use of only the term "publisher" in § 230 indicates a purpose to immunize service providers only from publisher liability. He argues that distributors are left unprotected by § 230 and, therefore, his suit should be permitted to proceed against AOL. We disagree. Assuming arguendo that Zeran has satisfied the requirements for imposition of distributor liability, this theory of liability is merely a subset, or a species, of publisher liability, and is therefore also foreclosed by § 230.

The terms "publisher" and "distributor" derive their legal significance from the context of defamation law. Although Zeran attempts to artfully plead his claims as ones of negligence, they are indistinguishable from a garden-variety defamation action. Because the publication of a statement is a necessary element in a defamation action, only one who publishes can be subject to this form of tort liability. Publication does not only describe the choice by an author to include certain information. In addition, both the negligent communication of a defamatory statement and the failure to remove such a statement when first communicated by another party—each alleged by Zeran here under a negligence label—constitute publication. In fact, every repetition of a defamatory statement is considered a publication.

In this case, AOL is legally considered to be a publisher. "Every one who takes part in the publication … is charged with publication." Even distributors are considered to be publishers for purposes of defamation law…. AOL falls squarely within this traditional definition of a publisher and, therefore, is clearly protected by § 230's immunity.

Zeran contends that decisions like *Stratton Oakmont and Cubby, Inc. v. CompuServe Inc.,* 776 F. Supp. 135 (S.D.N.Y. 1991), recognize a legal distinction between publishers and distributors. He misapprehends, however, the significance of that distinction for the legal issue we consider here. It is undoubtedly true that mere conduits, or distributors, are subject to a different standard of liability. As explained above, distributors must at a minimum have knowledge of the existence of a defamatory statement as a prerequisite to liability. But this distinction signifies only that different standards of liability may be applied within the larger publisher category, depending on the specific type of publisher concerned. To the extent that decisions like Stratton and Cubby utilize the terms "publisher" and "distributor" separately, the decisions correctly describe two different standards of liability. Stratton and Cubby do not, however, suggest that distributors are not also a type of publisher for purposes of defamation law.

Zeran simply attaches too much importance to the presence of the distinct notice element in distributor liability. The simple fact of notice surely cannot transform one from an original publisher to a distributor in the eyes of the law. To the contrary, once a computer service provider receives notice of a potentially defamatory posting, it is thrust into the role of a traditional publisher. The computer service provider must decide whether to publish, edit, or withdraw the posting. In this respect, Zeran seeks to impose liability on AOL for assuming the role for which § 230 specifically proscribes liability—the publisher role….

III.

The CDA was signed into law and became effective on February 8, 1996. Zeran did not file his complaint until April 23, 1996. Zeran contends that even if § 230 does bar the type of claim he brings here, it cannot be applied retroactively to bar an action arising from AOL's alleged misconduct prior to the CDA's enactment. We disagree. Section 230 applies by its plain terms to complaints brought after the CDA became effective…

For the foregoing reasons, we affirm the judgment of the district court.

GRACE V. EBAY INC.
Court of Appeal of California, 2004
120 Cal. App. 4th 984

THOMAS L. WILLHITE, Jr., Judge.

Roger M. Grace appeals a judgment of dismissal after the court sustained a demurrer to his complaint against eBay Inc. (eBay). The superior court concluded that title 47 United

States Code section 230 (section 230), part of the Communications Decency Act of 1996, immunizes eBay against liability for libel … as a publisher of information provided by another person. Grace challenges that conclusion.

Section 230 states that federal policy is to promote the continued development of the Internet and other interactive computer services, to encourage the development of technologies that enable user control over information received through the Internet, and to remove disincentives to the development and use of technologies that restrict children's access to objectionable Internet content. Section 230 provides immunity against civil liability for certain conduct in furtherance of those policies.

We conclude that section 230 provides no immunity against liability for a distributor of information who knew or had reason to know that the information was defamatory. We conclude further, however, that the written release in eBay's User Agreement relieves eBay of the liability alleged in the complaint. We therefore affirm the judgment.

FACTUAL AND PROCEDURAL BACKGROUND

eBay maintains an Internet Web site that describes goods for sale by third party sellers. Potential buyers bid on the goods by sending e-mail to eBay. After a sale is consummated, the buyer and seller may provide comments on each other and the transaction, or "feedback," which is displayed on the Web site. The website displays a "feedback profile" on each user, including the comments and a numerical rating. eBay discourages inflammatory language and libel and requires buyers and sellers to agree to a User Agreement that prohibits defamation, but eBay's stated policy is not to remove objectionable comments.

The User Agreement also states:

"Because we are a venue, in the event that you have a dispute with one or more users, you release eBay (and our officers, directors, …) from claims, demands and damages (actual and consequential) of every kind and nature, known and unknown, suspected and unsuspected, disclosed and undisclosed, arising out of or in any way connected with such disputes…."

Grace purchased several items from another individual and then posted negative comments on the seller pertaining to some of the transactions. The seller responded by commenting on Grace as to each transaction, "Complaint: SHOULD BE BANNED FROM EBAY!!!! DISHONEST ALL THE WAY!!!!" Grace notified eBay that the seller's comments were defamatory, but eBay refused to remove them.

Grace sued eBay and the seller, alleging counts against eBay for libel….

DISCUSSION

… Section 230 states that no provider or user of an interactive computer service can be held liable for an action taken in good faith to restrict access to material that the provider or user considers obscene or otherwise objectionable, or for an action taken to enable or make available the technical means to restrict access to such material.

Section 230 also states, "No provider or user of an interactive computer service shall be treated as the publisher or speaker of any information provided by another information content provider." …

Section 230(c)(1) Provides No Immunity Against Liability for Libel as a Distributor
a. Construction of Section 230(c)(1) in Light of the Common Law Background

Section 230(c)(1) states that a provider or user of an interactive computer service may not "be treated as the publisher or speaker" of information provided by another person. To understand the intended effect of this provision on the common law of libel requires an understanding of the common law of libel. We presume that Congress was aware of common law principles and intended those principles to apply absent some indication to the contrary....

The common law of libel distinguishes between liability as a primary publisher and liability as a distributor. A primary publisher, such as an author or a publishing company, is presumed to know the content of the published material, has the ability to control the content of the publication, and therefore generally is held liable for a defamatory statement, provided that constitutional requirements imposed by the First Amendment are satisfied. A distributor, such as a book seller, news vendor, or library, may or may not know the content of the published matter and therefore can be held liable only if the distributor knew or had reason to know that the material was defamatory.

Thus, although a distributor can be held liable for libel in certain circumstances, a distributor is subject to a different standard of liability from that of a primary publisher, and liability as a distributor ordinarily requires a greater showing of culpability. Section 230(c)(1) does not state that a provider or user of an interactive computer service may not be treated as a "distributor" or "transmitter" of information provided by another person, but only that a provider or user may not "be treated as the publisher or speaker." In light of the common law distinction between liability as a primary publisher and liability as a distributor, we conclude that section 230(c)(1) does not clearly and directly address distributor liability and therefore does not preclude distributor liability.

Legislative History of Section 230(c)(1)

The legislative history of section 230 supports our conclusion. The conference committee report on the Telecommunications Act of 1996, of which the Communications Decency Act of 1996 is a part, stated of section 230:

"This section provides 'Good Samaritan' protections from civil liability for providers or users of an interactive computer service for actions to restrict or to enable restriction of access to objectionable online material. One of the specific purposes of this section is to overrule *Stratton-Oakmont v. Prodigy* and any other similar decisions which have treated such providers and users as publishers or speakers of content that is not their own because they have restricted access to objectionable material. The conferees believe that such decisions create serious obstacles to the important federal policy of empowering parents to determine the content of communications their children receive through interactive computer services." ...

The conference committee report stated that one of the specific purposes of section 230 was to overrule *Stratton Oakmont* and any other decisions that treated providers and users of interactive computer services "as publishers or speakers" of information provided by another person "because they have restricted access to objectionable material." This statement reflects a legislative intent to repudiate the holding in *Stratton Oakmont* that an operator of a computer bulletin board, or other provider or user of an interactive computer service, can be held liable for libel without regard to whether the operator knew or had reason to know that the matter was defamatory (i.e., liable as a primary publisher rather than a distributor) because of the operator's efforts to control content (i.e., act as a "Good Samaritan"). There is no indication, however, that Congress intended to preclude liability where the provider or user knew or had reason to know that the matter was defamatory, that is, common law distributor liability.

Conclusion

We conclude that section 230 provides no immunity against liability as a distributor. We decline to follow *Zeran v. America Online, Inc.* (4th Cir. 1997) 129 F.3d 327 and its progeny.... For the reasons we have stated, we disagree with the *Zeran* court's conclusion that because the term "publication" can encompass any repetition of a defamatory statement, use of the term "publisher" in section 230(c)(1) indicates a clear legislative intention to abrogate common law distributor liability. In light of the well-established common law distinction between liability as a primary publisher and liability as a distributor and Congress's expressed intention to overrule an opinion that held the operator of a computer bulletin board liable as a primary publisher rather than a distributor (*Stratton Oakmont*), we cannot conclude that use of the term "publisher" in section 230(c)(1) discloses a clear legislative intention to abrogate distributor liability.

We also disagree with the *Zeran* court's conclusion that for providers and users of interactive computer services to be subject to distributor liability would defeat the purposes of the statute and therefore could not be what Congress intended. The *Zeran* court opined that the threat of distributor liability would encourage providers and users to remove potentially offensive material upon notice that the material is potentially offensive rather than risk liability for failure to do so. The *Zeran* court opined further that a provider or user who undertakes efforts to block and filter objectionable material is more likely to know or have reason to know of potentially defamatory material and therefore more likely to be held liable as a distributor, so the threat of distributor liability would discourage undertaking those efforts. The broad immunity provided under *Zeran*, however, would eliminate potential liability for providers and users even if they made no effort to control objectionable content and therefore would neither promote the development of technologies to accomplish that task nor remove disincentives to that development as Congress intended. Rather, the total elimination of distributor liability under *Zeran* would eliminate a potential incentive to the development of those technologies; that incentive being the threat of distributor liability. We conclude that Congress reasonably could have concluded that the threat of distributor liability together with the immunity provided for efforts to restrict access to objectionable material would encourage the development and application of technologies to block and filter access to objectionable material, consistent with the expressed legislative purposes....

The Release Relieves eBay of Liability

A written release ordinarily relieves a person of liability for all claims within the scope of the release, unless the release does not express the parties' mutual intention or is procured by fraud or other improper means....

The provision states that the user releases eBay from claims and demands "of every kind and nature, known and unknown, . . . arising out of or in any way connected with such disputes." This broad language encompasses a claim or demand against eBay based on its displaying of or failure to remove objectionable comments by another user posted on the Web site. Such a claim or demand against eBay arises out of or is connected with a dispute with another user. Thus, the plain meaning of the release encompasses Grace's claim for libel and his claim or demand for injunctive relief in connection with the alleged libel. No greater specificity is required of the release.

DISPOSITION

The judgment is affirmed.

Chapter Five
PRIVACY AND PEACE OF MIND

Legal protection for personal privacy is safeguarded primarily through four torts, or civil wrongs, that are typically referred to as (1) commercial appropriation, (2) disclosure of private facts, (3) false light, and (4) intrusion upon physical seclusion. This section includes cases dealing with each of these torts, as well as the related tort of intentional infliction of emotional distress.

Hoffman v. Capital Cities/ABC Inc. is a recent appropriation case that illustrates how a commercial objective, coupled with creativity and modern computer technology, can lead to illegal exploitation of an individual's image.

McNamara v. Freedom Newspapers, Inc., a recent Texas court decision, represents a line of cases in which the individual subjects of photographs have sued for public disclosure of embarrassing private facts.

Florida Star v. BJF is a much-cited U.S. Supreme Court opinion concerning the private-facts tort and its conflict with First Amendment rights. The case is important also because it involves a controversial issue with significant public policy implications—the extent to which a rape victim may keep her name out of the news.

Diaz v. Oakland Tribune, Inc. is a classic example of a private-facts case that the plaintiff won on the merits, and it serves as a warning against reckless humor at another's expense.

Shulman v. Group W Productions, Inc. is a very thorough decision from the California Supreme Court in a case that involved claims for both intrusion and disclosure of private facts.

Hustler Magazine v. Falwell is a highly significant case in which the Supreme Court put the brakes on lawsuits against the media for intentional infliction of emotional distress—at least in cases where the plaintiff is a public figure.

Finally, *Armstrong v. H & C Communications, Inc.* is a Florida case illustrating that, even after *Hustler,* in cases of extremely bad judgment the emotional distress tort remains viable against the media.

HOFFMAN V. CAPITAL CITIES/ABC INC.
U.S. District Court for the Central District of California, 1999
33 F. Supp. 2d 867

Opinion by: DICKRAN TEVRIZIAN Findings of Fact

Plaintiff, Dustin Hoffman, is a highly successful and recognizable motion picture actor. For the past thirty years he has appeared in scores of motion pictures and has received numerous honors, including six Academy Award nominations and two Academy Awards. . . .

The right to use Plaintiff's name and likeness is an extremely valuable commodity and privilege not only because of Mr. Hoffman's stature as an actor, but because he does not knowingly permit commercial uses of his identity. Since appearing in the film *The Graduate,* Mr. Hoffman has scrupulously guided and guarded the manner in which he has been shown to the public. Plaintiff maintains a strict policy of not endorsing commercial products for fear that he will be perceived in a negative light by his peers and motion picture industry executives, suggesting that his career is in decline and that he no longer has the business opportunities or the box office draw as before.

Defendant, ABC, Inc. (formerly known as Capital Cities/ABC, Inc.), is owned by the Walt Disney Company. ABC, Inc. owns one-hundred percent of Defendant, Los Angeles Magazine, Inc., the publisher of *Los Angeles Magazine.* . . .

At Page 118 of its March 1997 issue, *Los Angeles Magazine* published a photograph of Mr. Hoffman as he appeared to have appeared in the successful 1982 motion picture *Tootsie,* and through a process of technology employing computer imaging software, manipulated and altered the photograph to make it appear that Mr. Hoffman was wearing what appeared to be a contemporary silk gown designed by Richard Tyler and high-heel shoes designed by Ralph Lauren. Page 118 also contained the following text: "Dustin Hoffman isn't a drag in a butter-colored silk gown by Richard Tyler and Ralph Lauren heels."

Mr. Hoffman's photograph and name appeared in conjunction with an article entitled, "Grand Illusions," published on Pages 104 through 119 of the March 1997 issue of *Los Angeles Magazine.* The magazine article used computer technology to merge famous still photographs of famous actors/actresses, many of whom are now deceased, from classic films with photographs of body models wearing spring 1997 fashions identifying the designers of the articles of clothing used in the cannibalized photographs. Many of the articles of clothing used in the magazine article were designed by designers who were major advertisers in *Los Angeles Magazine* at the time of publication. . . .

. . . . The new composite computer-generated photograph that appeared in the "Grand Illusions" article incorporated only Mr. Hoffman's face and head and the American flag from the original still photograph, and a new photograph of a male model's body clothed in the silk gown designed by Richard Tyler and high-heel shoes designed by Ralph Lauren. . . .

Defendant, Los Angeles Magazine, Inc., did not seek or obtain permission from Mr. Hoffman to use his name or likeness in the March 1997 issue of *Los Angeles Magazine* and, in particular, did not obtain Mr. Hoffman's consent to commercially endorse or "shill" for any fashion designer or advertiser or the magazine. Defendant, Los Angeles Magazine, Inc., did not seek or obtain the permission of Columbia Pictures to use any image from *Tootsie* in the March 1997 issue of *Los Angeles Magazine.* . . .

Defendant, Los Angeles Magazine, Inc., was aware that celebrities are sensitive and particular regarding the manner in which they are depicted in photographs. Defendant, Los Angeles Magazine, Inc., did not want the celebrities they were going to use to be "upset" or "degraded" by the manner in which they were portrayed in the March 1997 issue of *Los Angeles Magazine.* Despite these purported concerns, Defendant, Los Angeles Magazine, Inc., made absolutely no effort to contact the celebrities to see if they would consent to being portrayed in clothes that they never actually wore. The reason permission was not sought is because Defendant, Los Angeles Magazine, Inc., knew, or should have known, that the celebrities either would not consent or, alternatively, would demand payment for the fair market value for the right to utilize their names and likenesses in this manner for commercial exploitation.

Defendant, Los Angeles Magazine, Inc., obtained the celebrity photographs used in the March 1997 issue from photo archive companies. One of the companies that supplied photographs for the article, the Motion Picture and Television Photo Archive, specifically included a provision in its contract with *Los Angeles Magazine* that prohibited the stills from being altered or digitized through the use of a computer. Defendant, Los Angeles Magazine, Inc., completely ignored this contractual restriction. . . .

Plaintiff, Dustin Hoffman, has been damaged by Defendant, Los Angeles Magazine, Inc., for the unauthorized use of his name and likeness to endorse and promote articles of clothing designed by Richard Tyler and Ralph Lauren. . . .

The fair market value of Plaintiff's damages is the value that a celebrity of Mr. Hoffman's reputation, appeal, talent, and fame would bring in the open market for this type of one-time use in a publication in a regional magazine, in the Los Angeles market area. . . .

. . . . [T]his Court finds the fair market value of Plaintiff's name and likeness used for endorsement purposes to be $ 1,500,000.

The Court also finds that Plaintiff has established by clear and convincing evidence that Plaintiff is entitled to an award of punitive damages. . . . The unauthorized use of Plaintiff's name and likeness to promote the interests of *Los Angeles Magazine* in the manner depicted by the evidence introduced during this trial crossed over the line between editorial content and advertising. The photographs were manipulated and cannibalized to such an extent that the celebrities were commercially exploited and were robbed of their dignity, professionalism, and talent. To be blunt, the celebrities were violated by technology.

Allowing this type of deceptive conduct to continue under the guise of First Amendment protection would lead to further technological mischief. The First Amendment provides extremely broad protection but does not permit unbridled exploitive speech at the expense of Mr. Hoffman and his distinguished career.

CONCLUSIONS OF LAW

1. Under the common law, the right of publicity protects a plaintiff from having his/her name and likeness appropriated for the defendant's advantage. "A common law cause of action for appropriation of name or likeness may be pleaded by alleging: (1) the defendant's use of the plaintiff's identity; (2) the appropriation of plaintiff's name or likeness to defendant's advantage, commercially or otherwise; (3) lack of consent; and (4) resulting injury."

2. Defendant, Los Angeles Magazine, Inc.'s conduct violates Mr. Hoffman's common law right of publicity, because: (a) Defendant, Los Angeles Magazine, Inc., used Mr. Hoffman's name and likeness at Page 118 of the March 1997 issue of *Los Angeles Magazine;* (b) Defendant, Los Angeles Magazine, Inc., used Mr. Hoffman's name and likeness for its own advantage to sell magazines, advertise, and promote designer clothing; (c) Defendant, Los Angeles Magazine, Inc., did not obtain Mr. Hoffman's consent to utilize his name or likeness in *Los Angeles Magazine;* and (d) Mr. Hoffman

has suffered injury and damage to his property rights as a result of the unauthorized use of his name and likeness by Defendant, Los Angeles Magazine, Inc., in that he was unable to reap the commercial value or control the use to which his name and likeness were put.

3. California Civil Code Section 3344 provides a remedy separate and distinct from the common law right of publicity. The right of publicity statute provides, in pertinent part:

Any person who knowingly uses another's name, voice, signature, photograph, or likeness, in any manner, on or in products, merchandise, or goods, or for purposes of advertising or selling, or soliciting purchases of products, merchandise, goods, or services, without such person's prior consent . . . shall be liable for any damages sustained by the person or persons injured as a result thereof.

4. Defendant, Los Angeles Magazine, Inc.'s conduct violates Mr. Hoffman's statutory right of publicity because: (a) Defendant, Los Angeles Magazine, Inc., knowingly used Mr. Hoffman's name and likeness; (b) Defendant, Los Angeles Magazine, Inc., used Mr. Hoffman's name and likeness on or in products, merchandise, or goods, namely, *Los Angeles Magazine;* (c) Defendant, Los Angeles Magazine, Inc., used Mr. Hoffman's name and likeness for purposes of advertising or selling, or soliciting purchases of products, merchandise, or goods, namely, Richard Tyler gowns, Ralph Lauren shoes, and *Los Angeles Magazine;* (d) Defendant, Los Angeles Magazine, Inc., utilized Mr. Hoffman's name and likeness without obtaining his prior consent; and (e) Mr. Hoffman has suffered injury and damage to his property rights as a result of the unauthorized use of his name and likeness by Defendant, Los Angeles Magazine, Inc., in that he was unable to reap the commercial value or control the use to which his name and likeness were put. . . .

9. Defendant, Los Angeles Magazine, Inc.'s First Amendment defense is unavailing. The First Amendment does not protect the exploitative commercial use of Mr. Hoffman's name and likeness. The *Los Angeles Magazine* article provided no commentary on fashion trends and no coordinated or unified view of current fashions. The article contains no statement that any particular style of clothes is in vogue, that any particular color is becoming popular, or that any type of fabric is attracting the attention of designers. It merely used randomly selected designer clothes to attract attention when "worn" by the computer-manipulated, involuntary, celebrity models. Moreover, the use of Mr. Hoffman's name and likeness was wholly unnecessary to deliver whatever message Defendant, Los Angeles Magazine, Inc., claims the *Los Angeles Magazine* article contained. . . .

16. In connection with each of his four claims, Mr. Hoffman is entitled to compensatory damages in the amount of $ 1,500,000.00, which represents the fair market value of the right to utilize Mr. Hoffman's name and likeness in the manner in which it was used by *Los Angeles Magazine.*

17. Mr. Hoffman is entitled to punitive damages in an amount to be fixed by the Court after presentation of additional evidence on the ground that Defendant, Los Angeles Magazine, Inc.'s unauthorized use of his name and likeness was willful and was done in conscious disregard of Mr. Hoffman's rights.

MCNAMARA V. FREEDOM NEWSPAPERS, INC.
Court of Appeals of Texas, 1991
802 S.W.2d 901

Judge BENAVIDES:

Larry McNamara appeals a summary judgment in favor of Freedom Newspapers d/b/a *Brownsville Herald* (hereafter "Newspaper"). . . . We affirm the trial court's judgment.

The underlying action arises out of the publication by the Newspaper of a photograph taken during a high school soccer game. The photograph in question accurately depicted McNamara and a student from the opposing school running full stride and chasing a soccer ball. The picture further shows McNamara's genitalia which happened to be exposed at the exact moment that the photograph was taken. [The exposure was apparently caused by McNamara's failure to wear the customary athletic supporter.] The photograph was published in conjunction with an article reporting on the soccer game.

At issue in this case is whether the Newspaper's publication of the photograph is protected by the First Amendment of the United States Constitution and Article 1, Section 8, of the Texas Constitution such that McNamara's suit for invasion of privacy . . . as a result of the publication of the photograph is precluded. . . .

The Newspaper asserts that the publication of the photograph is protected by the First Amendment of the United States Constitution and Article I, Section 8, of the Texas Constitution because the constitutional provisions do not allow civil damages against a newspaper for the publication of a photograph taken at a public event. . . .

Article I, Section 8, of the Texas Constitution provides:

Every person shall be at liberty to speak, write, or publish his opinions on any subject, being responsible for the abuse of that privilege; and no law shall ever be passed curtailing the liberty of speech or of the press.

. . . . Arguably, the rights of free speech and press guaranteed by our Texas Constitution are more extensive than those guaranteed by the United States Constitution. . . . We determine first whether the Newspaper would be entitled to protection under the First Amendment from McNamara's claims.

First Amendment protection for publications covers a vast spectrum of tastes, views, and expressions, all of which fall within a broad definition of newsworthy. The First Amendment sometimes protects what would otherwise be an actionable invasion of privacy when a publication by the media is involved. See *Cox Broadcasting Corp. v. Cohn,* 420 U.S. 469, (1975). This constitutional privilege applies to the public disclosure of private facts, which in this case is alleged to have resulted in the invasion of privacy. . . .

The First Amendment privilege immunizes the reporting of private facts when discussed in connection with matters of the kind customarily regarded as news. Under this privilege, a factually accurate public disclosure is not tortious when connected with a newsworthy event even though offensive to ordinary sensibilities. This standard provides a privilege for truthful publications that ceases to operate only when an editor abuses his broad discretion to publish matters that are of legitimate public interest.

Publication in a newspaper does not lose its protected character simply because it may embarrass the persons to whom the publication refers. "The risk of this exposure is an essential incident of life in a society which places a primary value on freedom of speech and of press." When an individual is photographed at a public place for a newsworthy article and that photograph is published, the entity publishing the photograph is entitled to the protection of the First Amendment.

McNamara argues that the Newspaper could have used one of its other numerous photographs in its article. The mere existence of an alternative means of expression cannot by itself justify a restraint on some particular means that the speaker finds more effective. . . .

McNamara further contends that by the publication of his photograph, the Newspaper violated the bounds of public decency and, in such a situation, he is entitled to protection of the law. He argues that the Newspaper should have provided a mechanism that would have prevented the publication of this photograph. In support of his position, McNamara relies extensively on *Daily Times Democrat v. Graham,* 276 Ala. 380, 162 So.2d 474 (1964). We do not find *Graham* persuasive. In *Graham,* the Alabama Supreme Court allowed a woman to recover for invasion of privacy for the publication of a photograph (in which her body was exposed from the waist down, except for her panties) but did not discuss or analyze the availability of First Amendment protection for the newspaper. The key issue in the case at hand, however, is whether the publication of McNamara's photograph is protected by the First Amendment.

The uncontroverted facts in this case establish that the photograph of McNamara was taken by a newspaper photographer for media purposes. The picture accurately depicted a public event and was published as part of a newspaper article describing the game. At the time the photograph was taken, McNamara was voluntarily participating in a spectator sport at a public place. None of the persons involved in the publishing procedure actually noticed that McNamara's genitals were exposed.

We hold that because the published photograph accurately depicts a public, newsworthy event, the First Amendment provides the Newspaper with immunity from liability for damages resulting from its publication of McNamara's photograph. Since immunity under Article I, Section 8, of the Texas Constitution is at least as extensive as that under the First Amendment, we conclude that the Newspaper is also protected by Article I, Section 8, which affords another basis for the trial court's judgment. . . .

The trial court's judgment is AFFIRMED.

THE FLORIDA STAR V. B.J.F.
Supreme Court of the United States, 1989
491 U.S. 524

Justice MARSHALL delivered the opinion of the Court.

Florida Stat. § 794.03 (1987) makes it unlawful to "print, publish, or broadcast . . . in any instrument of mass communication" the name of the victim of a sexual offense. Pursuant to this statute, appellant the *Florida Star* was found civilly liable for publishing the name of a rape victim that it had obtained from a publicly released police report. The issue presented here is whether this result comports with the First Amendment. We hold that it does not.

I

. . . .

On October 20, 1983, appellee B.J.F. reported to the Duval County, Florida, Sheriff's Department (the Department) that she had been robbed and sexually assaulted by an unknown assailant. The Department prepared a report on the incident that identified B.J.F. by her full name. The Department then placed the report in its press-room. The Department does not restrict access either to the pressroom or to the reports made available therein.

A *Florida Star* reporter-trainee sent to the pressroom copied the police report verbatim, including B.J.F.'s full name, on a blank duplicate of the Department's forms. A *Florida Star* reporter then prepared a one-paragraph article about the crime, derived entirely from the trainee's copy of the police report. The article included B.J.F.'s full name. It appeared in the "Robberies" subsection of the "Police Reports" section. . . . In printing B.J.F.'s full name, the *Florida Star* violated its internal policy of not publishing the names of sexual offense victims.

. . . B.J.F. filed suit in the Circuit Court of Duval County against the Department and the *Florida Star,* alleging that these parties negligently violated § 794.03. Before trial, the Department settled with B.J.F. for $2,500. The *Florida Star* moved to dismiss, claiming, *inter alia,* that imposing civil sanctions on the newspaper pursuant to § 794.03 violated the First Amendment. The trial judge rejected the motion.

At the ensuing daylong trial, B.J.F. testified that she had suffered emotional distress from the publication of her name. She stated that she had heard about the article from fellow workers and acquaintances; that her mother had received several threatening phone calls from a man who stated that he would rape B.J.F. again; and that these events had forced B.J.F. to change her phone number and residence, to seek police protection, and to obtain mental health counseling. In defense, the *Florida Star* put forth evidence indicating that the newspaper had learned B.J.F.'s name from the incident report released by the Department, and that the newspaper's violation of its internal rule against publishing the names of sexual offense victims was inadvertent.

. . . The jury awarded B.J.F. $75,000 in compensatory damages and $25,000 in punitive damages. . . .

II

The tension between the right which the First Amendment accords to a free press, on the one hand, and the protections that various statutes and common-law doctrines accord to personal privacy against the publication of truthful information, on the other, is a subject we have addressed several times in recent years. . . .

The parties to this case frame their contentions in light of a trilogy of cases which have presented, in different contexts, the conflict between truthful reporting and state-protected privacy interests. In *Cox Broadcasting Corp. v. Cohn,* 420 U.S. 469 (1975), we found unconstitutional a civil damages award entered against a television station for broadcasting the name of a rape-murder victim which the station had obtained from courthouse records.

In *Oklahoma Publishing Co. v. District Court,* 430 U.S. 308 (1977), we found unconstitutional a state court's pretrial order enjoining the media from publishing the name or photograph of an eleven-year-old boy in connection with a juvenile proceeding involving that child which reporters had attended. Finally, in *Smith v. Daily Mail Publishing Co.,* 443 U.S. 97 (1979), we found unconstitutional the indictment of two newspapers for violating a state statute forbidding newspapers to publish, without written approval of the juvenile court, the name of any youth charged as a juvenile offender. The papers had learned about a shooting by monitoring a police band radio frequency, and had obtained the name of the alleged juvenile assailant from witnesses, the police, and a local prosecutor. . . .

We conclude that imposing damages on appellant for publishing B.J.F.'s name violates the First Amendment, although not for either of the reasons appellant urges. Despite the strong resemblance this case bears to *Cox Broadcasting,* that case cannot fairly be read as controlling here. The name of the rape victim in that case was obtained from courthouse records that were open to public inspection, a fact that Justice WHITE's opinion for the Court repeatedly noted. Significantly, one of the reasons we gave in *Cox Broadcasting* for invalidating the challenged damages award was the important role the press plays in subjecting trials to public scrutiny and thereby helping guarantee their fairness. That role is not directly comprised where, as here, the information in question comes from a police report prepared and disseminated at a time at which not only had no adversarial criminal proceedings begun, but no suspect had been identified.

Nor need we accept appellant's invitation to hold broadly that truthful publication may never be punished consistent with the First Amendment. Our cases have carefully eschewed reaching this ultimate question, mindful that the future may bring scenarios which prudence counsels our not resolving anticipatorily. . . . We continue to believe that the sensitivity and significance of the interests presented in clashes between First Amendment and privacy rights counsel relying on limited principles that sweep no more broadly than the appropriate context of the instant case.

In our view, this case is appropriately analyzed with reference to such a limited First Amendment principle. It is the one, in fact, which we articulated in *Daily Mail* in our synthesis of prior cases involving attempts to punish truthful publication: "[I]f a newspaper lawfully obtains truthful information about a matter of public significance, then state officials may not constitutionally punish publication of the information, absent a need to further a state interest of the highest order." According to the press the ample protection provided by the principle is supported by at least three separate considerations, in addition to, of course, the overarching "'public interest, secured by the Constitution, in the dissemination of truth.'" . . .

First, because the *Daily Mail* formulation only protects the publication of information which a newspaper has "lawfully obtain[ed]," the government retains ample means of safeguarding significant interests upon which publication may impinge, including protecting a rape victim's anonymity. To the extent sensitive information rests in private hands, the government may under some circumstances forbid its nonconsensual acquisition, thereby bringing outside of the *Daily Mail* principle the publication of any information so acquired. To the extent sensitive information is in the government's custody, it has even greater power to forestall or mitigate the injury caused by its release. The government may classify certain information, establish and enforce procedures ensuring its redacted release, and extend a damages remedy against the government or its officials where the government's mishandling of sensitive information leads to its dissemination. Where information is entrusted to the government, a less drastic means than punishing truthful publication almost always exists for guarding against the dissemination of private facts. . . .

A second consideration undergirding the *Daily Mail* principle is the fact that punishing the press for its dissemination of information that is already publicly available is relatively unlikely to advance the interests in the service of which the State seeks to act. It is not, of course, always the case that information lawfully acquired by the press is known, or accessible, to others. But where the government has made certain information publicly available, it is highly anomalous to sanction persons other than the source of its release. We noted this anomaly in *Cox Broadcasting:* "By placing the information in the public domain on official court records, the State must be presumed to have concluded that the public interest was thereby being served." . . .

A third and final consideration is the "timidity and self-censorship" which may result from allowing the media to be punished for publishing certain truthful information. . . .

Applied to the instant case, the *Daily Mail* principle clearly commands reversal. The first inquiry is whether the newspaper "lawfully obtain[ed] truthful information about a matter of public significance." It is undisputed that the news article describing the assault on B.J.F. was accurate. In addition, appellant lawfully obtained B.J.F.'s name. . . . It is clear, furthermore, that the news article concerned "a matter of public significance," in the sense in which the *Daily Mail* synthesis of prior cases used that term. That is, the article generally, as opposed to the specific identity contained within it, involved a matter of paramount public import: the commission, and investigation, of a violent crime which had been reported to authorities.

The second inquiry is whether imposing liability on appellant pursuant to § 794.03 serves "a need to further a state interest of the highest order." Appellee argues that a rule punishing publication furthers three closely related interests: the privacy of victims of sexual offenses; the physical safety of such victims, who may be targeted for retaliation if their names become known to their assailants; and the goal of encouraging victims of such crimes to report these offenses without fear of exposure.

At a time in which we are daily reminded of the tragic reality of rape, it is undeniable that these are highly significant interests, a fact underscored by the Florida Legislature's explicit attempt to protect these interests by enacting a criminal statute prohibiting much dissemination of victim identities. We accordingly do not rule out the possibility that, in a proper case, imposing civil sanctions for publication of the name of a rape victim might be so overwhelmingly necessary to advance these interests as to satisfy the *Daily Mail* standard. For three independent reasons, however, imposing liability for publication under the circumstances of this case is too precipitous a means of advancing these interests to convince us that there is a "need" within the meaning of the *Daily Mail* formulation for Florida to take this extreme step.

First is the manner in which appellant obtained the identifying information in question. As we have noted, where the government itself provides information to the media, it is most appropriate to assume that the government had, but failed to utilize, far more limited means of guarding against dissemination than the extreme step of punishing truthful speech. . . . Florida's policy against disclosure of rape victims' identities, reflected in § 794.03, was undercut by the Department's failure to abide by this policy. Where, as here, the government has failed to police itself in disseminating information, it is clear under *Cox Broadcasting, Oklahoma Publishing,* and *Landmark Communications* that the imposition of damages against the press for its subsequent publication can hardly be said to be a narrowly tailored means of safeguarding anonymity. . . .

A second problem with Florida's imposition of liability for publication is the broad sweep of the negligence *per se* standard applied under the civil cause of action implied from § 794.03. Unlike claims based on the common law tort of invasion of privacy, see Restatement (Second) of Torts § 652D (1977), civil actions based on § 794.03 require no case-by-case findings that the disclosure of a fact about a person's private life was one that a reasonable person would find highly offensive. On the contrary, under the *per se* theory of negligence adopted by the courts below, liability follows automatically from publication. This is so regardless of whether the identity of the victim is already known throughout the community; whether the victim has voluntarily called public attention to the offense; or whether the identity of the victim has otherwise become a reasonable subject of public concern—because, perhaps, questions have arisen whether the victim fabricated an assault by a particular person. . . . We have previously noted the impermissibility of categorical prohibitions upon media access where important First Amendment interests are at stake. . . .

Third, and finally, the facial underinclusiveness of § 794.03 raises serious doubts about whether Florida is, in fact, serving, with this statute, the significant interests which appellee invokes in support of affirmance. Section 794.03 prohibits the publication of identifying information only if this information appears in an "instrument of mass communication," a term the statute does not define. Section 794.03 does not prohibit the spread by other means of the identities of victims of sexual offenses. . . .

When a State attempts the extraordinary measure of punishing truthful publication in the name of privacy, it must demonstrate its commitment to advancing this interest by applying its prohibition evenhandedly, to the smalltime disseminator as well as the media giant. . . .

III

Our holding today is limited. We do not hold that truthful publication is automatically constitutionally protected, or that there is no zone of personal privacy within which the State may protect the individual from intrusion by the press, or even that a State may never punish publication of the name of a victim of a sexual offense. We hold only that where a newspaper publishes truthful information which it has lawfully obtained, punishment may lawfully be imposed, if at all, only when narrowly tailored to a state interest of the highest order, and that no such interest is satisfactorily served by imposing liability under § 794.03 to appellant under the facts of this case. The decision below is therefore *Reversed.*

DIAZ V. OAKLAND TRIBUNE, INC.
Court of Appeal of California, First Appellate District, 1983
139 Cal. App. 3d 118

Opinion by: BARRY-DEAL, J.

Plaintiff Toni Ann Diaz (Diaz) sued the Oakland Tribune, Inc., owners and publishers of the *Oakland Tribune* (the *Tribune*), and Sidney Jones (Jones), one of its columnists, for invasion of privacy. Diaz claimed that the publication of highly embarrassing private facts in Jones' March 26, 1978, newspaper column was unwarranted and malicious and caused her to suffer severe emotional distress. The jury awarded Diaz $250,000 in compensatory damages and $525,000 in punitive damages. . . .

The facts are for the most part undisputed. Diaz is a transsexual. She was born in Puerto Rico in 1942 as Antonio Diaz, a male. She moved to California from New York in 1964. Suffice it to say that for most of her life Diaz suffered from a gender-identification problem and the anxiety and depression that accompanied it. She testified that since she was young she had had the feeling of being a woman. In 1968 Diaz began receiving psychological counseling and hormone therapy. In 1970 or 1971 Diaz embarked on the lengthy process of evaluation as a candidate for gender corrective surgery at the Stanford University Gender Dysphoria Clinic. . . . In 1975 gender-corrective surgery was performed by the Stanford staff.

According to Diaz the surgery was a success. By all outward appearances she looked and behaved as a woman and was accepted by the public as a woman. . . .

Diaz scrupulously kept the surgery a secret from all but her immediate family and closest friends. She never sought to publicize the surgery. She changed her name to Toni Ann Diaz and made the necessary changes in her high school records, her social security records, and on her driver's license. She tried unsuccessfully to change her Puerto Rican birth certificate. . . .

. . . . In 1975 she enrolled in the College of Alameda (the College), a two-year college. . . .

In spring 1977, she was elected student body president for the 1977–1978 academic year, the first woman to hold that office. Her election and an unsuccessful attempt to unseat her were reported in the College newspaper, the *Reporter*, in the May 17, June 1, and June 14, 1977, editions. At no time during the election did Diaz reveal any information about her sex-change operation. . . .

Near the middle of her term as student body president, Diaz became embroiled in a controversy in which she charged the College administrators with misuse of student funds. The March 15, 1978, issue of the *Tribune* quoted Diaz's charge that her signature had improperly been "rubber stamped" on checks drawn from the associated students' account. . . .

Shortly after the controversy arose, Jones was informed by several confidential sources that Diaz was a man. Jones considered the matter newsworthy if he could verify the information. Jones testified that he inspected the *Tribune's* own files and spoke with an unidentified number of persons at the College to confirm this information. . . .

On March 26, 1978, the following item appeared in Jones' newspaper column:

"More Education Stuff: The students at the College of Alameda will be surprised to learn that their student body president, Toni Diaz, is no lady, but is in fact a man whose real name is Antonio.

"Now I realize, that in these times, such a matter is no big deal, but I suspect his female classmates in P.E. 97 may wish to make other showering arrangements."

Upon reading the article, Diaz became very depressed and was forced to reveal her status, which she had worked hard to conceal. Diaz testified that as a result of the article she suffered from insomnia, nightmares, and memory lapses. She also delayed her enrollment in Mills College, scheduled for that fall.

In her complaint Diaz did not charge that any of the information was untrue, only that defendants invaded her privacy by the unwarranted publicity of intimate facts. Defendants defended on the ground that the matter was newsworthy and hence was constitutionally protected.

At trial the jury returned a special verdict and found that (1) defendants did publicly disclose a fact concerning Diaz; (2) the fact was private and not public; (3) the fact was not newsworthy; (4) the fact was highly offensive to a reasonable person of ordinary sensibilities; (5) defendants disclosed the fact with knowledge that it was highly offensive or with reckless disregard of whether it was highly offensive; and (6) the disclosure proximately caused injury or damage to Diaz.

In this appeal defendants challenge the jury's finding on issues Nos. (2) and (3) above. Defendants also urge instructional error and attack the awards of compensatory and punitive damages. . . .

Background

The concept of a common law right to privacy was first developed in a landmark article by Warren and Brandeis, The Right to Privacy (1890) 4 Harv.L.Rev. 193, and has been adopted in virtually every state. The specific privacy right with which we are concerned is the right to be free from public disclosure of private embarrassing facts, in short, "the right to be let alone." . . .

The public disclosure cause of action is distinct from a suit for libel or "false light," since the plaintiff herein does not challenge the accuracy of the information published, but asserts that the publicity is so intimate and unwarranted as to outrage the community's notion of decency.

Of course, the right to privacy is not absolute and must be balanced against the often competing constitutional right of the press to publish newsworthy matters. The First Amendment protection from tort liability is necessary if the press is to carry out its constitutional obligation to keep the public informed so that they may make intelligent decisions on matters important to a self-governing people.

However, the newsworthy privilege is not without limitation. Where the publicity is so offensive as to constitute a "'morbid and sensational prying into private lives for its own sake, . . . '" it serves no legitimate public interest and is not deserving of protection.

    . . . .

1. Private Facts

Defendants argue that the evidence establishes as a matter of law that the fact of Diaz's original gender was a matter of public record, and therefore its publicity was not actionable. In support of their contention defendants rely on *Cox Broadcasting Corp. v. Cohn,* 420 U.S. 469. That reliance is misplaced.

Generally speaking, matter that is already in the public domain is not private, and its publication is protected.

In *Cox Broadcasting Corp.,* the Supreme Court ruled that Cohn, the father of a deceased rape victim, could not maintain a disclosure action against media defendants who identified Cohn's daughter as the victim during the television coverage of the murder trial. Central to the court's conclusion was the fact that the reporter obtained the victim's name from the indictment, which had been shown to him in open court. . . .

Here there is no evidence to suggest that the fact of Diaz's gender-corrective surgery was part of the public record. To the contrary, the evidence reveals that Diaz took affirmative steps to conceal this fact by changing her driver's license, social security, and high school records, and by lawfully changing her name. The police records, upon which Jones relied, contained information concerning one Antonio Diaz. No mention was made of Diaz's new name or gender. In order to draw the connection, Jones relied upon unidentified confidential sources. Under these circumstances, we conclude that Diaz's sexual identity was a private matter. . . .

2. Newsworthiness

As discussed above, whether the fact of Diaz's sexual identity was newsworthy is measured along a sliding scale of competing interests: the individual's right to keep private facts from the public's gaze versus the public's right to know. In an effort to reconcile these competing interests, our courts have settled on a three-part test for determining whether matter published is newsworthy: "[1] the social value of the facts published, [2] the depth of the article's intrusion into ostensibly private affairs, and [3] the extent to which the party voluntarily acceded to a position of public notoriety." Defendants argue that in light of Diaz's position as the first female student body president of the College, her "questionable gender" was a newsworthy item. . . .

It is well settled that persons who voluntarily seek public office or willingly become involved in public affairs waive their right to privacy of matters connected with their public conduct. However, the extent to which Diaz voluntarily acceded to a position of public notoriety and the degree to which she opened her private life are questions of fact. As student body president, Diaz was a public figure for some purposes. However, applying the three-part test . . . we cannot state that the fact of her gender was newsworthy per se.

Contrary to defendants' claim, we find little if any connection between the information disclosed and Diaz's fitness for office. The fact that she is a transsexual does not adversely reflect on her honesty or judgment.

Nor does the fact that she was the first woman student body president, in itself, warrant that her entire private life be open to public inspection. The public arena entered by Diaz is concededly small. Public figures more celebrated than she are entitled to keep some information of their domestic activities and sexual relations private.

Nor is there merit to defendants' claim that the changing roles of women in society make this story newsworthy. This assertion rings hollow. The tenor of the article was by no means an attempt to enlighten the public on a contemporary social issue. Rather, as Jones himself admitted, the article was directed to the students at the College about their newly elected president. Moreover, Jones' attempt at humor at Diaz's expense removes all pretense that the article was meant to educate the reading public. The social utility of the information must be viewed in context, and not based upon some arguably meritorious and unintended purpose.

Therefore, we conclude that the jury was the proper body to answer the question whether the article was newsworthy or whether it extended beyond the bounds of decency.
Insufficient Evidence of Malice

Defendants next urge that the award of punitive damages was improper, since there was insufficient evidence to support a finding of malice on the part of either defendant. The evidence demonstrated that Jones published the article without first contacting Diaz, although he knew that the information contained therein would have a "devastating" impact on her. He testified that he attempted to obtain Diaz's telephone number from his unidentified sources but was unsuccessful. He admitted that he never telephoned the College in order to contact Diaz. Jones also stated that his comment about Diaz's classmates in "P.E. 97" making other shower arrangements was a joke, an attempt to be "flip."

In order to justify the imposition of punitive damages, "the defendant" " . . . must act with the intent to vex, injure, or annoy, or with a conscious disregard of the plaintiff's rights."

Viewing the article as a whole, as well as Jones' conduct in preparing the article, we cannot say as a matter of law that there was insufficient evidence to support a finding of malice.

Here Jones knew that Diaz would certainly suffer severe emotional distress from the publicity alone. Nevertheless, he added to the indignity by making Diaz the brunt of a joke. The defendants' knowledge of the extent and severity of plaintiff's injuries is relevant to a finding of malice. The jury could reasonably have inferred from these facts that Jones acted with the intent to outrage or humiliate Diaz or that he published the article with a conscious disregard of her rights. . . .

[The judgment for Plaintiff was sent back to the lower court because of a procedural error in instructing the jury on newsworthiness. Ultimately the case was settled out of court.]

SHULMAN V. GROUP W PRODUCTIONS, INC.
Supreme Court of California, 1998
955 P.2d 469

WERDEGAR, J.

More than 100 years ago, Louis Brandeis and Samuel Warren complained that the press, armed with the then recent invention of "instantaneous photographs" and under the influence of new "business methods," was "overstepping in every direction the obvious bounds of propriety and of decency." (Warren & Brandeis, The Right to Privacy (1890) 4 Harv. L.Rev. 193, 195–196.) Even more ominously, they noted the "numerous mechanical devices" that "threaten to make good the prediction that 'what is whispered in the closet shall be proclaimed from the house-tops.' " . . .

The sense of an ever-increasing pressure on personal privacy notwithstanding, it has long been apparent that the desire for privacy must at many points give way before our right to know, and the news media's right to investigate and relate facts about the events and individuals of our time. . . . As early as 1931, in the first California case recognizing invasion of privacy as a tort, the court observed that the right of privacy "does not exist in the dissemination of news and news events." (Melvin v. Reid (1931) 112 Cal. App. 285, 290 [297 P. 91].)

Also clear is that the freedom of the press, protected by the supreme law of the First and Fourteenth Amendments to the United States Constitution, extends far beyond simple accounts of public proceedings and abstract commentary on well-known events. . . .

. . . .

In the present case, we address the balance between privacy and press freedom in the commonplace context of an automobile accident. . . .

FACTS AND PROCEDURAL HISTORY

On June 24, 1990, plaintiffs Ruth and Wayne Shulman, mother and son, were injured when the car in which they and two other family members were riding on interstate 10 in Riverside County flew off the highway and tumbled down an embankment into a drainage ditch on state-owned property, coming to rest upside down. Ruth, the most seriously injured of the two, was pinned under the car. Ruth and Wayne both had to be cut free from the vehicle by the device known as "the jaws of life."

A rescue helicopter operated by Mercy Air was dispatched to the scene. The flight nurse, who would perform the medical care at the scene and on the way to the hospital, was Laura Carnahan. Also on board were the pilot, a medic, and Joel Cooke, a video camera operator employed by defendants Group W Productions, Inc., and 4MN Productions. Cooke was recording the rescue operation for later broadcast.

Cooke roamed the accident scene, videotaping the rescue. Nurse Carnahan wore a wireless microphone that picked up her conversations with both Ruth and the other rescue personnel. Cooke's tape was edited into a piece approximately nine minutes long, which, with the addition of narrative voice-over, was broadcast on September 29, 1990, as a segment of *On Scene: Emergency Response*.

The segment begins with the Mercy Air helicopter shown on its way to the accident site. The narrator's voice is heard in the background, setting the scene and describing in general terms what has happened. The pilot can be heard speaking with rescue workers on the ground in order to prepare for his landing. . . . After Carnahan steps from the helicopter, she can be seen and heard speaking about the situation with various rescue workers. . . .

The videotape shows only a glimpse of Wayne, and his voice is never heard. Ruth is shown several times, either by brief shots of a limb or her torso, or with her features blocked by others or obscured by an oxygen mask. She is also heard speaking several times. Carnahan calls her "Ruth," and her last name is not mentioned on the broadcast.

. . . . During her extrication from the car, Ruth asks at least twice if she is dreaming. At one point she asks Carnahan, who has told her she will be taken to the hospital in a helicopter: "Are you teasing?" At another point she says: "This is terrible. Am I dreaming?" She also asks what happened and where the rest of her family is, repeating the questions even after being told she was in an accident and the other family members are being cared for. While being loaded into the helicopter on a stretcher, Ruth says: "I just want to die." Carnahan reassures her that she is "going to do real well," but Ruth repeats: "I just want to die. I don't want to go through this."

Ruth and Wayne are placed in the helicopter, and its door is closed. The narrator states: "Once airborne, Laura and [the flight medic] will update their patients' vital signs and establish communications with the waiting trauma teams at Loma Linda." Carnahan, speaking into what appears to be a radio microphone, transmits some of Ruth's vital signs and states that Ruth cannot move her feet and has no sensation. The video footage during the helicopter ride includes a few seconds of Ruth's face, covered by an oxygen mask. . . .

The accident left Ruth a paraplegic. When the segment was broadcast, Wayne phoned Ruth in her hospital room and told her to turn on the television because "Channel 4 is showing our accident now." Shortly afterward, several hospital workers came into the room to mention that a videotaped segment of her accident was being shown. Ruth was "shocked, so to speak, that this would be run and I would be exploited, have my privacy invaded, which is what I felt had happened." She did not know her rescue had been recorded in this manner and had never consented to the recording or broadcast. Ruth had the impression from the broadcast "that I was kind of talking nonstop, and I remember hearing some of the things I said, which were not very pleasant." Asked at deposition what part of the broadcast material she considered private, Ruth explained: "I think the whole scene was pretty private. It was pretty gruesome, the parts that I saw, my knee sticking out of the car. I certainly did not look my best, and I don't feel it's for the public to see. I was not at my best in what I was thinking and what I was saying and what was being shown, and it's not for the public to see this trauma that I was going through."

Ruth and Wayne sued the producers of *On Scene: Emergency Response,* as well as others. The first amended complaint included two causes of action for invasion of privacy, one based on defendants' unlawful intrusion by videotaping the rescue in the first instance and the other based on the public disclosure of private facts, i.e., the broadcast.

Defendants moved for summary judgment, contending primarily that their conduct was protected by the First Amendment because of the broadcast's newsworthy content. . . .

The trial court granted the media defendants' summary judgment motion, basing its ruling on plaintiffs' admissions that the accident and rescue were matters of public interest and public affairs. . . .

We conclude . . . that the material broadcast was newsworthy as a matter of law and, therefore, cannot be the basis for tort liability under a private facts claim. Summary judgment thus was proper as to both plaintiffs on the private facts cause of action.

As to intrusion . . . triable issues exist as to whether defendants invaded plaintiffs' privacy by accompanying plaintiffs in the helicopter. Contrary to the holding below, we also hold triable issues exist as to whether defendants tortiously intruded by listening to Ruth's confidential conversations with Nurse Carnahan at the rescue scene without Ruth's consent. Moreover, we hold defendants had no constitutional privilege so to intrude on plaintiffs' seclusion and private communications.

DISCUSSION

. . . .

I. Publication of Private Facts

The claim that a publication has given unwanted publicity to allegedly private aspects of a person's life is one of the more commonly litigated and well-defined areas of privacy law. . . .

The element critical to this case is the presence or absence of legitimate public interest, i.e., newsworthiness, in the facts disclosed. After reviewing the decisional law regarding newsworthiness, we conclude, *inter alia,* that lack of newsworthiness is an element of the "private facts" tort, making newsworthiness a complete bar to common law liability. We further conclude that the analysis of newsworthiness inevitably involves accommodating conflicting interests in personal privacy and in press freedom as guaranteed by the First Amendment to the United States Constitution, and that in the circumstances of this case—where the facts disclosed about a private person involuntarily caught up in events of public interest bear a logical relationship to the newsworthy subject of the broadcast and are not intrusive in great disproportion to their relevance—the broadcast was of legitimate public concern, barring liability under the private facts tort. . . .

Newsworthiness—constitutional or common law—is also difficult to define because it may be used as either a descriptive or a normative term. "Is the term 'newsworthy' a descriptive predicate, intended to refer to the fact there is widespread public interest? Or is it a value predicate, intended to indicate that the publication is a meritorious contribution and that the public's interest is praiseworthy?" A position at either extreme has unpalatable consequences. If "newsworthiness" is completely descriptive—if all coverage that sells papers or boosts ratings is deemed newsworthy—it would seem to swallow the publication of private facts tort, for "it would be difficult to suppose that publishers were in the habit of reporting occurrences of little interest." At the other extreme, if newsworthiness is viewed as a purely normative concept, the courts could become to an unacceptable degree editors of the news and self-appointed guardians of public taste.

The difficulty of finding a workable standard in the middle ground between the extremes of normative and descriptive analysis, and the variety of factual circumstances in which the issue has been presented, have led to considerable variation in judicial descriptions of the newsworthiness concept. . . .

Our prior decisions have not explicitly addressed the type of privacy invasion alleged in this case: the broadcast of embarrassing pictures and speech of a person who, while generally not a public figure, has become involuntarily involved in an event or activity of legitimate public concern. . . .

. . . . [C]ourts have generally protected the privacy of otherwise private individuals involved in events of public interest "by requiring that a logical nexus exist between the complaining individual and the matter of legitimate public interest." The contents of the publication or broadcast are protected only if they have "some substantial relevance to a matter of legitimate public interest." Thus, recent decisions have generally tested newsworthiness with regard to such individuals by assessing the logical relationship or nexus, or the lack thereof, between the events or activities that brought the person into the public eye and the particular facts disclosed. . . .

An analysis measuring newsworthiness of facts about an otherwise private person involuntarily involved in an event of public interest by their relevance to a newsworthy subject matter incorporates considerable deference to reporters and editors, avoiding the likelihood of unconstitutional interference with the freedom of the press to report truthfully on matters of legitimate public interest. In general, it is not for a court or jury to say how a particular story is best covered. . . .

Turning now to the case at bar, we consider whether the possibly private facts complained of here—broadly speaking, Ruth's appearance and words during the rescue and evacuation—were of legitimate public interest. If so, summary judgment was properly entered. . . .

We agree at the outset with defendants that the subject matter of the broadcast as a whole was of legitimate public concern. Automobile accidents are by their nature of interest to that great portion of the public that travels frequently by automobile. The rescue and medical treatment of accident victims is also of legitimate concern to much of the public, involving as it does a critical service that any member of the public may someday need. The story of Ruth's difficult extrication from the crushed car, the medical attention given her at the scene, and her evacuation by helicopter was of particular interest because it highlighted some of the challenges facing emergency workers dealing with serious accidents.

The more difficult question is whether Ruth's appearance and words as she was extricated from the overturned car, placed in the helicopter, and transported to the hospital were of legitimate public concern. . . . [W]e conclude the disputed material was newsworthy as a matter of law. One of the dramatic and interesting aspects of the story as a whole is its focus on flight nurse Carnahan, who appears to be in charge of communications with other emergency workers, the hospital base, and Ruth, and who leads the medical assistance to Ruth at the scene. Her work is portrayed as demanding and important and as involving a measure of personal risk (e.g., in crawling under the car to aid Ruth despite warnings that gasoline may be dripping from the car). The broadcast segment makes apparent that this type of emergency care requires not only medical knowledge, concentration, and courage, but also an ability to talk and listen to severely traumatized patients. One of the challenges Carnahan faces in assisting Ruth is the confusion, pain, and fear that Ruth understandably feels in the aftermath of the accident. For that reason the broadcast video depicting Ruth's injured physical state (which was not luridly shown) and audio showing her disorientation and despair were substantially relevant to the segment's newsworthy subject matter.

Plaintiffs argue that showing Ruth's "intimate private, medical facts and her suffering was not necessary to enable the public to understand the significance of the accident or the rescue as a public event." The standard, however, is not necessity. That the broadcast could have been edited to exclude some of Ruth's words and images and still excite a minimum degree of viewer interest is not determinative. Nor is the possibility that the members of this or another court, or a jury, might find a differently edited broadcast more to their taste or even more interesting. The courts do not, and constitutionally could not, sit as superior editors of the press. . . .

The challenged material was thus substantially relevant to the newsworthy subject matter of the broadcast and did not constitute a "morbid and sensational prying into private lives for its own sake." . . . Summary judgment was therefore also proper on Wayne's cause of action for publication of private facts.

II. Intrusion

. . . . [T]he tort of intrusion into private places, conversations, or matter . . . encompasses unconsented-to physical intrusion into the home, hospital room, or other place the privacy of which is legally recognized, as well as unwarranted sensory intrusions such as eavesdropping, wiretapping, and visual or photographic spying. . . .

Despite its conceptual centrality, the intrusion tort has received less judicial attention than the private facts tort, and its parameters are less clearly defined. The leading California decision is *Miller v. National Broadcasting Co.*, 187 Cal. App. 3d 1463. *Miller,* which like the present case involved a news organization's videotaping the work of emergency medical personnel, adopted the Restatement's formulation of the cause of action: "One who intentionally intrudes, physically or otherwise, upon the solitude or seclusion of another or his private affairs or concerns, is subject to liability to the other for invasion of his privacy, if the intrusion would be highly offensive to a reasonable person." (Rest.2d Torts, § 652B).

As stated in *Miller* and the Restatement, therefore, the action for intrusion has two elements: (1) intrusion into a private place, conversation, or matter, (2) in a manner highly offensive to a reasonable person. We consider the elements in that order.

. . . . To prove actionable intrusion, the plaintiff must show the defendant penetrated some zone of physical or sensory privacy surrounding, or obtained unwanted access to data about, the plaintiff. The tort is proven only if the plaintiff had an objectively reasonable expectation of seclusion or solitude in the place, conversation, or data source.

Cameraman Cooke's mere presence at the accident scene and filming of the events occurring there cannot be deemed either a physical or sensory intrusion on plaintiffs' seclusion. Plaintiffs had no right of ownership or possession of the property where the rescue took place, nor any actual control of the premises. Nor could they have had a reasonable expectation that members of the media would be excluded or prevented from photographing the scene; for journalists to attend and record the scenes of accidents and rescues is in no way unusual or unexpected.

Two aspects of defendants' conduct, however, raise triable issues of intrusion on seclusion. First, a triable issue exists as to whether both plaintiffs had an objectively reasonable expectation of privacy in the interior of the rescue helicopter, which served as an ambulance. Although the attendance of reporters and photographers at the scene of an accident is to be expected, we are aware of no law or custom permitting the press to ride in ambulances or enter hospital rooms during treatment without the patient's consent. Other than the two patients and Cooke, only three people were present in the helicopter, all Mercy Air staff. As the Court of Appeal observed, "[i]t is neither the custom nor the habit of our society that any member of the public at large or its media representatives may hitch a ride in an ambulance and ogle as paramedics care for an injured stranger."

Second, Ruth was entitled to a degree of privacy in her conversations with Carnahan and other medical rescuers at the accident scene, and in Carnahan's conversations conveying medical information regarding Ruth to the hospital base. Cooke, perhaps, did not intrude into that zone of privacy merely by being present at a place where he could hear such conversations with unaided ears. But by placing a microphone on Carnahan's person, amplifying and recording what she said and heard, defendants may have listened in on conversations the parties could reasonably have expected to be private. . . .

Whether Ruth expected her conversations with Nurse Carnahan or the other rescuers to remain private and whether any such expectation was reasonable are, on the state of the record before us, questions for the jury. . . .

We turn to the second element of the intrusion tort, offensiveness of the intrusion. In a widely followed passage, the Miller court explained that determining offensiveness requires consideration of all the circumstances of the intrusion, including its degree and setting and the intruder's "motives and objectives." The *Miller* court concluded that reasonable people could regard the camera crew's conduct in filming a man's emergency medical treatment in his home, without seeking or obtaining his or his wife's consent, as showing "a cavalier disregard for ordinary citizens' rights of privacy" and, hence, as highly offensive.

We agree with the *Miller* court that all the circumstances of an intrusion, including the motives or justification of the intruder, are pertinent to the offensiveness element. Motivation or justification becomes particularly important when the intrusion is by a member of the print or broadcast press in the pursuit of news material. Although, as will be discussed more fully later, the First Amendment does not immunize the press from liability for torts or crimes committed in an effort to gather news, the constitutional protection of the press does reflect the strong societal interest in effective and complete reporting of events, an interest that may—as a matter of tort law—justify an intrusion that would otherwise be considered offensive. . . .

On this summary judgment record, we believe a jury could find defendants' recording of Ruth's communications to Carnahan and other rescuers, and filming in the air ambulance, to be "'highly offensive to a reasonable person.'" With regard to the depth of the intrusion, a reasonable jury could find highly offensive the placement of a microphone on a medical rescuer in order to intercept what would otherwise be private conversations with an injured patient. In that setting, as defendants could and should have foreseen, the patient would not know her words were being recorded and would not have occasion to ask about, and object or consent to, recording. Defendants, it could reasonably be said, took calculated advantage of the patient's "vulnerability and confusion." Arguably, the last thing an injured accident victim should have to worry about while being pried from her wrecked car is that a television producer may be recording everything she says to medical personnel for the possible edification and entertainment of casual television viewers.

For much the same reason, a jury could reasonably regard entering and riding in an ambulance—whether on the ground or in the air—with two seriously injured patients to be an egregious intrusion on a place of expected seclusion. Again, the patients, at least in this case, were hardly in a position to keep careful watch on who was riding with them, or to inquire as to everyone's business and consent or object to their presence. A jury could reasonably believe that fundamental respect for human dignity requires the patients' anxious journey be taken only with those whose care is solely for them and out of sight of the prying eyes (or cameras) of others.

Nor can we say as a matter of law that defendants' motive—to gather usable material for a potentially newsworthy story—necessarily privileged their intrusive conduct as a matter of common law tort liability. A reasonable jury could conclude the producers' desire to get footage that would convey the "feel" of the event—the real sights and sounds of a difficult rescue—did not justify either placing a microphone on Nurse Carnahan or filming inside the rescue helicopter. Although defendants' purposes could scarcely be regarded as evil or malicious (in the colloquial sense), their behavior could, even in light of their motives, be thought to show a highly offensive lack of sensitivity and respect for plaintiffs' privacy. . . .

Turning to the question of constitutional protection for newsgathering, one finds the decisional law reflects a general rule of nonprotection: the press in its newsgathering activities enjoys no immunity or exemption from generally applicable laws. (*Cohen v. Cowles Media Co.,* 501 U.S. at pp. 669–670; see *Branzburg v. Hayes,* 408 U.S. at pp. 680–695 [extensive discussion, concluding press enjoys no special immunity from questioning regarding sources with information on criminal activities under investigation by grand jury].)

. . . . These laws serve the undisputedly substantial public interest in allowing each person to maintain an area of physical and sensory privacy in which to live. Thus, defendants enjoyed no constitutional privilege, merely by virtue of their status as members of the news media, to eavesdrop in violation of section 632 or otherwise to intrude tortiously on private places, conversations, or information. . . .

As should be apparent from the above discussion, the constitutional protection accorded newsgathering, if any, is far narrower than the protection surrounding the publication of truthful material; consequently, the fact that a reporter may be seeking

"newsworthy" material does not in itself privilege the investigatory activity. The reason for the difference is simple: The intrusion tort, unlike that for publication of private facts, does not subject the press to liability for the contents of its publications. Newsworthiness, as we stated earlier, is a complete bar to liability for publication of private facts and is evaluated with a high degree of deference to editorial judgment. The same deference is not due, however, when the issue is not the media's right to publish or broadcast what they choose, but their right to intrude into secluded areas or conversations in pursuit of publishable material. At most, the Constitution may preclude tort liability that would "place an impermissible burden on newsgatherers "by depriving them of their "'indispensable tools.'"
. . .

CONCLUSION

The claim of these accident victims that their privacy was invaded by the production and broadcast of a documentary segment on their rescue raises questions about how the news media obtain their material (the intrusion claim), as well as about what they choose to publish or broadcast (the publication of private facts claim). Largely for constitutional reasons, the paths we have taken in analyzing these two privacy claims have diverged and led to different results.

The broadcast details of Ruth's rescue of which she complains were, as a matter of law, of legitimate public concern because they were substantially relevant to the newsworthy subject of the piece and their intrusiveness was not greatly disproportionate to their relevance. That analytical path is dictated by the danger of the contrary approach; to allow liability because this court, or a jury, believes certain details of the story as broadcast were not important or necessary to the purpose of the documentary, or were in poor taste, or overly sensational in impact, would be to assert impermissible supervisory power over the press.

The intrusion claim calls for a much less deferential analysis. In contrast to the broad privilege the press enjoys for publishing truthful, newsworthy information in its possession, the press has no recognized constitutional privilege to violate generally applicable laws in pursuit of material. Nor, even absent an independent crime or tort, can a highly offensive intrusion into a private place, conversation, or source of information generally be justified by the plea that the intruder hoped thereby to get good material for a news story. . . .

Hustler Magazine v. Falwell
Supreme Court of the United States, 1988
485 U.S. 46

Chief Justice REHNQUIST delivered the opinion of the Court.

Petitioner Hustler Magazine, Inc., is a magazine of nationwide circulation. Respondent Jerry Falwell, a nationally known minister who has been active as a commentator on politics and public affairs, sued petitioner and its publisher, petitioner Larry Flynt, to recover damages for invasion of privacy, libel, and intentional infliction of emotional distress. . . .

The inside front cover of the November 1983 issue of *Hustler Magazine* featured a "parody" of an advertisement for Campari Liqueur that contained the name and picture of respondent and was entitled "Jerry Falwell talks about his first time." . . . The *Hustler* parody portrays respondent and his mother as drunk and immoral, and suggests that respondent is a hypocrite who preaches only when he is drunk. In small print at the bottom of the page, the ad contains the disclaimer, "ad parody—not to be taken seriously." . . .

. . . [T]he District Court granted a directed verdict for petitioners on the invasion of privacy claim. The jury then found against respondent on the libel claim, specifically finding that the ad parody could not "reasonably be understood as describing actual facts about [respondent] or actual events in which [he] participated." The jury ruled for respondent on the intentional infliction of emotional distress claim, however, and stated that he should be awarded $100,000 in compensatory damages, as well as $50,000 each in punitive damages from petitioners. . . .

This case presents us with a novel question involving First Amendment limitations upon a State's authority to protect its citizens from the intentional infliction of emotional distress. We must decide whether a public figure may recover damages for emotional harm caused by the publication of an ad parody offensive to him, and doubtless gross and repugnant in the eyes of most. Respondent would have us find that a State's interest in protecting public figures from emotional distress is sufficient to deny First Amendment protection to speech that is patently offensive and is intended to inflict emotional injury, even when that speech could not reasonably have been interpreted as stating actual facts about the public figure involved. This we decline to do. . . .

The sort of robust political debate encouraged by the First Amendment is bound to produce speech that is critical of those who hold public office or those public figures who are "intimately involved in the resolution of important public questions or, by reason of their fame, shape events in areas of concern to society at large." Justice Frankfurter put it succinctly in *Baumgartner v. United States* when he said that "[o]ne of the prerogatives of American citizenship is the right to criticize public men and measures." Such criticism, inevitably, will not always be reasoned or moderate; public figures as well as public officials will be subject to "vehement, caustic, and sometimes unpleasantly sharp attacks." . . .

Of course, this does not mean that *any* speech about a public figure is immune from sanction in the form of damages. Since *New York Times Co. v. Sullivan,* we have consistently ruled that a public figure may hold a speaker liable for the damage to reputation caused by publication of a defamatory falsehood, but only if the statement was made "with knowledge that it was false or with reckless disregard of whether is was false or not." . . .

Respondent argues, however, that a different standard should apply in this case because here the State seeks to prevent not reputational damage, but the severe emotional distress suffered by the person who is the subject of an offensive publication. In respondent's view, and in the view of the Court of Appeals, so long as the utterance was intended to inflict emotional distress, was outrageous, and did in fact inflict serious emotional distress, it is of no constitutional import whether the statement was a fact or an opinion, or whether it was true or false. . . .

Generally speaking the law does not regard the intent to inflict emotional distress as one which should receive much solicitude, and it is quite understandable that most if not all jurisdictions have chosen to make it civilly culpable where the conduct in question is sufficiently "outrageous." But in the world of debate about public affairs, many things done with motives that are less than admirable are protected by the First Amendment. . . . Thus while such a bad motive may be deemed controlling for purposes of tort liability in other areas of the law, we think the First Amendment prohibits such a result in the area of public debate about public figures.

Were we to hold otherwise, there can be little doubt that political cartoonists and satirists would be subjected to damages awards without any showing that their work falsely defamed its subject. . . . The appeal of the political cartoon or caricature is often based on exploration of unfortunate physical traits or politically embarrassing events—an exploration often calculated to injure the feelings of the subject of the portrayal. The art of the cartoonist is often not reasoned or evenhanded, but slashing and one-sided. . . . Several famous examples of this type of intentionally injurious speech were drawn by Thomas Nast, probably the greatest American cartoonist to date, who was associated for many years during the post-Civil War era with *Harper's Weekly*. In the pages of that publication Nast conducted a graphic vendetta against William M. "Boss" Tweed and his corrupt associates in New York City's "Tweed Ring." . . .

. . . There is no doubt that the caricature of respondent and his mother published in *Hustler* is at best a distant cousin of the political cartoons described above, and a rather poor relation at that. If it were possible by laying down a principled standard to separate the one from the other, public discourse would probably suffer little or no harm. But we doubt that there is any such standard, and we are quite sure that the pejorative description "outrageous" does not supply one. "Outrageousness" in the area of political and social discourse has an inherent subjectiveness about it that would allow a jury to impose liability on the basis of the jurors' tastes or views, or perhaps on the basis of their dislike of a particular expression. An "outrageousness" standard thus runs afoul of our longstanding refusal to allow damages to be awarded because the speech in question may have an adverse emotional impact on the audience. . . .

. . . [T]his Court has "long recognized that not all speech is of equal First Amendment importance." But the sort of expression involved in this case does not seem to us to be governed by any exception to the general First Amendment principles stated above.

We conclude that public figures and public officials may not recover for the tort of intentional infliction of emotional distress by reason of publications such as the one here at issue without showing in addition that the publication contains a false statement of fact that was made with "actual malice." . . .

. . . The judgment of the Court of Appeals is accordingly
Reversed.

ARMSTRONG V. H & C COMMUNICATIONS, INC.
Court of Appeal of Florida, Fifth District, 1991
575 So. 2d 280

Opinion by: COBB, J.

This appeal concerns the trial court's determination to dismiss with prejudice the plaintiffs' first amended complaint that claimed invasion of privacy and outrage by the defendant below, Channel 2. . . .

The six-year-old child of Robert and Donna Armstrong, Regina Mae Armstrong, was abducted from Orlando, Florida, in June, 1985. She was wearing a sundress at the time. In September, 1987, a construction worker in nearby Oviedo, Florida, discovered a sundress meeting the description and a child's skull. The Oviedo Police Department took possession of the sundress and the skull, but failed to make the connection with Regina Mae until July, 1988, some ten months later, at which time the Orlando Police and the Armstrongs were notified. It was determined that the remains were those of Regina Mae.

On August 2, 1988, a memorial service was held for Regina Mae. On that same day, a reporter from Channel 2, Michelle Meredith, went to the Oviedo Police Department and asked the police chief to allow her to see Regina Mae's skull. He complied by lifting the skull from a box and displaying it to Meredith, who then asked to videotape it. She staged this by having the police chief replace the skull and again remove it from the box for the camera, and had the skull tilted for a close-up. Upon obtaining the videotape of the skull, Meredith called the Channel 2 studio and informed the 6:00 p.m. news producer, one Carolyn Reitz, that she had obtained videotape of the skull. Reitz expressed her aversion to broadcasting such a videotape, but agreed to allow Meredith to present the matter to the news director, one Steve Ramsey.

A meeting was held that afternoon at which time Reitz adamantly argued that broadcast of the skull would be offensive to the public and the Armstrong family, and would cause resentment and outrage. Anchor person Steve Rondinaro agreed with Reitz. Ramsey overruled the dissenters, stating "Fuck it! We are going to run it." At this time, no one at the station had seen the film, which was still in the field with reporter Meredith. No one bothered to review or edit the film once it arrived at the station and the editors and journalists there saw it for the first time as it was broadcast live throughout Central Florida on the 6:00 p.m. news. No one at the station made any effort to contact the Armstrongs and warn them of the broadcast, although it is now admitted by the personnel of Channel 2 that such a call should have been made. The editors of Channel 2 also admit that the close-up of the skull was not newsworthy, was wrongfully aired, would not have been aired if properly reviewed before the broadcast, and was likely to cause resentment and outrage with members of the community and the Armstrongs. . . .

The close-up of the skull was intentionally included to create sensationalism for the report. The close-up was gruesome and macabre, and was broadcast to thousands of viewers, including the Armstrongs. The broadcast opened with an emotional story on the memorial services with the photographs of Regina Mae and film footage of the family. Immediately following was a close-up of animal remains, originally thought to have been those of Regina Mae. Then, the cameraman cut directly to the Oviedo Police Chief removing her skull from the box, zoomed in for a frontal close-up of the tilted skull facing directly at the camera, and the audio identified the skull as that of Regina Mae Armstrong.

At the time of the broadcast, it was being watched by the unsuspecting Armstrong family. The emotional impact was devastating. Regina Mae's twelve-year-old sister, Christina, fled from the room screaming "that cannot be my sister." Many members of the public, including journalists and experienced police officials, have expressed outrage at the broadcast of the skull. . . .

The independent tort of outrage has been recognized in Florida. . . .

We have no difficulty in concluding that reasonable persons in the community could find that the alleged conduct of Channel 2 was outrageous in character and exceeded the bounds of decency so as to be intolerable in a civilized community. An average member of the community might well exclaim, "Outrageous!" Indeed, if the facts as alleged herein do not constitute the tort of outrage, then there is no such tort. . . .

. . . . The factual disclosure by Channel 2 does not fit into any of the four general categories comprising the tort of invasion of privacy as recognized by Prosser in his Law of Torts, p. 804–14 (4th ed. 1971): (1) Intrusion, i.e., invading plaintiffs' physical solitude, or seclusion; (2) Public Disclosure of Private Facts; (3) False Light in the Public Eye, i.e., a privacy theory analogous to the law of defamation; and (4) Appropriation, i.e., commercial exploitation of the property value of one's name. . . .

Accordingly, we reverse the trial court's dismissal of the Armstrongs' action based on the tort of outrage in Count II of their first amended complaint, and affirm the dismissal of their action based on the tort of invasion of privacy in Count I.

AFFIRMED IN PART, REVERSED IN PART, AND REMANDED FOR FURTHER PROCEEDINGS CONSISTENT WITH THIS OPINION.

DISSENT: SHARP, W. J., concurs in part and dissents in part.

I concur with the majority opinion that the tort of intentional infliction of severe emotional distress was sufficiently pled in the Armstrongs' amended complaint to withstand Channel 2's motion to dismiss for failure to state a cause of action. However, I would also reverse the dismissal of count I, invasion of privacy, although in this case the two counts may prove to be identical and require an election by the Armstrongs at a subsequent point, as to which tort to pursue.

The invasion of privacy tort is a much older common law creation than the tort of "outrage" now encompassed in section 46, Restatement of Torts. . . .

In an attempt to limit the invasion of privacy tort, a majority of the courts ruled that only persons whose privacy rights are invaded have standing to bring this cause of action. But, the Restatement of Torts and other authorities do not foreclose a suit by close family members where their emotional psyches have suffered injury due to unwarranted publicity concerning a deceased relative. Indeed, the long famous and often cited cases of *Douglas v. Stokes,* 149 Ky. 506, 149 S.W. 849 (Ky. 1912) and *Bazemore v. Savannah Hospital,* 171 Ga. 257, 155 S.E. 194 (Ga. 1930) were both decided on the basis of unwarranted invasion of the parent's right of privacy by publicizing pictures of the nude bodies of the plaintiffs' deceased children. . . .

Most of the suits involving mishandling the remains of deceased persons have been brought under the banner of the newer tort (intentional infliction of emotional distress) in Florida. But, I can find no Florida case on point that expressly holds that parents do not have a right of privacy action for the unwarranted and outrageous publication of pictures of their deceased child's body or body parts. . . .

Chapter Six
ACCESS TO PLACES AND INFORMATION

Here we look at cases concerning the ability of journalists to gain access to newsworthy places and information. On a day-to-day basis, clashes over access are the most common legal battles that journalists encounter. Access rights in the United States are primarily of statutory, not constitutional, origin. Each state and the federal government has its own rules, and each is unique, particularly with respect to the extensive rules that guarantee access to government records and meetings. The cases in this section, however, address relatively broad principles of access law rather than the statutory schemes of individual states. Also, the right of access to *court proceedings* is a topic reserved for the next chapter.

Miller v. National Broadcasting Co. deals with access to private property and the general law of trespass, which is virtually identical in all jurisdictions. The case illustrates, in particular, the danger of tagging along with paramedics, police, or other authorities.

Houchins v. KQED, Inc. is representative of the U.S. Supreme Court's general position that the Constitution does not guarantee media access to newsworthy places, even if those places are owned and operated by the government.

U.S. Dept. of Justice v. Reporters Committee for Freedom of the Press is a Supreme Court decision that interprets a key provision in the federal Freedom of Information Act. This is a particularly good FOIA case because it discusses Congress' underlying intent for the Act.

Griffis v. Pinal County & Phoenix Newspapers, Inc. is illustrative of an issue that many states' courts are wrestling with: Are pubic officials' private e-mails considered public documents, subject to disclosure under the states' public-records laws?

Finally, *Borreca v. Fasi*, a federal trial court opinion, illustrates that when access *is* granted by government, it usually must be granted in a nondiscriminatory manner.

MILLER V. NATIONAL BROADCASTING CO.
California Court of Appeal, 1986
232 Cal. Rptr. 668

L. THAXTON HANSON, Associate Justice.

INTRODUCTION

The events giving rise to this action occurred on the night of October 30, 1979, when an NBC television camera crew entered the apartment of Dave and Brownie Miller in Los Angeles, without their consent to film the activities of Los Angeles Fire

121

Department paramedics called to the Miller home to administer life-saving techniques to Dave Miller, who had suffered a heart attack in his bedroom. The NBC television camera crew not only filmed the paramedics' attempts to assist Miller, but NBC used the film on its nightly news without obtaining anyone's consent....

The paramedics were unable to successfully resuscitate Dave Miller; he died that October evening at Mount Sinai Hospital. His widow, Brownie... brought suit against defendants National Broadcasting Company (NBC), doing business as KNBC, a Los Angeles television station, Ruben Norte (Norte), a producer employed by NBC, and the City of Los Angeles (City) for damages, alleging trespass, invasion of privacy, and infliction of emotional distress against all defendants....

THE SCENARIO

Defendant Norte, an NBC news field producer in charge of news stories and projects, was assigned a mini-documentary on fire department paramedics and their work....

Norte contacted Tony De Domenico, the Los Angeles City Fire Department medical representative, and discussed the feasibility of having a news crew accompany a unit of paramedics, and was advised that it would be acceptable with the City ... Norte testified that "My intent was to film and document whatever their work was and whatever it happened to be when we filmed." He told the paramedics' media representative, Brown, that he wanted to film something "dramatic." He personally accompanied his film crew, consisting of a cameraman and a soundman, and between ten to fifteen times entered private residences with the film crew while filming with the paramedics. He testified that about half of the times someone asked what they were doing, that he always responded, and that no one objected. Norte also testified that it was standard practice in the television industry to secure consent before entering someone's home to film, but that he had not considered the necessity for such permission when accompanying the paramedics on their rounds.

... When they arrived at the Miller home, all three NBC personnel immediately followed the two paramedics into the apartment and the bedroom, where they filmed the paramedics performing CPR on Dave Miller. At no time did Norte or any other NBC employee seek or obtain consent to follow the paramedic team into the residence. The cameraman and soundman left with the paramedics, who placed the heart attack victim on a gurney and took him to Mount Sinai Hospital, where he subsequently died....

While Norte conceded it was normal procedure to get permission to enter a house, because of the emergency situation "there was no one to ask."...

Plaintiff ... testified substantially as follows: that on October 30, 1979, she and her husband Dave Miller resided in apartment 3, 8211 Blackburn; that at about 10 p.m. on that date, Dave Miller collapsed onto the bedroom floor; and that she screamed and a neighbor came and called the paramedics. Although aware that the paramedics arrived and were administering CPR to her husband, she was completely unaware that the NBC filming unit had arrived and left with them. A police officer that had arrived escorted her to another room while the paramedics were working on her husband. She at no time asked anyone to leave the apartment and no one asked her permission to film the paramedics.

Plaintiff Miller saw the film of her husband and the paramedics weeks after his death; at 10:30 a.m., while she was "flipping" channels looking for a "soap opera" to watch, suddenly the film was shown. She screamed and turned the television off. That was the only time she saw the film.

I.
TRESPASS: PLAINTIFF WIFE'S FIRST CAUSE OF ACTION

Plaintiff wife has alleged, and it is undisputed, that defendants made an unauthorized entry into her apartment on October 30, 1979. Common law defined such entry as a trespass. "The essence of the cause of action for trespass is an 'unauthorized entry' onto the land of another. Such invasions are characterized as intentional torts, regardless of the actor's motivation."...

The trial court awarded summary judgment to the defendants on this cause of action "because (1) there is no evidence that Defendants entered Plaintiff Miller's property *maliciously*; and (2) Plaintiff Miller suffered no actual damages as a result of the alleged entry." (Emphasis added.)

The trial court's ruling concerning the "trespass" was based on the notion that it was "technical" in nature due to the lack of specific malice directed against the Millers by the NBC camera crew. The trial court ignored the fact that the trespass was intentional in the sense that the law understands and uses that word: the defendants intended to cross the threshold of the Miller home. Thus, they committed an intentional tort, which rendered that actors' more refined motivation or intentions immaterial in terms of establishing that commission. As Prosser and Keeton on Torts explained, "[t]he intent required as a basis for liability as a trespasser is simply an intent to be at the place on the land where the trespass allegedly occurred.... The defendant is liable for an intentional entry although he has acted in good faith, under the mistaken belief, however reasonable, that he is committing no wrong."...

Under California law, the "consequences" flowing from an intentional tort such as a trespass may include emotional distress neither accompanied by a physical injury to the person or the land.... The basic statutory provision concerning tort damages reflects this view, in providing that "[f]or the breach of an obligation not arising from contract, the measure of damages, except where otherwise expressly provided by this Code, is the amount which will compensate for all the detriment proximately caused thereby, whether it could have been anticipated or not." In the case at bench, the "consequences" would include plaintiff wife's anguish, i.e., her emotional distress when NBC broadcast her husband's dying moments.

Thus, pursuant to common law principles accepted in California law, plaintiff wife has stated a cause of action for trespass unless First Amendment rights preclude it....

. . . .

V.
CONSTITUTIONAL RIGHTS

Defendants have vigorously defended against liability in the instant case, relying, on two propositions: (1) that by calling for the paramedics, the Millers impliedly consented to the entry of the NBC camera crew, and (2) plaintiff wife's cause of action was precluded by NBC's constitutionally recognized and protected First Amendment right to gather news.

The first proposition is devoid of merit. One seeking emergency medical attention does not thereby "open the door" for persons without any clearly identifiable and justifiable official reason who may wish to enter the premises where the medical aid is being administered. In *A.A. Dieterman v. Time, Inc.* 449 F.2d 245, the court held that newsgatherers cannot immunize their conduct by purporting to act jointly with public officials such as the police or paramedics. The clear line of demarcation between the public interest served by public officials and that served by private business must not be obscured.

The second argument, however, merits discussion.... We assume, for the purpose of discussion here, that public education about paramedics, as well as about the use of cardiopulmonary resuscitation (CPR) as a lifesaving technique almost anyone might either need or be called upon to administer to another, qualifies as "news."

The First Amendment of the United States Constitution declares that "Congress shall make no law ... abridging the freedom of speech, or of the press."... The protection afforded the disseminators of the news, be they reporters, broadcasters, or television newspersons, has been perceived throughout our history as of the utmost importance in maintaining a free society. The protection extends not only to prohibit direct state action, but must be considered when any private citizen seeks to impose civil liability for invasion of privacy by the press or media through access to state courts.

Newsgathering, as well as news dissemination, may be within the protective ambit of the First Amendment....

Where the United States Supreme Court has addressed the problem of providing adequate constitutional protection for newsgathering, however, it has been careful to point out that the protection is limited, rather than absolute....

We conclude, in the case before us, that the obligation not to make unauthorized entry into the private premises of individuals like the Millers does not place an impermissible burden on newsgatherers, nor is it likely to have a chilling effect on the exercise of First Amendment rights. To hold otherwise might have extraordinarily chilling implications for all of us; instead of a zone of privacy protecting our secluded moments, a climate of fear might surround us instead. Others besides the media have rights, and those rights prevail when they are considered in the context of the events at the Miller home on October 30, 1979.

In summary, we hold that plaintiff wife, Brownie Miller, has stated three causes of action against defendants and that since there are triable issues of material fact, the trial court erred in awarding summary judgment to the defendants....

HOUCHINS V. KQED, INC.
Supreme Court of the United States, 1978
438 U.S. 1

Chief Justice BURGER announced the judgment of the Court....

The question presented is whether the news media have a constitutional right of access to a county jail, over and above that of other persons, to interview inmates and make sound recordings, films, and photographs for publication and broadcasting by newspapers, radio, and television.

I

Petitioner Houchins, as Sheriff of Alameda County, California, controls all access to the Alameda County Jail at Santa Rita. Respondent KQED operates licensed television and radio broadcasting stations that have frequently reported newsworthy events relating to penal institutions in the San Francisco Bay Area. On March 31, 1975, KQED reported the suicide of a prisoner in the Greystone portion of the Santa Rita jail....

KQED requested permission to inspect and take pictures within the Greystone facility. After permission was refused, KQED and the Alameda and Oakland branches of the National Association for the Advancement of Colored People (NAACP) filed suit. They alleged that petitioner had violated the First Amendment by refusing to permit media access and failing to provide any effective means by which the public could be informed of conditions prevailing in the Greystone facility or learn of the prisoners' grievances....

The complaint requested a preliminary and permanent injunction to prevent petitioner from "excluding KQED news personnel from the Greystone cells and Santa Rita facilities and generally preventing full and accurate news coverage of the conditions prevailing therein." On June 17, 1975, when the complaint was filed, there appears to have been no formal policy regarding public access to the Santa Rita jail. However, according to petitioner, he had been in the process of planning a program of regular monthly tours since he took office six months earlier. On July 8, 1975, he announced the program and invited all interested persons to make arrangements for the regular public tours....

Each tour was limited to twenty-five persons and permitted only limited access to the jail. The tours did not include the disciplinary cells or the portions of the jail known as "Little Greystone," the scene of alleged rapes, beatings, and adverse physical conditions....

After considering the testimony, affidavits, and documentary evidence presented by the parties, the District Court preliminarily enjoined petitioner from denying KQED news personnel and "responsible representatives" of the news media access to the Santa Rita facilities, including Greystone, "at reasonable times and hours" and "from preventing KQED news personnel and responsible representatives of the news media from utilizing photographic and sound equipment or from utilizing inmate interviews in providing full and accurate coverage of the Santa Rita facilities."...

.... The court of Appeals ... concluded, albeit in three separate opinions, that the public and the media had a First and Fourteenth Amendment right of access to prisons and jails, and sustained the District Court's order.

II

.... Respondents assert that the right recognized by the Court of Appeals flows logically from our decisions construing the First Amendment. They argue that there is a constitutionally guaranteed right to gather news under *Pell v. Procunier,* 417 U.S., at 835, 94 S.Ct., at 2810, and *Branzburg v. Hayes,* 408 U.S. 665, 681, 707, 92 S.Ct. 2646, 2656—2669, 33 L.Ed.2d 626 (1972). From the right to gather news and the right to receive information, they argue for an implied special right of access to government-controlled sources of information. This right, they contend, compels access as a *constitutional* matter....

III

We can agree with many of the respondents' generalized assertions; conditions in jails and prisons are clearly matters "of great public importance." Penal facilities are public institutions that require large amounts of public funds, and their mission is crucial in our criminal justice system.... Beyond question, the role of the media is important; acting as the "eyes and ears" of the public, they can be a powerful and constructive force, contributing to remedial action in the conduct of public business. They have served that function since the beginning of the Republic, but like all other components of our society media representatives are subject to limits.

The media are not a substitute for or an adjunct of government and, like the courts, they are "ill equipped" to deal with problems of prison administration. We must not confuse the role of the media with that of government; each has special, crucial functions, each complementing—and sometimes conflicting with—the other.

The public importance of conditions in penal facilities and the media's role of providing information afford no basis for reading into the Constitution a right of the public or the media to enter these institutions, with camera equipment, and take moving and still pictures of inmates for broadcast purposes. This Court has never intimated a First Amendment guarantee of a right of access to all sources of information within government control. Nor does the rationale of the decisions upon which respondents rely lead to the implication of such a right.

Grosjean v. American Press Co. and *Mills v. Alabama* emphasized the importance of informed public opinion and the traditional role of a free press as a source of public information. But an analysis of those cases reveals that the Court was concerned with the freedom of the media to *communicate* information once it is obtained; neither case intimated that the Constitution *compels* the government to provide the media with information or access to it on demand....

Branzburg v. Hayes offers even less support for the respondents' position. Its observation, in dictum, that "newsgathering is not without its First Amendment protections," in no sense implied a constitutional right of access to news sources.... There is an undoubted right to gather news "from any source by means within the law," but that affords no basis for the claim that the First Amendment compels others—private persons or governments—to supply information....

Pell v. Procunier and *Saxbe v. Washington Post Co.* also assumed that there is no constitutional right of access such as the Court of Appeals conceived. In those cases the Court declared, explicitly and without reservation, that the media have "no constitutional right of access to prisons or their inmates beyond that afforded the general public," and on that premise the Court sustained prison regulations that prevented media interviews with inmates....

IV

The respondents' argument is flawed, not only because it lacks precedential support and is contrary to statements in this Court's opinions, but also because it invites the Court to involve itself in what is clearly a legislative task, which the Constitution has left to the political processes. Whether the government should open penal institutions in the manner sought by respondents is a question of policy which a legislative body might appropriately resolve one way or the other....

There is no discernible basis for a constitutional duty to disclose, or for standards governing disclosure of, or access to information. Because the Constitution affords no guidelines, absent statutory standards, hundreds of judges would, under the Court of Appeals' approach, be at large to fashion ad hoc standards, in individual cases, according to their own ideas of what seems "desirable" or "expedient." We, therefore, reject the Court of Appeals' conclusory assertion that the public and the media have a First Amendment right to government information regarding the conditions of jails and their inmates and presumably all other public facilities such as hospitals and mental institutions....

The judgment of the Court of Appeals is reversed, and the case is remanded for further proceedings.

U.S. DEPT. OF JUSTICE V. REPORTERS COMMITTEE FOR FREEDOM OF THE PRESS
Supreme Court of the United States, 1989
489 U.S.749

Justice STEVENS delivered the opinion of the Court.

The Federal Bureau of Investigation (FBI) has accumulated and maintained criminal identification records, sometimes referred to as "rap sheets," on over twenty-four million persons. The question presented by this case is whether the disclosure of the contents of such a file to a third party "could reasonably be expected to constitute an unwarranted invasion of personal privacy" within the meaning of the Freedom of Information Act (FOIA), 5 U.S.C. § 552(b)(7)(C)(1982 ed., Supp. IV).

I

In 1924 Congress appropriated funds to enable the Department of Justice (Department) to establish a program to collect and preserve fingerprints and other criminal identification records. That statue authorized the Department to exchange such information with "officials of States, cities, and other institutions." Six years later Congress created the FBI's identification division, and gave it responsibility for "acquiring, collecting, classifying, and preserving criminal identification and other crime records and the exchanging of said criminal identification records with the duly authorized officials of governmental agencies, of States, cities, and penal institutions." Rap sheets compiled pursuant to such authority contain certain descriptive information, such as date of birth and physical characteristics, as well as a history of arrests, charges, convictions, and incarcerations of the subject. Normally a rap sheet is preserved until its subject attains age eighty. Because of the volume of rap sheets, they are sometimes incorrect or incomplete and sometimes contain information about other persons with similar names.

The local, state, and federal law enforcement agencies throughout the Nation that exchange rap-sheet data with the FBI do so on a voluntary basis. The principal use of the information is to assist in the detection and prosecution of offenders; it is also used by courts and corrections officials in connection with sentencing and parole decisions. As a matter of executive policy, the Department has generally treated rap sheets as confidential and, with certain exceptions, has restricted their use to governmental purposes....

As a matter of Department policy, the FBI has made two exceptions to its general practice of prohibiting unofficial access to rap sheets. First, it allows the subject of a rap sheet to obtain a copy, and second, it occasionally allows rap sheets to be used in the preparation of press releases and publicity designed to assist in the apprehension of wanted persons or fugitives....

Although much rap-sheet information is a matter of public record, the availability and dissemination of the actual rap sheet to the public is limited....

II

The statute known as the FOIA is actually a part of the Administrative Procedure Act (APA). Section 3 of the APA as enacted in 1946 gave agencies broad discretion concerning the publication of governmental records. In 1966, Congress amended that section to implement "'a general philosophy of full agency disclosure.'" The amendment required agencies to publish their rules of procedure in the Federal Register, 5 U.S.C. § 552(a)(1)(C), and to make available for public inspection and copying their opinions, statements of policy, interpretations, and staff manuals and instructions that are not published in the Federal Register, § 552(a)(2). In addition, § 552(a)(3) requires every agency "upon any request for records which ... reasonably describes such records" to make such records "promptly available to any person."...

Congress exempted nine categories of documents from the FOIA's broad disclosure requirements.... Exemption 7(C) excludes records or information compiled for law enforcement purposes, "but only to the extent that the production of such [materials] ... could reasonably be expected to constitute an unwarranted invasion of personal privacy." § 552(b)(7)(C)....

III

This case arises out of requests made by a CBS news correspondent and the Reporters Committee for Freedom of the Press (respondents) for information concerning the criminal records of four members of the Medico family. The Pennsylvania Crime Commission had identified the family's company, Medico Industries, as a legitimate business dominated by organized crime figures. Moreover, the company allegedly had obtained a number of defense contracts as a result of an improper arrangement with a corrupt Congressman.

The FOIA requests sought disclosure of any arrests, indictments, acquittals, convictions, and sentences of any four Medicos. Although the FBI originally denied the requests, it provided the requested data concerning three of the Medicos after their deaths. In their complaint in the District Court, respondents sought the rap sheet for the fourth, Charles Medico (Medico), insofar as it contained "matters of public record."…

The District Court granted the Department's motion for summary judgment …

The Court of Appeals reversed. It held that an individual's privacy interest in criminal-history information that is a matter of public record was minimal at best.…

Exemption 7(C) requires us to balance the privacy interest in maintaining, as the Government puts it, the "practical obscurity" of the rap sheets, against the public interest in their release.

The preliminary question is whether Medico's interest in the nondisclosure of any rap sheet the FBI might have on him is the sort of "personal privacy" interest that Congress intended Exemption 7(C) to protect.… Because events summarized in a rap sheet have been previously disclosed to the public, respondents contend that Medico's privacy interest in avoiding disclosure of a federal compilation of these events approaches zero. We reject respondents' cramped notion of personal privacy.

To begin with, both the common law and the literal understandings of private encompass the individual's control of information concerning his or her person. In an organized society, there are few facts that are not at one time or another divulged to another. Thus the extent of the protection accorded a privacy right at common law rested in part on the degree of dissemination of the allegedly private fact and the extent to which the passage of time rendered it private.… Recognition of this attribute of a privacy interest supports the distinction, in terms of personal privacy, between scattered disclosure of the bits of information contained in a rap sheet and revelation of the rap sheet as a whole. The very fact that federal funds have been spent to prepare, index, and maintain these criminal-history files demonstrates that the individual items of information in the summaries would not otherwise be "freely available" either to the officials who have access to the underlying files or to the general public.… Granted, in many contexts the fact that information is not freely available is no reason to exempt that information from a statute generally requiring its dissemination. But the issue here is whether the compilation of otherwise hard-to-obtain information alters the privacy interest implicated by disclosure of that information. Plainly there is a vast difference between the public records that might be found after a diligent search of courthouse files, county archives, and local police stations throughout the country and a computerized summary located in a single clearinghouse of information.…

Also supporting our conclusion that a strong privacy interest inheres in the nondisclosure of compiled computerized information is the Privacy Act, codified at 5 U.S.C. § 552a (1982 ed. and Supp. IV). The Privacy Act was passed in 1974 largely out of concern over "the impact of computer data banks on individual privacy." The Privacy Act provides generally that "[n]o agency shall disclose any record which is contained in a system of records … except pursuant to a written request by, or with the prior written consent of, the individual to whom the record pertains." Although the Privacy Act

Contains a variety of exceptions to this rule, including an Exemption for information required to be disclosed under the FOIA, Congress' basic policy concern regarding the implications of computerized data banks for personal privacy is certainly relevant in our consideration of the privacy interest affected by dissemination of rap sheets from the FBI....

V

Exemption 7(C), by its terms, permits an agency to withhold a document only when revelation "could reasonably be expected to constitute an *unwarranted* invasion of personal privacy." We must next address what factors might *warrant* an invasion of the interest described in Part IV.

Our previous decisions establish that whether an invasion of privacy is warranted cannot turn on the purposes for which the request for information is made. Except for cases in which the objection to disclosure is based on a claim of privilege and the person requesting disclosure is the party protected by the privilege, the identity of the requesting party has no bearing on the merits of his or her FOIA request.... [T]he rights of the two press respondents in this case are no different from those that might be asserted by any other third party, such as a neighbor or prospective employer. As we have repeatedly stated, Congress "clearly intended" the FOIA "to give any member of the public as much right to disclosure as one with a special interest [in a particular document]."

Thus whether disclosure of a private document under Exemption 7(C) is warranted must turn on the nature of the requested document and its relationship to "the basic purpose of the Freedom of Information Act 'to open agency action to the light of public scrutiny'" rather than on the particular purpose for which the document is being requested.... This basic policy of "'full agency disclosure unless information is exempted under clearly delineated statutory language,'" indeed focuses on the citizens' right to be informed about "what their government is up to." Official information that sheds light on an agency's performance of its statutory duties falls squarely within that statutory purpose. That purpose, however, is not fostered by disclosure of information about private citizens that is accumulated in various governmental files but that reveals little or nothing about an agency's own conduct. In this case—and presumably in the typical case in which one private citizen is seeking information about another—the requester does not intend to discover anything abut the conduct of the agency that has possession of the requested records. Indeed, response to this request would not shed any light on the conduct of any Government agency or official....

Respondents argue that there is a two-fold public interest in learning about Medico's past arrests or convictions: He allegedly had improper dealings with a corrupt Congressman and he is an officer of a corporation with defense contracts. But if Medico has, in fact, been arrested or convicted of certain crimes, the information would neither aggravate nor mitigate his allegedly improper relationship with the Congressman; more specifically, it would tell us nothing directly about the character of the *Congressman's* behavior. Nor would it tell us anything about the conduct of the *Department of Defense* (DOD) in awarding one or more contracts to the Medico Company. Arguably of FOIA request to the DOD for records relating to those contracts, or for documents describing the agency's procedures, if any, for determining whether officers of a prospective contractor have criminal records, would constitute an appropriate request for "official information." Conceivably Medico's rap sheet would provide details to include in a news story, but, in itself, this is not the kind of public interest for which Congress enacted the FOIA. In other words, although there is undoubtedly some public interest in anyone's criminal history, especially if the history is in some way related to the subject's dealing with a public official or agency, the FOIA's central purpose is to ensure that the *Government's* activities be opened to the sharp eye of public scrutiny, not that information about *private citizens* that happens to be in the warehouse of the Government be so disclosed....

What we have said should make clear that the public interest in the release of any rap sheet on Medico that may exist is not the type of interest protected by the FOIA....

... The judgment of the Court of Appeals is reversed.

Justice BLACKMUN, with whom Justice BRENNAN joins, concurring in the judgment.

I concur in the result the Court reaches in this case, but I cannot follow the route the Court takes to reach that result. In other words, the Court's use of "categorical balancing" under Exemption 7(C), I think, is not basically sound. Such a bright-line rule obviously has its appeal, but I wonder whether it would not run aground on occasion, such as in a situation where a rap sheet discloses a congressional candidate's conviction of tax fraud five years before. Surely, the FBI's disclosure of that information could not "reasonably be expected" to constitute an invasion of personal privacy, much less an unwarranted invasion, inasmuch as the candidate relinquished any interest in preventing the dissemination of this information when he chose to run for Congress. In short, I do not believe that Exemption 7(C)'s language and its legislative history, or the case law, support interpreting that provision as exempting *all* rap-sheet information from FOIA's disclosure requirements.

GRIFFIS V. PINAL COUNTY & PHOENIX NEWSPAPERS, INC.
Supreme Court of Arizona, 2007
156 P.3d 418

McGREGOR, Chief Justice

We granted review to consider whether purely personal e-mails generated or maintained on a government e-mail system are, as a matter of law, public records under Arizona's public records law, Arizona Revised Statutes sections 39-121 to 39-121.03. We hold that such e-mails do not necessarily qualify as public records. We further hold that when a government entity withholds documents generated or maintained on a government-owned computer system on the grounds that the documents are personal, the requesting party may ask the trial court to perform an in camera inspection to determine whether the documents fall within the public records law.

I.

In late 2005, the Pinal County Sheriff's Office began an investigation of then-County Manager Stanley Griffis after learning of Griffis' unauthorized purchase of sniper rifles and other equipment with county funds. Phoenix Newspapers, Inc. filed a public records request with Pinal County ... seeking release of all e-mails sent to or received by Griffis on the County's e-mail system from October 1 to December 2, 2005. The County released 706 e-mails, but withheld others it and Griffis considered personal or confidential. After PNI threatened to sue, the County agreed to release the previously withheld e-mails and notified Griffis of its decision.

Griffis obtained a preliminary injunction blocking release of e-mails that both he and the County initially had agreed were personal. PNI moved to intervene and dissolve the injunction, and the County joined this motion. The County then prepared a log identifying each e-mail subject to the injunction and allowed Griffis to redact any personal information before providing the log to PNI. Griffis chose to disclose approximately thirty of the e-mails listed in the log.

The superior court granted PNI's motion to dissolve the injunction, ruling that the remaining e-mails should be disclosed, but giving Griffis the opportunity to redact any personal information. The superior court noted that "everything that is on a computer of the Pinal County . . . governmental entity is presumed to be a public record" and that "any records generated on a public computer are presumptively open to public inspection." Although it found the e-mails to be presumptively public records, the superior court offered to conduct an in camera inspection of the disputed e-mails to determine whether Griffis could establish an expectation of privacy that would overcome that presumption. Griffis declined and appealed the decision.

The court of appeals reversed the superior court's judgment, holding that personal e-mails are not "public records or other matters" under Arizona's public records law and, therefore, need not be disclosed. The court of appeals, like the superior court, did not review the content of the disputed e-mails.

PNI petitioned for review, arguing that the court of appeals misapplied [precedent] and ignored Arizona's longstanding presumption in favor of providing public access to government records. Alternatively, PNI urges us to remand for an in camera inspection of the disputed e-mails to determine whether they fall within the scope of the public records law....

II.

Whether a document is a public record under Arizona's public records law presents a question of law, which we review de novo.

A.

We have set forth the legal principles that control the issue raised here in previous public records cases. As an initial matter, Arizona law defines "public records" broadly and creates a presumption requiring the disclosure of public documents. Section 39-121 of the Arizona Revised Statutes affirms the presumption of openness, stating that "[p]ublic records and other matters in the custody of any officer shall be open to inspection by any person at all times during office hours." Although the phrase "public records and other matters" is not expressly defined by statute, [the code section] requires that "[a]ll officers and public bodies shall maintain all records . . . reasonably necessary or appropriate to maintain an accurate knowledge of their official activities and of any of their activities which are supported by monies from the state or any political subdivision of the state."

[T]his Court [has] articulated three alternative definitions of public records: A public record is one "made by a public officer in pursuance of a duty, the immediate purpose of which is to disseminate information to the public, or to serve as a memorial of official transactions for public reference"; a record that is "required to be kept, or necessary to be kept in the discharge of a duty imposed by law or directed by law to serve as a memorial and evidence of something written, said or done"; or any "written record of transactions of a public officer in his office, which is a convenient and appropriate method of discharging his duties, and is kept by him as such, whether required by . . . law or not."

The broad definition of public records, however, is not unlimited. The public records law requires all public officials to make and maintain records "reasonably necessary to provide knowledge of all activities they undertake in the furtherance of their duties." That definition does not encompass documents of a purely private or personal nature. Instead, only those documents having a "substantial nexus" with a government agency's activities qualify as public records. "[T]he nature and purpose of the document" determine its status as a public record. Determining a document's status, therefore, requires a content-driven inquiry.

Because the nature and purpose of the document determine its status, mere possession of a document by a public officer or agency does not by itself make that document a public record, nor does expenditure of public funds in creating the document. To hold otherwise would create an absurd result: Every note made on government-owned paper, located in a government office, written with a government-owned pen, or composed on a government-owned computer would presumably be a public record. Under that analysis, a grocery list written by a government employee while at work, a communication to schedule a family dinner, or a child's report card stored in a desk drawer in a government employee's office would be subject to disclosure. The public records law was never intended to encompass such documents; the purpose of the law is to open government activity to public scrutiny, not to disclose information about private citizens.

Although the public records law creates a strong presumption in favor of disclosure, that presumption applies only when a document first qualifies as a public record. To apply a presumption of disclosure when a question exists as to the nature of the document is inappropriate: The initial inquiry must be whether the document is subject to the statute. The reason for this requirement is clear: Disclosure of purely private documents does nothing to advance the purposes underlying the public records law. The contents of purely private documents shed no light on how the government is conducting its business or spending taxpayer money.

Determining whether the public records law requires disclosure, then, involves a two-step process. When the facts of a particular case "raise a substantial question as to the threshold determination of whether the document is subject to the statute," the court must first determine whether that document is a public record. If a document falls within the scope of the public records statute, then the presumption favoring disclosure applies and, when necessary, the court can perform a balancing test to determine whether privacy, confidentiality, or the best interests of the state outweigh the policy in favor of disclosure.

B.

Applying the principles discussed above, we reject PNI's argument that all e-mails generated or maintained on a government-owned computer system are automatically public records. Some e-mails will relate solely to personal matters and will not, therefore, reflect the requisite substantial nexus with government activities. On the other hand, many e-mails generated or retained on a government computer system are public records because they relate to government business. The issue, then, is how a court should determine whether requested e-mails are subject to disclosure under the public records law when the facts raise a substantial question as to the nature of the document.

III.

Comparing the nature and purpose of a document with an official's or agency's activities to determine whether the required nexus exists necessarily requires a fact-specific inquiry. To make that inquiry, while maintaining the privacy of personal, non-public documents, a court should perform an in camera review. In camera review of disputed documents also reinforces this Court's previous holding that the courts, rather than government officials, are the final arbiter of what qualifies as a public record.

To further Arizona's strong policy of public access and disclosure of public records, the threshold showing needed to raise a "substantial question" about a document's status must be relatively low. When, as in this case, the question is whether e-mails from or to a public official are public records, we hold that a party can raise a substantial question by showing that a government agency or public official withheld documents generated or maintained on a government-owned computer on the grounds that those documents are personal or private. Once a requesting party makes this basic showing, that party can ask the court to conduct an in camera inspection of any withheld documents to determine whether they possess the requisite nexus with official duties that is required of all public records. The party claiming that the disputed documents are not public records bears the burden of establishing its claim. If the party cannot establish that the documents are not public records, the trial judge can still consider whether privacy, confidentiality, or the best interests of the state outweigh the policy in favor of disclosure.

In this case, no court has reviewed the e-mails at issue. Absent such a review, we have no record on which we can determine the nature and content of the requested documents. We therefore remand this case to permit the superior court to review the content of the disputed e-mails in camera to determine whether they are subject to the public records law. Griffis bears the burden of establishing that the e-mails are not public records.

IV.

For the foregoing reasons, we reverse the ruling of the superior court, vacate the opinion of the court of appeals, and remand to the superior court for further proceedings consistent with this opinion.

Borreca v. Fasi

U.S. District Court, District of Hawaii, 1974
309 F. Supp. 906

SAMUEL P. KING, District Judge.

Statement of the Case

On December 21, 1973, city hall news reporter Richard Borreca and his employer Gannett Pacific Corporation, doing business as *Honolulu Star-Bulletin,* filed an action in this court … requesting an injunction and damages against Frank F. Fasi, Mayor of the City and the County of Honolulu, and James Lee Loomis, Administrative Assistant of the Mayor and Director Information and Complaint Office, for alleged actions of defendants denying Borreca access to city hall news.

….

Findings of Fact:

The *Honolulu Star-Bulletin* is Hawaii's leading newspaper of general circulation. Richard Borreca came to Hawaii in 1968, attended the University of Hawaii for two years, then started working for the *Honolulu Star-Bulletin* as a news reporter in 1970. For the past two years, his assignment has been Honolulu's city hall, which includes attending the mayor's news conferences….

During 1973, Mayor Fasi concluded that Borreca was irresponsible, inaccurate, biased, and malicious in reporting on the mayor and the city administration. This conclusion was based on the news stories written by Borreca, and was reinforced by a report that Borreca had said that the mayor was a "crook" and that Borreca was going to "shaft" the mayor at every opportunity. Mayor Fasi expressed his dislike for Borreca personally and stated that he would not talk to Borreca "until Hell freezes over." He declared Borreca persona non grata at city hall and instructed his staff, and specifically his administrative assistant James Lee Loomis, to keep Borreca out of the mayor's office.

Loomis, on behalf of the mayor and as part of his usual duties, announced general news conferences in the mayor's office for November 2 and 22 and December 13 and 19, 1873.

A general news conference was defined by Loomis as a conference "where all media generally are informed of the mayor's intention to hold a news conference and all are free to attend." …

Borreca presented himself at the mayor's office on November 2, 1973, as the *Honolulu Star-Bulletin's* representative at the news conference. Loomis informed Borreca that Borreca would not be allowed to attend that news conference. Borreca was in fact blocked and denied entry and no one from the *Honolulu Star-Bulletin* was in attendance at this conference.

Borreca again presented himself at the mayor's office on November 22, 1973, as the *Honolulu Star-Bulletin's* representative at the news conference. It is a fair inference from the evidence that Borreca expected to be excluded and purposely sought a confrontation with Loomis, which confrontation occurred and the verbal parts of which

Borreca recorded on a portable tape recorder, transcribed, and wrote up for the next day's afternoon newspaper.

Borreca was in fact excluded from this news conference and the two December news conferences and no one from the *Honolulu Star-Bulletin* was in attendance at the news conferences.

Mayor Fasi informed the *Honolulu Star-Bulletin* that any other reporter from that newspaper would be welcome, but the newspaper declined to change Borreca's assignment or to send another representative to the mayor's news conferences....

Sufficiency of the Complaint and Evidence:

Mayor Fasi argues that his ostracism of Borreca and ultimatum to the *Honolulu Star-Bulletin* are not invasions of freedom of the press or do not involve state action.

With respect to the first point, the mayor argues that nothing he has done "subjects, or causes to be subjected [Borreca or the *Honolulu Star-Bulletin*] to the deprivation of any rights, privileges, or immunities secured by the Constitution and laws" of the United States, because the *Honolulu Star-Bulletin* is not prevented from having a representative at a news conference as anyone other than Borreca would be admitted, Borreca is not denied access to news as he may obtain a copy of each news release and any other written material, and the right of access to news does not include a requirement that Mayor Fasi respond to Borreca's questioning.

… Requiring a newspaper's reporter to pass a subjective compatibility-accuracy test as a condition precedent to the right of that reporter to gather news is no different in kind from requiring a newspaper to submit its proposed news stories for editing as a precondition precedent to the right of that newspaper to have a reporter cover the news. Each is a form of censorship....

As a general proposition, the mayor is quite correct in his position that he is not required to respond in any way to any question put to him by any representative of any news media. Whether repeated selective discriminatory unreasonable refusal to respond to all questions by an individual reporter would form the basis of an action for damages is not before the court at this time....

With respect to the mayor's second point, he argues that his news conferences are private affairs held in his private office at his discretion and his actions in connection with such conferences are not "under color of any statute, ordinance, regulation, custom, or usage," of the State of Hawaii.

The mayor is too modest. As the chief executive of the City and County of Honolulu, his statements on municipal and county operations and concerns are embryonic executive directives. They are public communications put forth by him and his official capacity.... When he uses public buildings and public employees to call and hold general news conferences on public matters he is operating in the public and not the private sector of his activities. His oral order to his staff to exclude Borreca from his office is an executive directive by him in the exercise of his authority as mayor which authority he derives from the constitution and laws of the State of Hawaii....

A free press is not necessarily an angelic press. Newspapers take sides, especially in political contests. Newspaper reporters are not always accurate and objective. They are subject to criticism, and the right of a governmental official to criticize is within First Amendment guarantees.

But when criticism transforms into an attempt to use the powers of governmental office to intimidate or to discipline the press or one of its members because of what appears in print, a compelling governmental interest that cannot be served by less restrictive means must be shown for such use to meet Constitutional standards. No compelling governmental interest has been shown or even claimed here....

Conclusions of Law:

Plaintiffs are entitled to a preliminary injunction enjoining Defendant Frank F. Fasi from preventing, or from instructing or advising any person to prevent, Plaintiff Richard Borreca from attending any press conference on the same basis and to the same extent that other news reporters attend press conferences.

Chapter Seven
MEDIA AND THE JUSTICE SYSTEM

The eight cases in this section pertain to the often-tense relationship between the mass media and the justice system. Of course, one of the traditional roles of journalists is to report on crime, prosecution efforts, and ...courtroom proceedings. On the other hand, officials in the justice system—including judges—often see journalists as a threat to courtroom protocol and a hindrance to the efficient administration of justice. This relationship between the media and the justice system is a topic upon which the Supreme Court has had much to say. The cases here are noteworthy samples from the key battlegrounds.

Rideau v. State of Louisiana is one of a handful of 1960s cases in which the Court pronounced that journalistic activities could indeed impinge upon the Sixth Amendment, fair-trial rights of criminal defendants.

Nebraska Press Association v. Stuart, decided in 1976, made it clear, however, that trial judges were not at liberty to utilize just *any* method of controlling journalistic coverage of criminal proceedings. Specifically, prior restraints on speech must be a last resort.

The People v. Bryant is a 2004 Colorado decision that upheld a prior restraint on the media in connection with a notorious and short-lived criminal prosecution of basketball star Kobe Bryant.

Press-Enterprise Co. v. Superior Court of Cal. (Press-Enterprise II) represents a series of cases in which the Court has declared that a First Amendment, public right of access applies to some legal proceedings.

Chandler v. Florida was a criminal defendant's challenge to the constitutionality of cameras in the courtroom. Although cameras may pose a danger in some cases, the Court decided their presence does not automatically violate a defendant's right to a fair trial.

Branzburg v. Hayes is the Supreme Court's one, fractured pronouncement on a different sort of problem: the right of a journalist to keep confidences when it is the *journalist* who is ordered to testify in a formal legal proceeding.

In re: Grand Jury Subpoena, Judith Miller is one federal circuit's recent interpretation of *Branzburg*, and the case serves as a warning that while some courts have recognized a limited First Amendment right of reporters to keep confidences, other courts may decline to recognize any such right.

Cohen v. Cowles Media Co. presents a twist on the issue of confidential media sources: If a news reporter *promises* that a source's name will remain confidential, but the medium discloses the name anyway, may the source pursue a breach of contract claim against the medium?

RIDEAU V. STATE OF LOUISIANA
Supreme Court of the United States, 1963
373 U.S. 723

Justice STEWART delivered the opinion of the Court.

On the evening of February 16, 1961, a man robbed a bank in Lake Charles, Louisiana, kidnapped three of the bank's employees, and killed one of them. A few hours later the petitioner, Wilbert Rideau, was apprehended by the police and lodged in the Calcasieu Parish jail in Lake Charles. The next morning a moving picture film with a sound track was made of an "interview" in the jail between Rideau and the sheriff of Calcasieu Parish. This "interview" lasted approximately twenty minutes. It consisted of interrogation by the sheriff and admissions by Rideau that he had perpetrated the bank robbery, kidnapping, and murder. Later the same day the filmed "interview" was broadcast over a television station in Lake Charles, and some 24,000 people in the community saw and heard it on television. The sound film was again shown on television the next day to an estimated audience of 53,000 people. The following day the film was again broadcast by the same television station, and this time approximately 20,000 people saw and heard the "interview" on their television sets. Calcasieu Parish has a population of approximately 150,000 people.

Some two weeks later, Rideau was arraigned on charges of armed robbery, kidnapping, and murder, and two lawyers were appointed to represent him. His lawyers promptly filed a motion for a change of venue, on the ground that it would deprive Rideau of rights guaranteed to him by the United States Constitution to force him to trial in Calcasieu Parish after the three television broadcasts there of his "interview" with the sheriff. After a hearing, the motion for change of venue was denied, and Rideau was accordingly convicted and sentenced to death on the murder charge in the Calcasieu Parish trial court.

Three members of the jury that convicted him had stated on *voir dire* that they had seen and heard Rideau's television "interview" with the sheriff on at least one occasion....

...What the people of Calcasieu Parish saw on their television sets was Rideau, in jail, flanked by the sheriff and two state troopers, admitting in detail the commission of the robbery, kidnapping, and murder, in response to leading questions by the sheriff. The record fails to show whose idea it was to make the sound film, and broadcast it over the local television station, but we know from the conceded circumstances that the plan was carried out with the active cooperation and participation of the local law enforcement officers. And certainly no one has suggested that it was Rideau's idea, or even that he was aware of what was going on when the sound film was being made.

In the view we take of this case, the question of who originally initiated the idea of the televised interview is, in any event, a basically irrelevant detail. For we hold that it was a denial of due process of law to refuse the request for a change of venue, after the people of Calcasieu Parish had been exposed repeatedly and in depth to the spectacle of Rideau personally confessing in detail to the crimes with which he was later to be charged. For anyone who has ever watched television the conclusion cannot be avoided that this spectacle, to the tens of thousands of people who saw and heard it, in a very real sense *was* Rideau's trial— at which he pleaded guilty to murder. Any subsequent court proceedings in a community so pervasively exposed to such a spectacle could be but a hollow formality....

The case now before us does not involve physical brutality. The kangaroo court proceedings in this case involved a more subtle but no less real deprivation of due process of law. Under our Constitution's guarantee of due process, a person accused of committing a crime is vouchsafed basic minimal rights. Among these are the right to counsel, the right to plead not guilty, and the right to be tried in a courtroom presided over by a judge. Yet in this case the people of Calcasieu Parish saw and heard, not once but three times, a "trial" of Rideau in a jail, presided over by a sheriff, where there was no lawyer to advise Rideau of his right to stand mute.

… [W]e do not hesitate to hold, without pausing to examine a particularized transcript of the *voir dire* examination of the members of the jury, that due process of law in this case required a trial before a jury drawn from a community of people who had not seen and heard Rideau's televised "interview." …

Reversed.

Justice CLARK, with whom Justice HARLAN joins, dissenting.

….

I agree fully with the Court that one is deprived of due process of law when he is tried in an environment so permeated with hostility that judicial proceedings can be "but a hollow formality." This proposition, and my position with regard thereto, are established in *Irvin v. Dowd,* 366 U.S. 717 (1961). At this point I must part company with the Court, however, not so much because it deviates from the principles established in *Irvin* but because it applies no principles at all. It simply stops at this point, without establishing any substantial nexus between the televised "interview" and petitioner's trial, which occurred almost two months later. Unless the adverse publicity is shown by the record to have fatally infected the trial, there is simply no basis for the Court's inference that the publicity, epitomized by the televised interview … [made] petitioner's trial a meaningless formality.…

NEBRASKA PRESS ASSOCIATION V. STUART
Supreme Court of the United States, 1976
427 U.S. 539

Chief Justice BURGER delivered the opinion of the Court.

I

On the evening of October 18, 1975, local police found the six members of the Henry Kellie family murdered in their home in Sutherland, Nebraska, a town of about 850 people. Police released the description of a suspect, Erwin Charles Simants, to the reporters who had hastened to the scene of the crime. Simants was arrested and arraigned in Lincoln County Court the following morning, ending a tense night for this small rural community.

The crime immediately attracted widespread news coverage, by local, regional, and national newspapers, radio, and television stations. Three days after the crime, the County Attorney and Simants' attorney joined in asking the County Court to enter a restrictive order relating to "matters that may or may not be publicly reported or disclosed to the public," because of the "mass coverage by news media" and the "reasonable likelihood of prejudicial news which would make difficult, if not impossible, the impaneling of an impartial jury and tend to prevent a fair trial." …The County Court granted the prosecutor's motion for a restrictive order…. The order prohibited everyone in attendance from "releasing or authorizing the release for public dissemination in any form or manner whatsoever any testimony given or evidence adduced." …

Petitioners—several press and broadcast associations, publishers, and individual reporters—moved … to intervene in the District Court, asking that the restrictive order imposed by the County Court be vacated…. The District Judge entered his own restrictive order. The judge found "because of the nature of the crimes charged in the complaint that there is a clear and present danger that pretrial publicity could impinge upon the defendant's right to a fair trial." The order applied only until the jury was impaneled, and specifically prohibited petitioners from reporting five subjects: (1) the existence or contents of a confession Simants had made to law enforcement officers, which had been introduced in open court at arraignment; (2) the fact or nature of statements Simants had made to other persons; (3) the contents of a note he had written the night of the crime; (4) certain aspects of the medical testimony at the preliminary hearing; and (5) the identity of the victims of the alleged sexual assault and the nature of the assault…. Like the County Court's order, this order incorporated the Nebraska Bar-Press Guidelines. [The guidelines were voluntary standards adopted by members of the state bar and news media to deal with the reporting of crimes and criminal trials.] ….

III

The problems presented by this case are almost as old as the Republic. Neither in the Constitution nor in contemporaneous writings do we find that the conflict between these two important rights was anticipated, yet it is inconceivable that the authors of the Constitution were unaware of the potential conflicts between the right to an unbiased jury and the guarantee of freedom of the press….

The speed of communication and the pervasiveness of the modern news media have exacerbated these problems…. The trial of Bruno Hauptmann in a small New Jersey community for the abduction and murder of the Charles Lindberghs' infant child probably was the most widely covered trial up to that time, and the nature of the coverage produced widespread public reaction. Criticism was directed at the "carnival" atmosphere that pervaded the community and the courtroom itself. Responsible leaders of the press and the legal profession—including other judges—pointed out that much of this sorry performance could have been controlled by a vigilant trial judge and by other public officers subject to the control of the court.

The excesses of press and radio and lack of responsibility of those in authority in the *Hauptmann* case and others of that era led to efforts to develop voluntary guidelines for courts, lawyers, press, and broadcasters….

In practice, of course, even the most ideal guidelines are subjected to powerful strains when a case such as Simants' arises, with reporters from many parts of the country on the scene. Reporters from distant places are unlikely to consider themselves bound by local standards….

IV

....

In *Sheppard v. Maxwell*, 384 U.S. 333 (1966), the Court focused sharply on the impact of pretrial publicity and a trial court's duty to protect the defendant's constitutional right to a fair trial.... [T]he Court ordered a new trial for the petitioner, even though the first trial had occurred twelve years before. Beyond doubt the press had shown no responsible concern for the constitutional guarantee of a fair trial; the community from which the jury was drawn had been inundated by publicity hostile to the defendant.... The Court noted that "unfair and prejudicial news comment on pending trials has become increasingly prevalent," and issued a strong warning:

"Due process requires that the accused receive a trial by an impartial jury free from outside influences. Given the pervasiveness of modern communications and the difficulty of effacing prejudicial publicity from the minds of the jurors, *the trial courts must take strong measures to ensure that the balance is never weighed against the accused....* [W]here there is a reasonable likelihood that prejudicial news prior to trial will prevent a fair trial, the judge should *continue the case* until the threat abates, *or transfer it* to another county not so permeated with publicity. In addition, *sequestration of the jury* was something the judge should have raised."...

...

... [P]retrial publicity—even pervasive, adverse publicity—does not inevitably lead to an unfair trial. The capacity of the jury eventually impaneled to decide the case fairly is influenced by the tone and extent of the publicity, which is in part, and often in large part, shaped by what attorneys, police, and other officials do to precipitate news coverage. The trial judge has a major responsibility.... [T]he measures a judge takes or fails to take to mitigate the effects of pretrial publicity—the measures described in *Sheppard*—may well determine whether the defendant receives a trial consistent with the requirements of due process....

The state trial judge in the case before us acted responsibly, out of a legitimate concern, in an effort to protect the defendant's right to a fair trial. What we must decide is ... whether in the circumstances of this case the means employed were foreclosed by another provision of the Constitution.

V

... None of our decided cases on prior restraint involved restrictive orders entered to protect a defendant's right to a fair and impartial jury, but the opinions on prior restraint have a common thread relevant to this case....

The threat ... is that prior restraints on speech and publication are the most serious and the least tolerable infringement on First Amendment rights....

A prior restraint ... has an immediate and irreversible sanction. If it can be said that a threat of criminal or civil sanctions after publication "chills" speech, prior restraint "freezes" it at least for the time.

The damage can be particularly great when the prior restraint falls upon the communication of news and commentary on current events....

The authors of the Bill of Rights did not undertake to assign priorities as between First Amendment and Sixth Amendment rights, ranking one as superior to the other. In this case, the petitioners would have us declare the right of an accused subordinate to their right to publish in all circumstances. But if the authors of these guarantees, fully aware of the potential conflicts between them, were unwilling or unable to resolve the issue by assigning to one priority over the other, it is not for us to rewrite the Constitution by undertaking what they declined to do…. Yet it is nonetheless clear that the barriers to prior restraint remain high….

VI

We turn now to the record in this case to determine whether, as [Judge] Learned Hand put it, "the gravity of the 'evil,' discounted by its improbability, justifies such invasion of free speech as is necessary to avoid danger." To do so, we must examine the evidence before the trial judge when the order was entered to determine (a) the nature and extent of pretrial news coverage; (b) whether other measures would be likely to mitigate the effects of unrestrained pretrial publicity; and (c) how effectively a restraining order would operate to prevent the threatened danger….

A

In assessing the probable extent of publicity, the trial judge had before him newspapers demonstrating that the crime had already drawn intensive news coverage, and the testimony of the County Judge, who had entered the initial restraining order based on the local and national attention the case had attracted….

Our review of the pretrial record persuades us that the trial judge was justified in concluding that there would be intense and pervasive pretrial publicity concerning this case….

B

We find little in the record that goes to another aspect of our task, determining whether measures short of an order restraining all publication would have insured the defendant a fair trial. Although the entry of the order might be read as a judicial determination that other measures would not suffice, the trial court made no express findings to that effect….

Most of the alternatives to prior restraint of publication in these circumstances were discussed with obvious approval in *Sheppard v. Maxwell:* (a) change of trial venue to a place less exposed to the intense publicity that seemed imminent in Lincoln County; (b) postponement of the trial to allow public attention to subside; (c) searching questioning of prospective jurors … to screen out those with fixed opinions as to guilt or innocence; and (d) the use of emphatic and clear instructions on the sworn duty of each juror to decide the issues only on evidence presented in open court….

… There is no finding that alternative measures would not have protected Simants' rights, and the Nebraska Supreme Court did no more than imply that such measures might not be adequate. Moreover, the record is lacking in evidence to support such a finding.

We must also assess the probable efficacy of prior restraint on publication as a workable method of protecting Simants' right to a fair trial, and we cannot ignore the reality of the problems of managing and enforcing pretrial restraining orders….

[W]e note that the events disclosed by the record took place in a community of 850 people. It is reasonable to assume that, without any news accounts being printed or broadcast, rumors would travel swiftly by word of mouth. One can only speculate on the accuracy of such reports, given the generative propensities of rumors; they could well be more damaging than reasonably accurate news accounts. But plainly a whole community cannot be restrained from discussing a subject intimately affecting life within it.

Given these practical problems, it is far from clear that prior restraint on publication would have protected Simants' rights....

E

The record demonstrates, as the Nebraska courts held, that there was indeed a risk that pretrial news accounts, true or false, would have some adverse impact on the attitudes of those who might be called as jurors. But on the record now before us it is not clear that further publicity, unchecked, would so distort the views of potential jurors that twelve could not be found who would, under proper instructions, fulfill their sworn duty to render a just verdict exclusively on the evidence presented in open court. We cannot say on this record that alternatives to a prior restraint on petitioners would not have sufficiently mitigated the adverse effects of pretrial publicity so as to make prior restraint unnecessary. Nor can we conclude that the restraining order actually entered would serve its intended purpose....

[W]e conclude that the heavy burden imposed as a condition to securing a prior restraint was not met and the judgment of the Nebraska Supreme Court is therefore *Reversed.*

THE PEOPLE V. BRYANT
Supreme Court of Colorado, 2004
94 P.3d 624

Justice HOBBS delivered the opinion of the court.

... [W]e accepted jurisdiction in this original proceeding to review an order by the District Court for Eagle County in a criminal prosecution against Kobe B. Bryant for allegedly sexually assaulting a woman.

... [T]he District Court, on June 21 and 22, 2004, held *in camera* proceedings regarding the "relevancy and materiality of evidence of specific instances of the victim's ... prior or subsequent sexual conduct, or opinion evidence of the victim's ... sexual conduct."

On June 24, 2004, the court reporter mistakenly sent the transcripts of the *in camera* proceedings by electronic transmission to seven media entities ("Recipients") via an electronic mailing list for subscribers to public proceeding transcripts in the case, instead of using only the electronic mailing list for persons authorized to receive transcripts of *in camera* proceedings. There is no dispute that this was an error, and no dispute that the Recipients would otherwise not have received the transcripts....

Upon discovering the transmission mistake, the court reporter immediately notified the District Court, which promptly issued its June 24th order to the Recipients:

It has come to the Court's attention that the *in camera* portions of the hearings in this matter on the 21st and 22nd were erroneously distributed. These transcripts are not for public dissemination. Anyone who has received these transcripts is ordered to delete and destroy any copies and not reveal any contents thereof, or be subject to contempt of Court.

Four days later, the Recipients filed their original proceeding petition, asking that we exercise jurisdiction to review the District Court's order and set it aside as an unconstitutional prior restraint against publication, in violation of the First Amendment to the United States Constitution and article II, section 10 of the Colorado Constitution....

We determine that the District Court's order is a prior restraint against publishing the contents of the transcripts. We also determine that, narrowly tailored, the prior restraint is constitutional under both the United States and the Colorado Constitutions....

I. Facts and Procedural Background

By its Complaint/Information dated July 18, 2003, the state of Colorado alleges that Defendant Bryant, on June 30, 2003, committed forcible sexual penetration of a woman in Eagle County, Colorado, against her will ... a class 3 felony....

This criminal prosecution has received extraordinary media attention from the outset, fueled by Defendant Bryant's international reputation as an all-star professional basketball player and the sexual assault charge made against him. In order to facilitate public access to the proceedings in this case, the Eagle County District Court ... maintained an electronic scheduling archive on the Colorado Courts' webpage that contains links to publicly accessible documents.

Among these publicly accessible documents is the June 17, 2004, memorandum addressed by the District Court to "Members of the Media." It states that the District Court will hold hearings at the Eagle County Justice Center on the Bryant case on Monday, June 21, and Tuesday, June 22, 2004, a portion of which will be open to the public and a portion closed....

The court reporter mistakenly transmitted the transcribed *in camera* proceedings for June 21 and 22, along with the transcribed public proceedings for June 21, to the Recipients. The notation "** IN CAMERA PROCEEDINGS **" is marked on every page of the transcript containing information from the closed portions of the proceedings. The mistake occurred because the court reporter maintained an electronic list for media entities subscribing to transcripts of the public proceedings in the case.

Our review of the transcripts under seal demonstrates that the pages bearing the label "** IN CAMERA PROCEEDINGS **" are concerned with evidence and arguments relating to the victim's sexual conduct before and after her sexual encounter with the Defendant Bryant....

The District Court's order and the original proceeding before us involve only the *in camera* proceeding transcripts for June 21 and June 22, and do not concern any information the media may have obtained through its investigative capacities....

II. First Amendment Prior Restraint Law

The First Amendment limits the choices the government may make in its efforts to regulate or prohibit speech, but it does not bar all government attempts to regulate speech, and it does not absolutely prohibit prior restraints against publication. *Neb. Press Ass'n v. Stuart*, 427 U.S. 539, 570 (1976)....

In cases dealing with the conflict between truthful reporting and state-protected privacy interests, the Supreme Court–when reviewing the validity of sanctions following publication–has held unconstitutional a civil damages award entered against a television station for broadcasting the name of a rape-murder victim it had obtained from publicly available courthouse records. *Cox Broad. Corp. v. Cohn*, 420 U.S. 469 (1975)....

Nevertheless, the Supreme Court has recognized that protecting the privacy of rape victims is a highly significant state interest, requiring courts to consider both the First Amendment and the compelling privacy interests in the particular factual context of the case in reaching their decisions....

In *Florida Star v. BJF*, the Sheriff's Department publicly posted a police report containing a sexual assault victim's name. Under the circumstances, the Supreme Court determined that a civil damages award against the newspaper for revealing the name violated the First Amendment. But the Court said it was not holding that "truthful publication is automatically constitutionally protected, or that there is no zone of personal privacy within which the state may protect the individual from intrusion by the press, or even that a state may never punish publication of the name of a victim of a sexual offense."

We therefore turn to Colorado's rape shield statute, which serves purposes the Supreme Court identified in Florida Star as being of the highest order.

III. Colorado's Rape Shield Statute

Rape is among the most intimate and personally devastating invasions a person may experience in his or her lifetime. It typically produces emotionally destructive reverberations for the victim and the victim's family long after its occurrence. It can destroy the ability of a person to enjoy his or her sexuality with another.

The price of making a sexual assault victim's testimony available to courts of law historically exposed the victim to detailed questioning about his or her sexual relationships with others on the theory that a person who consented to a sexual relationship in the past was more likely to have consented in the case at hand. This tactic of "putting the victim on trial" attempts to characterize the accuser as a person who consented to the alleged unlawful sexual conduct. Due to the likelihood or possibility that this defense will be invoked, exposing the victim's most intimate life history to public view, victims often are deterred from reporting the crime, or having reported it, from following through in the role of complaining witness.

At the time the Colorado General Assembly enacted the rape shield statute, many sexual assaults were never reported because victims of rape were often ashamed, humiliated, or terrified about the specter of their most private hurt being publicly revealed. Therefore the offenses could not be prosecuted under the state's criminal laws....

The United States Department of Justice reported in 2002 that "[m]ost rapes and sexual assaults [are] not reported to the police .... Sixty-three percent of completed rapes, 65% of attempted rapes, and 74% of completed and attempted sexual assaults against females [are] not reported to the police."...

Because a defendant may seek to inject irrelevant details about the victim's personal sexual conduct into the case, the Colorado General Assembly has enacted a carefully-crafted judicial mechanism that allows the prosecution and defense–in private, that is, "*in camera*"–to explore and argue about the relevancy and materiality of evidence tendered to the trial judge for admission at the public trial of the case....

In summary, Colorado's rape shield statute: (1) protects the sexual assault victim's privacy; (2) allows the accused person to explore facts, examine witnesses, present testimony, and challenge expert opinion to uncover material evidence potentially helpful to the defendant; (3) enables the trial judge in pretrial proceedings to determine what shall be admitted or excluded at the public trial; (4) shelters all evidence in the *in camera* proceeding from being reported publicly; (5) keeps the evidence that is not material and relevant from being publicly reported in the future; and (6) serves the state's interest in prosecuting those accused of sexual assault and protecting the victims of sexual assault while affording defendants a fair opportunity to confront their accusers and hold prosecutors to the burden of proof at the public trial.

IV. Application to This Case

We determine that the District Court's order is a prior restraint because it prohibits specific entities possessing the *in camera* June 21 and June 22, 2004, transcripts from revealing the contents.

We also determine that, narrowly tailored, the prior restraint is constitutional. The state has an interest of the highest order in this case in providing a confidential evidentiary proceeding under the rape shield statute because such hearings protect victims' privacy, encourage victims to report sexual assault, and further the prosecution and deterrence of sexual assault.

We further determine that a narrowly tailored order can be fashioned in this case, and it is necessary to protect against an evil that is great and certain and would result from the reportage....

The District Court placed into effect reasonable procedures, in advance, to prevent the media from attending and reporting these proceedings. By a standing order entered in the case dated October 31, 2003, the District Court prohibited the parties, attorneys, and court personnel–including the court reporter–from publicly revealing the hearing contents.... To make the *in camera* evidence and arguments accessible to the court and the parties, so that the District Court could make its rape shield statute determinations, the court reporter transcribed the *in camera* proceedings, marking every page of the *in camera* transcripts with highly visible lettering: "** IN CAMERA PROCEEDINGS **." ...

Recipients, the few media entities on whose computer screens the electronic document appeared, obtained a private transmission placed under seal by the District Court. The District Court did not intend to make these transcripts publicly available, nor did the court reporter. The private and protected nature of these transcripts was manifest to the Recipients from the bold notation on each page and the District Court's prior orders and actions....

Recipients do not dispute the constitutionality of excluding the public and press from the *in camera* hearings, nor do they challenge the requirement that the parties, witnesses, and court personnel must maintain the secrecy of the proceedings. Rather, the Recipients argue in this case that at the moment the transcript arrived at their computers, they lawfully acquired the information and were entitled to publish it.

In conducting our analysis of whether the prior restraint is necessary to protect against an evil that is great and certain, would result from the reportage, and cannot be mitigated by less intrusive measures, we recognize that the Supreme Court has hypothesized that a valid restraint might occur in the intersection of First Amendment and privacy rights, but has not yet decided a case approving one....

In the case before us, the state's interest in protecting the victim's privacy is even stronger than in Florida Star. The Defendant Bryant is an internationally recognized professional basketball player. The press has been covering every minute detail of this case, and most of this coverage has been published or broadcast nationwide. In addition, the reported news is typically posted on the Internet, and thus available to computer users world-wide. The *in camera* transcribed proceedings of June 21 and 22 address the prior and subsequent sexual conduct of the victim apart from her encounter with Defendant Bryant. A victim's sexual conduct is even more private than a victim's identity, which the Court held was of utmost importance in Florida Star.

Moreover, in contrast to Florida Star, the contents of the *in camera* transcribed proceedings were not publicly available, there was no burden on the press to determine whether it should risk publication and sanctions in light of the District Court's prior restraint order, and the specter of the press having to impose self censorship was not an issue, as the transcripts were clearly marked private by the "In Camera" notation....

[T]he applicable standard of review requires us to determine whether publication of these transcripts would cause great and certain harm to a state interest of the highest order. We conclude that it would.

First, the evidence and the opinion testimony presented at these *in camera* proceedings were taken under oath in a court of law. Reporting these court proceedings will add a level of official legitimacy and detail to the information that does not attend press reports–the ring of authenticity, the stamp of authority. Because sworn testimony is viewed by the law and the public as having greater value and credibility than press reports of unsworn statements, this will cause great and certain harm to the victim's privacy interest. Unsworn statements often contain a mix of fact, conjecture, rumor, and unconfirmed assertions that a person might not make under oath, or that lack evidentiary value or relevance.

We do not accept the proposition that the greater the press attention to a case the less important it becomes to keep *in camera* rape shield transcripts from being published. If the contents of these transcripts are reported, the world will have access to graphic detail of sworn evidence and opinion testimony about the victim's sexual conduct that the public trial of the case may not reveal, because the District Court may determine it to be irrelevant and immaterial under the rape shield statute....

Second, the state's interests of the highest order in this case not only involve the victim's privacy interest, but also the reporting and prosecution of this and other sexual assault cases. Revealing the *in camera* rape shield evidence will not only destroy the utility of this very important legal mechanism in this case, but will demonstrate to other sexual assault victims that they cannot rely on the rape shield statute to prevent public airing of sexual conduct testimony the law deems inadmissible. This would directly undercut the reporting and prosecution of sexual assault cases, in contravention of the General Assembly's legislative purposes....

V. Order and Judgment

Accordingly, we uphold the prohibition against revealing the contents of the transcribed *in camera* proceedings of June 21 and 22, 2004, and affirm the District Court's order to that extent....

Justice BENDER, dissenting:

The question in this case is whether a court may prohibit publication of all or part of a transcript of an *in camera* rape shield hearing where the transcript was inadvertently released to the media by trial court personnel. In my view, two striking facts about this case make it obvious that the prior restraint issued by the district court is an unconstitutional violation of the freedom of the press guaranteed by the First Amendment. First, most of the private details of the alleged victim's sexual conduct around the time of the alleged rape, which is also the subject matter of the confidential hearings in this case, are already available through public court documents and other sources and have been widely reported by the media. Second, the media did nothing wrong in obtaining the transcripts. Under well-established prior restraint doctrine, these two factors alone require this Court to direct the district court to vacate its order immediately....

I sympathize with the majority's desire to offer some assurance that the alleged victim will not be subject to further unnecessary harm from invasive and even at times mean-spirited revelations about her private life. But as a court, our sole task is to determine whether this case presents one of those extraordinary circumstances where the harm to a state interest is so great and so sure to occur that the freedom of the media to publish what it sees fit, free from government interference, may be abridged....

Because the prior restraint issued in this case can accomplish nothing more than preventing, at best, incremental harm to the interests protected by the rape shield statute, I conclude that the district court has not overcome the heavy presumption against the constitutionality of prior restraints. The facts of this case are not so extraordinary that we as a court can overlook the fundamental importance of the media's right to decide for itself what it may or may not publish....

PRESS-ENTERPRISE CO. V. SUPERIOR COURT OF CALIFORNIA (PRESS-ENTERPRISE II)
Supreme Court of the United States, 1986
478 U.S. 1

Chief Justice BURGER delivered the opinion of the Court.

I

On December 23, 1981, the State of California filed a complaint in the Riverside County Municipal Court, charging Robert Diaz with twelve counts of murder and seeking the death penalty. The complaint alleged that Diaz, a nurse, murdered twelve patients by administering massive doses of the heart drug lidocaine. The preliminary hearing on the complaint commenced on July 6, 1982. Diaz moved to exclude the public from the proceedings under Cal. Penal Code Ann. § 868 (West 1985), which requires such proceedings to be open unless "exclusion of the public is necessary in order to protect the defendant's right to a fair and impartial trial." The Magistrate granted the unopposed motion, finding that closure was necessary because the case had attracted national publicity and "only one side may get reported in the media."

The preliminary hearing continued for forty-one days.... At the conclusion of the hearing, petitioner Press-Enterprise Company asked that the transcript of the proceedings be released. The Magistrate refused and sealed the record....

The California Supreme Court ... [held] that there is no general First Amendment right of access to preliminary hearings....

We reverse....

III

....

The right to an open public trial is a shared right of the accused and the public, the common concern being the assurance of fairness....

... The California Supreme Court concluded that the First Amendment was not implicated because the proceeding was not a criminal trial, but a preliminary hearing. However, the First Amendment question cannot be resolved solely on the label we give the event, i.e., "trial" or otherwise, particularly where the preliminary hearing functions much like a full-scale trial.

In cases dealing with the claim of a First Amendment right of access to criminal proceedings, our decisions have emphasized two complementary considerations. First, because a "'tradition of accessibility implies the favorable judgment of experiences'" *Globe Newspaper Co. v. Superior Court*, 457 U.S., at 605 [quoting *Richmond Newspapers, Inc. v. Virginia*, 448 U.S. 555 (1980)], we have considered whether the place and process have historically been open to the press and general public.

In *Press-Enterprise I*, for example [*Press-Enterprise Co. v. Superior Court*, 464 U.S. 501 (1984)], we observed that "since the development of trial by jury, the process of selection of jurors has presumptively been a public process with exceptions only for good cause shown." In *Richmond Newspapers*, we reviewed some of the early history of England's open trials from the day when a trial was much like a "town meeting." ... The public trial, "one of the essential qualities of a court of justice" in England, was recognized early on in the Colonies....

Second, in this setting the Court has traditionally considered whether public access plays a significant positive role in the functioning of the particular process in question.... [I]t takes little imagination to recognize that there are some kinds of government operations that would be totally frustrated if conducted openly. A classic example is that "the proper functioning of our grand jury system depends upon the secrecy of grand jury proceedings." Other proceedings plainly require public access. In *Press-Enterprise I*, we summarized the holdings of prior cases, noting that openness in criminal trials, including the selection of jurors, "enhances both the basic fairness of the criminal trial and the appearance of fairness so essential to public confidence in the system."

... If the particular proceeding in question passes these tests of experience and logic, a qualified First Amendment right of public access attaches. But even when a right of access attaches, it is not absolute.... In such cases, the trial court must determine whether the situation is such that the rights of the accused override the qualified First Amendment right of access....

IV

A

The considerations that led the Court to apply the First Amendment right of access to criminal trials in *Richmond Newspapers* and *Globe* and the selection of jurors in *Press-Enterprise I* lead us to conclude that the right of access applies to preliminary hearings as conducted in California.

First, there has been a tradition of accessibility to preliminary hearings of the type conducted in California....

The second question is whether public access to preliminary hearings as they are conducted in California plays a particularly significant positive role in the actual functioning of the process. We have already determined in *Richmond Newspapers*, *Globe*, and *Press-Enterprise I* that public access to criminal trials and the selection of jurors is essential to the proper functioning of the criminal justice system. California preliminary hearings are sufficiently like a trial to justify the same conclusion.

In California, to bring a felon to trial, the prosecutor has a choice of securing a grand jury indictment or a finding of probable cause following a preliminary hearing.... The accused has the right to personally appear at the hearing, to be represented by counsel, to cross-examine hostile witnesses, to present exculpatory evidence, and to exclude illegally obtained evidence....

... Because of its extensive scope, the preliminary hearing is often the final and most important step in the criminal proceeding....

Denying the transcript of a forty-one-day preliminary hearing would frustrate what we have characterized as the "community therapeutic value" of openness....

B

Since a qualified First Amendment right of access attaches to preliminary hearings in California ... the proceedings cannot be closed unless specific, on the record findings are made demonstrating that "closure is essential to preserve higher values and is narrowly tailored to serve that interest." If the interest asserted is the right of the accused to a fair trial, the preliminary hearing shall be closed only if specific findings are made demonstrating that, first, there is a substantial probability that the defendant's right to a fair trial will be prejudiced by publicity that closure would prevent and, second, reasonable alternatives to closure cannot adequately protect the defendant's fair trial rights.

The California Supreme Court, interpreting its access statute, concluded "the magistrate shall close the preliminary hearing upon finding a reasonable likelihood of substantial prejudice." As the court itself acknowledged, the "reasonable likelihood" test places a lesser burden on the defendant than the "substantial probability" test, which we hold is called for by the First Amendment. Moreover, the court failed to consider whether alternatives short of complete closure would have protected the interests of the accused....

[The] risk of prejudice does not automatically justify refusing public access to hearings on every motion to suppress. Through *voir dire*, cumbersome as it is in some circumstances, a court can identify those jurors whose prior knowledge of the case would disable them from rendering an impartial verdict. And even if closure were justified for the hearings on a motion to suppress, closure of an entire forty-one-day proceeding would rarely be warranted....

The standard applied by the California Supreme Court failed to consider the First Amendment right of access to criminal proceedings. Accordingly, the judgment of the California Supreme Court is reversed.

It is so ordered.

CHANDLER V. FLORIDA
Supreme Court of the United States, 1981
449 U.S. 560

Chief Justice BURGER delivered the opinion of the Court.

The question presented on this appeal is whether, consistent with constitutional guarantees, a state may provide for radio, television, and still photographic coverage of a criminal trial for public broadcast, notwithstanding the objection of the accused.

I

A

Background. Over the past fifty years, some criminal cases characterized as "sensational" have been subjected to extensive coverage by news media, sometimes seriously interfering with the conduct of the proceedings and creating a setting wholly inappropriate for the administration of justice. Judges, lawyers, and others soon became concerned, and in 1937, after study, the American Bar Association House of Delegates adopted Judicial Canon 35, declaring that all photographic and broadcast coverage of courtroom proceedings should be prohibited.... A majority of the states, including Florida, adopted the substance of the ABA provision and its amendments. In Florida, the rule was embodied in Canon 3A(7) of the Florida Code of Judicial Conduct....

The Florida Program. In January 1975 ... the Post-Newsweek Stations of Florida petitioned the Supreme Court of Florida urging a change in Florida's Canon 3A(7).... [I]n January 1976, [the court] announced an experimental program for televising one civil and one criminal trial under specific guidelines. These initial guidelines required the consent of all parties. It developed, however, that in practice such consent could not be obtained. The Florida Supreme Court then supplemented its order and established a new one-year pilot program during which the electronic media were permitted to cover all judicial proceedings in Florida without reference to the consent of participants, subject to detailed standards with respect to technology and the conduct of operators....

When the pilot program ended, the Florida Supreme Court received and reviewed briefs, reports, letters of comment, and studies.... The court also studied the experience of six States that had, by 1979, adopted rules relating to electronic coverage of trials, as well as that of ten other States that, like Florida, were experimenting with such coverage.

Following its review of this material, the Florida Supreme Court concluded "that on balance there [was] more to be gained than lost by permitting electronic media coverage of judicial proceedings subject to standards for such coverage." The Florida court was of the view that because of the significant effect of the courts on the day-to-day lives of the citizenry, it was essential that the people have confidence in the process. It felt that broadcast coverage of trials would contribute to wider public acceptance and understanding of decisions. Consequently, after revising the 1977 guidelines to reflect its evaluation of the pilot program, the Florida Supreme Court promulgated a revised Canon 3A(7). The Canon provides:

"Subject at all times to the authority of the presiding judge to (i) control the conduct of proceedings before the court, (ii) ensure decorum and prevent distractions, and (iii) ensure the fair administration of justice in the pending cause, electronic media and still photography coverage of public judicial proceedings in the appellate and trial courts of this state shall be allowed in accordance with standards of conduct and technology promulgated by the Supreme Court of Florida."

....

B

In July 1977, appellants were charged with conspiracy to commit burglary, grand larceny, and possession of burglary tools. The counts covered breaking and entering a well-known Miami Beach restaurant.

The details of the alleged criminal conduct are not relevant to the issue before us, but several aspects of the case distinguish it from a routine burglary. At the time of their arrest, appellants were Miami Beach policemen. The State's principal witness was John Sion, an amateur radio operator who, by sheer chance, had overheard and recorded conversations between the appellants over their walkie-talkie radios during the burglary. Not surprisingly, these novel factors attracted the attention of the media.

By pretrial motion, counsel for the appellants sought to have experimental Canon 3A(7) declared unconstitutional on its face and as applied. The trial court denied relief....

After several additional fruitless attempts by the appellants to prevent electronic coverage of the trial, the jury was selected....

A television camera was in place for one entire afternoon, during which the State presented the testimony of Sion, its chief witness. No camera was present for the presentation of any part of the case for the defense. The camera returned to cover closing arguments. Only two minutes and fifty-five seconds of the trial below were broadcast—and those depicted only the prosecution's side of the case.

The jury returned a guilty verdict on all counts. Appellants moved for a new trial, claiming that because of the television coverage, they had been denied a fair and impartial trial. No evidence of specific prejudice was tendered....

II

At the outset, it is important to note that in promulgating the revised Canon 3A(7), the Florida Supreme Court pointedly rejected any state or federal constitutional right of access on the part of photographers or the broadcast media to televise or electronically record and thereafter disseminate court proceedings. It carefully framed its holding as follows:

"While we have concluded that the due process clause does not prohibit electronic media coverage of judicial proceedings per se, by the same token we reject the argument of the

[Post-Newsweek stations] that the First and Sixth Amendments to the United States Constitution mandate entry of the electronic media into judicial proceedings."

....

The Florida Supreme Court predicated the revised Canon 3A(7) upon its supervisory authority over the Florida courts, and not upon any constitutional imperative. Hence, we have before us only the limited question of the Florida Supreme Court's authority to promulgate the Canon for the trial of cases in Florida courts.

III

Appellants rely chiefly on *Estes v. Texas*, 381 U.S. 532 (1965).... They argue that the televising of criminal trials is inherently a denial of due process, and they read *Estes* as announcing a per se constitutional rule to that effect....

... [I]t is fair to say that Justice Harlan viewed the holding as limited to the proposition that "*what was done in this case* infringed the fundamental right to a fair trial assured by the Due Process Clause of the Fourteenth Amendment," (emphasis added), he went on:

"At the present juncture I can only conclude that televised trials, at least in cases like this one, possess such capabilities for interfering with the even course of the judicial process that they are constitutionally banned." (Emphasis added.)

Justice Harlan's opinion, upon which analysis of the constitutional holding of *Estes* turns, must be read as defining the scope of that holding; we conclude that *Estes* is not to be read as announcing a constitutional rule barring still photographic, radio, and television coverage in all cases and under all circumstances. It does not stand as an absolute ban on state experimentation with an evolving technology, which, in terms of modes of mass communication, was in its relative infancy in 1964, and is, even now, in a state of continuing change.

IV

Since we are satisfied that *Estes* did not announce a constitutional rule that all photographic or broadcast coverage of criminal trials is inherently a denial of due process, we turn to consideration, as a matter of first impression, of the appellants' suggestion that we now promulgate such a per se rule.

A

Any criminal case that generates a great deal of publicity presents some risks that the publicity may compromise the right of the defendant to a fair trial. Trial courts must be especially vigilant to guard against any impairment of the defendant's right to a verdict based solely upon the evidence and the relevant law. Over the years, courts have developed a range of curative devices to prevent publicity about a trial from infecting jury deliberations.

An absolute constitutional ban on broadcast coverage of trials cannot be justified simply because there is a danger that, in some cases, prejudicial broadcast accounts of pretrial and trial events may impair the ability of jurors to decide the issue of guilt or innocence uninfluenced by extraneous matter.... The risk of juror prejudice is present in any publication of a trial, but the appropriate safeguard against such prejudice is the defendant's right to demonstrate that the media's coverage of his case—be it printed or broadcast— compromised the ability of the particular jury that heard the case to adjudicate fairly.

B

... [T]he concurring opinions in *Estes* expressed concern that the very presence of media cameras and recording devices at a trial inescapably gives rise to an adverse psychological impact on the participants in the trial. This kind of general psychological prejudice, allegedly present whenever there is broadcast coverage of a trial, is different from the more particularized problem of prejudicial impact discussed earlier. If it could be demonstrated that the mere presence of photographic and recording equipment and the knowledge that the event would be broadcast invariably and uniformly affected the conduct of participants so as to impair fundamental fairness, our task would be simple; prohibition of broadcast coverage of trials would be required....

Not unimportant to the position asserted by Florida and other states is the change in television technology since 1962, when *Estes* was tried. It is urged, and some empirical data are presented, that many of the negative factors found in *Estes*—cumbersome equipment, cables, distracting lighting, numerous camera technicians—are less substantial factors today than they were at that time.

It is also significant that safeguards have been built into the experimental programs in state courts, and into the Florida program, to avoid some of the most egregious problems envisioned by the six opinions in the *Estes* case. Florida admonishes its courts to take special pains to protect certain witnesses—for example, children, victims of sex crimes, some informants, and even the very timid witness or party—from the glare of publicity and the tensions of being "on camera."...

Whatever may be the "mischievous potentialities [of broadcast coverage] for intruding upon the detached atmosphere which should always surround the judicial process," at present no one has been able to present empirical data sufficient to establish that the mere presence of the broadcast media inherently has an adverse effect on that process. The appellants have offered nothing to demonstrate that their trial was subtly tainted by broadcast coverage—let alone that all broadcast trials would be so tainted....

To demonstrate prejudice in a specific case a defendant must show something more than juror awareness that the trial is such as to attract the attention of broadcasters. No doubt the very presence of a camera in the courtroom made the jurors aware that the trial was thought to be of sufficient interest to the public to warrant coverage. Jurors, forbidden to watch all broadcasts, would have had no way of knowing that only fleeting seconds of the proceeding would be reproduced. But the appellants have not attempted to show with any specificity that the presence of cameras impaired the ability of the jurors to decide the case on only the evidence before them or that their trial was affected adversely by the impact on any of the participants of the presence of cameras and the prospect of broadcast....

V

It is not necessary either to ignore or to discount the potential danger to the fairness of a trial in a particular case in order to conclude that Florida may permit the electronic media to cover trials in its state courts. Dangers lurk in this, as in most experiments, but unless we were to conclude that television coverage under all conditions is prohibited by the Constitution, the states must be free to experiment....

... We hold that the Constitution does not prohibit a state from experimenting with the program authorized by revised Canon 3A(7).
Affirmed.

BRANZBURG V. HAYES
Supreme Court of the United States, 1972
408 U.S. 665

Opinion of the Court by Justice WHITE….

The issue in these cases is whether requiring newsmen to appear and testify before state or federal grand juries abridges the freedom of speech and press guaranteed by the First Amendment. We hold that it does not.

I

The writ of certiorari in No. 70-85, *Branzburg v. Hayes and Meigs,* brings before us two judgments of the Kentucky Court of Appeals, both involving petitioner Branzburg, a staff reporter for the *Courier-Journal,* a daily newspaper published in Louisville, Kentucky.

On November 15, 1969, the *Courier-Journal* carried a story under petitioner's byline describing in detail his observations of two young residents of Jefferson County synthesizing hashish from marijuana, an activity which, they asserted, earned them about $5,000 in three weeks. The article included a photograph of a pair of hands working above a laboratory table on which was a substance identified by the caption as hashish. The article stated that petitioner had promised not to reveal the identity of the two hashish makers. Petitioner was shortly subpoenaed by the Jefferson County grand jury; he appeared, but refused to identify the individuals he had seen possessing marijuana …

The second case involving petitioner Branzburg arose out of his later story published on January 10, 1971, which described in detail the use of drugs in Frankfort, Kentucky. The article reported that in order to provide a comprehensive survey of the "drug scene" in Frankfort, petitioner had "spent two weeks interviewing several dozen drug users in the capital city" and had seen some of them smoking marijuana. A number of conversations with and observations of several unnamed drug users were recounted. Subpoenaed to appear before a Franklin County grand jury "to testify in the matter of violation of statutes concerning use and sale of drugs," petitioner Branzburg moved to quash the summons; the motion was denied …

In re Pappas, No. 70-94, originated when petitioner Pappas, a television newsman-photographer working out of the Providence, Rhode Island, office of a New Bedford, Massachusetts, television station, was called to New Bedford on July 30, 1970, to report on civil disorders there which involved fires and other turmoil. He intended to cover a Black Panther news conference at that group's headquarters in a boarded-up store. Petitioner found the streets around the store barricaded, but he ultimately gained entrance to the area…. [H]e was allowed to enter and remain inside Panther headquarters. As a condition of entry, Pappas agreed not to disclose anything he saw or heard inside the store except an anticipated police raid, which Pappas, "on his own," was free to photograph and report as he wished. Pappas stayed inside the headquarters for about three hours, but there was no police raid, and petitioner wrote no story and did not otherwise reveal what had occurred in the store while he was there. Two months later, petitioner was summoned before the Bristol County Grand Jury and appeared, answered questions as to his name, address, employment, and what he had seen and heard outside Panther headquarters, but refused to answer any questions about what had taken place inside headquarters while he was there, claiming that the First Amendment afforded him a privilege to protect confidential informants and their information....

United States v. Caldwell, No. 70-57, arose from subpoenas issued by a federal grand jury in the Northern District of California to respondent Earl Caldwell, a reporter for the *New York Times* assigned to cover the Black Panther Party and other black militant groups. A subpoena *duces tecum* was served on respondent on February 2, 1970, ordering him to appear before the grand jury to testify and to bring with him notes and tape recordings of interviews given him for publication by officers and spokesmen of the Black Panther Party concerning the aims, purposes, and activities of that organization.... Respondent and his employer, the *New York Times,* moved to quash on the ground that the unlimited breadth of the subpoenas and the fact that Caldwell would have to appear in secret before the grand jury would destroy his working relationship with the Black Panther Party and "suppress vital First Amendment freedoms ... by driving a wedge of distrust and silence between the news media and the militants." ...

II

Petitioners Branzburg and Pappas and respondent Caldwell press First Amendment claims that may be simply put: that to gather news it is often necessary to agree either not to identify the source of information published or to publish only part of the facts revealed, or both; that if the reporter is nevertheless forced to reveal these confidences to a grand jury, the source so identified and other confidential sources of other reporters will be measurably deterred from furnishing publishable information, all to the detriment of the free flow of information protected by the First Amendment. Although the newsmen in these cases do not claim an absolute privilege against official interrogation in all circumstances, they assert that the reporter should not be forced either to appear or to testify before a grand jury or at trial until and unless sufficient grounds are shown for believing that the reporter possesses information relevant to a crime the grand jury is investigating, that the information the reporter has is unavailable from other sources, and that the need for the information is sufficiently compelling.... The heart of the claim is that the burden on newsgathering resulting from compelling reporters to disclose confidential information outweighs any public interest in obtaining the information.

We do not question the significance of free speech, press, or assembly to the country's welfare. Nor is it suggested that newsgathering does not qualify for First Amendment protection; without some protection for seeking out the news, freedom of the press could be eviscerated. But these cases involve no intrusions upon speech or assembly, no prior restraint or restriction on what the press may publish, and no express or implied command that the press publish what it prefers to withhold.... The use of confidential sources by the press is not forbidden or restricted; reporters remain free to seek news from any source by means within the law....

The sole issue before us is the obligation of reporters to respond to grand jury subpoenas as other citizens do and to answer questions relevant to an investigation into the commission of crime....

It is clear that the First Amendment does not invalidate every incidental burdening of the press that may result from the enforcement of civil or criminal statutes of general applicability. Under prior cases, otherwise valid laws serving substantial public interests may be enforced against the press as against others, despite the possible burden that may be imposed. The Court has emphasized that "[t]he publisher of a newspaper has no special immunity from the application of general laws. He has no special privilege to invade the rights and liberties of others." ...

Despite the fact that newsgathering may be hampered, the press is regularly excluded from grand jury proceedings, our own conferences, the meetings of other official bodies gathered in executive session, and the meetings of private organizations. Newsmen have no constitutional right of access to the scenes of crime or disaster when the general public is excluded ...

It is thus not surprising that the great weight of authority is that newsmen are not exempt from the normal duty of appearing before a grand jury and answering questions relevant to a criminal investigation.... The opinions of the state courts in *Branzburg* and *Pappas* are typical of the prevailing view, although a few recent cases, such as *Caldwell*, have recognized and given effect to some form of constitutional newsman's privilege....

A number of States have provided newsmen a statutory privilege of varying breadth, but the majority has not done so, and none has been provided by federal statute. Until now the only testimonial privilege for unofficial witnesses that is rooted in the Federal Constitution is the Fifth Amendment privilege against compelled self-incrimination. We are asked to create another by interpreting the First Amendment to grant newsmen a testimonial privilege that other citizens to not enjoy. This we decline to do. Fair and effective law enforcement aimed at providing security for the person and property of the individual is a fundamental function of government, and the grand jury plays an important, constitutionally mandated role in this process. On the records now before us, we perceive no basis for holding that the public interest in law enforcement and in ensuring effective grand jury proceedings is insufficient to override the consequential, but uncertain, burden on newsgathering that is said to result from insisting that reporters, like other citizens, respond to relevant questions put to them in the course of a valid grand jury investigation or criminal trial....

Thus, we cannot seriously entertain the notion that the First Amendment protects a newsman's agreement to conceal the criminal conduct of his source, or evidence thereof, on the theory that it is better to write about crime than to do something about it. Insofar as any reporter in these cases undertook not to reveal or testify about the crime he witnessed, his claim of privilege under the First Amendment presents no substantial question. The crimes of news sources are no less reprehensible and threatening to the public interest when witnessed by a reporter than when they are not....

Accepting the fact, however, that an undetermined number of informants not themselves implicated in crime will nevertheless, for whatever reason, refuse to talk to newsmen if they fear identification by a reporter in an official investigation, we cannot accept the argument that the public interest in possible future news about crime from undisclosed, unverified sources must take precedence over the public interest in pursuing and prosecuting those crimes reported to the press by informants and in thus deterring the commission of such crimes in the future....

Of course, the press has the right to abide by its agreement not to publish all the information it has, but the right to withhold news is not equivalent to a First Amendment exemption from the ordinary duty of all other citizens to furnish relevant information to a grand jury performing an important public function....

We are admonished that refusal to provide a First Amendment reporter's privilege will undermine the freedom of the press to collect and disseminate news. But this is not the lesson history teaches us. As noted previously, the common law recognized no such privilege, and the constitutional argument was not even asserted until 1958. From the beginning of our country the press has operated without constitutional protection for press informants, and the press has flourished....

... The administration of a constitutional newsman's privilege would present practical and conceptual difficulties of a high order. Sooner or later, it would be necessary to define those categories of newsmen who qualified for the privilege, a questionable procedure in light of the traditional doctrine that liberty of the press is the right of the lonely pamphleteer who uses carbon paper or a mimeograph just as much as of the large metropolitan publisher who utilizes the latest photocomposition methods....

At the federal level, Congress has freedom to determine whether a statutory newsman's privilege is necessary and desirable and to fashion standards and rules as narrow or broad as deemed necessary to deal with the evil discerned and, equally important, to refashion those rules as experience from time to time may dictate. There is also merit in leaving state legislatures free, within First Amendment limits, to fashion their own standards in light of the conditions and problems with respect to the relations between law enforcement officials and press in their own areas. It goes without saying, of course, that we are powerless to bar state courts from responding in their own way and construing their own constitutions so as to recognize a newsman's privilege, either qualified or absolute....

Finally, as we have earlier indicated, newsgathering is not without its First Amendment protections, and grand jury investigations if instituted or conducted other than in good faith, would pose wholly different issues for resolution under the First Amendment. Official harassment of the press undertaken not for purposes of law enforcement but to disrupt a reporter's relationship with his news sources would have no justification....

[The *Branzburg* and *Pappas* decisions, which declined to recognize a constitutional reporter's privilege, were affirmed. The lower court decision in *Caldwell,* which had granted the reporter a privilege, was reversed. Three other justices agreed with Justice White's opinion. Justice Powell agreed with the ultimate disposition of the cases, but wrote a separate, concurring opinion. Four justices dissented.]

Justice POWELL, concurring.

I add this brief statement to emphasize what seems to me to be the limited nature of the Court's holding....

As indicated in the concluding portion of the opinion, the Court states that no harassment of newsmen will be tolerated. If a newsman believes that the grand jury investigation is not being conducted in good faith he is not without a remedy.... The asserted claim to privilege should be judged on its facts by the striking of a proper balance between freedom of the press and the obligation of all citizens to give relevant testimony with respect to criminal conduct. The balance of these vital constitutional and societal interests on a case-by-case basis accords with the tried and traditional way of adjudicating such questions.

Justice STEWART, with whom Justice BRENNAN and Justice MARSHALL join, dissenting.

The Court's crabbed view of the First Amendment reflects a disturbing insensitivity to the critical role of an independent press in our society. The question whether a reporter has a constitutional right to a confidential relationship with his source is of first impression here, but the principles that should guide our decision are as basic as any to be found in the Constitution. While Mr. Justice POWELL'S enigmatic concurring opinion gives some hope of a more flexible view in the future, the Court in these cases holds that a newsman has no First Amendment right to protect his sources when called before a grand jury. The Court thus invites state and federal authorities to undermine the historic independence of the press by attempting to annex the journalistic profession as an investigative arm of government. Not only will this decision impair performance of the press' constitutionally protected functions, but it will, I am convinced, in the long run, harm rather than help the administration of justice.

I

A

    … [W]e have held that the right to publish is central to the First Amendment and basic to the existence of constitutional democracy.

    A corollary of the right to publish must be the right to gather news. The full flow of information to the public protected by the free-press guarantee would be severely curtailed if no protection whatever was afforded to the process by which news is assembled and disseminated.…

B

    The right to gather news implies, in turn, a right to a confidential relationship between a reporter and his source. This proposition follows as a matter of simple logic once three factual predicates are recognized: (1) newsmen require informants to gather news; (2) confidentiality—the promise or understanding that names or certain aspects of communications will be kept off the record—is essential to the creation and maintenance of a news-gathering relationship with informants; and (3) an unbridled subpoena power—the absence of a constitutional right protecting, in *any* way, a confidential relationship from compulsory process—will either deter sources from divulging information or deter reporters from gathering and publishing information.…

II

    ….

    In striking the proper balance between the public interest in the efficient administration of justice and the First Amendment guarantee of the fullest flow of information, we must begin with the basic proposition that because of their "delicate and vulnerable" nature, and their transcendent importance for the just functioning of our society, First Amendment rights require special safeguards.

A

    ….

    Accordingly, when a reporter is asked to appear before a grand jury and reveal confidences, I would hold that the government must (1) show that there is probable cause to believe that the newsman has information that is clearly relevant to a specific probable violation of law; (2) demonstrate that the information sought cannot be obtained by alternative means less destructive of First Amendment rights; and (3) demonstrate a compelling and overriding interest in the information.

This is not to say that a grand jury could not issue a subpoena until such a showing were made, and it is not to say that a newsman would be in any way privileged to ignore any subpoena that was issued. Obviously, before the government's burden to make such a showing were triggered, the reporter would have to move to quash the subpoena, asserting the basis on which he considered the particular relationship a confidential one....

IN RE: GRAND JURY SUBPOENA, JUDITH MILLER
U.S. Court of Appeals for the D.C. Circuit, 2005
397 F.3d 964

SENTELLE, Circuit Judge:

An investigative reporter for the New York Times; the White House correspondent for the weekly news magazine, Time; and Time, Inc., the publisher of Time, appeal from orders of the District Court for the District of Columbia finding all three appellants in civil contempt for refusing to give evidence in response to grand jury subpoenas served by Special Counsel Patrick J. Fitzgerald. Appellants assert that the information concealed by them, specifically the identity of confidential sources, is protected by a reporter's privilege arising from the First Amendment, or failing that, by federal common law privilege. The District Court held that neither the First Amendment nor the federal common law provides protection for journalists' confidential sources in the context of a grand jury investigation. For the reasons set forth below, we agree with the District Court that there is no First Amendment privilege protecting the evidence sought. We further conclude that if any such common law privilege exists, it is not absolute, and in this case has been overcome by the filings of the Special Counsel with the District Court. ... We therefore affirm the decision of the District Court.

I. Background

According to the briefs and record before us, the controversy giving rise to this litigation began with a political and news media controversy over a sixteen-word sentence in the State of the Union Address of President George W. Bush on January 28, 2003. In that address, President Bush stated: "The British government has learned that Saddam Hussein recently sought significant quantities of uranium from Africa." The ensuing public controversy focused ... on the accuracy of the proposition that Saddam Hussein had sought uranium, a key ingredient in the development of nuclear weaponry, from Africa. Many publications on the subject followed. On July 6, 2003, the New York Times published an op-ed piece by former Ambassador Joseph Wilson, in which he claimed to have been sent to Niger in 2002 by the Central Intelligence Agency ("CIA") in response to inquiries from Vice President Cheney to investigate whether Iraq had been seeking to purchase uranium from Niger. Wilson claimed that he had conducted the requested investigation and reported on his return that there was no credible evidence that any such effort had been made.

On July 14, 2003, columnist Robert Novak published a column in the Chicago Sun-Times in which he asserted that … "two senior administration officials" told him that Wilson's selection was at the suggestion of Wilson's wife, Valerie Plame, whom Novak described as a CIA "operative on weapons of mass destruction." After Novak's column was published, various media accounts reported that other reporters had been told by government officials that Wilson's wife worked at the CIA monitoring weapons of mass destruction, and that she was involved in her husband's selection for the mission to Niger. …

The Department of Justice undertook an investigation into whether government employees had violated federal law by the unauthorized disclosure of the identity of a CIA agent. As the investigation proceeded, in December of 2003, the Attorney General recused himself from participation and delegated his full authority in the investigation to the Deputy Attorney General as Acting Attorney General. The Deputy, in turn, appointed Patrick J. Fitzgerald, United States Attorney for the Northern District of Illinois, as Special Counsel and delegated full authority concerning the investigation to him. As part of the ongoing investigation, a grand jury investigation began in January of 2004.

In cooperation with Special Counsel Fitzgerald, the grand jury conducted an extensive investigation. On May 21, 2004, a grand jury subpoena was issued to appellant Matthew Cooper, seeking testimony and documents related to two specific articles dated July 17, and July 21, 2003, to which Cooper had contributed. Cooper refused to comply with the subpoena, even after the Special Counsel offered to narrow its scope to cover only conversations between Cooper and a specific individual identified by the Special Counsel. Instead, Cooper moved to quash the subpoena on June 3, 2004. On July 6, the Chief Judge of the United States District Court for the District of Columbia denied Cooper's motion.…

A further grand jury subpoena was issued to Time, Inc., seeking the same documents requested in the subpoena to Cooper. Time also moved to quash its subpoena. On August 6, 2004, the District Court denied Time's motion. Both Cooper and Time refused to comply with the subpoenas despite the District Court's denial of their motions to quash. The District Court thereafter found that Cooper and Time had refused to comply with the subpoenas without just cause and held them in civil contempt of court. After both Cooper and Time had filed appeals, and further negotiations between Special Counsel and the two had proceeded, Cooper agreed to provide testimony and documents relevant to a specific source who had stated that he had no objection to their release. Cooper and Time fulfilled their obligations under the agreement, the Special Counsel moved to vacate the District Court's contempt order, and the notices of appeal were voluntarily dismissed.

On September 13, 2004, the grand jury issued a further subpoena to Cooper seeking "any and all documents … [relating to] conversations between Matthew Cooper and official source(s) prior to July 14, 2003, concerning in any way: former Ambassador Joseph Wilson; the 2002 trip by former Ambassador Wilson to Niger; Valerie Wilson Plame, a/k/a Valerie Wilson, a/k/a Valerie Plame (the wife of former Ambassador Wilson); and/or any affiliation between Valerie Wilson Plame and the CIA." An August 2, 2004 subpoena to Time requested "all notes, tape recordings, e-mails, or other documents of Matthew Cooper relating to the July 17, 2003 Time.com article entitled 'A War on Wilson?' and the July 21,

2003 Time Magazine article entitled, 'A Question of Trust.'" Cooper and Time again moved to quash the subpoenas, and on October 7, 2004, the District Court denied the motion. The two refused to comply with the subpoenas, and on October 13, 2004, the District Court held that their refusal was without just cause and held both in contempt.

In the meantime, on August 12 and August 14, grand jury subpoenas were issued to Judith Miller, seeking documents and testimony related to conversations between her and a specified government official "occurring from on or about July 6, 2003, to on or about July 13, 2003, ... concerning Valerie Plame Wilson (whether referred to by name or by description as the wife of Ambassador Wilson) or concerning Iraqi efforts to obtain uranium." Miller refused to comply with the subpoenas and moved to quash them. The District Court denied Miller's motion to quash. Thereafter, the court found that Miller had refused to comply without just cause and held her in civil contempt of court also. She also has appealed.

The appellants have proceeded ... in a consolidated proceeding before this court....

II. Analysis

The First Amendment Claim

In his opinion below, the Chief District Judge held that "a reporter called to testify before a grand jury regarding confidential information enjoys no First Amendment protection." Appellants argue that "this proposition of law is flatly contrary to the great weight of authority in this and other circuits." Appellants are wrong. The governing authority in this case, as the District Court correctly held, comes not from this or any other circuit, but the Supreme Court of the United States. In *Branzburg v. Hayes* the Highest Court considered and rejected the same claim of First Amendment privilege on facts materially indistinguishable from those at bar....

On the record before us, there is at least sufficient allegation to warrant grand jury inquiry that one or both journalists received information concerning the identity of a covert operative of the United States from government employees acting in violation of the law by making the disclosure. Each petitioner in *Branzburg* and each journalist before us claimed or claims the protection of a First Amendment reporter's privilege. The Supreme Court in no uncertain terms rejected the existence of such a privilege. As we said at the outset of this discussion, the Supreme Court has already decided the First Amendment issue before us today.

In rejecting the claim of privilege, the Supreme Court made its reasoning transparent and forceful. The High Court recognized that "the grand jury's authority to subpoena witnesses is not only historic . . . but essential to its task."...

Lest there be any mistake as to the breadth of the rejection of the claimed First Amendment privilege, the High Court went on to recognize that "there remain those situations where a source is not engaged in criminal conduct but has information suggesting illegal conduct by others." As to this category of informants, the Court was equally adamant in rejecting the claim of First Amendment privilege:

We cannot accept the argument that the public interest in possible future news about crime from undisclosed, unverified sources must take precedence over the public interest in pursuing and prosecuting those crimes reported to the press by informants and in thus deterring the commission of such crimes in the future.

The *Branzburg* Court further supported the rejection of this claimed privilege by the commonsense observation that "it is obvious that agreements to conceal information relevant to the commission of crime have very little to recommend them from the standpoint of public policy."... We have pressed appellants for some distinction between the facts before the Supreme Court in *Branzburg* and those before us today. They have offered none, nor have we independently found any. ... The Highest Court has spoken and never revisited the question. Without doubt, that is the end of the matter.

Despite the absolute and unreversed answer to the question of constitutional privilege by the Supreme Court in *Branzburg*, appellants nonetheless persist in arguing that the District Court erred in concluding that journalists subpoenaed to reveal their confidential sources before federal grand juries enjoy no First Amendment protection. They base this argument on the concurring opinion of Justice Powell in *Branzburg* and a case from this circuit, *Zerilli v. Smith*. These authorities, either separately or together, provide no support for the existence of such a privilege protecting reporters subpoenaed to a grand jury. ...

Justice Powell's concurring opinion was not the opinion of a justice who refused to join the majority. He joined the majority by its terms, rejecting none of Justice White's reasoning on behalf of the majority. He wrote separately "to emphasize" what seemed to him "to be the limited nature of the Court's holding." Justice White's opinion is not a plurality opinion of four justices joined by a separate Justice Powell to create a majority; it is the opinion of the majority of the Court. As such it is authoritative precedent. It says what it says. It rejects the privilege asserted by appellants....

Zerilli cannot possibly help appellants, although they assert that *Zerilli*, citing Justice Powell's "deciding vote" in *Branzburg*, recognized, at least in dicta, a reporter's privilege in civil cases and held that *Branzburg* was not controlling as to that issue. Indeed, the *Zerilli* Court expressly distinguished its case from *Branzburg*. ... Even if *Zerilli* states the law applicable to civil cases, this is not a civil case....

The Common Law Privilege

Appellants argue that even if there is no First Amendment privilege protecting their confidential source information, we should recognize a privilege under federal common law, arguing that regardless of whether a federal common law privilege protecting reporters existed in 1972 when *Branzburg* was decided, in the intervening years much has changed. While appellants argue for an absolute privilege under the common law, they wisely recognize the possibility that a court not recognizing such an absolute privilege might nonetheless find a qualified privilege. They therefore also argue that if there is a qualified privilege, then the government has not overcome that qualified privilege. The Court is not of one mind on the existence of a common law privilege. Judge Sentelle would hold that there is no such common law privilege .... Judge Tatel would hold that there is such a common law privilege. Judge Henderson believes that we need not, and therefore should not, reach that question. However, all believe that if there is any such privilege, it is not absolute and may be overcome by an appropriate showing. All further believe ... that if such a privilege applies here, it has been overcome. Therefore, the common law privilege, even if one exists, does not warrant reversal....

Department of Justice Guidelines

In their final argument for reversal of the District Court's contempt finding, appellants contend that the Special Counsel did not comply with the Department of Justice guidelines for issuing subpoenas to news media and that such failure provides an independent basis for reversal. The District Court expressed its doubt that the DOJ guidelines were enforceable, but found that even if they were, Special Counsel had fully complied with the guidelines. Because we conclude that the guidelines create no enforceable right, we need not reach the question of the Special Counsel's compliance. The guidelines in question are set forth in 28 C.F.R. § 50.10.... Those guidelines provide that subpoenas for testimony by news media must be approved by the Attorney General, a requirement not pertinent in the present case as the Special Counsel had received delegation of all the Attorney General's authority, and should meet the following standards:

(a) "In criminal cases, there should be reasonable grounds to believe, based on information obtained from nonmedia sources, that a crime has occurred, and that the information sought is essential to a successful investigation-particularly with reference to establishing guilt or innocence. The subpoena should not be used to obtain peripheral, nonessential, or speculative information."

(b) Before issuing a subpoena to a member of the news media, all reasonable efforts should be made to obtain the desired information from alternative sources.

(c) Wherever possible, subpoenas should be directed at information regarding a limited subject matter and a reasonably limited period of time. Subpoenas should avoid requiring production of a large volume of unpublished materials and provide reasonable notice of the demand for documents.

(d) "The use of subpoenas to members of the news media should, except under exigent circumstances, be limited to the verification of published information and to such surrounding circumstances as relate to the accuracy of the published information."

(e) When issuance of a subpoena to a member of the media is contemplated, the government shall pursue negotiations with the relevant media organization. The negotiations should seek accommodation of the interests of the grand jury and the media. Where the nature of the investigation permits, the government should make clear what its needs are in a particular case as well as its willingness to respond to particular problems of the media.

However, as the District Court correctly observed, the guidelines expressly state that they do "not create or recognize any legally enforceable right in any person."...

III. Conclusion

For the reasons set forth above, the judgment of the District Court is affirmed.

COHEN V. COWLES MEDIA CO.

Supreme Court of the United States, 1991
501 U.S. 663

Justice WHITE delivered the opinion of the Court.

The question before us is whether the First Amendment prohibits a plaintiff from re-covering damages, under state promissory estoppel law, for a newspaper's breach of a promise of confidentiality given to the plaintiff in exchange for information. We hold that it does not.

During the closing days of the 1982 Minnesota gubernatorial race, Dan Cohen, an active Republican associated with Wheelock Whitney's Independent-Republican gubernatorial campaign, approached reporters from the *St. Paul Pioneer Press Dispatch* (*Pioneer Press*) and the *Minneapolis Star and Tribune* (*Star Tribune*) and offered to provide documents relating to a candidate in the upcoming election. Cohen made clear to the reporters that he would provide the information only if he was given a promise of confidentiality. Reporters from both papers promised to keep Cohen's identity anonymous and Cohen turned over copies of two public court records concerning Marlene Johnson, the Democratic-Farmer-Labor candidate for Lieutenant Governor. The first record indicated that Johnson had been charged in 1969 with three counts of unlawful assembly, and the second that she had been convicted in 1970 of petit theft.... As it turned out, the unlawful assembly charges arose out of Johnson's participation in a protest of an alleged failure to hire minority workers on municipal construction projects and the charges were eventually dismissed. The petit theft conviction was for leaving a store without paying for $6.00 worth of sewing materials. The incident apparently occurred at a time during which Johnson was emotionally distraught, and the conviction was later vacated.

After consultation and debate, the editorial staffs of the two newspapers independently decided to publish Cohen's name as part of their stories concerning Johnson. In their stories, both papers identified Cohen as the source of the court records, indicated his connection to the Whitney campaign, and included denials by Whitney campaign officials of any role in the matter. The same day the stories appeared, Cohen was fired by his employer.

Cohen sued respondents, the publishers of the *Pioneer Press* and *Star Tribune,* in Minnesota state court, alleging ... breach of contract. The trial court rejected respondents' argument that the First Amendment barred Cohen's lawsuit. A jury returned a verdict in Cohen's favor, awarding him $200,000 in compensatory damages ...

A divided Minnesota Supreme Court reversed the compensatory damages award.... [T]he court considered his breach of contract claim and concluded that "a contract cause of action is inappropriate for these particular circumstances." The court then went on to address the question whether Cohen could establish a cause of action under Minnesota law on a promissory estoppel theory....

... After a brief discussion, the court concluded that "in this case enforcement of the promise of confidentiality under a promissory estoppel theory would violate defendants' First Amendment rights."...

Respondents rely on the proposition that "if a newspaper lawfully obtains truthful information about a matter of public significance then state officials may not constitutionally punish publication of the information, absent a need to further a state interest of the highest order." *Smith v. Daily Mail Publishing Co.*, 443 U.S. 97, 103 (1979). That proposition is unexceptionable, and it has been applied in various cases that have found insufficient the asserted state interests in preventing publication of truthful, lawfully obtained information. See, e.g., *The Florida Star v. B.J.F.*, 491 U.S. 524 (1989); *Smith v. Daily Mail, supra*; *Landmark Communications, Inc. v. Virginia*, 435 U.S. 829 (1978).

This case, however, is not controlled by this line of cases but rather by the equally well-established line of decisions holding that generally applicable laws do not offend the First Amendment simply because their enforcement against the press has incidental effects on its ability to gather and report the news. As the cases relied on by respondents recognize, the truthful information sought to be published must have been lawfully acquired. The press may not with impunity break and enter an office or dwelling to gather news. Neither does the First Amendment relieve a newspaper reporter of the obligation shared by all citizens to respond to a grand jury subpoena and answer questions relevant to a criminal investigation, even though the reporter might be required to reveal a confidential source. *Branzburg v. Hayes*, 408 U.S. 665 (1972). The press, like others interested in publishing, may not publish copyrighted material without obeying the copyright laws. See *Zacchini v. Scripps-Howard Broadcasting Co.*, 433 U.S. 562, 576-579 (1977).... It is therefore beyond dispute that "[t]he publisher of a newspaper has no special immunity from the application of general laws. He has no special privilege to invade the rights and liberties of others." Accordingly, enforcement of such general laws against the press is not subject to stricter scrutiny than would be applied to enforcement against other persons or organizations.

There can be little doubt that the Minnesota doctrine of promissory estoppel is a law of general applicability. It does not target or single out the press. Rather, insofar as we are advised, the doctrine is generally applicable to the daily transactions of all the citizens of Minnesota. The First Amendment does not forbid its application to the press....

... Unlike the situation in *The Florida Star*, where the rape victim's name was obtained through lawful access to a police report, respondents obtained Cohen's name only by making a promise that they did not honor....

Respondents ... argue that permitting Cohen to maintain a cause of action for promissory estoppel will inhibit truthful reporting because news organizations will have legal incentives not to disclose a confidential source's identity even when that person's identity is itself newsworthy.... But if this is the case, it is no more than the incidental, and constitutionally insignificant, consequence of applying to the press a generally applicable law that requires those who make certain kinds of promises to keep them.... Accordingly, the judgment of the Minnesota Supreme Court is reversed, and the case is remanded for further proceedings not inconsistent with this opinion.

Chapter Eight
CREATIVE PROPERTY

The communications industries are based, to a significant extent, on the production and marketing of creative property—mainly copyrights, and to some degree also trademarks. For most communicators the primary aim is not the manufacture of physical property, be it videocassettes or pieces of paper. Rather, it is the creative, "intellectual" material embodied *on* the videotape or paper that is of paramount value. It could be a news story, a screenplay, or an advertising jingle. The law recognizes these intangible creations as specialized forms of property. In this section are several cases dealing with the creation and protection of such property.

Eldred v. Ashcroft is the Supreme Court's most recent copyright case, and a good one to begin with because it looks at Congress' constitutional authority to enact copyright statutes as it sees fit.

Feist Publications v. Rural Telephone Service Co. examines the essential ingredients necessary for copyright. In particular, the Court in this case explains the degree of "originality" that must be evident.

Community for Creative Non-Violence v. Reid is the Supreme Court's key case on the "work made for hire" doctrine which, in the absence of an agreement, determines who owns a copyright.

Harper & Row Publishers v. Nation Enterprises is a highly instructive case for understanding the fair use doctrine—a limited exception to the exclusive control normally enjoyed by a copyright owner.

Campbell v. Acuff-Rose Music, Inc., a recent Supreme Court decision, concerns the important fair use doctrine and its application to works of parody.

MGM Studios v. Grokster was a much-anticipated Supreme Court decision in 2005, dealing with the hugely popular practice of "peer-to-peer" digital file sharing of copyrighted works – and whether the providers of such file sharing technology may be held liable for the resulting infringements.

Time, Inc. v. Petersen Publishing Co. is a recent trademark infringement case illustrating the kind of legal analysis that may be necessary when two media companies lay claim to the same name for a magazine.

ELDRED V. ASHCROFT
Supreme Court of the United States, 2003
537 U.S. 186

Justice GINSBURG delivered the opinion of the Court.

This case concerns the authority the Constitution assigns to Congress to prescribe the duration of copyrights. The Copyright and Patent Clause of the Constitution, Art. I, §8, cl.

169

8, provides as to copyrights: "Congress shall have Power … [t]o promote the Progress of Science … by securing [to Authors] for limited Times … the exclusive Right to their … Writings." In 1998, in the measure here under inspection, Congress enlarged the duration of copyrights by twenty years. Copyright Term Extension Act (CTEA) (amending 17 U. S. C. §§302, 304). As in the case of prior extensions, principally in 1831, 1909, and 1976, Congress provided for application of the enlarged terms to existing and future copyrights alike.

Petitioners are individuals and businesses whose products or services build on copyrighted works that have gone into the public domain. They seek a determination that the CTEA fails constitutional review under both the Copyright Clause's "limited Times" prescription and the First Amendment's free speech guarantee. Under the 1976 Copyright Act, copyright protection generally lasted from the work's creation until fifty years after the author's death. Under the CTEA, most copyrights now run from creation until seventy years after the author's death. Petitioners do not challenge the "life-plus-seventy-years" time span itself. "Whether fifty years is enough, or seventy years too much," they acknowledge, "is not a judgment meet for this Court." Congress went awry, petitioners maintain, not with respect to newly created works, but in enlarging the term for published works with existing copyrights. The "limited Tim[e]" in effect when a copyright is secured, petitioners urge, becomes the constitutional boundary, a clear line beyond the power of Congress to extend. As to the First Amendment, petitioners contend that the CTEA is a content-neutral regulation of speech that fails inspection under the heightened judicial scrutiny appropriate for such regulations….

I

A

We evaluate petitioners' challenge to the constitutionality of the CTEA against the backdrop of Congress' previous exercises of its authority under the Copyright Clause. The Nation's first copyright statute, enacted in 1790, provided a federal copyright term of fourteen years from the date of publication, renewable for an additional fourteen years if the author survived the first term. The 1790 Act's renewable fourteen-year term applied to existing works (i.e., works already published and works created but not yet published) and future works alike. Congress expanded the federal copyright term to forty-two years in 1831 (twenty-eight years from publication, renewable for an additional fourteen years), and to fifty-six years in 1909 (twenty-eight years from publication, renewable for an additional twenty-eight years). Both times, Congress applied the new copyright term to existing and future works.

In 1976, Congress altered the method for computing federal copyright terms. For works created by identified natural persons, the 1976 Act provided that federal copyright protection would run from the work's creation, not—as in the 1790, 1831, and 1909 Acts—its publication; protection would last until fifty years after the author's death. In these respects, the 1976 Act aligned United States copyright terms with the then-dominant international standard adopted under the Berne Convention for the Protection of Literary and Artistic Works. For anonymous works, pseudonymous works, and works made for hire, the 1976 Act provided a term of seventy-five years from publication or 100 years from creation, whichever expired first.

These new copyright terms, the 1976 Act instructed, governed all works not published by its effective date of January 1, 1978, regardless of when the works were created. For published works with existing copyrights as of that date, the 1976 Act granted a copyright term of seventy-five years from the date of publication, a nineteen-year increase over the fifty-six-year term applicable under the 1909 Act.

The measure at issue here, the CTEA, installed the fourth major duration extension of federal copyrights. Retaining the general structure of the 1976 Act, the CTEA enlarges the terms of all existing and future copyrights by twenty years…. This standard harmonizes the baseline United States copyright term with the term adopted by the European Union in 1993….

… For works published before 1978 with existing copyrights as of the CTEA's effective date, the CTEA extends the term to ninety-five years from publication. Thus, in common with the 1831, 1909, and 1976 Acts, the CTEA's new terms apply to both future and existing copyrights.

B

… [T]he District Court entered judgment for the Attorney General (respondent here)…. The Court of Appeals for the District of Columbia Circuit affirmed….

We granted certiorari to address two questions: whether the CTEA's extension of existing copyrights exceeds Congress' power under the Copyright Clause; and whether the CTEA's extension of existing and future copyrights violates the First Amendment. We now answer those two questions in the negative and affirm.

II

A

We address first the determination of the courts below that Congress has authority under the Copyright Clause to extend the terms of existing copyrights. Text, history, and precedent, we conclude, confirm that the Copyright Clause empowers Congress to prescribe "limited Times" for copyright protection and to secure the same level and duration of protection for all copyright holders, present and future.

The CTEA's baseline term of life plus seventy years, petitioners concede, qualifies as a "limited Tim[e]" as applied to future copyrights. Petitioners contend, however, that existing copyrights extended to endure for that same term are not "limited." Petitioners' argument essentially reads into the text of the Copyright Clause the command that a time prescription, once set, becomes forever "fixed" or "inalterable." The word "limited," however, does not convey a meaning so constricted…. [A] time span appropriately "limited" as applied to future copyrights does not automatically cease to be "limited" when applied to existing copyrights….

To comprehend the scope of Congress' power under the Copyright Clause, "a page of history is worth a volume of logic." History reveals an unbroken congressional practice of granting to authors of works with existing copyrights the benefit of term extensions so that all under copyright protection will be governed evenhandedly under the same regime. As earlier recounted, the First Congress accorded the protections of the Nation's first federal copyright statute to existing and future works alike….

Congress' consistent historical practice of applying newly enacted copyright terms to future and existing copyrights reflects a judgment stated concisely by Representative Huntington at the time of the 1831 Act: "[J]ustice, policy, and equity alike forb[id]" that an "author who had sold his [work] a week ago, be placed in a worse situation than the author who should sell his work the day after the passing of [the] act." The CTEA follows this historical practice by keeping the duration provisions of the 1976 Act largely in place and simply adding twenty years to each of them. Guided by text, history, and precedent, we cannot agree with petitioners' submission that extending the duration of existing copyrights is categorically beyond Congress' authority under the Copyright Clause.

Satisfied that the CTEA complies with the "limited Times" prescription, we turn now to whether it is a rational exercise of the legislative authority conferred by the Copyright Clause. On that point, we defer substantially to Congress....

The CTEA reflects judgments of a kind Congress typically makes, judgments we cannot dismiss as outside the Legislature's domain. As respondent describes, a key factor in the CTEA's passage was a 1993 European Union (EU) directive instructing EU members to establish a copyright term of life plus seventy years. Consistent with the Berne Convention, the EU directed its members to deny this longer term to the works of any non-EU country whose laws did not secure the same extended term. By extending the baseline United States copyright term to life plus seventy years, Congress sought to ensure that American authors would receive the same copyright protection in Europe as their European counterparts....

In sum, we find that the CTEA is a rational enactment; we are not at liberty to second-guess congressional determinations and policy judgments of this order, however debatable or arguably unwise they may be. Accordingly, we cannot conclude that the CTEA—which continues the unbroken congressional practice of treating future and existing copyrights in parity for term extension purposes—is an impermissible exercise of Congress' power under the Copyright Clause.

B

Petitioners' Copyright Clause arguments rely on several novel readings of the Clause. We next address these arguments and explain why we find them unpersuasive.

Petitioners contend that even if the CTEA's twenty-year term extension is literally a "limited Tim[e]," permitting Congress to extend existing copyrights allows it to evade the "limited Times" constraint by creating effectively perpetual copyrights through repeated extensions. We disagree.

As the Court of Appeals observed, a regime of perpetual copyrights "clearly is not the situation before us." Nothing before this Court warrants construction of the CTEA's twenty-year term extension as a congressional attempt to evade or override the "limited Times" constraint. Critically, we again emphasize, petitioners fail to show how the CTEA crosses a constitutionally significant threshold with respect to "limited Times" that the 1831, 1909, and 1976 Acts did not....

...

... [P]etitioners contend that the CTEA's extension of existing copyrights does not "promote the Progress of Science" as contemplated by the preambular language of the Copyright Clause. ... [T]hey maintain that the preambular language identifies the sole end to which Congress may legislate; accordingly, they conclude, the meaning of "limited Times" must be "determined in light of that specified end." The CTEA's extension of existing copyrights categorically fails to "promote the Progress of Science," petitioners argue, because it does not stimulate the creation of new works but merely adds value to works already created.

As petitioners point out, we have described the Copyright Clause as "both a grant of power and a limitation" and have said that "[t]he primary objective of copyright" is "[t]o promote the Progress of Science." The "constitutional command," we have recognized, is that Congress, to the extent it enacts copyright laws at all, create a "system" that "promote[s] the Progress of Science."

We have also stressed, however, that it is generally for Congress, not the courts, to decide how best to pursue the Copyright Clause's objectives. The justifications we earlier set out for Congress' enactment of the CTEA provide a rational basis for the conclusion that the CTEA "promote[s] the Progress of Science."...

For the several reasons stated, we find no Copyright Clause impediment to the CTEA's extension of existing copyrights.

III

Petitioners separately argue that the CTEA is a content-neutral regulation of speech that fails heightened judicial review under the First Amendment. We reject petitioners' plea for imposition of uncommonly strict scrutiny on a copyright scheme that incorporates its own speech-protective purposes and safeguards. The Copyright Clause and First Amendment were adopted close in time. This proximity indicates that, in the Framers' view, copyright's limited monopolies are compatible with free speech principles. Indeed, copyright's purpose is to promote the creation and publication of free expression. As *Harper & Row* observed: "[T]he Framers intended copyright itself to be the engine of free expression. By establishing a marketable right to the use of one's expression, copyright supplies the economic incentive to create and disseminate ideas."

In addition to spurring the creation and publication of new expression, copyright law contains built-in First Amendment accommodations. First, it distinguishes between ideas and expression and makes only the latter eligible for copyright protection. Specifically, 17 U. S. C. §102(b) provides: "In no case does copyright protection for an original work of authorship extend to any idea, procedure, process, system, method of operation, concept, principle, or discovery, regardless of the form in which it is described, explained, illustrated, or embodied in such work." As we said in *Harper & Row*, this "idea/expression dichotomy strike[s] a definitional balance between the First Amendment and the Copyright Act by permitting free communication of facts while still protecting an author's expression." Due to this distinction, every idea, theory, and fact in a copyrighted work becomes instantly available for public exploitation at the moment of publication.

Second, the "fair use" defense allows the public to use not only facts and ideas contained in a copyrighted work, but also expression itself in certain circumstances. Codified at 17 U. S. C. §107, the defense provides: "[T]he fair use of a copyrighted work, including such use by reproduction in copies ... , for purposes such as criticism, comment, news reporting, teaching (including multiple copies for classroom use), scholarship, or research, is not an infringement of copyright." The fair use defense affords considerable "latitude for scholarship and comment," *Harper & Row,* 471 U. S., at 560, and even for parody, see *Campbell v. Acuff-Rose Music, Inc.,* 510 U. S. 569 (1994) (rap group's musical parody of Roy Orbison's "Oh, Pretty Woman" may be fair use).

The CTEA itself supplements these traditional First Amendment safeguards. First, it allows libraries, archives, and similar institutions to "reproduce" and "distribute, display, or perform in facsimile or digital form" copies of certain published works "during the last twenty years of any term of copyright ... for purposes of preservation, scholarship, or research" if the work is not already being exploited commercially and further copies are unavailable at a reasonable price. 17 U. S. C. §108(h). Second, Title II of the CTEA, known as the Fairness in Music Licensing Act of 1998, exempts small businesses, restaurants, and like entities from having to pay performance royalties on music played from licensed radio, television, and similar facilities. 17 U. S. C. §110(5)(B)....

IV

...

As we read the Framers' instruction, the Copyright Clause empowers Congress to determine the intellectual property regimes that, overall, in that body's judgment, will serve the ends of the Clause. Beneath the facade of their inventive constitutional interpretation, petitioners forcefully urge that Congress pursued very bad policy in prescribing the CTEA's long terms. The wisdom of Congress' action, however, is not within our province to second guess. Satisfied that the legislation before us remains inside the domain the Constitution assigns to the First Branch, we affirm the judgment of the Court of Appeals.
It is so ordered.

FEIST PUBLICATIONS V. RURAL TELEPHONE SERVICE CO.
Supreme Court of the United States, 1991
499 U.S. 340

Justice O' CONNOR delivered the opinion of the court.

This case requires us to clarify the extent of copyright protection available to telephone directory white pages.

I

Rural Telephone Service Company is a certified public utility that provides service to several communities in northwest Kansas to issue annually an updated telephone directory.... The white pages list in alphabetical order the names of Rural's subscribers, together with their towns and telephone numbers. The yellow pages list Rural's business subscribers alphabetically by category and feature classified advertisements of various sizes....
Feist Publications, Inc., is a publishing company that specializes in area-wide telephone directories. Unlike a typical directory, which covers only a particular calling area, Feist's area-wide directories cover a much larger geographical range, reducing the need to call directory assistance or consult multiple directories. The Feist directory that is subject of this

litigation covers eleven different telephone service areas in fifteen counties and contains 46,878 white pages listings—compared to Rural's approximately 7,700 listings. Like Rural's directory, Feist's is distributed free of charge and includes both white pages and yellow pages. Feist and Rural compete vigorously for yellow pages advertising.

As the sole provider of telephone service in its service area, Rural obtains subscriber information quite easily. Persons desiring telephone service must apply to Rural and provide their name and addresses; Rural then assigns them a telephone number. Feist is not a telephone company, let alone one with monopoly status, and therefore lacks independent access to any subscriber information. To obtain white pages listings for its area-wide directory, Feist approaches each of the eleven telephone companies operating in northwest Kansas and offers to pay for the right to use its white pages.

Of the eleven telephone companies, only Rural refused to license its listings to Feist. Rural's refusal created a problem for Feist as omitting these listings would have left a gaping hole in its area-wide directory, rendering it less attractive to potential yellow pages advertisers....

Unable to license Rural's white pages listings, Feist used them without Rural's consent. Feist began by removing several thousand listings that fell outside the geographic range of its area-wide directory, then hired personnel to investigate the 4,935 that remained. These employees verified the data reported by Rural and sought to obtain additional information. As a result, a typical Feist listing includes the individual's street address; most of Rural's listings do not. Notwithstanding these additions, however, 1309 of the 46,878 listings in Feist's 1983 directory were identical to the listings in Rural's 1982-1983 white pages. Four of these were fictitious listings that Rural had inserted into its directory to detect copying.

Rural sued for copyright infringement in the District Court for the District of Kansas taking the position Feist, in compiling its own directory, could not use the information contained in Rural's white pages.... The District Court granted summary judgment to Rural, explaining that "[c]ourts have consistently held that telephone directories are copyrightable" and citing a string of lower court decisions. In an unpublished opinion, the Court of Appeals for the Tenth Circuit affirmed "for substantially the reasons given by the district court." ...

II

A

This case concerns the interaction of two well-established propositions. The first is that facts are not copyrightable; the other, that compilations of facts generally are. Each of these propositions possesses an impeccable pedigree. That there can be no valid copyright in facts is universally understood. The most fundamental axiom of copyright laws is that "[n]o author may copyright his ideas or the facts he narrates." ... At the same time, however, it is beyond dispute that compilations of facts are within the subject matter of copyright. Compilations were expressly mentioned in the Copyright Act of 1909, and again in the Copyright Act of 1979.

There is an undeniable tension between these two propositions. Many compilations consist of nothing but raw data—i.e., wholly factual information not accompanied by any original written expression. On what basis may one claim a copyright in such a work? Common sense tells us that 100 uncopyrightable facts do not magically change their status when gathered together in one place. Yet copyright law seems to contemplate that compilations that consist exclusively of facts are potentially within its scope.

The key to resolving the tension lies in understanding why facts are not copyrightable.... To qualify for copyright protection, a work must be original to the author.... Original, as the term is used in copyright, means only that the work has been independently created by the author (as opposed to copied from other works), and that it possesses at least some minimal degree of creativity. To be sure, the requisite level of creativity is extremely low; even a slight amount will suffice. The vast majority of works make the grade quite easily, as they possess some creative spark, "no matter how crude, humble, or obvious" it might be. Originality does not signify novelty. A work may be original even though it closely resembles other works so long as the similarities are fortuitous, and not the result of copy....

Originality is a constitutional requirement....

It is this bedrock principle of copyright that mandates the law's seemingly disparate treatment of facts and factual compilations. "No one may claim originality as to facts." This is because facts do not owe their origin to an act of authorship. The distinction is one between creation and discovery: the first has not created the fact; he or she has merely discovered its existence.... Census-takers, for example, do not "create" the population figures that emerge from their efforts: in a sense, they copy these figures from the world around them. Census data therefore do not trigger copyright because these data are not "original" in the constitutional sense. The same is true of all facts—scientific, historical, biographical, and news of the day....

Factual compilations, on the other hand, may possess the requisite originality. The compilation author typically chooses which facts to include, in what order to place them, and how to arrange the collected data so that they may be used effectively by readers. These choices as to selection and arrangement, so long as they are made independently by the compiler and are sufficiently original that Congress may protect such compilations through the copyright laws. Thus, even a directory that contains absolutely no protectable written expression, only facts, meets the constitution minimum for copyright protection if it features an original selection or arrangement.

This protection is subject to an important limitation. The mere fact that a work is copyrighted does not mean that every element of the work may be protected.... [C]opyright protection may extend only to those components of a work that are original to the author....

This inevitably means that the copyright in a factual compilation is thin. Notwithstanding a valid copyright, a subsequent compiler remains free to use the facts contained in another's publication to aid in preparing a competing work, so long as the competing work does not feature the same selection and arrangement....

C

The definition of "compilation" is found in § 101 of the 1976 Act. It defines a "compilation" in the copyright sense as "a work formed by the collection and assembly of preexisting materials or of data *that* are selected, coordinated, or arranged *in such a way that* the resulting work as a whole constitutes an original work of authorship" (emphasis added).

The purpose of the statutory definition is to emphasize that collections of facts are not copyrightable per se. It conveys this message through its tripartite structure, as emphasized above by italics. The statute identifies three distinct elements and requires each to be met for a work to qualify as a copyrightable compilation: (1) the collection and assembly of preexisting material, facts, or data; (2) the selection, coordination, or arrangement of those materials; and (3) the creation, by virtue of the particular selection, coordination, or arrangement, of an "original" work of authorship....

Not every selection, coordination, or arrangement will pass muster. This is plain from the statute. It states that, to merit protection, the facts must be selected, coordinated, or arranged "in such a way" as to render the work as a whole original. This implies that some "ways" will trigger copyright, but others will not....

III

There is no doubt that Feist took from the white pages of Rural's directory a substantial amount of factual information. At a minimum, Feist copied the names, towns, and telephone numbers of 1,309 of Rural's subscribers. Not all copying, however, is copyright infringement. To establish infringement, two elements must be proven: (1) ownership of a valid copyright, and (2) copying of constituent elements of the work that are original. The first element is not at issue here; Feist appears to concede that Rural's directory, considered as a whole, is subject to a valid copyright because it contains some forward text, as well as original materials in its yellow pages advertisements.

The question is whether Rural has proved the second element. In other words, did Feist, by taking 1309 names, towns, and telephone numbers from Rural's white pages, copy anything that was "original" to Rural? Certainly, the raw data does not satisfy the originality requirement. Rural may have been the first to discover and report the names, towns, and telephone numbers of its subscribers, but this data does not "'ow[e] its origin'" to Rural. Rather, these bits of information are uncopyrightable facts; they existed before Rural reported them and would have continued to exist if Rural had never published a telephone directory....

The question that remains is whether Rural selected, coordinated, or arranged these uncopyrightable facts in an original way. As mentioned, originality is not a stringent standard; it does not require that facts be presented in an innovative or surprising way. It is equally true, however, that the selection and arrangement of facts cannot be so mechanical or routine as to require no creativity whatsoever....

The selection, coordination, and arrangement of Rural's white pages do not satisfy the minimum constitutional standard for copyright protection.... Rural's white pages are entirely typical. Persons desiring telephone service in Rural's service area fill out an application and Rural issues them a telephone number. In preparing its white pages, Rural simply takes the data provided by its subscribers and lists it alphabetically by surname. The end product is a garden-variety white pages directory, devoid of even the slightest trace of creativity.

Rural's selection of listings could not be more obvious: it publishes the most basic information—about each person who applies to it for telephone service. This is "selection" of a sort, but it lacks the modicum of creativity necessary to transform the mere selection into copyrightable expression. Rural extended sufficient effort to make the white pages directory useful, but insufficient creativity to make it original....

Nor can Rural claim originality in its coordination and arrangement of facts. The white pages can do nothing more than list Rural's subscribers in alphabetical order. This arrangement may, technically speaking, owe its origin to Rural; no one disputes that Rural undertook the task of alphabetizing the names itself. But there is nothing remotely creative about arranging names alphabetically in a white pages directory....

We conclude that the names, towns, and telephone numbers copied by Feist were not original to Rural and therefore not protected by the copyright in Rural's combined white and yellow pages directory....

Because Rural's white pages lack the requisite originality, Feist's uses of listings cannot constitute infringement. This decision should not be construed as a demeaning of Rural's efforts in compiling its directory, but rather as making clear that copyright rewards originality, not effort.

COMMUNITY FOR CREATIVE NON-VIOLENCE V. REID
Supreme Court of the United States, 1989
490 U.S. 730

Justice MARSHALL delivered the opinion of the Court.

In this case, an artist and the organization that hired him to produce a sculpture contest the ownership of the copyright in that work. To resolve this dispute, we must construe the "work made for hire" provisions of the Copyright Act of 1976, and in particular, the provision in § 101, which defines as a "work made for hire" a "work prepared by an employee within the scope of his or her employment."

I

Petitioners are the Community for Creative Non-Violence (CCNV), a nonprofit, unincorporated association dedicated to eliminating homelessness in America, and Mitch Snyder, a member and trustee of CCNV. In the fall of 1985, CCNV decided to participate in the annual Christmastime Pageant of Peace in Washington, D. C., by sponsoring a display to dramatize the plight of the homeless. As the District Court recounted:

> "Snyder and fellow CCNV members conceived the idea for the nature of the display: a sculpture of a modern Nativity scene in which, in lieu of the traditional Holy Family, the two adult figures and the infant would appear as contemporary homeless people huddled on a street-side steam grate."...

Snyder made inquiries to locate an artist to produce the sculpture. He was referred to respondent James Earl Reid, a Baltimore, Maryland, sculptor. In the course of two telephone calls, Reid agreed to sculpt the three human figures. CCNV agreed to make the steam grate and pedestal for the statue. Reid proposed that the work be cast in bronze, at a total cost of approximately $100,000 and taking six to eight months to complete. Snyder rejected that proposal because CCNV did not have sufficient funds, and because the statue had to be completed by December 12 to be included in the pageant. Reid then suggested, and Snyder agreed, that the sculpture would be made of a material known as "Design Cast 62," a synthetic substance that could meet CCNV's monetary and time constraints, could be tinted to resemble bronze, and could withstand the elements. The parties agreed that the project would cost no more than $15,000, not including Reid's services, which he offered to donate. The parties did not sign a written agreement. Neither party mentioned copyright.

After Reid received an advance of $3,000, he made several sketches of figures in various poses. At Snyder's request, Reid sent CCNV a sketch of a proposed sculpture showing the family in a crèche-like setting: the mother seated, cradling a baby in her lap; the father standing behind her, bending over her shoulder to touch the baby's foot. Reid testified that Snyder asked for the sketch to use in raising funds for the sculpture. Snyder testified that it was also for his approval....

Throughout November and the first two weeks of December 1985, Reid worked exclusively on the statue.... On a number of occasions, CCNV members visited Reid to check on his progress and to coordinate CCNV's construction of the base.... Reid and CCNV members did not discuss copyright ownership on any of these visits.

On December 24, 1985, twelve days after the agreed-upon date, Reid delivered the completed statue to Washington. There it was joined to the steam grate and pedestal prepared by CCNV and placed on display near the site of the pageant. Snyder paid Reid the final installment of the $15,000.... In late January 1986, CCNV members returned it to Reid's studio in Baltimore for minor repairs. Several weeks later, Snyder began making plans to take the statue on a tour of several cities to raise money for the homeless. Reid objected, contending that the Design Cast 62 material was not strong enough to withstand the ambitious itinerary....

In March 1986, Snyder asked Reid to return the sculpture. Reid refused. He then filed a certificate of copyright registration for "Third World America" in his name and announced plans to take the sculpture on a more modest tour than the one CCNV had proposed. Snyder, acting in his capacity as CCNV's trustee, immediately filed a competing certificate of copyright registration.

Snyder and CCNV then commenced this action against Reid ... seeking return of the sculpture and a determination of copyright ownership.... [T]he District Court declared that "Third World America" was a "work made for hire" under § 101 of the Copyright Act and that Snyder, as trustee for CCNV, was the exclusive owner of the copyright in the sculpture....

The Court of Appeals for the District of Columbia Circuit reversed and remanded, holding that Reid owned the copyright because "Third World America" was not a work for hire....

II

The Copyright Act of 1976 provides that copyright ownership "vests initially in the author or authors of the work." As a general rule, the author is the party who actually creates the work, that is, the person who translates an idea into a fixed, tangible expression entitled to copyright protection. The Act carves out an important exception, however, for "works made for hire." If the work is for hire, "the employer or other person for whom the work was prepared is considered the author" and owns the copyright, unless there is a written agreement to the contrary.... The contours of the work for hire doctrine therefore carry profound significance for freelance creators—including artists, writers, photographers, designers, composers, and computer programmers—and for the publishing, advertising, music, and other industries which commission their works.

Section 101 of the 1976 Act provides that a work is "for hire" under two sets of circumstances:

"(1) a work prepared by an employee within the scope of his or her employment; or
(2) a work specially ordered or commissioned for use as a contribution to a collective work, as a part of a motion picture or other audiovisual work, as a translation, as a supplementary work, as a compilation, as an instructional text, as a test, as answer material for a test, or as an atlas, if the parties expressly agree in a written instrument signed by them that the work shall be considered a work made for hire."

Petitioners do not claim that the statue satisfies the terms of § 101(2). Quite clearly, it does not. Sculpture does not fit within any of the nine categories of "specially ordered or commissioned" works enumerated in that subsection, and no written agreement between the parties establishes "Third World America" as a work for hire.

The dispositive inquiry in this case therefore is whether "Third World America" is "a work prepared by an employee within the scope of his or her employment" under § 101(1). The Act does not define these terms....

.... It is, however, well established that "[w]here Congress uses terms that have accumulated settled meaning under ... the common law, a court must infer, unless the statute otherwise dictates, that Congress means to incorporate the established meaning of these terms." ... We thus agree with the Court of Appeals that the term "employee" should be understood in light of the general common law of agency....

... In determining whether a hired party is an employee under the general common law of agency, we consider the hiring party's right to control the manner and means by which the product is accomplished. Among the other factors relevant to this inquiry are the skill required; the source of the instrumentalities and tools; the location of the work; the duration of the relationship between the parties; whether the hiring party has the right to assign additional projects to the hired party; the extent of the hired party's discretion over when and how long to work; the method of payment; the hired party's role in hiring and paying assistants; whether the work is part of the regular business of the hiring party; whether the hiring party is in business; the provision of employee benefits; and the tax treatment of the hired party.

Examining the circumstances of this case in light of these factors, we agree with the Court of Appeals that Reid was not an employee of CCNV but an independent contractor. True, CCNV members directed enough of Reid's work to ensure that he produced a sculpture that met their specifications. But the extent of control the hiring party exercises over the details of the product is not dispositive. Indeed, all the other circumstances weigh heavily against finding an employment relationship. Reid is a sculptor, a skilled occupation. Reid supplied his own tools. He worked in his own studio in Baltimore, making daily supervision of his activities from Washington practicably impossible. Reid was retained for less than two months, a relatively short period of time. During and after this time, CCNV had no right to assign additional projects to Reid. Apart from the deadline for completing the sculpture, Reid had absolute freedom to decide when and how long to work. CCNV paid Reid $15,000, a sum dependent on "completion of a specific job, a method by which independent contractors are often compensated." Reid had total discretion in hiring and paying assistants. "Creating sculptures was hardly 'regular business' for CCNV." Indeed,

CCNV is not a business at all. Finally, CCNV did not pay payroll or Social Security taxes, provide any employee benefits, or contribute to unemployment insurance or workers' compensation funds.

... Thus, CCNV is not the author of "Third World America" by virtue of the work for hire provisions of the Act....

For the aforestated reasons, we affirm the judgment of the Court of Appeals for the District of Columbia Circuit.

HARPER & ROW PUBLISHERS V. NATION ENTERPRISES
Supreme Court of the United States, 1985
471 U.S. 539

Justice O' CONNOR delivered the opinion of the Court.

This case requires us to consider to what extent the "fair use" provision of the Copyright Revision Act of 1976 sanctions the unauthorized use of quotations from a public figure's unpublished manuscript....

I

In February 1977, shortly after leaving the White House, former President Gerald R. Ford contracted with petitioners Harper & Row and *Reader's Digest,* to publish his as yet unwritten memoirs. The memoirs were to contain "significant hitherto unpublished material" concerning the Watergate crisis, Mr. Ford's pardon of former President Nixon, and "Mr. Ford's reflections on this period of history and the morality and personalities involved." In addition to the right to publish the Ford memoirs in book form, the agreement gave petitioners the exclusive right to license prepublication excerpts, known in the trade as "first serial rights." Two years later, as the memoirs were nearing completion, petitioners negotiated a prepublication licensing agreement with *Time,* a weekly news magazine. *Time* agreed to pay $25,000; $12,500 in advance and an additional $12,500 at publication, in exchange for the right to excerpt 7,500 words from Mr. Ford's account of the Nixon pardon. The issue featuring the excerpts was timed to appear approximately one week before shipment of the full-length book version to bookstores. Exclusivity was an important consideration; Harper & Row instituted procedures designed to maintain the confidentiality of the manuscript, and *Time* retained the right to renegotiate the second payment should the material appear in print prior to its release of the excerpts.

Two to three weeks before the *Time* article's scheduled release, an unidentified person secretly brought a copy of the Ford manuscript to Victor Navasky, editor of *The Nation,* a political commentary magazine.... He hastily put together what he believed was "a real hot news story" composed of quotes, paraphrases, and facts drawn exclusively from the manuscript. Mr. Navasky attempted no independent commentary, research, or criticism, in part because of the need for speed if he was to "make news" by "publish[ing]" in advance of "publication of the Ford book." The 2,250-word article ... appeared on April 3, 1979. As a result of *The Nation's* article, *Time* cancelled its piece and refused to pay the remaining $12,500.

Petitioners brought suit in District Court for the Southern District of New York, alleging ... violations of the Copyright Act. After a six-day bench trial, the District Judge found that *A Time to Heal* was protected by copyright at the time of *The Nation* publication and that respondents' use of the copyrighted material constituted an infringement....
A divided panel of the Court of Appeals for the Second Circuit reversed....
... The Court of Appeals was especially influenced by the "politically significant" nature of the subject matter and its conviction that it is not "the purpose of the Copyright Act to impede that harvest of knowledge so necessary to a democratic state" or "chill the activities of the press by forbidding a circumscribed use of copyrighted words."

II

We agree with the Court of Appeals that copyright is intended to increase and not to impede the harvest of knowledge. But we believe the Second Circuit gave insufficient difference to the scheme to establish by the Copyright Act for fostering the original works that provide the seed and substance of this harvest. The rights conferred by copyright are designed to assure contributors to the store of knowledge a fair return for their labors
Article I § 8, of the Constitution provides:
"The Congress shall have Power ... to Promote the Progress of Science and useful Arts, by securing for limited Times to Authors and Inventors the exclusive Right to their respective Writings and Discoveries."
As we noted last Term "[This] limited grant is a means by which an important public purpose may be achieved. It is intended to motivate the creative activity of authors and inventors by the provision of a special reward, and to allow the public access to the products of their genius after the limited period of exclusive control has expired." *Sony Corp. of America v. Universal City Studios, Inc.,* 464 U.S. 417, 429, 104 S.Ct. 774, 782, 78 L.Ed.2d 574 (1984). "The monopoly created by copyright thus rewards the individual author in order to benefit the public." ...
Section 106 of the Copyright Act confers a bundle of exclusive rights to the owner of the copyright. Under the Copyright Act, these rights—to publish, copy, and distribute the author's work from the time of its creation.... The copyright owner's rights, however, are subject of certain statutory exceptions. Among these is § 107 that codifies the traditional privilege of other authors to make "fair use" of an earlier writer's work. In addition, no author may copyright facts or ideas. The copyright is limited to those aspects of the work— termed "expression"—that display the stamp of the author's originality....
... *The Nation* has admitted to lifting verbatim quotes of the author's original language totaling between 300 and 400 words and constituting some thirteen percent of *The Nation* article. In using generous verbatim excerpts of Mr. Ford's unpublished manuscript to lend authenticity to its account of the forthcoming memoirs, *The Nation* effectively arrogated to itself the right of first publication, an important marketable subsidiary right. For the reasons set forth below, we find that this use of copyrighted manuscript ... was not a fair use within the meaning of the Copyright Act.

III

A

Fair use was traditionally defined as "a privilege in others than the owner of the copyright to the use of the copyrighted material in a reasonable manner without his consent." … The statutory formulation of the defense of fair use in the Copyright Act reflects the intent of Congress to codify the common law doctrine. Section 107 requires a case-by-case determination whether a particular use is fair, and the statute notes four nonexclusive factors to be considered….

Through the right of first publication, like the other rights enumerated in § 106, is expressly made subject to the fair use provision of § 107, fair use analysis must always be tailored to the individual case. The nature of interest at stake is highly relevant to whether a given use is fair…. The right of first publication implicates a threshold decision by the author whether and in what form to release his work. First publication is inherently different from other § 106 rights in that only one person can be the first publisher; as the contract with *Time* illustrates, the commercial value of the right lies primarily in exclusivity. Because the potential damage to the author from judicially enforced "sharing" of the first publication right with unauthorized users of his manuscript is substantial, the balance of equities in evaluating such a claim of fair use inevitably shifts….

… We conclude that the unpublished nature of a work is "[a] key, though not necessarily determinative, factor" tending to negate a defense of fair use….

B

Respondents, however, contend that First Amendment values require a different rule under the circumstances of this case. The thrust of the decision below is that "[t]he scope of [fair use] is undoubtedly wider when the information conveyed relates to matters of high public concern." Respondents advance the substantial public import of the subject matter of the Ford memoirs as grounds for excusing a use that would ordinarily not pass muster as a fair use—the privacy of verbatim quotations for the purpose of "scooping" the authorized first serialization. Respondents explain their copying of Mr. Ford's expression as essential to reporting the news story it claims the book itself represents. In respondents' view, not only the facts contained in Mr. Ford's memoirs, but "the precise manner in which [he] expressed himself [were] as newsworthy as what he had to say." Respondents argue that the public's interest in learning the news as fast as possible outweighs the right of the author to control its first publication….

Respondents' theory, however, would expand fair use to effectively destroy any expectation of copyright protection in the work of a public figure. Absent such protection, there would be little incentive to create or profit in financing such memoirs, and the public would be denied an important source of significant historical information. The promise of copyright would be an empty one if it could be avoided merely by dubbing the infringement of a fair use "news report" of the book….

In view of the First Amendment protections already embodied in the Copyright Act's distinction between copyrightable expression and uncopyrightable facts and ideas, and the latitude for scholarship and comment traditionally afforded by fair use, we see no warrant for expanding the doctrine of fair use to create what amounts to a public figure exception to copyright. Whether verbatim copying from a public figure's manuscript in a given case is or is not fair must be judged according to the traditional equities of fair use.

IV

... The four factors identified by Congress especially relevant in determining whether the use was fair are: (1) the purpose and character of the use; (2) the nature of the copyrighted work; (3) the substantiality of the portion used in relation to the copyrighted work as a whole; and (4) the effect on the potential market for or value of the copyright work. We address each one separately.

Purpose of the Use. The Second Circuit correctly identified news reporting as the general purpose of *The Nation's* use. News reporting is one of the examples enumerated in § 107 to "give some idea of the sort of activities the courts might regard as fair use under the circumstances." ... The fact than an article arguably is "news" and therefore a productive use is simply one factor in a fair use analysis....

The fact that a publication was commercial as opposed to nonprofit is a separate factor that tends to weigh against a finding of fair use.... In arguing that the purpose of news reporting is not purely commercial, *The Nation* misses the point entirely. The crux of the profit/nonprofit distinction is not whether the sole motive of the use is monetary gain but whether the user stands to profit from exploitation of the copyrighted material without paying the customary price.

In evaluating character and purpose we cannot ignore *The Nation's* stated purpose of scooping the forthcoming hardcover and *Time* abstracts. *The Nation's* use had not merely the incidental effect but the *intended purpose* of supplanting the copyright holder's commercially valuable right of first publication. Also relevant to the "character" of the use is "the propriety of the defendant's conduct." ...The trial court found that *The Nation* knowingly exploited a purloined manuscript....

Nature of the Copyrighted Work. Second, the Act directs attention to the nature of the copyrighted work. *A Time to Heal* may be characterized as an unpublished historical narrative or autobiography. The law generally recognizes a greater need to disseminate factual works than works of fiction or fantasy.... Some of the briefer quotes from the memoirs are arguably necessary to adequately convey the facts; for example, Mr. Ford's characterization of the White House tapes as the "smoking gun" is perhaps so integral to the idea expressed as to be inseparable from it. But *The Nation* did not stop at isolated phrases and instead excerpted subjective descriptions and portraits of public figures whose power lies in the author's individualized expression. Such use, focusing on the most expressive elements of the work, exceeds that necessary to disseminate the facts.

The fact that a work is unpublished is a critical element of its "nature." Our prior discussion establishes that the scope of fair use is narrower with respect of unpublished works. While even substantial quotations might qualify as fair use in a review of a published work or a news account of a speech that had been delivered to the public or disseminated to the press, the author's right to control the first public appearance of his expression weighs against such use of the work before its release....

Amount and Substantiality of the Portion Used. Next, the Act direct us to examine the amount and substantiality of the portion used in relation to the copyrighted work as a whole. In absolute terms, the words actually quoted were an insubstantial portion of *A Time to Heal.* The District Court, however, found that "*[T]he Nation* took what was essentially the heart of the book."… A *Time* editor described the chapters on the pardon as "the most interesting and moving parts of the entire manuscript." The portions actually quoted that were selected by Mr. Navasky are among the most powerful passages in those chapters.…

… *The Nation* article is structured around the quoted excerpts that serve as its dramatic focal points. In view of the expressive value of the excerpts and their key role in the infringing work, we cannot agree with the Second Circuit that the "magazine took a meager, indeed, an infinitesimal amount of Ford's original language."

Effect on the Market. Finally, the Act focuses on the effect of the use upon the potential market for or value of the copyrighted work. This last factor is undoubtedly the single most important element of fair use.… The trial court found not merely a potential but an actual effect on the market. *Time's* cancellation of its projected serialization and its refusal to pay the $12,500 were the direct effect of infringement.… Rarely will a case of copyright infringement present such clear-cut evidence of actual damage. Petitioners assured *Time* that there would be no other authorized publication of *any* portion of the unpublished manuscript prior to April 23, 1979. *Any* publication of material from chapters one and three would permit *Time* to renegotiate its final payment. *Time* cited *The Nation's* article, which contained verbatim quotes from the unpublished manuscript, as a reason for its nonperformance.…

More important, to negate fair use one need only show that if the challenged use "should become widespread, it would adversely affect the *potential* market for the copyright work." …

… The excerpts were employed as featured episodes in a story about the Nixon pardon—precisely the use petitioners had licensed to *Time.* The borrowing of these verbatim quotes from the unpublished manuscript lent to *The Nation's* piece a special air of authenticity—as Navasky expressed it, the reader would know it was Ford speaking and not *The Nation.* Thus it directly competed for a share of the market for prepublication excerpts.…

Placed in a broader perspective, a fair use doctrine that permits extensive prepublication quotations from an unreleased manuscript without the copyright owner's consent poses substantial potential for damage to the marketability of first serialization rights in general. "Isolated instances of minor infringements, when multiplied many times, becomes in the aggregate a major inroad on copyright that must be prevented."

V

The Court of Appeals erred in concluding that *The Nation's* use of the copyrighted material was excused by the public's interest in the subject matter. It erred, as well, in overlooking the unpublished nature of the work and the resulting impact on the potential market for first serial rights of permitting unauthorized prepublication excerpts under the rubric of fair use. Finally, in finding the taking "infinitesimal," the Court of Appeals accorded too little weight to the qualitative importance of the quoted passages of original expression.…

… Because we find that *The Nation's* use of these verbatim excerpts from the unpublished manuscript was not a fair use, the judgment of the Court of Appeals is reversed.…

CAMPBELL V. ACUFF-ROSE MUSIC, INC.
Supreme Court of the United States, 1994
510 U.S. 569

Justice SOUTER delivered the opinion of the Court.

I

In 1964, Roy Orbison and William Dees wrote a rock ballad called "Oh, Pretty Woman" and assigned their rights in it to respondent Acuff-Rose Music, Inc....

Petitioners Luther R. Campbell, Christopher Wongwon, Mark Ross, and David Hobbs, are collectively known as 2 Live Crew, a popular rap music group. In 1989, Campbell wrote a song entitled "Pretty Woman," which he later described in an affidavit as intended, "through comical lyrics, to satirize the original work.".... On July 5, 1989, 2 Live Crew's manager informed Acuff-Rose that 2 Live Crew had written a parody of "Oh, Pretty Woman" that they would afford all credit for ownership and authorship of the original song to Acuff-Rose, Dees, and Orbison, and that they were willing to pay a fee for the use they wished to make of it.... Acuff-Rose's agent refused permission, stating that "I am aware of the success enjoyed by 'The 2 Live Crews,' but I must inform you that we cannot permit the use of a parody of 'Oh, Pretty Woman.'" Nonetheless, in June or July 1989, 2 Live Crew releases cassette tapes and compact discs of "Pretty Woman" in a collection of songs entitled "As Clean As They Wanna Be."...

Almost a year later, after nearly a quarter of a million copies of the recording had been sold, Acuff-Rose sued 2 Live Crew and its record company, Luke Skyywalker Records, for copyright infringement. The District Court granted summary judgment for 2 Live Crew, reasoning that the commercial purpose of 2 Live Crew's song was no bar to fair use; that 2 Live Crew's version was a parody, which "quickly degenerates into a play on words, substituting predictable lyrics with shocking ones" to show "how bland and banal the Orbison song" is; that 2 Live Crew had taken no more than was necessary to "conjure up" the original in order to parody it; and that it was "extremely unlikely that 2 Live Crew's song could adversely affect the market for the original." The District Court weighed these factors and held that 2 Live Crew's song made fair use of Orbison's original.

The Court of Appeals for the Sixth Circuit reversed and remanded. Although it assumed for the purpose of its opinion that 2 Live Crew's song was a parody of the Orbison original, the Court of Appeals thought the District Court had put too little emphasis on the fact that "every commercial use ... is presumptively ... unfair."...

We granted certiorari to determine whether 2 Live Crew's commercial parody could be a fair use.

II

It is uncontested here that 2 Live Crew's song would be an infringement of Acuff-Rose's rights in "Oh, Pretty Woman," under the Copyright Act of 1976, but for a finding of fair use through parody....

... The fair use doctrine ... "permits [and requires] courts to avoid rigid application of the copyright statute when, on occasion, it would stifle the very creativity which that law is designed to foster."

The task is not to be simplified with bright-line rules, for [§ 107 of] the statute, like the doctrine it recognizes, calls for case-by-case analysis....

A

The first factor in a fair use inquiry is "the purpose and character of the use, including whether such use is of a commercial nature or is for nonprofit educational purposes."... The enquiry here may be guided by the examples given in the preamble to § 107, looking to whether the use is for criticism, or comment, or news reporting, and the like. The central purpose of this investigation is to see ... whether the new work merely supersedes the objects of the original creation ("supplanting" the original), or instead adds something new, with a further purpose or different character, altering the first with new expression, meaning, or message; it asks, in other words, whether and to what extent the new work is "transformative." Although such transformative use is not absolutely necessary for a finding of fair use, the goal of copyright, to promote science and the arts, is generally furthered by the creation of transformative works. Such works thus lie at the heart of the fair use doctrine's guarantee of breathing space within the confines of copyright, and the more transformative the new work, the less will be the significance of other factors, like commercialism, that may weigh against a finding of fair use.

... [P]arody has an obvious claim to transformative value, as Acuff-Rose itself does not deny. Like less ostensibly humorous forms of criticism, it can provide social benefit, by shedding light on an earlier work, and, in the process, creating a new one. We thus line up with the courts that have held that parody, like other comment or criticism, may claim fair use under § 107.

... For the purposes of copyright law ... the heart of any parodist's claim to quote from existing material is the use of some elements of a prior author's composition to create a new one that, at least in part, comments on that author's works. If, on the contrary, the commentary has no critical bearing on the substance or style of the original composition, which the alleged infringer merely uses to get attention or to avoid the drudgery in working up something fresh, the claim to fairness in borrowing from another's work diminishes accordingly.... Parody needs to mimic an original to make its point, and so has some claim to use the creation of its victim's (or collective victims') imagination....

The fact that parody can claim legitimacy for some appropriation does not, of course, tell either parodist or judge much about where to draw the line. Like a book review quoting the copyrighted material criticized, parody may or may not be fair use, and petitioner's suggestion that any parodic use is presumptively fair has no more justification in law or fact than the equally hopeful claim that any use for news reporting should be presumed fair....

... Although the majority below had difficulty discerning any criticism of the original in 2 Live Crew's song, it assumed for purposes of its opinion that there was some.

We have less difficulty in finding that critical element in 2 Live Crew's song than the Court of Appeals did, although having found it we will not take the further step of evaluating its quality....

While we might not assign a high rank to the parodic element here, we think it fair to say that 2 Live Crew's song reasonably could be perceived as commenting on the original or criticizing it, to some degree. 2 Live Crew juxtaposes the romantic musings of a man whose fantasy comes true, with degrading taunts, a bawdy demand for sex, and a sigh of relief from paternal responsibility. The later words can be taken as a comment on the naivete of the original of an earlier day, as a rejection of its sentiment that ignores the ugliness of street life and the debasement that it signifies....

The Court of Appeals, however, immediately cut short the enquiry into 2 Live Crew's fair use claim by confining its treatment of the first [fair use] factor essentially to one relevant fact, the commercial nature of the use....

The language of the statute makes clear that the commercial or nonprofit educational purpose of a work is only one element of the first factor enquiry into its purpose and character.... Accordingly, the mere fact that a use is educational and not for profit does not insulate it from a finding of infringement, and more than the commercial character of a use bars a finding of fairness....

B

The second statutory factor, "the nature of the copyrighted work," ... calls for recognition that some works are closer to the core of intended copyright protection than others, with the consequence that fair use is more difficult to establish when the former works are copied. We agree with both the District Court and the Court of Appeals that Orbison's original creative expression for public dissemination falls within the core of the copyright's protective purposes. This fact, however, is not much help in this case, or ever likely to help much in separating the fair use sheep from the infringing goats in a parody case, since parodies almost invariably copy publicly known, expressive works.

C

The third factor asks whether "the amount and substantiality of the portion used in relation to the copyrighted work as a whole" are reasonable in relation to the purpose of the copying. Here, attention turns to the persuasiveness of a parodist's justification for the particular copying done ...

... Parody presents a difficult case. Parody's humor, or in any event its comment, necessarily springs from recognizable allusion to its object through distorted imitation. Its art lies in the tension between a known original and its parodic twin. When parody takes aim at a particular original work, the parody must be able to "conjure up" at least enough of that original to make the object of its critical writ recognizable....

We think the Court of Appeals was insufficiently appreciative of parody's need for the recognizable sight or sound when it ruled 2 Live Crew's use unreasonable as a matter of law. It is true, of course, that 2 Live Crew copied the characteristic opening bass riff (or musical phrase) of the original, and true that the words of the first line copy the Orbison lyrics. But if quotation of the opening riff and the first line may be said to go the the "heart" of the original, the heart is also what most readily conjures up the song for parody, and it is the heart at which parody takes aim....

This is not, or course, to say that anyone who calls himself a parodist can skim the cream and get away scot-free. In parody, as in news reporting, context is everything, and the question of fairness asks what else the parodist did besides go to the heart of the original. It is significant that 2 Live Crew not only copied the first line of the original, but thereafter departed markedly from the Orbison lyrics for its own ends....

D

The fourth fair use factor is "the effect of the use upon the potential market for or value of the copyrighted work." …

… The [Court of Appeals] reasoned that because "the use of the copyrighted work is wholly commercial, … we presume a likelihood of future harm to Acuff-Rose exists." In so doing, the court resolved the fourth factor against 2 Live Crew, just as it had the first, by applying a presumption about the effect of commercial use, a presumption which as applied here we hold to be error.

… [W]hen … the second use is transformative, market substitution is at least less certain, and market harm may not be so readily inferred. Indeed, as to parody pure and simple, it is more likely that the new work will not affect the market for the original in a way cognizable under this factor, that is, by acting as a substitute for it. This is so because the parody and the original usually serve different market functions.…

… 2 Live Crew's song comprises not only parody but also rap music, and the derivative market for rap music is a proper focus of enquiry. Evidence of substantial harm to it would weigh against a finding of fair use, because the licensing of derivatives is an important economic incentive to the creation of originals.…

Although 2 Live Crew submitted uncontroverted affidavits on the question of market harm to the original, neither they, nor Acuff-Rose, introduced evidence or affidavits addressing the likely effect of 2 Live Crew's parodic rap song on the market for a non-parody, rap version of "Oh, Pretty Woman."

III

It was error for the Court of Appeals to conclude that the commercial nature of 2 Live Crew's parody of "Oh, Pretty Woman" rendered it presumptively unfair.… The court also erred in holding that 2 Live Crew had necessarily copied excessively from the Orbison original, considering the parodic purpose of the use. We therefore reverse the judgment of the Court of Appeals and remand for further proceedings consistent with this opinion.

MGM STUDIOS, ET AL. V. GROKSTER, ET AL.
Supreme Court of the United States, 2005
545 U.S. 913

Justice SOUTER delivered the opinion of the Court.

The question is under what circumstances the distributor of a product capable of both lawful and unlawful use is liable for acts of copyright infringement by third parties using the product. We hold that one who distributes a device with the object of promoting its use to infringe copyright, as shown by clear expression or other affirmative steps taken to foster infringement, is liable for the resulting acts of infringement by third parties.

I

A

Respondents, Grokster, Ltd., and StreamCast Networks, Inc., defendants in the trial court, distribute free software products that allow computer users to share electronic files through peer-to-peer networks, so called because users' computers communicate directly with each other, not through central servers. The advantage of peer-to-peer networks over information networks of other types shows up in their substantial and growing popularity. Because they need no central computer server to mediate the exchange of information or files among users, the high-bandwidth communications capacity for a server may be dispensed with, and the need for costly server storage space is eliminated. Since copies of a file (particularly a popular one) are available on many users' computers, file requests and retrievals may be faster than on other types of networks, and since file exchanges do not travel through a server, communications can take place between any computers that remain connected to the network without risk that a glitch in the server will disable the network in its entirety. Given these benefits in security, cost, and efficiency, peer-to-peer networks are employed to store and distribute electronic files by universities, government agencies, corporations, and libraries, among others.

Other users of peer-to-peer networks include individual recipients of Grokster's and StreamCast's software, and although the networks that they enjoy through using the software can be used to share any type of digital file, they have prominently employed those networks in sharing copyrighted music and video files without authorization. A group of copyright holders (MGM for short, but including motion picture studios, recording companies, songwriters, and music publishers) sued Grokster and StreamCast for their users' copyright infringements, alleging that they knowingly and intentionally distributed their software to enable users to reproduce and distribute the copyrighted works in violation of the Copyright Act .... MGM sought damages and an injunction....

... Grokster and StreamCast use no servers to intercept the content of the search requests or to mediate the file transfers conducted by users of the software, there being no central point through which the substance of the communications passes in either direction.

Although Grokster and StreamCast do not therefore know when particular files are copied, a few searches using their software would show what is available on the networks the software reaches. MGM commissioned a statistician to conduct a systematic search, and his study showed that nearly 90% of the files available for download ... were copyrighted works. Grokster and StreamCast dispute this figure, raising methodological problems and arguing that free copying even of copyrighted works may be authorized by the rightholders.
...

... [N]o one can say how often the software is used to obtain copies of unprotected material. But MGM's evidence gives reason to think that the vast majority of users' downloads are acts of infringement, and because well over 100 million copies of the software in question are known to have been downloaded, and billions of files are shared across the ... networks each month, the probable scope of copyright infringement is staggering....

Grokster and StreamCast are not ... merely passive recipients of information about infringing use. The record is replete with evidence that from the moment Grokster and StreamCast began to distribute their free software, each one clearly voiced the objective that recipients use it to download copyrighted works, and each took active steps to encourage infringement.

After the notorious file-sharing service, Napster, was sued by copyright holders for facilitation of copyright infringement, *A & M Records, Inc. v. Napster, Inc.*, StreamCast gave away a software program of a kind known as OpenNap, designed as compatible with the Napster program and open to Napster users for downloading files from other Napster and OpenNap users' computers. Evidence indicates that "[i]t was always [StreamCast's] intent to use [its OpenNap network] to be able to capture e-mail addresses of [its] initial target market so that [it] could promote [its] StreamCast Morpheus interface to them."…

… StreamCast developed promotional materials to market its service as the best Napster alternative. One proposed advertisement read: "Napster Inc. has announced that it will soon begin charging you a fee. That's if the courts don't order it shut down first. What will you do to get around it?" Another proposed ad touted StreamCast's software as the "#1 alternative to Napster" and asked "[w]hen the lights went off at Napster … where did the users go?" StreamCast even planned to flaunt the illegal uses of its software; when it launched the OpenNap network, the chief technology officer of the company averred that "[t]he goal is to get in trouble with the law and get sued. It's the best way to get in the new[s]."

The evidence that Grokster sought to capture the market of former Napster users is sparser but revealing, for Grokster launched its own OpenNap system called Swaptor and inserted digital codes into its Web site so that computer users using Web search engines to look for "Napster" or "[f]ree filesharing" would be directed to the Grokster Web site, where they could download the Grokster software. …

In addition to this evidence of express promotion, marketing, and intent to promote further, the business models employed by Grokster and StreamCast confirm that their principal object was use of their software to download copyrighted works. Grokster and StreamCast receive no revenue from users, who obtain the software itself for nothing. Instead, both companies generate income by selling advertising space, and they stream the advertising to … users while they are employing the programs. As the number of users of each program increases, advertising opportunities become worth more. … [T]he evidence shows that substantive volume is a function of free access to copyrighted work. Users seeking Top 40 songs, for example, or the latest release by Modest Mouse, are certain to be far more numerous than those seeking a free Decameron, and Grokster and StreamCast translated that demand into dollars.

Finally, there is no evidence that either company made an effort to filter copyrighted material from users' downloads or otherwise impede the sharing of copyrighted files. …

B

After discovery, the parties on each side of the case cross-moved for summary judgment. … The District Court held that those who used the Grokster and [StreamCast] software to download copyrighted media files directly infringed MGM's copyrights, a conclusion not contested on appeal, but the court nonetheless granted summary judgment in favor of Grokster and StreamCast as to any liability arising from distribution of the then current versions of their software. Distributing that software gave rise to no liability in the court's view, because its use did not provide the distributors with actual knowledge of specific acts of infringement.

The Court of Appeals affirmed. In the court's analysis, a defendant was liable as a contributory infringer when it had knowledge of direct infringement and materially contributed to the infringement. But the court read *Sony Corp. of America v. Universal City Studios, Inc.*, 464 U. S. 417 (1984), as holding that distribution of a commercial product capable of substantial noninfringing uses could not give rise to contributory liability for infringement unless the distributor had actual knowledge of specific instances of infringement and failed to act on that knowledge. The fact that the software was capable of substantial noninfringing uses in the Ninth Circuit's view meant that Grokster and StreamCast were not liable, because they had no such actual knowledge, owing to the decentralized architecture of their software. The court also held that Grokster and StreamCast did not materially contribute to their users' infringement because it was the users themselves who searched for, retrieved, and stored the infringing files, with no involvement by the defendants beyond providing the software in the first place....

II

A

MGM and many of the *amici* fault the Court of Appeals' holding for upsetting a sound balance between the respective values of supporting creative pursuits through copyright protection and promoting innovation in new communication technologies by limiting the incidence of liability for copyright infringement. The more artistic protection is favored, the more technological innovation may be discouraged; the administration of copyright law is an exercise in managing the trade-off.

The tension between the two values is the subject of this case, with its claim that digital distribution of copyrighted material threatens copyright holders as never before, because every copy is identical to the original, copying is easy, and many people (especially the young) use file-sharing software to download copyrighted works. ... As the case has been presented to us, these fears are said to be offset by the different concern that imposing liability, not only on infringers but on distributors of software based on its potential for unlawful use, could limit further development of beneficial technologies.

The argument for imposing indirect liability in this case is, however, a powerful one, given the number of infringing downloads that occur every day using StreamCast's and Grokster's software. When a widely shared service or product is used to commit infringement, it may be impossible to enforce rights in the protected work effectively against all direct infringers, the only practical alternative being to go against the distributor of the copying device for secondary liability on a theory of contributory or vicarious infringement.

One infringes contributorily by intentionally inducing or encouraging direct infringement and infringes vicariously by profiting from direct infringement while declining to exercise a right to stop or limit it....

B

Despite the currency of these principles of secondary liability, this Court has dealt with secondary copyright infringement in only one recent case, and because MGM has tailored its principal claim to our opinion there, a look at our earlier holding is in order. In *Sony Corp. v. Universal City Studios*, this Court addressed a claim that secondary liability for infringement can arise from the very distribution of a commercial product. There, the product, novel at the time, was what we know today as the videocassette recorder, or VCR. Copyright holders sued Sony as the manufacturer, claiming it was contributorily liable for infringement that occurred when VCR owners taped copyrighted programs because it supplied the means used to infringe, and it had constructive knowledge that infringement would occur. At the trial on the merits, the evidence showed that the principal use of the VCR was for "'time-shifting,'" or taping a program for later viewing at a more convenient time, which the Court found to be a fair, not an infringing, use. There was no evidence that Sony had expressed an object of bringing about taping in violation of copyright or had taken active steps to increase its profits from unlawful taping....

On those facts, with no evidence of stated or indicated intent to promote infringing uses, the only conceivable basis for imposing liability was on a theory of contributory infringement arising from its sale of VCRs to consumers with knowledge that some would use them to infringe. But because the VCR was "capable of commercially significant noninfringing uses," we held the manufacturer could not be faulted solely on the basis of its distribution....

We agree with MGM that the Court of Appeals misapplied *Sony*, which it read as limiting secondary liability quite beyond the circumstances to which the case applied. ... The Ninth Circuit has read *Sony*'s limitation to mean that whenever a product is capable of substantial lawful use, the producer can never be held contributorily liable for third parties' infringing use of it; it read the rule as being this broad, even when an actual purpose to cause infringing use is shown by evidence independent of design and distribution of the product, unless the distributors had "specific knowledge of infringement at a time at which they contributed to the infringement, and failed to act upon that information." ...
This view of *Sony*, however, was error ....

C

Sony's rule limits imputing culpable intent as a matter of law from the characteristics or uses of a distributed product. But nothing in *Sony* requires courts to ignore evidence of intent if there is such evidence, and the case was never meant to foreclose rules of fault-based liability derived from the common law....

The rule on inducement of infringement as developed in the early cases is no different today. Evidence of "active steps ... taken to encourage direct infringement," such as advertising an infringing use or instructing how to engage in an infringing use, show an affirmative intent that the product be used to infringe, and a showing that infringement was encouraged overcomes the law's reluctance to find liability when a defendant merely sells a commercial product suitable for some lawful use.

... [T]he inducement rule ... is a sensible one for copyright. We adopt it here, holding that one who distributes a device with the object of promoting its use to infringe copyright, as shown by clear expression or other affirmative steps taken to foster infringement, is liable for the resulting acts of infringement by third parties. ...

III

A

The only apparent question about treating MGM's evidence as sufficient to withstand summary judgment under the theory of inducement goes to the need on MGM's part to adduce evidence that StreamCast and Grokster communicated an inducing message to their software users. The classic instance of inducement is by advertisement or solicitation that broadcasts a message designed to stimulate others to commit violations. MGM claims that such a message is shown here. It is undisputed that StreamCast beamed onto the computer screens of users of Napster-compatible programs ads urging the adoption of its OpenNap program, which was designed, as its name implied, to invite the custom of patrons of Napster, then under attack in the courts for facilitating massive infringement. ... Grokster distributed an electronic newsletter containing links to articles promoting its software's ability to access popular copyrighted music. ...

... Here, the summary judgment record is replete with other evidence that Grokster and StreamCast, unlike the manufacturer and distributor in *Sony*, acted with a purpose to cause copyright violations by use of software suitable for illegal use. ...

B

In addition to intent to bring about infringement and distribution of a device suitable for infringing use, the inducement theory of course requires evidence of actual infringement by recipients of the device, the software in this case. As the account of the facts indicates, there is evidence of infringement on a gigantic scale, and there is no serious issue of the adequacy of MGM's showing on this point in order to survive the companies' summary judgment requests. Although an exact calculation of infringing use, as a basis for a claim of damages, is subject to dispute, there is no question that the summary judgment evidence is at least adequate to entitle MGM to go forward with claims for damages and equitable relief.

***

In sum, this case is significantly different from *Sony* and reliance on that case to rule in favor of StreamCast and Grokster was error. ...

MGM's evidence in this case most obviously addresses a different basis of liability for distributing a product open to alternative uses. Here, evidence of the distributors' words and deeds going beyond distribution as such shows a purpose to cause and profit from third-party acts of copyright infringement. If liability for inducing infringement is ultimately found, it will not be on the basis of presuming or imputing fault, but from inferring a patently illegal objective from statements and actions showing what that objective was.

There is substantial evidence in MGM's favor on all elements of inducement, and summary judgment in favor of Grokster and StreamCast was error. On remand, reconsideration of MGM's motion for summary judgment will be in order.

The judgment of the Court of Appeals is vacated, and the case is remanded for further proceedings consistent with this opinion.

It is so ordered.

TIME, INC. V. PETERSEN PUBLISHING CO.
U.S. Court of Appeals for the Second Circuit, 1999
173 F.3d 113

WALKER, Circuit Judge:

Petersen Publishing Company L.L.C., the publisher of *Teen* magazine, appeals from the March 27, 1998, judgment of the United States District Court for the Southern District of New York ... that was entered after a jury found that Time, Inc., the publisher of *People* magazine, had not infringed Petersen's *Teen* trademark by publishing a new magazine entitled *Teen People*.
.... We ... affirm the judgment of the district court.

BACKGROUND

Petersen has published *Teen* magazine since 1957. Time has published *People* magazine since 1974. In 1997, seeking to expand their businesses, each publisher was working separately on a new magazine, and each wanted to name its new magazine *Teen People*. We need not concern ourselves over whether this desire to use the same name was driven by mutual admiration, or simply a shared lack of creativity. The fact is that, when each learned of the other's plans, both were displeased at the prospect of sharing the name and decided to do something about it.

Time, the first to reach the courthouse door, filed this action on August 7, 1997, to enjoin Petersen's use of the name Teen People. Time claimed the right to use the name due to its marketing and publicity efforts, and also alleged that Petersen's use of the name Teen People would infringe Time's *People* trademark. Petersen responded by agreeing not to use the contested title without giving advance notice to Time, and at one point was prepared to abandon the name entirely. However, after Time indicated its continuing intention to launch its own *Teen People* magazine, Petersen's answer pleaded counterclaims against Time that specifically asserted that Time's *Teen People* would infringe Petersen's *Teen* trademark.

Petersen moved for a temporary restraining order and a preliminary injunction. The district court held a hearing on the motion ... and denied the TRO and the preliminary injunction after Time stipulated to the appearance of its forthcoming Teen People logo. On February 13, 1998, the district court denied Time's motion for summary judgment and set down the case for trial.

The cause was tried to a jury in March of 1998. Petersen's central contention was that Time was improperly attempting to profit from the strength of Petersen's *Teen* mark; Time's defense was that its only intention was to build on the strength of its own *People* magazine. During the trial, the district court dismissed Petersen's claims for licensing royalties, diminution of trademark value, and trademark dilution. Petersen's claims for trademark infringement and unfair competition went to the jury.

After deliberating for a few hours, the jury sent to the district court the following question: "Does changing *Teen's* trademark from Teen with the apostrophe to Teen without the apostrophe mean that it is still a valid trademark for Petersen's *Teen* or does it weaken it/void it?" This question referred to a change Petersen made in July of 1997, when it switched its logo from one in all capital letters, preceded by an apostrophe ('TEEN), to one with no apostrophe and a single, initial capital letter (Teen). Over Petersen's objection, the district court responded with the following supplemental instruction:

> Petersen's federal trademark registration is for the word teen and the particular design depicted in its federal registration, i.e., with an apostrophe and in italicized capital letters. This trademark registration is still valid and in effect. As to the new logo that Petersen adopted in July 1997, Petersen may have common law rights in the new design. It is for you to determine whether Petersen has acquired common law trademark rights in that new design. And to determine from, you will see in my charges at least in one aspect of the charges, to determine how strong those rights are.
>
> Keep in mind, too, the scope of protection for a trademark is not limited to an exact replication of the mark as it appears on the registration certificate. Rather, the scope of protection of the mark is bounded by the line at which there is a likelihood of confusion of the people who are in fact buying the product caused by another's use of the same or similar mark.

The district court also referred the jury back to its earlier instructions.

After receiving the supplemental charge, the jury returned to its deliberations. Later that afternoon the jury sent a note to the district court to the effect that it was having difficulty reaching a verdict. The district court sent the jury home for the night. The next day the jury reached a unanimous verdict in favor of Time. This appeal followed.

DISCUSSION

I. Trademark Infringement Generally

Before discussing the specific question presented on this appeal, it is useful to outline the law of trademark infringement. The Lanham Act prohibits the use in commerce, without consent, of any "registered mark in connection with the sale, offering for sale, distribution, or advertising of any goods," in a way that is likely to cause confusion. 15 U.S.C. § 1114(1)(a). The Act similarly prohibits the infringement of unregistered, common law trademarks. Petersen brought counterclaims of trademark infringement against Time under both of these provisions.

To prevail on a trademark infringement claim under either of these provisions, a plaintiff must demonstrate that "'it has a valid mark entitled to protection and that the defendant's use of it is likely to cause confusion.'" A mark is entitled to protection when it is inherently distinctive; if the mark is "merely descriptive," it qualifies for protection only if it has acquired secondary meaning, i.e., if it "has become distinctive of the . . . goods in commerce." "Secondary meaning attaches when 'the name and the business have become synonymous in the mind of the public, submerging the primary meaning of the term in favor of its meaning as a word identifying that business.'"

If a mark is valid, its possessor, in order to succeed on its infringement claim, must prove that "numerous ordinary prudent purchasers are likely to be misled or confused as to the source of the product in question because of the entrance in the marketplace of defendant's mark." Under the law of this circuit, courts must consider Judge Henry Friendly's Polaroid factors to decide whether a plaintiff has established a likelihood of confusion:

> (1) the strength of the mark; (2) the degree of similarity between the two marks; (3) the proximity of the products; (4) the likelihood that the prior owner will 'bridge the gap';... (5) actual confusion; (6) the defendant's good faith in adopting its mark; (7) the quality of the defendant's product; and (8) the sophistication of the buyers.

Many of these factors received considerable attention at trial. Petersen and Time introduced consumer studies, documentary evidence, and witnesses in an effort to prove the presence or lack of good faith, consumer confusion, and similarity between the Teen and Teen People marks (as well as the similarity between Time's People and Teen People marks). On appeal, however, Petersen's sole challenge is to the district court's supplemental instruction. This instruction related only to the first Polaroid factor, the strength of Petersen's trademark, and to it we now turn.

The strength, or distinctiveness, of a mark is its power to identify the source of a product. In somewhat circular fashion, consideration of this factor includes an evaluation of the same characteristics that initially determined a mark's validity: inherent distinctiveness, descriptiveness, and secondary meaning.

There are four categories along the spectrum of possible trademarks: generic, descriptive, suggestive, and arbitrary or fanciful. A generic mark (e.g., "Magazine" as a magazine title) receives no trademark protection. The other three categories of marks may be valid trademarks deserving of protection, and the mark's classification is also relevant in determining the strength of the mark.

The strongest marks are arbitrary or fanciful marks, which are entitled to the fullest protection against infringement. The next strongest are suggestive marks, which require "imagination, thought, and perception to reach a conclusion as to the nature of goods." A mark that is merely descriptive of its product is entitled to somewhat less protection. At common law, a merely descriptive mark could not be a valid trademark, but as trademark law developed, these marks were accorded legal protection if they had acquired secondary meaning. With regard to all valid marks, the stronger the secondary meaning, the stronger the mark....

Along with the inherent distinctiveness of a mark, the mark's distinctiveness in the marketplace also must be considered in determining its strength. The use of part or all of the mark by third parties weakens its overall strength....

It is also relevant that the law of trademark accords stronger protection to the stylized version of certain words used as trademarks than to those words themselves....

II. The Jury Charge In This Case

"A jury charge is erroneous if it misleads the jury as to the correct legal standard, or if it does not adequately inform the jury of the law." ....

In his original charge regarding the strength of the mark, Judge Baer instructed the jury about the different categories of marks, and about the need to prove secondary meaning in order to protect a descriptive mark. He instructed that the sales success of *Teen* magazine could contribute to a finding of secondary meaning, and significantly, that the "length and exclusivity" of the mark's use was also a consideration. At the end of his original charge relating to the strength of the mark, Judge Baer underscored that "the ultimate issue is whether the defendant's use of the mark is likely to cause confusion among ordinary purchasers of the magazine as to the source of the product." Petersen takes no issue with any of these instructions.

Petersen contends that the district court erred, however, when it stated in its supplemental charge, with reference to Petersen's adoption of a new logo in July, 1997, that "it is for you to determine whether Petersen has acquired common law trademark rights in that new design." Petersen insists that this charge "effectively instructed the jury that it should disregard the previous forty years of Petersen's continuous use" of the Teen mark. Petersen argues that the district court's charge compelled the jury to ignore the common law rights that accrued over that period of use. Reviewing the entire charge, both original and supplemental, in light of the applicable legal standards, we disagree.

The district court was correct to distinguish between the new stylized logo and the previous one.... [T]rademark rights in the stylized appearance of a word are distinct from trademark rights in the word itself. The earlier registered trademark held by Petersen protects not only the word Teen, but also a particular stylized version of that word, a version no longer employed by Petersen. To the extent that Petersen acquired common law rights in the new design of the word, they could only have been acquired after use of that new design commenced.

Petersen also possesses trademark rights in the word itself that began accruing from its earliest use of the word Teen. The district court's instructions did not preclude the jury from considering whether these rights had been infringed. Judge Baer's supplemental charge made it clear that protection from infringement was "not limited to an exact replication of the mark." And by referring back to his original charge, he reiterated that the entire history of Petersen's use was legally significant.

The district court might have done better to emphasize more clearly the difference between rights in a word and rights in a particular version of that word. It is not at all certain whether, if this had occurred, Petersen's case would have been assisted. We remain unpersuaded that the supplemental charge did any of the damage of which Petersen complains. Judge Baer made plain to the jury that "the bottom line" in the case, as in most trademark cases, was whether there was a likelihood of consumer confusion. The jury found in favor of Time, and the charge was neither so prejudicial nor so confusing as to warrant reversal.

CONCLUSION

For the foregoing reasons, the judgment of the district court is affirmed.

Chapter Nine
THE FCC AND BROADCAST LICENSING

This chapter features cases that deal with government licensing of the broadcast media. From these cases it is evident that broadcast media are accorded narrower First Amendment rights than other media. Therefore, broadcasters are subject to application procedures, operating procedures, public-access rules, ownership limitations, and other restrictions that would be unconstitutional if applied to the print media. On the other hand, not all of these restrictions on the broadcast media can pass constitutional muster, as we will see.

Hoover v. Intercity Radio Co. is a classic case from the early days of broadcast, illustrating the government's predicament – and lack of discretion under earlier law—in trying to deal with signal interference.

Red Lion Broadcasting Co. v. FCC is the landmark case in which the Supreme Court thoroughly established the *scarcity rationale* as the constitutional underpinning for broadcast licensing as well as broadcast content controls.

MD/DC/DE Broadcasters Ass'n v. FCC utilized strict scrutiny to hold unconstitutional the FCC's equal employment opportunity (EEO) rules for broadcasters.

Fox Television Stations, Inc. v. FCC is a D.C. Circuit case concerning the FCC's TV ownership restrictions. It illustrates the demanding oversight that the FCC now receives from some in Congress and from the Court of Appeals.

Comcast Corp. v. FCC is a similar case in which the D.C. Circuit in 2009 examined the FCC's long-running – and awkward – attempt to limit the size of cable TV companies.

HOOVER V. INTERCITY RADIO CO., INC.
Court of Appeals of District of Columbia, 1923
286 F. 1003

VAN ORSDEL, Associate Justice.

This appeal is from an order of the Supreme Court of the District of Columbia, directing the issuance of a writ of mandamus requiring appellant, Secretary of Commerce, to issue to plaintiff company, a license to operate a radio station in the city of New York.

The plaintiff alleged that it has been engaged in the business of wireless telegraphy between New York and other cities of the United States since January 16, 1920, under licenses issued from time to time by defendant, pursuant to the Act of Congress approved August 13, 1912. It was further alleged that the last license expired on November 12, 1921; that defendant refused to grant plaintiff a new license for the operation of its station; that appellee, in all respects, complied with the requirements of the act of Congress and of the regulations contained therein; and that the duty imposed upon defendant of granting licenses is purely a ministerial one.

Defendant answered, admitting the refusal of the license, but defending on the ground that he had been unable to ascertain a wavelength for use by plaintiff, which would not interfere with government and private stations, and that under the provisions of the act of Congress the issuance or refusal of a license is a matter wholly within his discretion.

Section 1 of the act forbids the operation of radio apparatus, where interferences would be caused with receipt of messages or signals from beyond the jurisdiction of the state or territory in which it is situated, "except under and in accordance with a license, revocable for cause, in that behalf granted by the Secretary of Commerce and Labor upon application therefore." The license shall be in form prescribed by the Secretary, containing the restrictions pursuant to the act "on and subject to which the license is granted." The license also "shall state the wavelength or the wavelengths authorized for use by the station for the prevention of interference and the hours for which the station is licensed for work." The license is further made subject to the regulations of the act and such regulations as may be made by the authority of the act.

The Secretary of Commerce is given authority, for the purpose of preventing or minimizing interference with communication between stations, to enforce the regulations established by the act through the collectors of customs and other officers of the government, with power, however, in his discretion, to waive the provisions of the regulations when no interference obtains.

The act further provides as follows:

"All stations are required to give absolute priority to signals and radiograms relating to ships in distress; to cease all sending on hearing a distress signal; and, except when engaged in answering or aiding the ship in distress, to refrain from sending until all signals and radiograms relating thereto are completed."

Private or commercial shore stations, so situated that their operation interferes with naval and military stations, are forbidden to "use their transmitters during the first fifteen minutes of each hour, local standard time," during which time the military and naval stations shall transmit signals or radiograms, "except in case of signals or radiograms relating to vessels in distress." The Secretary is forbidden to license private or commercial stations to adopt a wavelength between 600 meters and 1,600 meters, the wavelengths between these figures being reserved for governmental agencies. Penalties are prescribed for violations of the act.

Congress seems to have legislated on the subject of radio telegraphy with reference to the undeveloped state of the art. Interference in operation is conceded; hence the act undertakes to prescribe regulations by which the interference may be minimized rather than prevented. It regulates the preferences to be accorded distress signals and government business. It specifically subjects private and commercial stations to the regulations prescribed by the act, the enforcement of which is imposed upon the Secretary of Commerce, acting "through the collectors of customs and other officers of the government." Indeed, the impossibility of totally eliminating interference was recognized internationally by the London Convention that resulted in the Treaty of July 8, 1913.

Complete control of the whole subject was reserved by Congress in the provision of section 2 that "such license shall be subject to the regulations contained herein, and such regulations as may be established from time to time by authority of this act or subsequent acts or treaties of the United States," and the further provision that "such license shall provide that the President of the United States in time of war or public peril or disaster may cause the closing of any station for ratio communication and the removal therefrom of all radio apparatus, or may authorize the use or control of any such station or apparatus by any department of the government, upon just compensation to the owners."

We are in accord with the construction placed upon the act by the Attorney General on October 24, 1912, in response to an inquiry from the Secretary of Commerce and Labor, as follows:

> *"The language of the act, the nature of the subject-matter regulated, as well as the general scope of the statute, negative the idea that Congress intended to repose any such discretion in you in the matter of licenses. It is apparent from the act as a whole that Congress determined thereby to put the subject of radio communication under federal supervision, so far as it was interstate or foreign in its nature. It is also apparent therefrom that that supervision and control is taken by Congress upon itself, and that the Secretary of Commerce and Labor is only authorized to deal with the matter as provided in the act, and is given no general regulative power in respect thereto. The act prescribes the condition under which the licensees shall operate, containing a set of regulations, with penalties for their violation."*

That Congress intended to fully regulate the business of radio telegraphy, without leaving it to the discretion of an executive officer, is apparent from the report of the House committee in recommending the passage of the bill to the House of Representatives, as follows:

> *"The first section of the bill defines its scope within the commerce clause of the Constitution, and requires all wireless stations, ship and shore, public and private, to be licensed by the Secretary of Commerce and Labor. This section does not give the head of that department discretionary power over the issue of licenses, but in fact provides for an enumeration of the wireless stations of the United States and on vessels under the American flag. The license system proposed is substantially the same as that in use for the documenting upward of 25,000 merchant vessels."*

It was further stated by the chairman of the committee on commerce in the Senate, when the bill was under consideration, that "it is compulsory with the Secretary of Commerce and Labor that upon application these licenses shall be issued."...

In the present case the duty of naming a wavelength is mandatory upon the Secretary. The only discretionary act is in selecting a wavelength, within the limitations prescribed in the statute, which, in his judgment, will result in the least possible interference. The issuing of a license is not dependent upon the fixing of a wavelength. It is a restriction entering into the license. The wavelength named by the Secretary merely measures the extent of the privilege granted to the licensee.

It logically follows that the duty of issuing licenses to persons or corporations coming within the classification designated in the act reposes no discretion whatever in the Secretary of Commerce. The duty is mandatory; hence the courts will not hesitate to require its performance.

The judgment is affirmed, with costs.

RED LION BROADCASTING CO. V. FCC
Supreme Court of the United States, 1969
395 U.S. 367

Justice WHITE delivered the opinion of the Court.

The Federal Communications Commission has for many years imposed on radio and television broadcasters the requirement that discussion of public issues be presented on broadcast stations, and that each side of those issues must be given fair coverage. This is known as the fairness doctrine.... Two aspects of the fairness doctrine, relating to personal attacks in the context of controversial public issues and to political editorializing, were codified more precisely in the form of FCC regulations in 1967. The two cases before us now, which were decided separately below, challenge the constitutional and statutory bases of the doctrine and component rules....

II

The history of the emergence of the fairness doctrine and of the related legislation shows that the Commission's action in the *Red Lion* case did not exceed its authority, and that in adopting the new regulations the Commission was implementing congressional policy rather than embarking on a frolic of its own.

Before 1927, the allocation of frequencies was left entirely to the private sector, and the result was chaos. It quickly became apparent that broadcast frequencies constituted a scarce resource whose use could be regulated and rationalized only by the Government. Without government control, the medium would be of little use because of the cacophony of competing voices, none of which could be clearly and predictably heard. Consequently, the Federal Radio Commission was established to allocate frequencies among competing applicants in a manner responsive to the public "convenience, interest, or necessity."

Very shortly thereafter the Commission expressed its view that the "public interest requires ample play for the free and fair competition of opposing views, and the commission believes that the principle applies ... to all discussions of issues of importance to the public." ...

When a personal attack has been made on a figure involved in a public issue [the regulations] require that the individual attacked himself be offered an opportunity to respond. Likewise, where one candidate is endorsed in a political editorial, the other candidates must themselves be offered reply time to use personally of through a spokesman....

The statutory authority of the FCC to promulgate these regulations derives from the mandate to the "Commission from time to time, as public convenience, interest, or necessity requires" to promulgate "such rules and regulations and prescribe such restrictions and conditions ... as may be necessary to carry our the provisions of this chapter ."... 47 U.S.C. § 303 and § 303(r)....

III

The broadcasters challenge the fairness doctrine and its specific manifestations in the personal attack and political editorial rules on conventional First Amendment grounds, alleging that the rules abridge their freedom of speech and press. Their contention is that the First Amendment protects their desire to use their allotted frequencies continuously to broadcast whatever they choose, and to exclude whomever they choose from ever using that frequency. No man may be prevented from saying or publishing what he thinks, or from refusing in his speech or other utterances to give equal weight to the views of his opponents. This right, they say, applies equally to broadcasters.

A

Although broadcasting is clearly a medium affected by a First Amendment interest, differences in the characteristics of new media justify differences in the First Amendment standards applied to them. For example, the ability of new technology to produce sounds more raucous than those of the human voice justifies restrictions on the sound level, and on the hours and places of use, of sound trucks so long as the restrictions are reasonable and applied without discrimination.

Just as the Government may limit the use of sound-amplifying equipment potentially so noisy that it drowns out civilized private speech, so may the Government limit the use of broadcast equipment. The right of free speech of a broadcaster, the user of a sound truck, or any other individual does not embrace a right to snuff out the free speech of others.

... The lack of know-how and equipment may keep many from the air, but only a tiny fraction of those with resources and intelligence can hope to communicate by radio at the same time if intelligible communication is to be had, even if the entire radio spectrum is utilized in the present state of commercially acceptable technology.

It is this fact, and the chaos that ensued from permitting anyone to use any frequency at whatever power level he wished, which made necessary the enactment of the Radio Act of 1927 and the Communications Act of 1934.... It was this reality which at the very least necessitated first the division of the radio spectrum into portions reserved respectively for public broadcasting and for other important radio uses such as amateur operation, aircraft, police, defense, and navigation; and then the subdivision of each portion, and assignment of specific frequencies to individual users or groups of users. Beyond this, however, because the frequencies reserved for public broadcasting were limited in number, it was essential for the Government to tell some applicants that they could not broadcast at all because there was room for only a few.

Where there are substantially more individuals who want to broadcast than there are frequencies to allocate, it is idle to posit an unabridgeable First Amendment right to broadcast comparable to the right of every individual to speak, write, or publish....

... A license permits broadcasting, but the licensee has no constitutional right to be the one who holds the license or to monopolize a radio frequency to the exclusion of his fellow citizens. There is nothing in the First Amendment which prevents the Government from requiring a licensee to share his frequency with others and to conduct himself as a proxy or fiduciary with obligations to present those views and voices which are representative of his community and which would otherwise, by necessity, be barred from the airwaves.

This is not to say that the First Amendment is irrelevant to public broadcasting. On the contrary, it has a major role to play as the Congress itself recognized in § 326, which forbids FCC interference with "the right of free speech by means of radio communication." Because of the scarcity of radio frequencies, the Government is permitted to put restraints on licensees in favor of others whose views should be expressed on this unique medium.

But the people as a whole retain their interest in free speech by radio and their collective right to have the medium function consistently with the ends and purposes of the First Amendment. It is the right of the viewers and listeners, not the right of the broadcasters, which is paramount. It is the purpose of the First Amendment to preserve an uninhibited marketplace of ideas in which truth will ultimately prevail, rather than to countenance monopolization of that market, whether it be by the Government itself or a private license....

B

Rather than confer frequency monopolies on a relatively small number of licensees, in a Nation of 200,000,000, the Government could surely have decreed that each frequency should be shared among all or some of those who wish to use it, each being assigned a portion of the broadcast day or the broadcast week. The ruling and regulations at issue here do not go quite so far. They assert that under specified circumstances, a licensee must offer to make available a reasonable amount of broadcast time to those who have a view different from that which has already been expressed on his station. The expression of a political endorsement, or of a personal attack while dealing with a controversial public issue, simply triggers this time-sharing. As we have said, the First Amendment confers no right on licensees to prevent others from broadcasting on "their" frequencies and no right to an unconditional monopoly of a scarce resource which the Government has denied others a right to use.

In terms of constitutional principle, and as enforced sharing of a scarce resource, the personal attack and political editorial rules are indistinguishable from the equal-rime provision of § 315, a specific enactment of Congress requiring stations to set aside reply time under specified circumstances and to which the fairness doctrine and these constituent regulations are important complements. That provision, which has been part of the law since 1927, has been held valid by this Court....

In view of the scarcity of broadcast frequencies, the Government's role in allocating those frequencies, and the legitimate claims of those unable, without government assistance, to gain access to those frequencies for expression of their views, we hold the regulations and ruling at issue here are both authorized by statute and constitutional.

MD/DC/DE Broadcasters Ass'n v. FCC
U.S. Court of Appeals for the D.C. Circuit, 2001
236 F.3d 13

GINSBURG, Circuit Judge:

Fifty state broadcasters associations (Broadcasters) petition for review of an Equal Employment Opportunity (EEO) rule promulgated by the Federal Communications Commission. The Broadcasters argue that the rule violates: (1) the Administrative Procedure Act by creating an arbitrary and capricious reporting burden; and (2) the equal protection component of the Due Process Clause of the Fifth Amendment to the Constitution of the United States by granting preferences to women and minorities....

We hold first that the Broadcasters fail to substantiate their claim that the rule is arbitrary and capricious. We further hold that the rule does put official pressure upon broadcasters to recruit minority candidates, thus creating a race-based classification that is not narrowly tailored to support a compelling governmental interest and is therefore unconstitutional. Because we find that the unconstitutional portion of the rule is not severable, we vacate the rule in its entirety....

I. BACKGROUND

The Federal Communications Commission draws its authority to issue EEO rules from the Communications Act of 1934, which authorizes the Commission, in considering whether to grant a license or renewal to a broadcast station, to determine "whether the public interest, convenience, and necessity will be served by the granting of such application." In 1969 the Commission determined that it would not serve the public interest to grant licenses to broadcasters with discriminatory hiring practices. The Commission therefore prohibited licensees from discriminating in employment on the basis of race or sex and required them to establish EEO programs. In 1992 the Congress prohibited the Commission from "revising ... the regulations concerning equal employment opportunity ... as such regulations apply to television broadcast station licensees."

The regulations then in effect required all broadcast licensees—both radio and television stations—not only to refrain from invidious discrimination but also to "establish, maintain, and carry out a positive continuing program of specific practices designed to ensure equal opportunity and nondiscrimination in every aspect of station employment policy and practice." The regulations required stations to seek out sources likely to refer female and minority applicants for employment, to track the source of each referral, and to record the race and sex of each applicant and of each person hired. If these data indicated that a station employed a lower percentage of women and minorities than were employed in the local workforce, then the Commission would take that into account in determining whether to renew the station's license.

In *Lutheran Church-Missouri Synod v. FCC*, 141 F.3d 344 (D.C. Cir. 1998), we held that the Commission's EEO rule was an unconstitutional race-based classification. (The question whether the rule was an unconstitutional sex-based classification was not before the court.) We held first that the rule was subject to strict constitutional scrutiny because it was "built on the notion that stations should aspire to a workforce that attains, or at least approaches, proportional [racial] representation" and "obliged stations to grant some degree of preference to minorities in hiring." We further held that the Commission's sole rationale for its rule, promoting "diversity of programming," was not a compelling governmental justification....

On remand, the Commission suspended the EEO rule in its entirety and issued a Notice of Proposed Rulemaking soliciting comments on a draft replacement rule.... [T]he Commission issued a new EEO rule requiring licensees to achieve a "broad outreach" in their recruiting efforts. To this end, the new EEO rule states that a licensee must make a good faith effort to disseminate widely any information about job openings and, in order to "afford broadcasters flexibility in designing their EEO programs," the rule allows them to select either of two options entailing "supplemental measures" for accomplishing that goal. Under Option A the licensee (if it has more than ten employees) must undertake four approved recruitment initiatives in each two-year period.... A licensee that selects Option A need not report the race and sex of job applicants. Under Option B the licensee may design its own outreach program but must report the race and sex of each job applicant and the source by which the applicant was referred to the station.

In addition, the new EEO rule reinstates the requirement that each licensee file an Annual Employment Report. See 47 C.F.R. § 73.2080(i). That report, the filing of which the Commission had suspended following the decision in *Lutheran Church,* requires the station to identify each employee by race and sex. The Commission stated that it would use the data from the Annual Employment Reports only to monitor industry trends and not (as it had under the prior EEO rule) to screen renewal applications or to assess a licensee's compliance with its EEO obligations.

II. ANALYSIS

The Broadcasters argue that the new EEO rule favors women and minorities and, in so doing, is arbitrary and capricious as well as unconstitutional....

A. The Broadcasters' statutory claim

The Broadcasters argue the new rule is arbitrary and capricious for two reasons, neither of which is persuasive. The Broadcasters first attack the Commission's claim, in the preamble to the new rule, that the rule will promote "programming diversity"; they point out that this court questioned the legitimacy of such a goal in *Lutheran Church.* On review, however, the Commission acknowledges the constitutional cloud over "programming diversity" as a justification for making race a consideration in employment and states that its primary and assertedly sufficient goal in issuing the EEO rule was to prevent invidious discrimination. The preamble to the rule supports the Commission's point. The Broadcasters' attack on the rule as an effort to promote diversity in programming is beside the point, therefore.

The Broadcasters next contend that the new EEO rule arbitrarily and capriciously increases the "regulatory burden" on stations: Under the old rule "broadcasters filed only nine reports in each eight-year license term, while the [new regulations] require broadcast licensees to prepare and file twenty-one reports during a license term." The Broadcasters also argue that the Commission acted arbitrarily and capriciously in eliminating the exemption from filing for stations in areas where minorities are a small percentage of the workforce. In response, the Commission states first that despite the increased number of reports, the time and effort required to complete them has decreased. In their reply the Broadcasters do not disagree and we take the Commission's point as conceded. Second, the Commission reasonably explains that it eliminated the filing exemption in areas with a low percentage of minority group members in the workforce because it no longer takes enforcement action against broadcasters that indicate in their Annual Reports that they have a "low" percentage of minority employees. The Commission's explanation is reasonable; hence the Broadcasters have not shown that the new rule creates an arbitrary and capricious regulatory burden.

B. The Broadcasters' constitutional challenge

The Broadcasters argue next that the new EEO rule puts official pressure on them to favor minorities in the hiring process. This pressure, they claim, violates the Fifth Amendment because it employs a race-based classification that does not withstand strict scrutiny.

1. Does the rule require recruitment or hiring of women and minorities?

The Broadcasters argue that the new EEO rule requires them to recruit and to hire women and minorities. Because we conclude that the rule does create pressure to recruit women and minorities, which pressure ultimately does not withstand constitutional review, we do not reach the question whether the rule creates pressure to hire those women and minorities who are recruited.

For purposes of their constitutional challenge, the Broadcasters focus upon application of the EEO rule to minorities. The Broadcasters argue that both Option A and Option B of the new rule pressure them to recruit minorities. In fact, however, only Option B actually seems to create such pressure. Under Option A, a licensee is not required to report the race or sex of job applicants or interviewees. Instead, the licensee selects from a list of thirteen types of recruitment measures, only two of which pay special attention to women and minorities. Because, as the Commission points out, licensees remain free under Option A to select recruitment measures that do not place a special emphasis upon the presence of women and minorities in the target audience, we do not believe the Broadcasters are meaningfully pressured under Option A to recruit women and minorities.

Option B, however, as FCC Commissioner Furchtgott-Roth pointed out in his dissent from the EEO rule, clearly does create pressure to focus recruiting efforts upon women and minorities in order to induce more applications from those groups. Licensees selecting Option B must report the race, sex, and source of referral for each applicant. The Commission made clear, moreover, in adopting the rule, that "if the data collected does [sic] not confirm that notifications are reaching the entire community, we expect a broadcaster to modify its program as warranted so that it is more inclusive." In determining whether recruitment efforts have reached the "entire community," the Commission considers the number of women and minorities in the applicant pool. If a licensee reports "few or no" women and minorities in its applicant pool, then the Commission will investigate the broadcaster's recruitment efforts.

A regulatory agency may be able to put pressure upon a regulated firm in a number of ways, some more subtle than others. The Commission in particular has a long history of employing: a variety of *sub silentio* pressures and "raised eyebrow" regulation of program content…. The practice of forwarding viewer or listener complaints to the broadcaster with a request for a formal response to the FCC, the prominent speech or statement by a Commissioner or Executive official, the issuance of notices of inquiry … all serve as means for communicating official pressures to the licensee.

Under Option B the Commission promises to investigate any licensee that reports "few or no" applications from women or minorities. Investigation by the licensing authority is a powerful threat, almost guaranteed to induce the desired conduct….

Indeed, the Commission's focus upon the race and sex of applicants belies its statement—or so a licensee reasonably might (and prudently would) conclude—that its only goal is that licensees recruit with a "broad outreach." Were that the Commission's only goal, then it would scrutinize the licensee's outreach efforts, not the job applications those efforts generate. Measuring outputs to determine whether readily measurable inputs were used is more than self-evidently illogical; it is evidence that the agency with life and death power over the licensee is interested in results, not process, and is determined to get them. As a consequence, the threat of being investigated creates an even more powerful incentive for licensees to focus their recruiting efforts upon women and minorities, at least until those groups generate a safe proportion of the licensee's job applications.

2. The level of scrutiny

...

In *Adarand Constructors, Inc. v. Pena*, the Supreme Court held that "any person, of whatever race, has the right to demand that any governmental actor subject to the Constitution justify any racial classification subjecting that person to unequal treatment under the strictest judicial scrutiny." 515 U.S. 200 (1995). The question before the court today, therefore, is whether a government mandate for recruitment targeted at minorities constitutes a "racial classification" that subjects persons of different races to "unequal treatment."...

Under Option B the Commission has compelled broadcasters to redirect their necessarily finite recruiting resources so as to generate a larger percentage of applications from minority candidates. As a result, some prospective non-minority applicants who would have learned of job opportunities but for the Commission's directive now will be deprived of an opportunity to compete simply because of their race. While the Commission's intentions are to benefit minorities rather than to disadvantage non-minorities, *Adarand* clearly holds that the standard of constitutional review does not turn upon the race of those benefited by a particular government action.

... The new rule is therefore subject to strict scrutiny for compliance with the constitutional requirement that all citizens receive equal protection under the law.

3. Does the rule survive strict scrutiny?

For a government action to withstand strict scrutiny it must "serve a compelling governmental interest, and must be narrowly tailored to further that interest."...

We need not resolve the issue of a compelling governmental interest in preventing discrimination, however, because the Broadcasters argue convincingly that the new EEO rule is not narrowly tailored to further that interest. First, Option B places pressure upon each broadcaster to recruit minorities without a predicate finding that the particular broadcaster discriminated in the past or reasonably could be expected to do so in the future. Quite apart from the question of a compelling governmental interest, such a sweeping requirement is the antithesis of a rule narrowly tailored to meet a real problem.

The requirement in Option B that licensees report the race of each applicant is another departure from the norm of narrow tailoring and a corollary, no doubt, of the Commission's true interest in results rather than mere outreach. The race of each job applicant is relevant to the prevention of discrimination only if the Commission assumes that minority groups will respond to non-discriminatory recruitment efforts in some predetermined ratio, such as in proportion to their percentage representation in the local workforce. Any such assumption stands in direct opposition to the guarantee of equal protection, however. The racial data required by Option B simply are not probative on the question of a licensee's efforts to achieve "broad outreach," much less narrowly tailored to further the Commission's stated goal of non-discrimination in the broadcast industry. Because Option B of the new EEO rule is not narrowly tailored, it does not withstand strict scrutiny, and we hold that it violates the equal protection component of the Due Process Clause of the Fifth Amendment.

III. CONCLUSION

...

For the reasons stated in the opinion, the Broadcasters' petition for review is granted and the rule is vacated in its entirety....
So ordered.

[Note: The FCC in 2002 again issued revised EEO rules in an effort to comply with the Constitution. The latest version requires broad-based employee recruitment efforts but aims to be race-neutral.]

FOX TV STATIONS, INC. v. FCC
U.S. Court of Appeals for the D.C. Circuit, 2002
280 F.3d 1027

GINSBURG, Chief Judge:

Before the court are five consolidated petitions to review the Federal Communications Commission's 1998 decision not to repeal or to modify the national television station ownership rule, 47 C.F.R. § 73.3555(e), and the cable/broadcast cross-ownership rule, 47 C.F.R. § 76.501(a). Petitioners challenge the decision as a violation of both the Administrative Procedure Act (APA) and § 202(h) of the Telecommunications Act of 1996. They also contend that both rules violate the First Amendment to the Constitution of the United States. The network petitioners—Fox Television Stations, Inc., National Broadcasting Company, Inc., Viacom Inc., and CBS Broadcasting Inc.—address the national television ownership rule, while petitioner Time Warner Entertainment Company, L.P. addresses the cable/broadcast cross-ownership rule....

We conclude that the Commission's decision to retain the rules was arbitrary and capricious and contrary to law. We remand the national television station ownership rule to the Commission for further consideration, and we vacate the cable/broadcast cross-ownership rule because we think it unlikely the Commission will be able on remand to justify retaining it.

I. BACKGROUND

In the Telecommunications Act of 1996 the Congress set in motion a process to deregulate the structure of the broadcast and cable television industries. The Act itself repealed the statutes prohibiting telephone/cable and cable/broadcast cross-ownership and overrode the few remaining regulatory limits upon cable/network cross-ownership. In radio it eliminated the national, and relaxed the local, restrictions upon ownership and eased the "dual network" rule. In addition, the Act directed the Commission to eliminate the cap upon the number of television stations any one entity may own and to increase to thirty-five from twenty-five the maximum percentage of American households a single broadcaster may reach.

Finally, and most important to this case, in s 202(h) of the Act, the Congress instructed the Commission, in order to continue the process of deregulation, to review each of the Commission's ownership rules every two years:

The Commission shall review its rules adopted pursuant to this section and all of its ownership rules biennially as part of its regulatory reform review under section 11 of the Communications Act of 1934 and shall determine whether any of such rules are necessary in the public interest as the result of competition. The Commission shall repeal or modify any regulation it determines to be no longer in the public interest.

The Commission first undertook a review of its ownership rules pursuant to this mandate in 1998. This case arises out of the resulting decision not to repeal or to modify two Commission rules: the national television station ownership rule and the cable/broadcast cross-ownership rule.

A. The National Television Station Ownership (NTSO) Rule

The NTSO Rule prohibits any entity from controlling television stations the combined potential audience reach of which exceeds thirty-five percent of the television households in the United States. As originally promulgated in the early 1940s, the Rule prohibited common ownership of more than three television stations; that number was later increased to seven. The stated purpose of the seven-station rule was "to promote diversification of ownership in order to maximize diversification of program and service viewpoints" and "to prevent any undue concentration of economic power."

In 1984 the Commission considered the effects of technological changes in the mass media and repealed the NTSO Rule subject to a six-year transition period during which the ownership limit was raised to twelve stations.

The Commission determined that repeal of the NTSO Rule would not adversely affect either the diversity of viewpoints available on the airwaves or competition among broadcasters. It concluded that diversity should be a concern only at the local level, as to which the NTSO Rule was irrelevant and that "[l]ooking at the national level [the Rule was unnecessary because] the U.S. enjoys an abundance of independently owned mass media outlets."...

Implementation of the 1984 Report was subsequently blocked by the Congress. The Commission thereupon reconsidered the matter and prohibited common ownership (1) of stations that in the aggregate reached more than twenty-five percent of the national television audience, and (2) of more than twelve stations regardless of their combined audience reach. These limitations remained in place until 1996, when the Congress directed the Commission to eliminate the twelve-station rule and to raise to thirty-five percent the cap upon audience reach, both of which actions the Commission promptly took.

B. The Cable/Broadcast Cross-Ownership (CBCO) Rule

The CBCO Rule prohibits a cable television system from carrying the signal of any television broadcast station if the system owns a broadcast station in the same local market. In conjunction with certain "must-carry" requirements to which cable operators are subject, the Rule has the effect of prohibiting common ownership of a broadcast station and a cable television system in the same local market.

The Commission first promulgated the CBCO Rule in 1970.... In 1984 the Congress codified the CBCO Rule....

In 1992 ... [t]he Commission ... revisited the CBCO Rule and concluded that "the rationale for an absolute prohibition on broadcast-cable cross-ownership is no longer valid in light of the ongoing changes in the video marketplace." Because the Congress had imposed a similar prohibition by statute, however, the Commission did not repeal the Rule; instead, the Commission recommended that the Congress repeal the statutory prohibition. In the 1996 Act the Congress did just that without, however, requiring the Commission to repeal the CBCO Rule.

C. Applying s 202(h) ...

1. The NTSO Rule

The Commission gave three primary reasons for retaining the NTSO Rule: (1) to observe the effects of recent changes to the rules governing local ownership of television stations; (2) to observe the effects of the increase in the national ownership cap to thirty-five percent; and (3) to preserve the power of affiliates in bargaining with their networks and thereby allow the affiliates to serve their local communities better. The Commission also stated that it believed repealing the rule would "increase concentration in the national advertising market"—presumably to the detriment of competition....

2. The CBCO Rule

In the 1998 Report the Commission decided that retaining the CBCO Rule was necessary to prevent cable operators from favoring their own stations and from discriminating against stations owned by others. The Commission also determined that the CBCO Rule was "necessary to further [the] goal of diversity at the local level."...

III. THE NTSO RULE

... The networks assert that the Commission's decision to retain the NTSO Rule was contrary to s 202(h) and arbitrary and capricious in violation of the APA; alternatively, they contend the Rule violates the First Amendment.

A. Section 202(h) and the APA

...

1. Is the Rule irrational?

...

... [T]he networks note that there is no evidence "that broadcasters have undue market power," such as to dampen competition, in any relevant market. The Commission attempts to rebut the point, but to no avail. In its brief the agency cites a single, barely relevant study by Phillip A. Beutel et al., entitled "Broadcast Television Networks and Affiliates: Economic Conditions and Relationship—1980 and Today" (1995). Insofar as there is any point of tangency between that study and the matter at hand, it is in the authors' conclusion that "the available evidence tends to refute the proposition that affiliates have gained negotiating power since ... 1980." The study plainly does not, however, suggest that broadcasters have undue market power.... Consequently, we must conclude, as the networks maintain, that the Commission has no valid reason to think the NTSO Rule is necessary to safeguard competition.

As to diversity, the networks contend there is no evidence that "the national ownership cap is needed to protect diversity."...

In the 1998 Report the Commission mentioned national diversity as a justification for retaining the NTSO Rule but never elaborated upon the point. This justification fails for two reasons. First, the Commission failed to explain why it was no longer adhering to the view it expressed in the 1984 Report that national diversity is irrelevant. Second, the Commission's passing reference to national diversity does nothing to explain why the Rule....

As to the Commission's three more specific reasons for retaining the NTSO Rule, the networks contend that each is inadequate. The Commission stated that retaining the cap was necessary so it could: (1) observe the effects of recent changes in the rules governing local ownership of television stations; (2) observe the effects of the national ownership cap having been raised to thirty-five percent; and (3) preserve the power of local affiliates to bargain with their networks in order to promote diversity of programming. We agree with the networks that these reasons cannot justify the Commission's decision.

... The Commission's wait-and-see approach cannot be squared with its statutory mandate promptly—that is, by revisiting the matter biennially—to "repeal or modify" any rule that is not "necessary in the public interest."...

Nor does the Commission's third reason—that the Rule is necessary to strengthen the bargaining power of network affiliates and thereby to promote diversity of programming—have sufficient support in the present record. ... [T]he Commission's failure to address itself to the contrary views it expressed in the 1984 Report effectively undermines its present rationale....

In sum, we agree with the networks that the Commission has adduced not a single valid reason to believe the NTSO Rule is necessary in the public interest, either to safeguard competition or to enhance diversity. Although we agree with the Commission that protecting diversity is a permissible policy, the Commission did not provide an adequate basis for believing the Rule would in fact further that cause. We conclude, therefore, that the 1998 decision to retain the NTSO Rule was arbitrary and capricious in violation of the APA.

2. Failure to comply with s 202(h)

The networks argue that the Commission's decision to retain the NTSO Rule was not only arbitrary and capricious but also contrary to s 202(h). As just discussed, we agree with the networks that two of the reasons the Commission gave for retaining the Rule did not even purport to show the Rule was necessary in the public interest, as required by the statute. Furthermore, we agree that the Commission "provided no analysis of the state of competition in the television industry to justify its decision to retain the national ownership cap." The Commission's brief description of the broadcasting market, a single paragraph of the 1998 Report under the heading "Status of Media Marketplace," is woefully inadequate…. [W]e agree with the networks that the Commission "failed even to address meaningfully the question that Congress required it to answer."…

B. The First Amendment

The networks contend that the NTSO Rule violates the First Amendment because it prevents them from speaking directly—that is, through stations they own and operate—to sixty-five percent of the potential television audience in the United States. They would have the court subject the Rule to "intermediate scrutiny," rather than to rationality review, on the grounds that: (a) in today's populous media marketplace the "scarcity" rationale associated with *Red Lion Broadcasting Co. v. FCC* … "makes no sense" as a reason for regulating ownership; (b) even if scarcity is still a valid concern, the NTSO Rule, which does not prevent an entity from owning more than one station in the same local market, does nothing to mitigate the effect of scarcity ….

… [T]his court is not in a position to reject the scarcity rationale even if we agree that it no longer makes sense. The Supreme Court has already heard the empirical case against that rationale and still "declined to question its continuing validity." Turner I, 512 U.S. 622, 638 (1994). In any event, it is not the province of this court to determine when a prior decision of the Supreme Court has outlived its usefulness.

Second, contrary to the networks' express protestations, the scarcity rationale is implicated in this case. The scarcity rationale is based upon the limited physical capacity of the broadcast spectrum, which limited capacity means that "there are more would-be broadcasters than frequencies available." In the face of this limitation, the national ownership cap increases the number of different voices heard in the nation (albeit not the number heard in any one market). But for the scarcity rationale, that increase would be of no moment….

… By limiting the number of stations each network (or other entity) may own, the NTSO Rule ensures that there are more owners than there would otherwise be. An industry with a larger number of owners may well be less efficient than a more concentrated industry. Both consumer satisfaction and potential operating cost savings may be sacrificed as a result of the Rule. But that is not to say the Rule is unreasonable because the Congress may, in the regulation of broadcasting, constitutionally pursue values other than efficiency—including in particular diversity in programming, for which diversity of ownership is perhaps an aspirational but surely not an irrational proxy. Simply put, it is not unreasonable—and therefore not unconstitutional—for the Congress to prefer having in the aggregate more voices heard, each in roughly one-third of the nation, even if the number of voices heard in any given market remains the same.

C. Remedy

We have concluded that, although the NTSO Rule is not unconstitutional, the Commission's decision to retain it was arbitrary and capricious and contrary to law because the

Commission failed to give an adequate reason for its decision, failed to comply with s 202(h), and failed to explain its departure from its previously expressed views....

Under the APA reviewing, courts generally limit themselves to remanding for further consideration an agency order wanting an explanation adequate to sustain it....

... Although the Commission's decision to retain the Rule was, as written, arbitrary and capricious and contrary to s 202(h), we cannot say with confidence that the Rule is likely irredeemable because the Commission failed to set forth the reasons—either analytical or empirical—for which it no longer adheres to the conclusions in its 1984 Report. We do not infer from this silence that the agency cannot justify its change of position....

... We therefore remand this case to the Commission for further consideration whether to repeal or to modify the NTSO Rule.

IV. THE CBCO RULE

Time Warner's principal contention is that the CBCO Rule is an unconstitutional abridgment of its First Amendment right to speak. Time Warner also argues that the Commission's decision to retain the Rule was arbitrary and capricious and contrary to s 202(h). Because we agree that the retention decision was arbitrary and capricious as well as contrary to s 202(h), and that this requires us to vacate the Rule, we do not reach Time Warner's First Amendment claim.

A. Section 202(h) and the APA

Time Warner raises a host of objections to the Commission's decision to retain the CBCO Rule. The Commission is largely unresponsive to these arguments; to the extent it is responsive, it is unpersuasive....

... Time Warner argues that the Commission applied too lenient a standard when it concluded only that the CBCO Rule "continues to serve the public interest," and not that it was "necessary" in the public interest. Again the Commission is silent, but nonetheless we do not reach the merits of Time Warner's argument. This important question was barely raised by the petitioners and was not addressed at all by the Commission.... Even if "necessary in the public interest" means simply "continues to serve the public interest," for the reasons given above and below, the Commission's decision not to repeal or to modify the NTSO and the CBCO Rules cannot stand.

Finally, Time Warner attacks the specific reasons the Commission gave for retaining the Rule. All three reasons relate either to competition or to diversity....

1. Competition

The Commission expressed concern that a cable operator that owns a broadcast station: (1) can "discriminate" against other broadcasters by offering cable/broadcast joint advertising sales and promotions; and (2) has an incentive not to carry, or to carry on undesirable channels, the broadcast signals—including the forthcoming digital signals—of competing stations. Addressing the first concern, Time Warner argues that the Commission failed both to explain why joint advertising rates constitute "discrimination—which is simply a pejorative way of referring to economies of scale and scope"—and to "point to substantial evidence that such 'discrimination' is a non-conjectural problem." Addressing the second concern (in part), Time Warner contends that refusals by cable operators to carry digital signals must not be a significant problem because the Commission has declined to impose must-carry rules for duplicate digital signals. Both of Time Warner's points are plausible—indeed, the first is quite persuasive—and we have no basis upon which to reject either inasmuch as the Commission does not respond to them.

Next, Time Warner gives four reasons for which the Commission's concern about discriminatory carriage of broadcast signals is unwarranted. First, must-carry provisions already ensure that broadcast stations have access to cable systems; indeed, the Commission pointed to only one instance in which a cable operator denied carriage to a broadcast station (Univision). Second, competition from direct broadcast satellite (DBS) providers makes discrimination against competing stations unprofitable. Third, the Commission failed to explain why it departed from the position it took in the 1992 Report, where it said that the CBCO Rule was not necessary to prevent carriage discrimination. Fourth, because a cable operator may lawfully be co-owned with a cable programmer or a network, the Rule does little to cure the alleged problem of cable operators having an incentive to discriminate against stations that air competing programming.

In response the Commission concedes it did not address Time Warner's second and third points....

We conclude that the Commission has failed to justify its retention of the CBCO Rule as necessary to safeguard competition....

2. Diversity

As for retaining the Rule in the interest of diversity, the Commission had this to say: "Cable/TV combinations ... would represent the consolidation of the only participants in the video market for local news and public affairs programming, and would therefore compromise diversity." Time Warner argues that this rationale is contrary to s 202(h), as well as arbitrary and capricious, for essentially three reasons.

First, Time Warner contends that s 202(h), by virtue of its exclusive concern with competition, plainly precludes consideration of diversity and that, in any event, it should be so interpreted in order to avoid the constitutional question raised by the burden the CBCO Rule places upon the company's right to speak. Second, Time Warner argues that the increase in the number of broadcast stations in each local market since the promulgation of the CBCO Rule in 1970 renders any marginal increase in diversity owing to the operation of the Rule too slight to justify retaining it. Finally, Time Warner asserts that the decision to retain the Rule cannot be reconciled with the TV Ownership Order, in which the Commission concluded that a single entity may own two local television stations as long as there are eight other stations in the market and one of the two stations coming under common ownership is not among the four most watched stations.

The Commission responds feebly.... [T]he Commission concedes that it decided to retain the Rule without considering the increase in the number of competing television stations since it had promulgated the Rule in 1970. The Commission gives no explanation for this omission, yet it is hard to imagine anything more relevant to the question whether the Rule is still necessary to further diversity.

Finally, the Commission makes no response to Time Warner's argument that the concern with diversity cannot support an across-the-board prohibition of cross-ownership in light of the Commission's conclusion in the TV Ownership Order that common ownership of two broadcast stations in the same local market need not unduly compromise diversity....

In sum, the Commission concedes it failed to consider the increased number of television stations now in operation, and it is clear that the Commission failed to reconcile the decision under review with the TV Ownership Order it had issued only shortly before. We conclude, therefore, that the Commission's diversity rationale for retaining the CBCO Rule is woefully inadequate.

B. Remedy

The only question left is whether, as Time Warner requests, we should order the Commission to vacate the CBCO Rule itself—as opposed merely to reversing the Commission's decision not to initiate a proceeding to repeal the Rule and remanding the matter for further consideration by the agency.... The Commission gave no reason to think it could adequately address its conclusions in the 1992 Report or in the TV Ownership Order.... Although the Commission presumably made its best effort, the reasons it gave in the 1998 Report for retaining the CBCO Rule were at best flimsy, and its half-hearted attempt to defend its decision in this court is but another indication that the CBCO Rule is a hopeless cause....

Because the probability that the Commission would be able to justify retaining the CBCO Rule is low and the disruption that *vacatur* will create is relatively insubstantial, we shall vacate the CBCO Rule.

V. CONCLUSION

The decision of the Commission not to repeal or to modify the NTSO Rule is vacated and the question whether to retain the Rule is remanded to the Commission for further proceedings consistent with this opinion.... The decision of the Commission not to repeal or to modify the CBCO Rule is also vacated, and the Commission is directed to repeal the CBCO Rule forthwith.

So ordered.

COMCAST CORP. V. FCC
U.S. Court of Appeals for the D.C. Circuit, 2009
579 F.3d 1

GINSBURG, Circuit Judge:

Comcast Corporation and several intervenors involved in the cable television industry petition for review of a rule in which the Federal Communications Commission capped at 30% of all subscribers the market share any single cable television operator may serve....

I. BACKGROUND

The Cable Television Consumer Protection and Competition Act of 1992 directed the FCC, "[i]n order to enhance effective competition," to "prescrib[e] rules and regulations ... [to] ensure that no cable operator or group of cable operators can unfairly impede, either because of the size of any individual operator or because of joint actions by a group of operators of sufficient size, the flow of video programming from the video programmer to the consumer." The Commission is to "make such rules and regulations reflect the dynamic nature of the communications marketplace."

Several cable operators immediately challenged certain provisions of the Act, in particular arguing the subscriber limit provision was facially unconstitutional as a content based restriction of speech. We "conclude[d] that the subscriber limits provision is not content-based." Applying "intermediate, rather than strict scrutiny," we upheld the relevant provision of the Act because the plaintiff "ha[d] not demonstrated that the subscriber limits provision is on its face either unnecessary or unnecessarily overburdensome" to speech protected by the First Amendment to the Constitution of the United States.

In 1993 the Commission first exercised its rulemaking authority and set the subscriber limit at 30%....

In 2001 we considered a petition for review of a then newly revised version of the 30% subscriber limit. *Time Warner Entm't Co. v. FCC* (*Time Warner II*), 240 F.3d 1126 (2001). Then, as now, the Commission established the subscriber limit through an "open field" analysis, in which the agency "determines whether a programming network would have access to alternative [video programming distributors] of sufficient size to allow it to successfully enter the market, if it were denied carriage by one or more of the largest cable operators." In *Time Warner II* we described the formula then used by the FCC:

> [T]he FCC determines that the average cable network needs to reach 15 million subscribers to be economically viable. This is 18.56% of the roughly 80 million ... subscribers, and the FCC rounds it up to 20% of such subscribers. The FCC then divines that the average cable programmer will succeed in reaching only about 50% of the subscribers linked to cable companies that *agree* to carry its programming, because of channel capacity,
> programming tastes of particular cable operators, or other factors. The average programmer therefore requires an open field of 40% of the market to be viable (.20/.50 = .40).
>
> Finally, to support the 30% limit that it says is necessary to assure this minimum, the Commission reasons as follows: With a 30% limit, a programmer has an open field of 40% of the market even if the two largest cable companies deny carriage, acting individually or collusively.

....

In establishing the subscriber limit we reviewed in *Time Warner II*, the Commission had sought to ensure a minimum open field of 40% and reasoned that a 30% cap, rather than the seemingly obvious 60% cap, was necessary because the Commission was concerned about the viability of a video programming network if the two largest cable operators denied it carriage. We granted the petition because the record contained no evidence of cable operators' colluding to deny a video programmer carriage and "the legitimate, independent editorial choices" of two or more cable operators could not be said to "unfairly impede, either because of the size of any individual operator or because of joint actions by a group of operators of sufficient size, the flow of video programming from the video programmer to the consumer." We directed the agency on remand to consider how the increasing market share of direct broadcast satellite (DBS) companies, such as DirecTV and Dish Network, diminished cable operators' ability to determine the economic fate of programming networks.

On remand, the Commission adopted the current version of the 30% subscriber limit. The Rule here under review was designed to ensure that no single cable operator "can, by simply refusing to carry a programming network, cause it to fail." Based upon the record before the court in *Time Warner II*, the subscriber limit under this standard could not have been lower than 60%. Based upon the present record, however, the Commission concluded no cable operator could safely be allowed to serve … more than 30% of all subscribers….

In re-calculating the minimum viable scale, the Commission relied upon a study's finding regarding the number of viewers a cable network needed to reach in order to have a 70% chance of survival after five years, using data
on the survival of cable networks between 1984 and 2001. Based upon the study, the FCC found the minimum viable scale was 19.03 million subscribers, about four million more than the agency had found were necessary in 1999.

To determine the total number of subscribers, the FCC counted all cable subscribers and DBS customers, totaling approximately 96 million (up from 80 million in 1999). In re-calculating the penetration rate, the
Commission observed, "many, if not most, new cable networks are placed on a digital tier. A consequence of being placed on a digital tier versus one of the basic levels of service ... is a much lower penetration rate." Using an in-house study of the tiering and subscribership data for a sample of cable operators and a linear regression model, the Commission determined the penetration rate of the average network was 27.42%, or slightly more than half the 50% penetration rate it found in 1999.

From these data, the Commission calculated that a video programming network, to be viable, required an open field of 70% (up from 40% in 1999). Therefore, no cable operator could serve more than 30% of all subscribers.

Although the Commission recognized "that competition in the downstream market [especially from DBS companies] may affect the ability of a large cable operator to prevent successful entry by a programming network, and that [the] open field analysis does not directly measure this," it decided not to adjust the subscriber limit to account for such competition because doing so would be "quite difficult." The FCC then gave four reasons it did not regard competition from DBS companies as significant: Customers are reluctant to switch from cable service to DBS because (1) switching is costly; and (2) cable operators offer non-video services, such as telephone and internet access, that are not available with DBS; and (3) "video programming is a product, the quality of which cannot be known with certainty until it is consumed." Additionally, (4) "[c]ompetitive pressures from DBS will not provide any assistance to networks that," not having a contract with the largest cable operator, are unable to "launch due to a lack of financing."

....

II. ANALYSIS

....

We may set aside the Commission's decision "only if [it] was 'arbitrary, capricious, an abuse of discretion, or otherwise not in accordance with law.'" We will not do so if the agency "examined the relevant data and articulated a satisfactory explanation for its action."

Whether a cable operator serving more than 30% of subscribers can exercise "bottleneck monopoly power," depends, as we observed in *Time Warner II*, "not only on its share of the market, but also on the elasticities of supply and demand, which in turn are determined by the *availability* of competition." A cable operator faces competition primarily from non-cable companies, such as those providing DBS service and, increasingly, telephone companies providing fiber optic service. As Comcast points out, DBS companies alone now serve approximately 33% of all subscribers. Recognizing the growing importance particularly of DBS, in *Time Warner II* we said in no uncertain terms that "in revisiting the horizontal rules the Commission will have to take account of the impact of DBS on [cable operators'] market power."

....

Comcast argues the Commission has offered no plausible reason for its failure to heed our explicit direction in *Time Warner II* to consider the competitive impact of DBS companies. Instead the Commission made the four nonempirical observations we enumerated above. As for the first, transaction costs undoubtedly do deter some cable customers from switching to satellite services, but Comcast points to record evidence that almost 50% of all DBS customers formerly subscribed to cable; in the face of that evidence, the Commission's observation that cost may deter some customers from switching to DBS is feeble indeed. With regard to the second—that some cable consumers may be reluctant to switch to a satellite television service because, unlike cable companies, DBS companies do not offer internet and telephone services—the Commission does not point to any evidence tending to show these inframarginal customers are numerous enough to confer upon cable operators their supposed bottleneck power over programming....

The Commission's third justification—that consumers will not switch providers to access new programming because they cannot know the quality of the programming before consuming it—warrants little discussion. As Comcast points out, there is no record support for this conjecture. In any event, it is common knowledge that new video programming is advertised on other television stations and in other media, and can be previewed over the internet, thus providing consumers with information about the quality of competing services. The FCC's fourth reason—that without its subscriber cap an upstart network will have trouble securing financing unless it has a contract with a cable company serving more than 30% of the market—is no more convincing than the other three when one recalls DBS companies already serve more than 30% of the market.

Finally, we note the Commission's observation that assessing competition from DBS companies is difficult—possibly true even if unexplained—does not justify the agency's failure to consider competition from DBS companies in important aspects of its model....

Comcast … points to evidence that the number of cable networks has increased by almost 500% since 1992 and has grown at an ever faster rate since 2000, and that a much lower percentage of cable networks are vertically integrated with cable operators than was the case when the Congress passed the 1992 Act. There can be no doubt that consumers are now able to receive far more channels than they could in 1999, let alone 1992.

In sum, the Commission has failed to demonstrate that allowing a cable operator to serve more than 30% of all cable subscribers would threaten to reduce either competition or diversity in programming. First, the record is replete with evidence of ever increasing competition among video providers: Satellite and fiber optic video providers have entered the market and grown in market share since the Congress passed the 1992 Act, and particularly in recent years. Cable operators, therefore, no longer have the bottleneck power over programming that concerned the Congress in 1992. Second, over the same period there has been a dramatic increase both in the number of cable networks and in the programming available to subscribers.

In view of the overwhelming evidence concerning "the dynamic nature of the communications marketplace," and the entry of new competitors at both the programming and the distribution levels, it was arbitrary and capricious for the Commission to conclude that a cable operator serving more than 30% of the market poses a threat either to competition or to diversity in programming….

….

The Commission's dereliction in this case is particularly egregious. In the previous round of this litigation we expressly instructed the agency on remand to consider fully the competition that cable operators face from DBS companies. The omission of this consideration was a major failing of the FCC's prior attempt to justify the 30% cap. The Commission nonetheless failed to heed our direction and we are again faced with the same objections to the rationale for the cap. It is apparent that the Commission either cannot or will not fully incorporate the competitive impact of DBS and fiber optic companies into its open field model….

….

…. Were the Rule left in place while the FCC tries a third time to rationalize the cap … it would continue to burden speech protected by the First Amendment….

The 30% subscriber cap has limited the ability of cable operators to communicate with the public for some 16 years despite our determination eight years ago that a prior version of the Rule was unconstitutional….

III. CONCLUSION

We hold the 30% subscriber limit is arbitrary and capricious because the Commission failed adequately to take account of the substantial competition cable operators face from noncable video programming distributors…. [T]he subscriber limit is, accordingly,

Vacated.

Chapter Ten
ELECTRONIC MEDIA CONTENT

In this chapter we look at a handful of cases that deal with government regulation of the content of electronic media. Generally speaking, the courts have upheld rational attempts by the federal government to control broadcast content, with a few exceptions. But in cable TV, without the airwave scarcity rationale as articulated in *Red Lion*, the First Amendment looms much larger. A key determination in cable can be whether the restriction is content-neutral or whether it is aimed at particular viewpoints or types of programming. You will note in this chapter, too, that the government controls often concern what programming electronic media outlets must carry, as opposed to what they must not.

FCC v. League of Women Voters of California illustrates that some broadcast content regulations may indeed be unconstitutional, particularly if they prevent licensees from broadcasting their own points of view.

CBS, Inc. v. FCC provides statutory interpretation of Communications Act section 312—a major content regulation that requires broadcasters to grant reasonable access time to federal political candidates. In this case the Supreme Court also dismissed a constitutional challenge to the statute.

Turner Broadcasting System v. FCC (Turner I) is a Supreme Court decision that established that cable operators are entitled to greater First Amendment protection than broadcasters. The case also illustrates the important distinction to be made between content-based and content-neutral restrictions on speech, however.

Turner Broadcasting System v. FCC (Turner II) revisits the complex litigation of *Turner I* and reaches an ultimate conclusion on the must-carry rules for cable TV.

FCC v. League of Women Voters of California
Supreme Court of the United States, 1984
468 U.S. 364

Justice BRENNAN delivered the opinion of the Court.

Moved to action by a widely felt need to sponsor independent sources of broadcast programming as an alternative to commercial broadcasting, Congress set out in 1967 to support and promote the development of noncommercial, educational broadcasting stations. A keystone of Congress' program was the Public Broadcasting Act of 1967, 47 U.S.C. § 390 *et seq.*, which established the Corporation for Public Broadcasting, a nonprofit corporation authorized to disburse federal funds to noncommercial television and radio stations in support of station operations and educational programming. Section 399 of that Act ... forbids any "noncommercial educational broadcasting station which receives a grant from the Corporation" to "engage in editorializing." In this case, we are called upon to decide whether Congress, by imposing that restriction, has passes a "law ... abridging the freedom of speech, or of the press" in violation of the First Amendment of the Constitution.

I

....

Appellee Pacifica Foundation [one of three appellees] is a nonprofit corporation that owns and operates several noncommercial, educational broadcasting stations in five major metropolitan areas. Its licensees have received and are presently receiving grants from the Corporation and are therefore prohibited from editorializing by the terms of § 399....

The District Court granted summary judgment in favor of appellees, holding that § 399's ban on editorializing violated the First Amendment. The court rejected the Federal Communications Commission's contention that "§ 399 serves a compelling government interest in ensuring that funded noncommercial broadcasters do not become propaganda organs for the government." ... The FCC appealed from the District Court judgment directly to this Court.... [W]e now affirm.

II

We begin by considering the appropriate standard of review. The District Court acknowledged that our decisions have generally applied a different First Amendment standard for broadcast regulation than in other areas, but after finding that no special characteristic of the broadcast media justified application of a less stringent standard in this case, it held that § 399 could survive constitutional scrutiny only if it served a "compelling" governmental interest.... [T]he Government contends that a less demanding standard is required. It argues that Congress may, consistently with the First Amendment, exercise broad power to regulate broadcast speech because the medium of broadcasting is subject to the "special characteristic" of spectrum scarcity—a characteristic not shared by other media—which calls for more exacting regulation....

At first glance, of course, it would appear that the District Court applied the correct standard. Section 399 plainly operates to restrict the expression of editorial opinion on matters of public importance, and, as we have repeatedly explained, communication of this kind is entitled to the most exacting degree of First Amendment protection. Were a similar ban on editorializing applied to newspapers and magazines, we would not hesitate to strike it down as violative of the First Amendment. But, as the Government correctly notes, because broadcast regulation involves unique considerations, our cases have not followed precisely the same approach that we have applied to other media and have never gone so far as to demand that such regulations serve "compelling" governmental interests....

... In *Red Lion*, for example, we upheld the FCC's "fairness doctrine"—which requires broadcasters to provide adequate coverage of public issues and to ensure that this coverage fairly and accurately reflects the opposing views—because the doctrine advanced the substantial governmental interest in ensuring balanced presentations of views in this limited medium and yet posed no threat that a "broadcaster [would be denied permission] to carry a particular program or to publish his own views." Similarly, in *CBS, Inc. v. FCC*, the Court upheld the right of access for federal candidates imposed by § 312(a)(7) of the Communications Act both because that provision "makes a significant contribution to freedom of expression by enhancing the ability of candidates to present, and the public to receive, information necessary for the effective operation of the democratic process," and because it defined a sufficiently "*limited* right of 'reasonable' access" so that "the discretion of broadcasters to present their views on any issue or to carry any particular type of programming" was not impaired....

Thus, although the broadcasting industry plainly operates under restraints not imposed upon other media, the thrust of these restrictions has generally been to secure the public's First Amendment interest in receiving a balanced presentation of views on diverse matters of public concern....

III

We turn now to consider whether the restraint imposed by § 399 satisfies the requirements established by our prior cases for permissible broadcast regulation. Before assessing the Government's proffered justifications for the statute, however, two central features of the ban against editorializing must be examined, since they help to illuminate the importance of the First Amendment interests at stake in this case.

A

First, the restriction imposed by § 399 is specifically directed at a form of speech— namely, the expression of editorial opinion—that lies at the heart of First Amendment protection....

... Because § 399 appears to restrict precisely that form of speech which the Framers of the Bill of Rights were most anxious to protect—speech that is "indispensable to the discovery and spread of political truth"—we must be especially careful in weighing the interests that are asserted in support of this restriction and in assessing the precision with which the ban is crafted.

Second, the scope of § 399's ban is defined solely on the basis of the content of the suppressed speech. A wide variety of noneditorial speech "by licensees, their management, or those speaking on their behalf," is plainly not prohibited by § 399. Examples of such permissible forms of speech include daily announcements of the station's program schedule or over-the-air appeals for contributions from listeners....

As Justice STEVENS observed in *Consolidated Edison Co. v. Public Service Comm'n of N.Y.,* 447 U.S. 530 (1980), however: "A regulation of speech that is motivated by nothing more than a desire to curtail expression of a particular point of view on controversial issues of general interest is the purest example of a 'law ... abridging the freedom of speech, or of the press.' A regulation that denies one group of persons the right to address a selected audience on 'controversial issues of public policy' is plainly such a regulation." Section 399 is just such a regulation, for it singles out noncommercial broadcasters and denies them the right to address their chosen audience on matters of public importance....

B

In seeking to defend the prohibition on editorializing imposed by § 399, the Government urges that the statute was aimed at preventing two principal threats to the overall success of the Public Broadcasting Act of 1967. According to this argument, the ban was necessary, first, to protect noncommercial, educational broadcasting stations from being coerced, as a result of federal financing, into becoming vehicles for Government propagandizing or the objects of governmental influence; and, second, to keep these stations from becoming convenient targets for capture by private interest groups wishing to express their own partisan viewpoints. By seeking to safeguard the public's right to a balanced presentation of public issues through the prevention of either governmental or private bias, these objectives are, of course, broadly consistent with the goals identified in our earlier broadcast regulation cases. But, in sharp contrast to the restrictions upheld in *Red Lion* or in *CBS, Inc. v. FCC,* which left room for editorial discretion and simply required broadcast editors to grant others access to the microphone, § 399 directly prohibits the broadcaster from speaking out on public issues even in a balanced and fair manner. The Government insists, however, that the hazards posed in the "special" circumstances of noncommercial, educational broadcasting are so great that § 399 is an indispensable means of preserving the public's First Amendment interests. We disagree.

(1)

   ....

   ... [A]n examination of both the overall legislative scheme established by the 1967 Act and the character of public broadcasting demonstrates that the interest asserted by the Government is not substantially advanced by § 399. First, to the extent that federal financial support creates a risk that stations will lose their independence through the bewitching power of governmental largesse, the elaborate structure established by the Public Broadcasting Act already operates to insulate local stations from governmental interference. Congress not only mandated that the new Corporation for Public Broadcasting would have a private, bipartisan structure, but also imposed a variety of important limitations on its powers....

   Even if these statutory protections were thought insufficient to the task, however, suppressing the particular category of speech restricted by § 399 is simply not likely, given the character of the public broadcasting system, to reduce substantially the risk that the Federal Government will seek to influence or put pressure on local stations.... There are literally hundreds of public radio and television stations in communities scattered throughout the United States and its territories. Given that central fact, it seems reasonable to infer that the editorial voices of these stations will prove to be as distinctive, varied, and idiosyncratic as the various communities they represent. More importantly, the editorial focus of any particular station can fairly be expected to focus largely on issues affecting only its community. Accordingly, absent some showing by the Government to the contrary, the risk that local editorializing will place all of public broadcasting in jeopardy is not sufficiently pressing to warrant § 399's broad suppression of speech.

   Indeed, what is far more likely than local station editorials to pose the kinds of dangers hypothesized by the Government are the wide variety of programs addressing controversial issues produced, often with substantial CPB funding, for national distribution to local stations....

   ....

   Finally, although the Government certainly has a substantial interest in ensuring that the audiences of noncommercial stations will not be led to think that the broadcaster's editorials reflect the official view of the government, this interest can be fully satisfied by less restrictive means that are readily available. To address this important concern, Congress could simply require public broadcasting stations to broadcast a disclaimer every time they editorialize which would state that the editorial represents only the view of the station's management and does not in any way represent the views of the Federal Government or any of the station's other sources of funding....

In sum, § 399's broad ban on all editorializing by every station that receives CPB funds far exceeds what is necessary to protect against the risk of governmental interference or to prevent the public from assuming that editorials by public broadcasting stations represent the official view of government. The regulation impermissibly sweeps within its prohibition a wide range of speech by wholly private stations on topics that do not take a directly partisan stand or that have nothing whatever to do with federal, state, or local government.

Assuming that the Government's second asserted interest in preventing noncommercial stations from becoming a "privileged outlet for the political and ideological opinions of station owners and managers," is legitimate, the substantiality of this asserted interest is dubious.... If it is true, as the Government contends, that noncommercial stations remain free, despite § 399, to broadcast a wide variety of controversial views through their power to control program selection, to select which persons will be interviewed, and to determine how news reports will be presented, then it seems doubtful that § 399 can fairly be said to advance any genuinely substantial government interest in keeping controversial or partisan opinions from being aired by noncommercial stations....

In short, § 399 does not prevent the use of noncommercial stations for the presentation of partisan views on controversial matters; instead, it merely bars a station from specifically communicating such views on its own behalf or on behalf of its management....

Finally, the public's interest in preventing public broadcasting stations from becoming forums for lopsided presentations of narrow partisan positions is already secured by a variety of other regulatory means that intrude far less drastically upon the "journalistic freedom" of noncommercial broadcasters....

IV

Although the Government did not present the argument in any form to the District Court, it now seeks belatedly to justify § 399 on the basis of Congress' spending power.... [T]he Government argues that by prohibiting noncommercial, educational stations that receive CPB grants from editorializing, Congress has, in the proper exercise of its spending power, simply determined that it "will not subsidize public broadcasting stations editorials." In *Taxation With Representation*, the Court found that Congress could, in the exercise of its spending power, reasonably refuse to subsidize the lobbying activities of tax-exempt charitable organizations by prohibiting such organizations from using tax-deductible contributions to support their lobbying efforts. In so holding, however, we explained that such organizations remained free "to receive [tax-]deductible contributions to support nonlobbying activit[ies]." Thus, a charitable organization could create ... an affiliate to conduct its nonlobbying activities using tax-deductible contributions, and, at the same time, establish a separate affiliate to pursue its lobbying efforts without such contributions.... [T]he Court concluded that "Congress has not infringed any First Amendment rights or regulated any First Amendment activity; [it] has simply chosen not to pay for TWR's lobbying."

In this case, however, unlike the situation faced by the charitable organization in *Taxation With Representation*, a noncommercial, educational station that receives only one percent of its overall income from CPB grants is barred absolutely from all editorializing. Therefore, in contrast to the appellee in *Taxation With Representation*, such a station is not able to segregate its activities according to the source of its funding. The station has no way of limiting the use of its federal funds to all noneditorializing activities, and, more importantly, it is barred from using even wholly private funds to finance its editorial activity.

....

In conclusion, we emphasize that our disposition of this case rests upon a narrow proposition. We do not hold that the Congress or the FCC is without power to regulate the content, timing, or character of speech by noncommercial educational broadcasting stations. Rather, we hold only that the specific interests sought to be advanced by § 399's ban on editorializing are either not sufficiently substantial or are not served in a sufficiently limited manner to justify the substantial abridgment of important journalistic freedoms which the First Amendment jealously protects....

CBS, INC. V. FCC
Supreme Court of the United States, 1981
453 U.S. 367

Chief Justice BURGER delivered the opinion of the Court.

We granted certiorari to consider whether the Federal Communications Commission properly construed 47 U.S.C. § 312(a)(7) and determined that petitioners failed to provide "reasonable access to ... the use of a broadcast station" as required by the statute.

I

A

On October 11, 1979, Gerald M. Rafshoon, President of the Carter-Mondale Presidential Committee, requested each of the three major television networks to provide time for a thirty-minute program between 8 p.m. and 10:30 p.m. on either the fourth, fifth, sixth, or seventh of December 1979. The Committee intended to present, in conjunction with President Carter's formal announcement of his candidacy, a documentary outlining the record of his administration.

The networks declined to make the requested time available. Petitioner CBS emphasized the large number of candidates for the Republican and Democratic Presidential nominations and the potential disruption of regular programming to accommodate requests for equal treatment, but it offered to sell two five-minute segments to the Committee, one at 10:55 p.m. on December 8 and one in the daytime. Petitioner American Broadcasting Co.

replied that it had not yet decided when it would begin selling political time for the 1980 Presidential campaign, but subsequently indicated that it would allow such sales in January 1980. Petitioner National Broadcasting Co., noting the number of potential requests for time from Presidential candidates, stated that it was not prepared to sell time for political programs as early as December 1979.

On October 29, 1979, the Carter-Mondale Presidential Committee filed a complaint with the Federal Communications Commission, charging that the networks had violated their obligation to provide "reasonable access" under § 312(a)(7) of the Communications Act of 1934, as amended. [The Act] states:

"The Commission may revoke any station license or construction permit—

. . . .

"(7) for willful or repeated failure to allow reasonable access or to permit purchase of reasonable amounts of time for the use of a broadcasting station by a legally qualified candidate for Federal elective office on behalf of his candidacy."

… [T]he Commission, by a 4-to-3 vote, ruled that the networks had violated § 312(a)(7)….

B

The Court of Appeals affirmed the Commission's orders, holding that the statute created a new, affirmative right of access to the broadcast media for individual candidates for federal elective office….

II

We consider first the scope of § 312(a)(7)….

A

…. It is clear on the face of the statute that Congress did not prescribe merely a general duty to afford some measure of political programming, which the public interest obligation of broadcasters already provided for. Rather, § 312(a)(7) focuses on the individual "legally qualified candidate" seeking air time to advocate "*his* candidacy," and guarantees him "reasonable access" enforceable by specific governmental sanction….

III

A

Although Congress provided in § 312(a)(7) for greater use of broadcasting stations by federal candidates, it did not give guidance on how the Commission should implement the statute's access requirement. Essentially, Congress adopted a "rule of reason" and charged the Commission with its enforcement…. The Commission has issued some general interpretative statements, but its standards implementing § 312(a)(7) have evolved principally on a case-by-case basis and are not embodied in formalized rules. The relevant criteria broadcasters must employ in evaluating access requests under the statute can be summarized from the Commission's 1978 Report and Order and the memorandum opinions and orders in these cases.

Broadcasters are free to deny the sale of air time prior to the commencement of a campaign, but once a campaign has begun, they must give reasonable and good faith attention to access requests from "legally qualified" candidates for federal elective office. Such requests must be considered on an individualized basis, and broadcasters are required to tailor their responses to accommodate, as much as reasonably possible, a candidate's stated purposes in seeking air time. In responding to access requests, however, broadcasters may also give weight to such factors as the amount of time previously sold to the candidate, the disruptive impact on regular programming, and the likelihood of requests for time by rival candidates under the equal opportunities provision of § 315(a). These considerations may not be invoked as pretexts for denying access; to justify a negative response, broadcasters must cite a realistic danger of substantial program disruption—perhaps caused by insufficient notice to allow adjustments in the schedule—or of an excessive number of equal time requests. Further, in order to facilitate review by the Commission, broadcasters must explain their reasons for refusing time or making a more limited counteroffer. If broadcasters take the appropriate factors into account and act reasonably and in good faith, their decisions will be entitled to deference even if the Commission's analysis would have differed in the first instance. But if broadcasters adopt "across-the-board policies" and do not attempt to respond to the individualized situation of a particular candidate, the Commission is not compelled to sustain their denial of access....

B

.... Based upon the Commission's prior decisions and 1978 Report and Order, we must conclude that petitioners had adequate notice that their conduct in responding to the Carter-Mondale Presidential Committee's request for access would contravene the statute.

In the 1978 Report and Order, the Commission stated that it could not establish a precise point at which § 312(a)(7) obligations would attach for all campaigns because each is unique:

> "For instance, *a presidential campaign may be in full swing almost a year before an election*; other campaigns may be limited to a short concentrated period.... [W]e believe that, generally, a licensee would be unreasonable if it refused to afford access to Federal candidates at least during those time periods [when the 'lowest unit charge' provision of § 315 applied]. Moreover, it may be required to afford reasonable access before these periods; however, the determination of whether 'reasonable access' must be afforded before these periods for particular races must be made in each case under all the facts and circumstances present.... [W]e expect licensees to afford access at a reasonable time prior to a convention or caucus. We will review a licensee's decisions in this area on a case-by-case basis." (Emphasis added by the Court.)

Here, the Carter-Mondale Presidential Committee sought broadcast time approximately eleven months before the 1980 Presidential election and eight months before the Democratic National Convention. In determining that a national campaign was underway at that point, the Commission stressed: (a) that ten candidates formally had announced their intention to seek the Republican nomination, and two candidates had done so for the Democratic nomination; (b) that various states had started the delegate selection process; (c) that candidates were traveling across the country making speeches and attempting to raise funds; (d) that national campaign organizations were established and operating; (e) that the Iowa caucus would be held the following month; (f) that public officials and private groups were making endorsements; and (g) that the national print media had given campaign activities prominent coverage for almost two months....

Nevertheless, petitioners ABC and NBC refused to sell the Carter-Mondale Presidential Committee any time in December 1979 on the ground that it was "too early in the political season." These petitioners made no counteroffers, but adopted "blanket" policies refusing access despite the admonition against such an approach in the 1978 Report and Order. Likewise, petitioner CBS, while not barring access completely, had an across-the-board policy of selling only five-minute spots to all candidates, not withstanding the Commission's directive in the 1978 Report and Order that broadcasters consider "a candidate's desires as to the method of conducting his or her media campaign" ... Moreover, the Committee's request was made almost two months before the intended date of broadcast, was flexible in that it could be satisfied with any prime time slot during a four-day period, was accompanied by an offer to pay the normal commercial rate, and was not preceded by other requests from President Carter for access. Although petitioners adverted to the disruption of regular programming and the potential equal time requests from rival candidates in their responses to the Carter-Mondale Presidential Committee's complaint, the Commission rejected these claims as "speculative and unsubstantiated at best."

Under these circumstances, we cannot conclude that the Commission abused its discretion in finding that petitioners failed to grant the "reasonable access" required by § 312(a)(7)....

IV

Finally, petitioners assert that § 312(a)(7) as implemented by the Commission violates the First Amendment rights of broadcasters by unduly circumscribing their editorial discretion. In *Columbia Broadcasting System, Ind. v. Democratic National Committee,* 412 U.S., at 117, we stated:

> "Th[e] role of the Government as an 'overseer' and ultimate arbiter and guardian of the public interest and the role of the licensee as a journalistic 'free agent' call for a delicate balancing of competing interests. The maintenance of this balance for more than forty years has called on both the regulators and the licensees to walk a 'tightrope' to preserve the First Amendment values written into the Radio Act and its successor, the Communications Act."

Petitioners argue that the Commission's interpretation of § 312(a)(7)'s access requirement disrupts the "delicate balance" that broadcast regulation must achieve. We disagree....

Petitioners are correct that the Court has never approved a *general* right of access to the media. See, e. g., *Miami Herald Publishing Co. v. Tornillo,* 418 U.S. 241 (1974). Nor do we do so today. Section 312(a)(7) creates a *limited* right to "reasonable" access that pertains only to legally qualified federal candidates and may be invoked by them only for the purpose of advancing their candidacies once a campaign has commenced....

Section 312(a)(7) represents an effort by Congress to assure that an important resource— the airwaves—will be used in the public interest. We hold that the statutory right of access, as defined by the Commission and applied in these cases, properly balances the First Amendment rights of federal candidates, the public, and broadcasters.

The judgment of the Court of Appeals is *Affirmed.*

TURNER BROADCASTING SYSTEM V. FCC (TURNER I)
Supreme Court of the United States, 1994
512 U.S. 622

Justice KENNEDY delivered the opinion of the Court.

I

....

On October 5, 1992, Congress overrode a Presidential veto to enact the Cable Television Consumer Protection and Competition Act of 1992.... At issue in this case is the constitutionality of the so-called must-carry provisions, contained in §§ 4 and 5 of the Act, which require cable operators to carry the signals of a specified number of local broadcast television stations....

... Congress concluded that unless cable operators are required to carry local broadcast stations, "[t]here is a substantial likelihood that ... additional local broadcast signals will be deleted, repositioned, or not carried"; the "market shift in market share" from broadcast to cable will continue to erode the advertising revenue base which sustains free local broadcast television; and that, as a consequence, "the economic viability of free local broadcast television and its ability to originate quality local programming will be seriously jeopardized."

Soon after the Act became law, appellants filed these five consolidated actions in the United States District Court for the District of Columbia against the United States and the Federal Communications Commission (hereinafter referred to collectively as the Government), challenging the constitutionality of the must-carry provisions. Appellants, plaintiffs below, are numerous cable programmers and cable operators....

II

....

By requiring cable systems to set aside a portion of their channels for local broadcasters, the must-carry rules regulate cable speech in two respects: The rules reduce the number of channels over which cable operators exercise unfettered control, and they render it more difficult for cable programmers to compete for carriage on the limited channels remaining. Nevertheless, because not every interference with speech triggers the same degree of scrutiny under the First Amendment, we must decide at the outset the level of scrutiny applicable to the must-carry provisions.

A

We address first the Government's contention that regulation of cable television should be analyzed under the same First Amendment standard that applies to regulation of broadcast television. It is true that our cases have permitted more intrusive regulation of broadcast speakers than of speakers in other media. Compare *Red Lion Broadcasting Co. v. FCC*, 395 U.S. 367 (1969) (television), and *National Broadcasting Co. v. United States*, 319 U.S. 190 (1943) (radio), with *Miami Herald Publishing Co. v. Tornillo*, 418 U.S. 241 (1974) (print), and *Riley v. National Federation of Blind of N.C., Inc.*, 487 U.S. 781 (1988) (personal solicitation). But the rationale for applying a less rigorous standard of First Amendment scrutiny to broadcast regulation, whatever its validity in the cases elaborating it, does not apply in the context of cable regulation.

The justification for our distinct approach to broadcast regulation rests upon the unique physical limitations of the broadcast medium....

... [c]able television does not suffer from the inherent limitations that characterize the broadcast medium. Indeed, given the rapid advances in fiber optics and digital compression technology, soon there may be no practical limitation on the number of speakers who may use the cable medium. Nor is there any danger of physical interference between two cable speakers attempting to share the same channel. In light of these fundamental technological differences between broadcast and cable transmission, application of the more relaxed standard of scrutiny adopted in *Red Lion* and the other broadcast cases is inapt when determining the First Amendment validity of cable regulation....

B

At the heart of the First Amendment lies the principle that each person should decide for him or herself the ideas and beliefs deserving of expression, consideration, and adherence. Our political system and cultural life rest upon this ideal. Government action that stifles speech on account of its message, or that requires the utterance of a particular message favored by the Government, contravenes this essential right....

For these reasons, the First Amendment, subject only to narrow and well-understood exceptions, does not countenance governmental control over the content of messages expressed by private individuals. Our precedents thus apply the most exacting scrutiny to regulations that suppress, disadvantage, or impose differential burdens upon speech because of its content. Laws that compel speakers to utter or distribute speech bearing a particular message are subject to the same rigorous scrutiny. In contrast, regulations that are unrelated to the content of speech are subject to an intermediate level of scrutiny because in most cases they pose a less substantial risk of excising certain ideas or viewpoints from the public dialogue.

Deciding whether a particular regulation is content-based or content-neutral is not always a simple task....

C

... [T]he must-carry rules, on their face, impose burdens and confer benefits without reference to the content of speech.... Nothing in the Act imposes a restriction, penalty, or burden by reason of the views, programs, or stations the cable operator has selected or will select. The number of channels a cable operator must set aside depends only on the operator's channel capacity.

The must-carry provisions also burden cable programmers by reducing the number of channels for which they can compete. But again, this burden is unrelated to content, for it extends to all cable programmers irrespective of the programming they choose to offer viewers....

....

That the must-carry provisions, on their face, do not burden or benefit speech of a particular content does not end the inquiry. Our cases have recognized that even a regulation neutral on its face may be content-based if its manifest purpose is to regulate speech because of the message it conveys.

Appellants contend, in this regard, that the must-carry regulations are content-based because Congress' purpose in enacting them was to promote speech of a favored content. We do not agree. Our review of the Act and its various findings persuades us that Congress' overriding objective in enacting must-carry was not to favor programming of a particular subject matter, viewpoint, or format, but rather to preserve access to free television programming for the forty percent of Americans without cable....

By preventing cable operators from refusing carriage to broadcast television stations, the must-carry rules ensure that broadcast television stations will retain a large enough potential audience to earn necessary advertising revenue—or, in the case of noncommercial broadcasters, sufficient viewer contributions, to maintain their continued operation. In so doing, the provisions are designed to guarantee the survival of a medium that has become a vital part of the Nation's communication system....

This overriding congressional purpose is unrelated to the content of expression disseminated by cable and broadcast speakers....

D

....

Appellants maintain that the must-carry provisions trigger strict scrutiny because they compel cable operators to transmit speech not of their choosing. Relying principally on *Miami Herald Publishing Co. v. Tornillo*, appellants say this intrusion on the editorial control of cable operators amounts to forced speech which, it not per se invalid, can be justified only if narrowly tailored to a compelling government interest. [In *Tornillo* the Court invalidated a statute that required newspapers to publish replies to their political editorials.] ....

Tornillo ... [does] not control this case for the following reasons. First, unlike the access rules struck down in [that case], the must-carry rules are content-neutral in application. They are not activated by any particular message spoken by cable operators and thus exact no content-based penalty. Likewise, they do not grant access to broadcasters on the ground that the content of broadcast programming will counterbalance the messages of cable operators. Instead, they confer benefits upon all full power, local broadcasters, whatever the content of their programming. Second, appellants do not suggest, nor do we think it the case, that must-carry will force cable operators to alter their own messages to respond to the broadcast programming they are required to carry. Given cable's long history of serving as a conduit for broadcast signals, there appears little risk that cable viewers would assume that the broadcast stations carried on a cable system convey ideas or messages endorsed by the cable operator....

Finally, the asserted analogy to *Tornillo* ignores an important technological difference between newspapers and cable television. Although a daily newspaper and a cable operator both may enjoy monopoly status in a given locale, the cable operator exercises far greater control over access to the relevant medium. A daily newspaper, no matter how secure its local monopoly, does not possess the power to obstruct readers' access to other competing publications—whether they be weekly local newspapers, or daily newspapers published in other cities....

The same is not true of cable. When an individual subscribes to cable, the physical connection between the television set and the cable network gives the cable operator bottleneck, or gatekeeper, control over most (if not all) of the television programming that is channeled into the subscriber's home....

III

In sum, the must-carry provisions do not pose such inherent dangers to free expression, or present such potential for censorship or manipulation, as to justify application of the most exacting level of First Amendment scrutiny. We agree with the District Court that the appropriate standard by which to evaluate the constitutionality of must-carry is the intermediate level of scrutiny applicable to content-neutral restrictions that impose an incidental burden on speech.

... [A] content-neutral regulation will be sustained if

> "it furthers an important or substantial governmental interest; if the governmental interest is unrelated to the suppression of free expression; and if the incidental restriction on alleged First Amendment freedoms is no greater than is essential to the furtherance of that interest."

....

... [B]ecause there are genuine issues of material fact still to be resolved on this record, we hold that the District Court erred in granting summary judgment in favor of the Government....

The judgment below is vacated, and the case is remanded for further proceedings consistent with this opinion.

TURNER BROADCASTING SYSTEM V. FCC (TURNER II)
Supreme Court of the United States, 1997
520 U.S. 180

Justice KENNEDY delivered the opinion of the Court.

Sections 4 and 5 of the Cable Television Consumer Protection and Competition Act of 1992 require cable television systems to dedicate some of their channels to local broadcast television stations. Earlier in this case, we held the so called "must-carry" provisions to be content-neutral restrictions on speech, subject to intermediate First Amendment scrutiny under *United States v. O'Brien*, 391 U.S. 367, 377 (1968). A plurality of the Court considered the record as then developed insufficient to determine whether the provisions were narrowly tailored to further important governmental interests, and we remanded the case to the District Court for the District of Columbia for additional fact-finding.

On appeal from the District Court's grant of summary judgment for appellees, the case now presents the two questions left open during the first appeal: First, whether the record as it now stands supports Congress' predictive judgment that the must-carry provisions further important governmental interests; and second, whether the provisions do not burden substantially more speech than necessary to further those interests. We answer both questions in the affirmative, and conclude the must-carry provisions are consistent with the First Amendment....

We begin where the plurality ended in *Turner*, applying the standards for intermediate scrutiny enunciated in *O'Brien*. A content-neutral regulation will be sustained under the First Amendment if it advances important governmental interests unrelated to the suppression of free speech and does not burden substantially more speech than necessary to further those interests. As noted in *Turner*, must-carry was designed to serve "three interrelated interests: (1) preserving the benefits of free, over-the-air local broadcast television, (2) promoting the widespread dissemination of information from a multiplicity of sources, and (3) promoting fair competition in the market for television programming." We decided then, and now reaffirm, that each of those is an important governmental interest. We have been most explicit in holding that "'protecting noncable households from loss of regular television broadcasting service due to competition from cable systems' is an important federal interest." Forty percent of American households continue to rely on over-the-air signals for television programming....

These alternative formulations are inconsistent with Congress' stated interests in enacting must-carry. The congressional findings do not reflect concern that, absent must-carry, "a few voices" would be lost from the television marketplace. In explicit factual findings, Congress expressed clear concern that the "marked shift in market share from broadcast television to cable television services," resulting from increasing market penetration by cable services, as well as the expanding horizontal concentration and vertical integration of cable operators, combined to give cable systems the incentive and ability to delete, reposition, or decline carriage to local broadcasters in an attempt to favor affiliated cable programmers. Congress predicted that "absent the reimposition of [must-carry], additional local broadcast signals will be deleted, repositioned, or not carried," with the end result that "the economic viability of free local broadcast television and its ability to originate quality local programming will be seriously jeopardized."

... Congress was under no illusion that there would be a complete disappearance of broadcast television nationwide in the absence of must-carry. Congress recognized broadcast programming (and network programming in particular) "remains the most popular programming on cable systems." Indeed, reflecting the popularity and strength of some broadcasters, Congress included in the Cable Act a provision permitting broadcasters to charge cable systems for carriage of the broadcasters' signals. Congress was concerned not that broadcast television would disappear in its entirety without must-carry, but that without it, "significant numbers of broadcast stations will be refused carriage on cable systems," and those "broadcast stations denied carriage will either deteriorate to a substantial degree or fail altogether."

... In short, Congress enacted must-carry to "preserve the existing structure of the Nation's broadcast television medium while permitting the concomitant expansion and development of cable television."...

We have no difficulty in finding a substantial basis to support Congress' conclusion that a real threat justified enactment of the must-carry provisions. We examine first the evidence before Congress and then the further evidence presented to the District Court on remand to supplement the congressional determination.

As to the evidence before Congress, there was specific support for its conclusion that cable operators had considerable and growing market power over local video programming markets. Cable served at least sixty percent of American households in 1992, and evidence indicated cable market penetration was projected to grow beyond seventy percent. As Congress noted, cable operators possess a local monopoly over cable households. Only one percent of communities are served by more than one cable system. Even in communities with two or more cable systems, in the typical case each system has a local monopoly over its subscribers. Cable operators thus exercise "control over most (if not all) of the television programming that is channeled into the subscriber's home... [and] can thus silence the voice of competing speakers with a mere flick of the switch."

Evidence indicated the structure of the cable industry would give cable operators increasing ability and incentive to drop local broadcast stations from their systems, or reposition them to a less viewed channel. Horizontal concentration was increasing as a small number of multiple system operators (MSO's) acquired large numbers of cable systems nationwide....

Vertical integration in the industry also was increasing. As Congress was aware, many MSO's owned or had affiliation agreements with cable programmers. Evidence indicated that before 1984 cable operators had equity interests in thirty-eight percent of cable programming networks. In the late 1980s, sixty-four percent of new cable programmers were held in vertical ownership. Congress concluded that "vertical integration gives cable operators the incentive and ability to favor their affiliated programming services."...

Cable systems also have more systemic reasons for seeking to disadvantage broadcast stations: Simply stated, cable has little interest in assisting, through carriage, a competing medium of communication. As one cable industry executive put it, "'our job is to promote cable television, not broadcast television.'"...

It was more than a theoretical possibility in 1992 that cable operators would take actions adverse to local broadcasters; indeed, significant numbers of broadcasters had already been dropped. The record before Congress contained extensive anecdotal evidence about scores of adverse carriage decisions against broadcast stations....

Additional evidence developed on remand supports the reasonableness of Congress' predictive judgment. Approximately eleven percent of local broadcasters were not carried on the typical cable system in 1989. The figure had grown to even more significant proportions by 1992. According to one of appellants' own experts, between nineteen and thirty-one percent of all local broadcast stations, including network affiliates, were not carried by the typical cable system. Based on the same data, another expert concluded that forty-seven percent of local independent commercial stations, and thirty-six percent of noncommercial stations, were not carried by the typical cable system. The rate of noncarriage was even higher for new stations....

This is not a case in which we are called upon to give our best judgment as to the likely economic consequences of certain financial arrangements or business structures, or to assess competing economic theories and predictive judgments, as we would in a case arising, say, under the antitrust laws.... The issue before us is whether, given conflicting views of the probable development of the television industry, Congress had substantial evidence for making the judgment that it did. We need not put our imprimatur on Congress' economic theory in order to validate the reasonableness of its judgment....

Considerable evidence, consisting of statements compiled from dozens of broadcasters who testified before Congress and the FCC, confirmed that broadcast stations had fallen into bankruptcy, curtailed their broadcast operations, and suffered serious reductions in operating revenues as a result of adverse carriage decisions by cable systems....

The second portion of the *O'Brien* inquiry concerns the fit between the asserted interests and the means chosen to advance them. Content-neutral regulations do not pose the same "inherent dangers to free expression" that content-based regulations do, and thus are subject to a less rigorous analysis, which affords the Government latitude in designing a regulatory solution. Under intermediate scrutiny, the Government may employ the means of its choosing "'so long as the . . . regulation promotes a substantial governmental interest that would be achieved less effectively absent the regulation,'" and does not "'burden substantially more speech than is necessary to further'" that interest.

The must-carry provisions have the potential to interfere with protected speech in two ways. First, the provisions restrain cable operators' editorial discretion in creating programming packages by "reduc[ing] the number of channels over which [they] exercise unfettered control." Second, the rules "render it more difficult for cable programmers to compete for carriage on the limited channels remaining."

Appellants say the burden of must-carry is great, but the evidence adduced on remand indicates the actual effects are modest. Significant evidence indicates the vast majority of cable operators have not been affected in a significant manner by must-carry. Cable operators have been able to satisfy their must-carry obligations eighty-seven percent of the time using previously unused channel capacity....

While the parties' evidence is susceptible of varying interpretations, a few definite conclusions can be drawn about the burdens of must-carry. It is undisputed that broadcast stations gained carriage on 5,880 channels as a result of must-carry. While broadcast stations occupy another 30,006 cable channels nationwide, this carriage does not represent a significant First Amendment harm to either system operators or cable programmers because those stations were carried voluntarily before 1992, and even appellants represent that the vast majority of those channels would continue to be carried in the absence of any legal obligation to do so. The 5,880 channels occupied by added broadcasters represent the actual burden of the regulatory scheme. Appellants concede most of those stations would be dropped in the absence of must-carry, so the figure approximates the benefits of must-carry as well.

Because the burden imposed by must-carry is congruent to the benefits it affords, we conclude must-carry is narrowly tailored to preserve a multiplicity of broadcast stations for the forty percent of American households without cable. Congress took steps to confine the breadth and burden of the regulatory scheme. For example, the more popular stations (which appellants concede would be carried anyway) will likely opt to be paid for cable carriage under the "retransmission consent" provision of the Cable Act; those stations will nonetheless be counted towards systems' must-carry obligations. Congress exempted systems of twelve or fewer channels, and limited the must-carry obligation of larger systems to one-third of capacity, allowed cable operators discretion in choosing which competing and qualified signals would be carried, and permitted operators to carry public stations on unused public, educational, and governmental channels in some circumstances....

Appellants posit a number of alternatives in an effort to demonstrate a less restrictive means to achieve the Government's aims. They ask us, in effect, to "sif[t] through all the available or imagined alternative means of regulating [cable television] in order to determine whether the [Government's] solution was 'the least intrusive means' of achieving the desired end," an approach we rejected in *Ward v. Rock Against Racism*. This "'less restrictive alternative analysis . . . has never been a part of the inquiry into the validity'" of content-neutral regulations on speech. Our precedents establish that when evaluating a content-neutral regulation that incidentally burdens speech, we will not invalidate the preferred remedial scheme because some alternative solution is marginally less intrusive on a speaker's First Amendment interests....

Judgments about how competing economic interests are to be reconciled in the complex and fast changing field of television are for Congress to make. Those judgments "cannot be ignored or undervalued simply because [appellants] cas[t] [their] claims under the umbrella of the First Amendment." Appellants' challenges to must-carry reflect little more than disagreement over the level of protection broadcast stations are to be afforded and how protection is to be attained. We cannot displace Congress' judgment respecting content-neutral regulations with our own, so long as its policy is grounded on reasonable factual findings supported by evidence that is substantial for a legislative determination. Those requirements were met in this case, and in these circumstances the First Amendment requires nothing more. The judgment of the District Court is affirmed.

It is so ordered.

Justice O'CONNOR, with whom Justice SCALIA, Justice THOMAS, and Justice GINSBURG join, dissenting.

In sustaining the must-carry provisions of the Cable Television Protection and Competition Act of 1992 against a First Amendment challenge by cable system operators and cable programmers, the Court errs in two crucial respects. First, the Court disregards one of the principal defenses of the statute urged by appellees on remand: that it serves a substantial interest in preserving "diverse, quality" programming that is "responsive" to the needs of the local community. The course of this litigation on remand and the proffered defense strongly reinforce my view that the Court adopted the wrong analytic framework in the prior phase of this case. See *Turner Broadcasting System, Inc. v. FCC*, 512 U.S. 622. Second, the Court misapplies the "intermediate scrutiny" framework it adopts. Although we owe deference to Congress' predictive judgments and its evaluation of complex economic questions, we have an independent duty to identify with care the Government interests supporting the scheme, to inquire into the reasonableness of congressional findings regarding its necessity, and to examine the fit between its goals and its consequences. The Court fails to discharge its duty here....

Chapter Eleven
OBSCENITY AND INDECENCY

The first few cases in this chapter deal with the concept of "obscenity" and the power of government to ban this narrow class of exapression. The remaining cases concern government authority to regulate expression that is not so reprehensible as to be obscene but that nevertheless is considered "pornographic" or "indecent." This can be done, under certain limited circumstances, with a type of time/place/manner restriction. Though some of these cases don't represent mainstream mass media, the legal principles involved go right to the heart of the First Amendment.

Miller v. California is a landmark case in which the Supreme Court refined its definition of obscenity. The definition in *Miller* remains the applicable standard today.

Paris Adult Theatre v. Slaton, decided by the Supreme Court on the same day as *Miller*, deals with the question of whether government prohibitions on obscenity are supported by sufficiently rational justifications.

Pope v. Illinois provides some insight into the sensitive, technical questions that arise in applying the *Miller* standard. Specifically, the case concerns proper application of the third prong of the three-part *Miller* test.

City of Renton v. Playtime Theatres is a highly significant case that paved the way for pornographic but nonobscene speech to nevertheless be controlled through zoning ordinances that the Supreme Court categorized as a brand of time/place/manner restriction.

FCC v. Pacifica Foundation is yet another landmark case in which the Supreme Court validated the power of Congress and the Federal Communications Commission to prohibit broadcasting of "indecent" speech under certain circumstances.

FCC v. Fox Television Stations is the Supreme Court's 2009 revisit to broadcast indecency regulations. The sharply divided Court examined the relatively narrow question of whether a sudden shift in FCC rules was impermissibly "arbitrary" under the federal statute that governs agency procedure.

And *Ashcroft v. American Civil Liberties Union* is the Supreme Court's pronouncement on the long-running attempt by Congress to block children's access to sexually explicit material on the Internet.

MILLER V. CALIFORNIA
Supreme Court of the United States, 1973
413 U.S. 15

Chief Justice BURGER delivered the opinion of the Court.

This is one of a group of "obscenity-pornography" cases being reviewed by the Court in a reexamination of standards enunciated in earlier cases involving what Mr. Justice Harlan called "the intractable obscenity problem."

Appellant conducted a mass mailing campaign to advertise the sale of illustrated books, euphemistically called "adult" material. After a jury trial, he was convicted of violating California Penal Code § 311.2(a), a misdemeanor, by knowingly distributing obscene matter....

The brochures advertise four books entitled *Intercourse, Man-Woman, Sex Orgies Illustrated,* and *An Illustrated History of Pornography,* and a film entitled *Marital Intercourse.* While the brochures contain some descriptive printed material, primarily they consist of pictures and drawings very explicitly depicting men and women in groups of two or more engaging in a variety of sexual activities, with genitals often prominently displayed.

I

....

... [S]ince the Court now undertakes to formulate standards more concrete than those in the past, it is useful for us to focus on two of the landmark cases in the somewhat tortured history of the Court's obscenity decisions. In *Roth v. United States,* 354 U.S. 476 (1957), the Court sustained a conviction under a federal statute punishing the mailing of "obscene, lewd, lascivious, or filthy..." materials. The key to that holding was the Court's rejection of the claim that obscene materials were protected by the First Amendment. Five Justices joined in the opinion stating: "... [I]mplicit in the history of the First Amendment is the rejection of obscenity as utterly without redeeming social importance."...

Nine years later, in *Memoirs v. Massachusetts,* 383 U.S. 413 (1966), the Court veered sharply away from the *Roth* concept and, with only three Justices in the plurality opinion, articulated a new test of obscenity. The plurality held that under the *Roth* definition

> as elaborated in subsequent cases, three elements must coalesce: it must be established that (a) the dominant theme of the material taken as a whole appeals to a prurient interest in sex; (b) the material is patently offensive because it affronts contemporary community standards relating to the description or representation of sexual matters; and (c) the material is utterly without redeeming social value.

The sharpness of the break with *Roth,* represented by the third element of the *Memoirs* test ... was further underscored when the *Memoirs* plurality went on to state:

> The Supreme Judicial Court erred in holding that a book need not be "unqualifiedly worthless before it can be deemed obscene." A book cannot be proscribed unless it is found to be *utterly* without redeeming social value.

While *Roth* presumed "obscenity" to be "utterly without redeeming social importance," *Memoirs* required that to prove obscenity it must be affirmatively established that the material is "*utterly* without redeeming social value." Thus, even as they repeated the words of *Roth,* the *Memoirs* plurality produced a drastically altered test that called on the prosecution to prove a negative, i.e., that the material was "*utterly* without redeeming social value"—a burden virtually impossible to discharge under our criminal standards of proof....

II

This much has been categorically settled by the Court, that obscene material is unprotected by the First Amendment. We acknowledge, however, the inherent dangers of undertaking to regulate any form of expression. State statutes designed to regulate obscene materials must be carefully limited. As a result, we now confine the permissible scope of such regulation to works that depict or describe sexual conduct. That conduct must be specifically defined by the applicable state law, as written or authoritatively construed. A state offense must also be limited to works which, taken as a whole, appeal to the prurient interest in sex, which portray sexual conduct in a patently offensive way, and which, taken as a whole, do not have serious literary, artistic, political, or scientific value.

The basic guidelines for the trier of fact must be: (a) whether "the average person, applying contemporary community standards" would find that the work, taken as a whole, appeals to the prurient interest; (b) whether the work depicts or describes, in a patently offensive way, sexual conduct specifically defined by the applicable state law; and (c) whether the work, taken as a whole, lacks serious literary, artistic, political, or scientific value....

We emphasize that it is not our function to propose regulatory schemes for the States. That must await their concrete legislative efforts. It is possible, however, to give a few plain examples of what a state statute could define for regulation under part (b) of the standard announced in this opinion, *supra*:

(a) Patently offensive representations or descriptions of ultimate sexual acts, normal or perverted, actual or simulated.

(b) Patently offensive representation or descriptions of masturbation, excretory functions, and lewd exhibition of the genitals.

....

Under the holdings announced today, no one will be subject to prosecution for the sale or exposure of obscene materials unless these materials depict or describe patently offensive "hard core" sexual conduct specifically defined by the regulating state law, as written or construed. We are satisfied that these specific prerequisites will provide fair notice to a dealer in such materials that his public and commercial activities may bring prosecution....

It is certainly true that the absence, since *Roth*, of a single majority view of this Court as to proper standards for testing obscenity has placed a strain on both state and federal courts. But today, for the first time since *Roth* was decided in 1957, a majority of this Court has agreed on concrete guidelines to isolate "hard core" pornography from expression protected by the First Amendment....

This may not be an easy road, free from difficulty. But no amount of "fatigue" should lead us to adopt a convenient "institutional" rationale—an absolutist, "anything goes" view of the First Amendment—because it will lighten our burdens....

III

Under a National Constitution, fundamental First Amendment limitations on the powers of the States do not vary from community to community, but this does not mean that there are, or should or can be, fixed, uniform national standards of precisely what appeals to the "prurient interest" or is "patently offensive." These are essentially questions of fact, and our Nation is simply too big and too diverse for this Court to reasonably expect that such standards could be articulated for all fifty States in a single formulation, even assuming the prerequisite consensus exists. When triers of fact are asked to decide whether "the average person, applying contemporary community standards" would consider certain materials "prurient," it would be unrealistic to require that the answer be based on some abstract formulation. The adversary system, with lay jurors as the usual ultimate fact-finders in criminal prosecutions, has historically permitted triers of fact to draw on the standards of their community, guided always by limiting instructions on the law. To require a State to structure obscenity proceedings around evidence of a *national* "community standard" would be an exercise in futility.

... [T]his case was tried on the theory that the California obscenity statute sought to incorporate the tripartite test of *Memoirs*. This, a "national" standard of First Amendment protection enumerated by a plurality of this Court, was correctly regarded at the time of trial as limiting state prosecution under the controlling state law....

... Nothing in the First Amendment requires that a jury must consider hypothetical and unascertainable "national standards" when attempting to determine whether certain materials are obscene as a matter of fact....

IV

The dissenting Justices sound the alarm of repression. But, in our view, to equate the free and robust exchange of ideas and political debate with commercial exploitation of obscene material demeans the grand conception of the First Amendment and its high purposes in the historic struggle for freedom.... The First Amendment protects works which, taken as a whole, have serious literary, artistic, political, or scientific value, regardless of whether the government or a majority of the people approve of the ideas these works represent.... But the public portrayal of hard core sexual conduct for its own sake, and for the ensuing commercial gain, is a different matter....

... The judgment of the Appellate Department of the Superior Court, Orange County, California, is vacated and the case remanded to that court for further proceedings not inconsistent with the First Amendment standards established by this opinion.

Paris Adult Theatre I v. Slaton
Supreme Court of the United States, 1973
413 U.S. 49

Chief Justice BURGER delivered the opinion of the Court.

Petitioners are two Atlanta, Georgia, movie theaters and their owners and managers, operating in the style of "adult" theaters. On December 28, 1970, respondents, the local state district attorney, and the solicitor for the local state trial court, filed civil complaints in that court alleging that petitioners were exhibiting to the public for paid admission two allegedly obscene films, contrary to Georgia Code Ann. § 26-2101. The two films in question, *Magic Mirror* and *It All Comes Out in the End,* depict sexual conduct characterized by the Georgia Supreme Court as "hard core pornography" leaving "little to the imagination."

... Certain photographs, [exhibited] at trial, were stipulated to portray the single entrance to both Paris Adult Theatre I and Paris Adult Theatre II as it appeared at the time of the complaints. These photographs show a conventional, inoffensive theater entrance, without any pictures, but with signs indicating that the theaters exhibit "Atlanta's Finest Mature Feature Films." On the door itself is a sign saying: "Adult Theatre—You must be 21 and able to prove it. If viewing the nude body offends you, Please Do Not Enter."

... On April 12, 1971, the trial judge dismissed respondents' complaints. He assumed "that obscenity is established," but stated:

It appears to the Court that the display of these films in a commercial theatre, when surrounded by requisite notice to the public of their nature and by reasonable protection against exposure of these films to minors, is constitutionally permissible.

On appeal, the Georgia Supreme Court unanimously reversed. It assumed that the adult theaters in question barred minors and gave a full warning to the general public of the nature of the films shown, but held that the films were without protection under the First Amendment....

I

It should be clear from the outset that we do not undertake to tell the States what they must do, but rather to define the area in which they may chart their own course in dealing with obscene material. This Court has consistently held that obscene material is not protected by the First Amendment as a limitation on the state police power by virtue of the Fourteenth Amendment. *Miller v. California,* 413 U.S. 15.

... Today, in *Miller v. California* we have sought to clarify the constitutional definition of obscene material subject to regulation by the States, and we vacate and remand this case for reconsideration in light of *Miller.*

This is not to be read as a disapproval of the Georgia civil procedure employed in this case, assuming the use of a constitutionally acceptable standard for determining what is unprotected by the First Amendment....

II

We categorically disapprove the theory, apparently adopted by the trial judge, that obscene, pornographic films acquire constitutional immunity from state regulation simply because they are exhibited for consenting adults only. This holding was properly rejected by the Georgia Supreme Court. Although we have often pointedly recognized the high importance of the state interest in regulating the exposure of obscene materials to juveniles and unconsenting adults, this Court has never declared these to be the only legitimate state interests permitting regulation of obscene material. The States have a long-recognized legitimate interest in regulating the use of obscene material in local commerce and in all places of public accommodation, as long as these regulations do not run afoul of specific constitutional prohibitions....

In particular, we hold that there are legitimate state interests at stake in stemming the tide of commercialized obscenity, even assuming it is feasible to enforce effective safeguards against exposure to juveniles and to passersby. Rights and interests "other than those of the advocates are involved." These include the interest of the public in the quality of life and the total community environment, the tone of commerce in the great city centers, and, possibly, the public safety itself. The Hill-Link Minority Report of the Commission on Obscenity and Pornography indicates that there is at least an arguable correlation between obscene material and crime. Quite apart from sex crimes, however, there remains one problem of large proportions aptly described by Professor Bickel:

> It concerns the tone of society, the mode, or to use terms that have perhaps greater currency, the style and quality of life, now and in the future. A man may be entitled to read an obscene book in his room, or expose himself indecently there.... We should protect his privacy. But if he demands a right to obtain the books and pictures he wants in the market, and to foregather in public places—discreet, if you will, but accessible to all—with others who share his tastes, *then to grant him his right is to affect the world about the rest of us, and to impinge on other privacies.* Even supposing that each of us can, if he wishes, effectively avert the eye and stop the ear (which, in truth, we cannot), what is commonly read and seen and heard and done intrudes upon us all, want it or not." 22 The Public Interest 25-26 (Winter 1971). (Emphasis added.)

....

But, it is argued, there are no scientific data that conclusively demonstrate that exposure to obscene material adversely affects men and women or their society. It is argued on behalf of the petitioners that, absent such a demonstration, any kind of state regulation is "impermissible." We reject this argument. It is not for us to resolve empirical uncertainties underlying state legislation, save in the exceptional case where that legislation plainly impinges upon rights protected by the Constitution itself.... Although there is no conclusive proof of a connection between antisocial behavior and obscene material, the legislature of Georgia could quite reasonably determine that such a connection does or might exist....

From the beginning of civilized societies, legislators and judges have acted on various unprovable assumptions. Such assumptions underlie much lawful state regulation of commercial and business affairs....

It is argued that individual "free will" must govern, even in activities beyond the protection of the First Amendment and other constitutional guarantees of privacy, and that government cannot legitimately impede an individual's desire to see or acquire obscene plays, movies, and books....

The States, of course, may follow such a "laissez-faire" policy and drop all controls on commercialized obscenity, if that is what they prefer, just as they can ignore consumer protection in the marketplace, but nothing in the Constitution *compels* the States to do so with regard to matters falling within state jurisdiction....

Our prior decisions recognizing a right to privacy guaranteed by the Fourteenth Amendment included "only personal rights that can be deemed 'fundamental' or 'implicit in the concept of ordered liberty.'" This privacy right encompasses and protects the personal intimacies of the home, the family, marriage, motherhood, procreation, and child rearing. Nothing, however, in this Court's decisions intimates that there is any "fundamental" privacy right "implicit in the concept of ordered liberty" to watch obscene movies in places of public accommodation.

POPE V. ILLINOIS
Supreme Court of the United States, 1987
481 U.S. 497

Justice WHITE delivered the opinion of the Court.

In *Miller v. California*, the Court set out a tripartite test for judging whether material is obscene. The third prong of the *Miller* test requires the trier of fact to determine "whether the work, taken as a whole, lacks serious literary, artistic, political, or scientific value." The issue in this case is whether, in a prosecution for the sale of allegedly obscene materials, the jury may be instructed to apply community standards in deciding the value question.

I

On July 21, 1983, Rockford, Illinois, police detectives purchased certain magazines from the two petitioners, each of whom was an attendant at an adult bookstore. Petitioners were subsequently charged separately with the offense of "obscenity" for the sale of these magazines. Each petitioner moved to dismiss the charges against him on the ground that the then-current version of the Illinois obscenity statute violated the First and Fourteenth Amendments to the United States Constitution. Both petitioners argued, among other things, that the statute was unconstitutional in failing to require that the value question be judged "solely on an objective basis as opposed to reference [*sic*] to contemporary community standards." ... Both petitioners were found guilty....

II

There is no suggestion in our cases that the question of the value of an allegedly obscene work is to be determined by reference to community standards. Indeed, our cases are to the contrary. *Smith v. United States*, 431 U.S. 291 (1977), held that, in a federal prosecution for mailing obscene materials, the first and second prongs of the *Miller* test—appeal to prurient interest and patent offensiveness—are issues of fact for the jury to determine applying contemporary community standards. The Court then observed that, unlike prurient appeal and patent offensiveness, "[l]iterary, artistic, political, or scientific value ... is not discussed in *Miller* in terms of contemporary community standards." This comment was not meant to point out an oversight in the *Miller* opinion, but to call attention to and approve a deliberate choice.

... Just as the ideas a work represents need not obtain majority approval to merit protection, neither, insofar as the First Amendment is concerned, does the value of the work vary from community to community based on the degree of local acceptance it has won. The proper inquiry is not whether an ordinary member of any given community would find serious literary, artistic, political, or scientific value in allegedly obscene material, but whether a reasonable person would find such value in the material, taken as a whole. The [jury] instruction at issue in this case was therefore unconstitutional.

III

The question remains whether the convictions should be reversed outright or are subject to salvage if the erroneous instruction is found to be harmless error....

... While it was error to instruct the juries to use a state community standard in considering the value question, if a reviewing court concludes that no rational juror, if properly instructed, could find value in the magazines, the convictions should stand.

... In this case the Illinois Appellate Court has not considered the harmless-error issue. We therefore vacate its judgment and remand so that it may do so.

CITY OF RENTON V. PLAYTIME THEATRES, INC.
Supreme Court of the United States, 1986
475 U.S. 41

Justice REHNQUIST delivered the opinion of the Court.

This case involves a constitutional challenge to a zoning ordinance, enacted by appellant city of Renton, Washington, that prohibits adult motion picture theaters from locating within 1,000 feet of any residential zone, single- or multiple-family dwelling, church, park, or school....

In early 1982, respondents acquired two existing theaters in downtown Renton, with the intention of using them to exhibit feature-length adult films. The theaters were located within the area proscribed by Ordinance No. 3526. At about the same time, respondents filed [a] lawsuit challenging the ordinance on First and Fourteenth Amendment grounds, and seeking declaratory and injunctive relief....

The District Court ... entered summary judgment in favor of Renton.... Relying on *Young v. American Mini Theatres, Inc.*, 427 U.S. 50 (1976), the court held that the Renton ordinance did not violate the First Amendment.

The Court of Appeals for the Ninth Circuit reversed. The Court of Appeals first concluded, contrary to the finding of the District Court, that the Renton ordinance constituted a substantial restriction on First Amendment interests....

In our view, the resolution of this case is largely dictated by our decision in *Young v. American Mini Theatres, Inc., supra*. There, although five Members of the Court did not agree on a single rationale for the decision, we held that the city of Detroit's zoning ordinance, which prohibited locating an adult theater within 1,000 feet of any two other "regulated uses" or within 500 feet of any residential zone, did not violate the First and Fourteenth Amendments. The Renton ordinance, like the one in *American Mini Theatres*, does not ban adult theaters altogether, but merely provides that such theaters may not be located within 1,000 feet of any residential zone, single- or multiple-family dwelling, church, park, or school. The ordinance is therefore properly analyzed as a form of time, place, and manner regulation.

Describing the ordinance as a time, place, and manner regulation is, of course, only the first step in our inquiry. This Court has long held that regulations enacted for the purpose of restraining speech on the basis of its content presumptively violate the First Amendment. On the other hand, so-called "content-neutral" time, place, and manner regulations are acceptable so long as they are designed to serve a substantial government interest and do not unreasonably limit alternative avenues of communication.

At first glance, the Renton ordinance, like the ordinance in *American Mini Theatres*, does not appear to fit neatly into either the "content-based" or the "content-neutral" category. To be sure, the ordinance treats theaters that specialize in adult films differently from other kinds of theaters. Nevertheless, as the District Court concluded, the Renton ordinance is aimed not at the *content* of the films shown at "adult motion picture theatres," but rather at the *secondary effects* of such theaters on the surrounding community. The District Court found that the City Council's "*predominate* concerns" were with the secondary effects of adult theaters, and not with the content of adult films themselves....

In short, the Renton ordinance is completely consistent with our definition of "content-neutral" speech regulations as those that "are *justified* without reference to the content of the regulated speech." The ordinance does not contravene the fundamental principle that underlies our concern about "content-based" speech regulations: that "government may not grant the use of a forum to people whose views it finds acceptable, but deny use to those wishing to express less favored or more controversial views."

It was with this understanding in mind that, in *American Mini Theatres*, a majority of this Court decided that, at least with respect to businesses that purvey sexually explicit materials, zoning ordinances designed to combat the undesirable secondary effects of such businesses are to be reviewed under the standards applicable to "content-neutral" time, place, and manner regulations....

The appropriate inquiry in this case, then, is whether the Renton ordinance is designed to serve a substantial governmental interest and allows for reasonable alternative avenues of communication. It is clear that the ordinance meets such a standard. As a majority of this Court recognized in *American Mini Theatres*, a city's "interest in attempting to preserve the quality of urban life is one that must be accorded high respect."

… The record in this case reveals that Renton relied heavily on the experience of, and studies produced by, the city of Seattle. In Seattle, as in Renton, the adult theater zoning ordinance was aimed at preventing the secondary effects caused by the presence of even one such theater in a given neighborhood. The opinion of the Supreme Court of Washington in *Northend Cinema*, which was before the Renton City Council when it enacted the ordinance in question here, described Seattle's experience as follows:

> The amendments to the City's zoning code that are at issue here are the culmination of a long period of study and discussion of the problems of adult movie theaters in residential areas of the City....
>
> … The court's detailed findings, which include a finding that the location of adult theaters has a harmful effect on the area and contribute to neighborhood blight, are supported by substantial evidence in the record.
>
> ….

We hold that Renton was entitled to rely on the experience of Seattle and other cities, and in particular on the "detailed findings" summarized in the Washington Supreme Court's *Northend Cinema* opinion, in enacting its adult theater zoning ordinance....

….

Finally, turning to the question whether the Renton ordinance allows for reasonable alternative avenues of communication, we note that the ordinance leaves some 520 acres, or more than five percent of the entire land area of Renton, open to use as adult theater sites. The District Court found, and the Court of Appeals did not dispute the finding, that the 520 acres of land consists of "[a]mple, accessible real estate," including "acreage in all stages of development from raw land to developed, industrial, warehouse, office, and shopping space that is crisscrossed by freeways, highways, and roads."…

… And although we have cautioned against the enactment of zoning regulations that have the "effect of suppressing, or greatly restricting access to, lawful speech," we have never suggested that the First Amendment compels the Government to ensure that adult theaters, or any other kinds of speech-related businesses for that matter, will be able to obtain sites at bargain prices. In our view, the First Amendment requires only that Renton refrain from effectively denying respondents a reasonable opportunity to open and operate an adult theater within the city, and the ordinance before us easily meets this requirement.

In sum, we find that the Renton ordinance represents a valid governmental response to the "admittedly serious problems" created by adult theaters. Renton has not used "the power to zone as a pretext for suppressing expression," but rather has sought to make some areas available for adult theaters and their patrons, while at the same time preserving the quality of life in the community at large by preventing those theaters from locating in other areas. This, after all, is the essence of zoning…. The judgment of the Court of Appeals is therefore

Reversed.

FCC v. PACIFICA FOUNDATION
Supreme Court of the United States, 1978
438 U.S. 726

Justice STEVENS delivered the opinion of the Court….

This case requires that we decide whether the Federal Communications Commission has any power to regulate a radio broadcast that is indecent but not obscene.

A satiric humorist named George Carlin recorded a twelve-minute monologue entitled "Filthy Words" before a live audience in a California theater. He began by referring to his thoughts about "the words you couldn't say on the public, ah, airwaves, um, the ones you definitely wouldn't say, ever." He proceeded to list those words and repeat them over and over again in a variety of colloquialisms. [The words were shit, piss, fuck, cunt, cocksucker, motherfucker, and tits.] …

At about 2 p.m. in the afternoon … a New York radio station, owned by respondent Pacifica Foundation, broadcast the "Filthy Words" monologue. A few weeks later a man, who stated that he had heard the broadcast while driving with his young son, wrote a letter complaining to the Commission….

The complaint was forwarded to the station for comment. In its response, Pacifica explained that the monologue had been played during a program about contemporary society's attitude toward language and that, immediately before its broadcast, listeners had been advised that it included "sensitive language which might be regarded as offensive to some."
...

... [T]he Commission issued a declaratory order ... holding that Pacifica "could have been the subject of administrative sanctions." The Commission did not impose formal sanctions, but it did state that the order would be "associated with the station's license file.";...

... [T]he Commission found a [statutory] power to regulate indecent broadcasting in ... 18 U.S.C. § 1464, which forbids the use of "any obscene, indecent, or profane language by means of radio communications." ...

The Commission characterized the language used in the Carlin monologue as "patently offensive," though not necessarily obscene, and expressed the opinion that it should be regulated by principles analogous to those found in the law of nuisance where the "law generally speaks to *channeling* behavior more than actually prohibiting it.... [T]he concept of 'indecent' is intimately connected with the exposure of children to language that describes, in terms patently offensive as measured by contemporary community standards for the broadcast medium, sexual or excretory activities and organs at times of the day when there is a reasonable risk that children may be in the audience."...

IV

Pacifica makes two constitutional attacks on the Commission's order. First, it argues that the Commission's construction of the statutory language broadly encompasses so much constitutionally protected speech that reversal is required even if Pacifica's broadcast of the "Filthy Words" monologue is not itself protected by the First Amendment. Second, Pacifica argues that inasmuch as the recording is not obscene, the Constitution forbids any abridgment of the right to broadcast it on the radio.

A

The first argument fails because our review is limited to the question whether the Commission has the authority to proscribe this particular broadcast. As the Commission itself emphasized, its order was "issued in a specific factual context." That approach is appropriate for courts as well as the Commission when regulation of indecency is at stake, for indecency is largely a function of context—it cannot be adequately judged in the abstract.
....

It is true that the Commission's order may lead some broadcasters to censor themselves. At most, however, the Commission's definition of indecency will deter only the broadcasting of patently offensive references to excretory and sexual organs and activities. While some of these references may be protected, they surely lie at the periphery of First Amendment concern....

B

When the issue is narrowed to the facts of this case, the question is whether the First Amendment denies government any power to restrict the public broadcast of indecent language in any circumstances. For if the government has any such power, this was an appropriate occasion for its exercise.

The words of the Carlin monologue are unquestionably "speech" within the meaning of the First Amendment. It is equally clear that the Commission's objections to the broadcast were based in part on its content. The order must therefore fall if, as Pacifica argues, the First Amendment prohibits all governmental regulation that depends on the content of speech. Our past cases demonstrate, however, that no such absolute rule is mandated by the Constitution.

The classic exposition of the proposition that both the content and the context of speech are critical elements of First Amendment analysis is Mr. Justice Holmes' statement for the Court in *Schenck v. United States,* 249 U.S. 47:

> "... [T]he character of every act depends upon the circumstances in which it is done.... The most stringent protection of free speech would not protect a man in falsely shouting fire in a theatre and causing a panic.... The question in every case is whether the words used are used in such circumstances and are of such a nature as to create a clear and present danger that they will bring about the substantive evils that Congress has a right to prevent."

Other distinctions based on content have been approved in the years since *Schenck....*

The question in this case is whether a broadcast of patently offensive words dealing with sex and excretion may be regulated because of its content. Obscene materials have been denied the protection of the First Amendment because their content is so offensive to contemporary moral standards. But the fact that society may find speech offensive is not a sufficient reason for suppressing it. Indeed, if it is the speaker's opinion that gives offense, that consequence is a reason for according it constitutional protection. For it is a central tenet of the First Amendment that the government must remain neutral in the marketplace of ideas. If there were any reason to believe that the Commission's characterization of the Carlin monologue as offensive could be traced to its political content—or even to the fact that it satirized contemporary attitudes about four-letter words—First Amendment protection might be required. But that is simply not the case....

Although these words ordinarily lack literary, political, or scientific value, they are not entirely outside the protection of the First Amendment. Some uses of even the most offensive words are unquestionably protected. Indeed, we may assume, *arguendo*, that this monologue would be protected in other contexts. Nonetheless, the constitutional protection accorded to a communication containing such patently offensive sexual and excretory language need not be the same in every context....

C

We have long recognized that each medium of expression presents special First Amendment problems. And of all forms of communication, it is broadcasting that has received the most limited First Amendment protection. Thus, although other speakers cannot be licensed except under laws that carefully define and narrow official discretion, a broadcaster may be deprived of his license and his forum if the Commission decides that such an action would serve "the public interest, convenience, and necessity." ...

The reasons for these distinctions are complex, but two have relevance to the present case. First, the broadcast media have established a uniquely pervasive presence in the lives of all Americans. Patently offensive, indecent material presented over the airwaves confronts the citizen, not only in public, but also in the privacy of the home, where the individual's right to be left alone plainly outweighs the First Amendment rights of an intruder. Because the broadcast audience is constantly tuning in and out, prior warnings cannot completely protect the listener or viewer from unexpected program content. To say that one may avoid further offense by turning off the radio when he hears indecent language is like saying that the remedy for an assault is to run away after the first blow. One may hang up on an indecent phone call, but that option does not give the caller a constitutional immunity or avoid a harm that has already taken place.

Second, broadcasting is uniquely accessible to children, even those too young to read.... Pacifica's broadcast could have enlarged a child's vocabulary in an instant. Other forms of offensive expression may be withheld from the young without restricting the expression at its source. Bookstores and motion picture theaters, for example, may be prohibited from making indecent material available to children. We held in *Ginsberg v. New York*, 390 U.S. 629, that the government's interest in the "well-being of its youth" and in supporting "parents' claim to authority in their own household" justified the regulation of otherwise protected expression. The ease with which children may obtain access to broadcast material, coupled with the concerns recognized in *Ginsberg*, amply justify special treatment of indecent broadcasting.

It is appropriate, in conclusion, to emphasize the narrowness of our holding.... We have not decided that an occasional expletive ... would justify any sanction or, indeed, that this broadcast would justify a criminal prosecution. The Commission's decision rested entirely on a nuisance rationale under which context is all-important. The concept requires consideration of a host of variables. The time of day was emphasized by the Commission. The content of the program in which the language is used will also affect the composition of the audience, and differences between radio, television, and perhaps closed-circuit transmissions, may also be relevant. As Mr. Justice Sutherland wrote, a "nuisance may be merely a right thing in the wrong place—like a pig in the parlor instead of the barnyard." We simply hold that when the Commission finds that a pig has entered the parlor, the exercise of its regulatory power does not depend on proof that the pig is obscene.

The judgment of the Court of Appeals is reversed.

FCC v. Fox Television Stations, Inc.
Supreme Court of the United States, 2009
173 L.Ed.2d 738

Justice SCALIA delivered the opinion of the Court.

Federal law prohibits the broadcasting of "any . . . indecent . . . language," 18 U.S.C. §1464, which includes expletives referring to sexual or excretory activity or organs, see *FCC v. Pacifica Foundation*. This case concerns the adequacy of the Federal Communications Commission's explanation of its decision that this sometimes forbids the broadcasting of indecent expletives even when the offensive words are not repeated.

I. STATUTORY AND REGULATORY BACKGROUND

The Communications Act of 1934 established a system of limited-term broadcast licenses subject to various "conditions" designed "to maintain the control of the United States over all the channels of radio transmission." Twenty-seven years ago we said that "[a]licensed broadcaster is granted the free and exclusive use of a limited and valuable part of the public domain; when he accepts that franchise it is burdened by enforceable public obligations." *CBS, Inc. v. FCC*, 453 U. S. 367, 395 (1981).

One of the burdens that licensees shoulder is the indecency ban—the statutory proscription against "utter[ing] any obscene, indecent, or profane language by means of radio communication," 18 U. S. C. §1464—which Congress has instructed the Commission to enforce between the hours of 6 a.m. and 10 p.m. ...

. . . .

In *FCC v. Pacifica Foundation*, we upheld the Commission's order against statutory and constitutional challenge....

In the ensuing years, the Commission took a cautious, but gradually expanding, approach to enforcing the statutory prohibition against indecent broadcasts. Shortly after *Pacifica*, the Commission expressed its "inten[tion] strictly to observe the narrowness of the *Pacifica* holding," which "relied in part on the repetitive occurrence of the 'indecent' words" contained in Carlin's monologue. When the full Commission next considered its indecency standard, however, it repudiated the view that its enforcement power was limited to "deliberate, repetitive use of the seven words actually contained in the George Carlin monologue."...

. . . .

Over a decade later, the Commission emphasized that the "full context" in which particular materials appear is "critically important," but that a few "principal" factors guide the inquiry, such as the "explicitness or graphic nature" of the material, the extent to which the material "dwells on or repeats" the offensive material, and the extent to which the material was presented to "pander," to "titillate," or to "shock." *In re Industry Guidance On the Commission's Case Law Interpreting 18 U.S.C. §1464 and Enforcement Policies Regarding Broadcast Indecency*, 16 FCC Rcd. 7999....

In 2004, the Commission took one step further by declaring for the first time that a nonliteral (expletive) use of the F- and S-Words could be actionably indecent, even when the word is used only once. The first order to this effect dealt with an NBC broadcast of the Golden Globe Awards, in which the performer Bono commented, "'This is really, really, f***ing brilliant.'" ....

The Commission first declared that Bono's use of the F-Word fell within its indecency definition, even though the word was used as an intensifier rather than a literal descriptor. "[G]iven the core meaning of the 'F-Word,'" it said, "any use of that word . . . inherently has a sexual connotation." The Commission determined, moreover, that the broadcast was "patently offensive" because the F-Word "is one of the most vulgar, graphic and explicit descriptions of sexual activity in the English language," because "[i]ts use invariably invokes a coarse sexual image," and because Bono's use of the word was entirely "shocking and gratuitous."

The Commission observed that categorically exempting such language from enforcement actions would "likely lead to more widespread use." ....

....

II. THE PRESENT CASE

This case concerns utterances in two live broadcasts aired by Fox Television Stations, Inc., and its affiliates prior to the Commission's *Golden Globes Order*. The first occurred during the 2002 Billboard Music Awards, when the singer Cher exclaimed, "I've also had critics for the last 40 years saying that I was on my way out every year. Right. So f*** 'em." The second involved a segment of the 2003 Billboard Music Awards, during the presentation of an award by Nicole Richie and Paris Hilton, principals in a Fox television series called "The Simple Life." Ms. Hilton began their interchange by reminding Ms. Richie to "watch the bad language," but Ms. Richie proceeded to ask the audience, "Why do they even call it 'The Simple Life?' Have you ever tried to get cow s*** out of a Prada purse? It's not so f***ing simple." Following each of these broadcasts, the Commission received numerous complaints from parents whose children were exposed to the language. On March 15, 2006, the Commission released Notices of Apparent Liability for a number of broadcasts that the Commission deemed actionably indecent, including the two described above....

The [FCC] order first explained that both broadcasts fell comfortably within the subject-matter scope of the Commission's indecency test because the 2003 broadcast involved a literal description of excrement and both broadcasts invoked the "F-Word," which inherently has a sexual connotation. The order next determined that the broadcasts were patently offensive under community standards for the medium. Both broadcasts, it noted, involved entirely gratuitous uses of "one of the most vulgar, graphic, and explicit words for sexual activity in the English language." .... The order relied upon the "critically important" context of the utterances, noting that they were aired during prime-time awards shows "designed to draw a large nationwide audience that could be expected to include many children interested in seeing their favorite music stars." ....

....

.... Although the Commission determined that Fox encouraged the offensive language by using suggestive scripting in the 2003 broadcast, and unreasonably failed to take adequate precautions in both broadcasts, the order again declined to impose any forfeiture or other sanction for either of the broadcasts.

Fox returned to the Second Circuit for review of the *Remand Order*, and various intervenors including CBS, NBC, and ABC joined the action. The Court of Appeals reversed the agency's orders, finding the Commission's reasoning inadequate under the Administrative Procedure Act. The majority was "skeptical that the Commission [could] provide a reasoned explanation for its 'fleeting expletive' regime that would pass constitutional muster," but it declined to reach the constitutional question....

III. ANALYSIS

A. Governing Principles

The Administrative Procedure Act, which sets forth the full extent of judicial authority to review executive agency action for procedural correctness,
permits (insofar as relevant here) the setting aside of agency action that is "arbitrary" or "capricious." Under what we have called this "narrow" standard of review, we insist that an agency "examine the relevant data and articulate a satisfactory explanation for its action." We have made clear, however, that "a court is not to substitute its judgment for that of the agency," and should "uphold a decision of less than ideal clarity if the agency's path may reasonably be discerned."

In overturning the Commission's judgment, the Court of Appeals here relied in part on Circuit precedent requiring a more substantial explanation for agency action that changes prior policy....

We find no basis in the Administrative Procedure Act or in our opinions for a requirement that all agency change be subjected to more searching review. The Act mentions no such heightened standard.... The statute makes no distinction ... between initial agency action and subsequent agency action undoing or revising that action.

....If the Commission's action here was not arbitrary or capricious in the ordinary sense, it satisfies the Administrative Procedure Act's "arbitrary [or] capricious" standard; its lawfulness under the Constitution is a separate question to be addressed in a constitutional challenge.

B. Application to This Case

Judged under the above described standards, the Commission's new enforcement policy and its order finding the broadcasts actionably indecent were neither arbitrary nor capricious. First, the Commission forthrightly acknowledged that its recent actions have broken new ground, taking account of inconsistent "prior Commission and staff action" and explicitly disavowing them as "no longer good law." .... There is no doubt that the Commission knew it was making a change. That is why it declined to assess penalties; and it relied on the *Golden Globes Order* as removing any lingering doubt. Moreover, the agency's reasons for expanding the scope of its enforcement activity were entirely rational....

....

The fact that technological advances have made it easier for broadcasters to bleep out offending words further supports the Commission's stepped-up enforcement policy. And the agency's decision not to impose any forfeiture or other sanction precludes any argument that it is arbitrarily punishing parties without notice of the potential consequences of their action.

D. Respondents' Arguments

.... The broadcasters ... make much of the fact that the Commission has gone beyond the scope of authority approved in *Pacifica*, which it once regarded as the farthest extent of its power. But we have never held that *Pacifica* represented the outer limits of permissible regulation, so that fleeting expletives *may not* be forbidden. To the contrary, we explicitly left for another day whether "an occasional expletive" in "a telecast of an Elizabethan comedy" could be prohibited....

Finally, the broadcasters claim that the Commission's repeated appeal to "context" is simply a smokescreen for a standardless regime of unbridled discretion. But we have previously approved Commission regulation based "on a nuisance rationale under which context is all-important," and we find no basis in the Administrative Procedure Act for mandating anything different.

....

IV. CONSTITUTIONALITY

The Second Circuit did not definitively rule on the constitutionality of the Commission's orders, but respondents nonetheless ask us to decide their validity under the First Amendment. This Court, however, is one of final review, "not of first view." It is conceivable that the Commission's orders may cause some broadcasters to avoid certain language that is beyond the Commission's reach under the Constitution. Whether that is so, and, if so, whether it is unconstitutional, will be determined soon enough, perhaps in this very case. Meanwhile, any chilled references to excretory and sexual material "surely lie at the periphery of First Amendment concern." .... We decline to address the constitutional questions at this time.

.... We decline to "substitute [our] judgment for that of the agency," and we find the Commission's orders neither arbitrary nor capricious.

The judgment of the United States Court of Appeals for the Second Circuit is reversed, and the case is remanded for further proceedings consistent with this opinion.

JUSTICE BREYER, with whom JUSTICE STEVENS, JUSTICE SOUTER, and JUSTICE GINSBURG join, dissenting.

In my view, the Federal Communications Commission failed adequately to explain *why* it *changed* its indecency policy from a policy permitting a single "fleeting use" of an expletive, to a policy that made no such exception. Its explanation fails to discuss two critical factors, at least one of which directly underlay its original policy decision. Its explanation instead discussed several factors well known to it the first time around, which by themselves provide no significant justification for a *change* of policy. Consequently, the FCC decision is "arbitrary, capricious, an abuse of discretion." And I would affirm the Second Circuit's similar determination.

I

I begin with applicable law. That law grants those in charge of independent administrative agencies broad authority to determine relevant policy. But it does not permit them to make policy choices for purely political reasons nor to rest them primarily upon unexplained policy preferences. Federal Communications Commissioners have fixed terms of office; they are not directly responsible to the voters; and they enjoy an independence expressly designed to insulate them, to a degree, from "'the exercise of political oversight.'" That insulation helps to secure important governmental objectives, such as the constitutionally related objective of maintaining broadcast regulation that does not bend too readily before the political winds. But that agency's comparative freedom from ballot-box control makes it all the more important that courts review its decision making to assure compliance with applicable provisions of the law—including law requiring that major policy decisions be based upon articulable reasons.

....

Moreover, an agency must act consistently. The agency must follow its own rules. And when an agency seeks to change those rules, it must focus on the fact of change and explain the basis for that change....

....

I recognize that *sometimes* the ultimate explanation for a change may have to be, "We now weigh the relevant considerations differently." But at other times, an agency can and should say more....

II

....

The FCC ... repeatedly made clear that it based its "fleeting expletive" policy upon the need to avoid treading too close to the constitutional line as set forth in Justice Powell's *Pacifica* concurrence. What then did it say, when it changed its policy, about *why* it abandoned this Constitution-based reasoning? .... They do not explain the transformation of what the FCC had long thought an insurmountable obstacle into an open door. The result is not simply *Hamlet* without the prince, but *Hamlet* with a prince who, in mid play and without explanation, just disappears.

....

ASHCROFT V. AMERICAN CIVIL LIBERTIES UNION
Supreme Court of the United States, 2004
542 U.S. 656

Justice KENNEDY delivered the opinion of the Court.

This case presents a challenge to a statute enacted by Congress to protect minors from exposure to sexually explicit materials on the Internet, the Child Online Protection Act (COPA). We must decide whether the Court of Appeals was correct to affirm a ruling by the District Court that enforcement of COPA should be enjoined because the statute likely violates the First Amendment.

In enacting COPA, Congress gave consideration to our earlier decisions on this subject, in particular the decision in *Reno v. American Civil Liberties Union*, 521 U.S. 844 (1997).

For that reason, "the Judiciary must proceed with caution and . . . with care before invalidating the Act." The imperative of according respect to the Congress, however, does not permit us to depart from well-established First Amendment principles. Instead, we must hold the Government to its constitutional burden of proof.

Content-based prohibitions, enforced by severe criminal penalties, have the constant potential to be a repressive force in the lives and thoughts of a free people. To guard against that threat the Constitution demands that content-based restrictions on speech be presumed invalid and that the Government bear the burden of showing their constitutionality. This is true even when Congress twice has attempted to find a constitutional means to restrict, and punish, the speech in question.

… [W]e affirm the decision of the Court of Appeals upholding the preliminary injunction, and we remand the case so that it may be returned to the District Court for trial on the issues presented.

I

A

COPA is the second attempt by Congress to make the Internet safe for minors by criminalizing certain Internet speech. The first attempt was the Communications Decency Act of 1996. The Court held the CDA unconstitutional because it was not narrowly tailored to serve a compelling governmental interest and because less restrictive alternatives were available. (*Reno.*)

In response to the Court's decision in *Reno*, Congress passed COPA. COPA imposes criminal penalties of a $50,000 fine and six months in prison for the knowing posting, for "commercial purposes," of World Wide Web content that is "harmful to minors." Material that is "harmful to minors" is defined as:

"any communication, picture, image, graphic image file, article, recording, writing, or other matter of any kind that is obscene or that--

"(A) the average person, applying contemporary community standards, would find, taking the material as a whole and with respect to minors, is designed to appeal to, or is designed to pander to, the prurientinterest;

"(B) depicts, describes, or represents, in a manner patently offensive with respect to minors, an actual or simulated sexual act or sexual contact, an actual or simulated normal or perverted sexual act, or a lewd exhibition of the genitals or post-pubescent female breast; and

"(C) taken as a whole, lacks serious literary, artistic, political, or scientific value for minors."

"Minors" are defined as "any person under 17 years of age." A person acts for "commercial purposes only if such person is engaged in the business of making such communications." …

While the statute labels all speech that falls within these definitions as criminal speech, it also provides an affirmative defense to those who employ specified means to prevent minors from gaining access to the prohibited materials on their Web site. A person may escape conviction under the statute by demonstrating that he

"has restricted access by minors to material that is harmful to minors--

"(A) by requiring use of a credit card, debit account, adult access code, or adult personal identification number;

"(B) by accepting a digital certificate that verifies age, or

"(C) by any other reasonable measures that are feasible under available technology." ...

B

Respondents, Internet content providers and others concerned with protecting the freedom of speech, filed suit in the United States District Court for the Eastern District of Pennsylvania. They sought a preliminary injunction against enforcement of the statute. After considering testimony from witnesses presented by both respondents and the Government, the District Court issued an order granting the preliminary injunction. ...

II

A

"This Court, like other appellate courts, has always applied the abuse of discretion standard on the review of a preliminary injunction."... If the underlying constitutional question is close, therefore, we should uphold the injunction and remand for trial on the merits. Applying this mode of inquiry, we agree with the Court of Appeals that the District Court did not abuse its discretion in entering the preliminary injunction....

The District Court, in deciding to grant the preliminary injunction, concentrated primarily on the argument that there are plausible, less restrictive alternatives to COPA. A statute that "effectively suppresses a large amount of speech that adults have a constitutional right to receive and to address to one another ... is unacceptable if less restrictive alternatives would be at least as effective in achieving the legitimate purpose that the statute was enacted to serve."...

In considering this question, a court assumes that certain protected speech may be regulated, and then asks what is the least restrictive alternative that can be used to achieve that goal. The purpose of the test is not to consider whether the challenged restriction has some effect in achieving Congress' goal, regardless of the restriction it imposes. The purpose of the test is to ensure that speech is restricted no further than necessary to achieve the goal, for it is important to assure that legitimate speech is not chilled or punished. ... [T]he court should ask whether the challenged regulation is the least restrictive means among available, effective alternatives.

... As the Government bears the burden of proof on the ultimate question of COPA's constitutionality, respondents must be deemed likely to prevail unless the Government has shown that respondents' proposed less restrictive alternatives are less effective than COPA....

The primary alternative considered by the District Court was blocking and filtering software. Blocking and filtering software is an alternative that is less restrictive than COPA, and, in addition, likely more effective as a means of restricting children's access to materials harmful to them....

Filters are less restrictive than COPA. They impose selective restrictions on speech at the receiving end, not universal restrictions at the source. Under a filtering regime, adults without children may gain access to speech they have a right to see without having to identify themselves or provide their credit card information. Even adults with children may obtain access to the same speech on the same terms simply by turning off the filter on their home computers. Above all, promoting the use of filters does not condemn as criminal any category of speech, and so the potential chilling effect is eliminated, or at least much diminished. All of these things are true, moreover, regardless of how broadly or narrowly the definitions in COPA are construed.

Filters also may well be more effective than COPA. First, a filter can prevent minors from seeing all pornography, not just pornography posted to the Web from America. The District Court noted in its fact findings that one witness estimated that 40% of harmful-to-minors content comes from overseas. COPA does not prevent minors from having access to those foreign harmful materials. That alone makes it possible that filtering software might be more effective in serving Congress' goals. Effectiveness is likely to diminish even further if COPA is upheld, because the providers of the materials that would be covered by the statute simply can move their operations overseas. It is not an answer to say that COPA reaches some amount of materials that are harmful to minors; the question is whether it would reach more of them than less restrictive alternatives....

That filtering software may well be more effective than COPA is confirmed by the findings of the Commission on Child Online Protection, a blue-ribbon commission created by Congress in COPA itself. Congress directed the Commission to evaluate the relative merits of different means of restricting minors' ability to gain access to harmful materials on the Internet. It unambiguously found that filters are more effective than age-verification requirements. Thus, not only has the Government failed to carry its burden of showing the District Court that the proposed alternative is less effective, but also a Government Commission appointed to consider the question has concluded just the opposite. That finding supports our conclusion that the District Court did not abuse its discretion in enjoining the statute.

Filtering software, of course, is not a perfect solution to the problem of children gaining access to harmful-to-minors materials. It may block some materials that are not harmful to minors and fail to catch some that are. Whatever the deficiencies of filters, however, the Government failed to introduce specific evidence proving that existing technologies are less effective than the restrictions in COPA....

B

... On a final point, it is important to note that this opinion does not hold that Congress is incapable of enacting any regulation of the Internet designed to prevent minors from gaining access to harmful materials. The parties, because of the conclusion of the Court of Appeals that the statute's definitions rendered it unconstitutional, did not devote their attention to the question whether further evidence might be introduced on the relative restrictiveness and effectiveness of alternatives to the statute. On remand, however, the parties will be able to introduce further evidence on this point. This opinion does not foreclose the District Court from concluding, upon a proper showing by the Government that meets the Government's constitutional burden as defined in this opinion, that COPA is the least restrictive alternative available to accomplish Congress' goal.

* * *

On this record, the Government has not shown that the less restrictive alternatives proposed by respondents should be disregarded. Those alternatives, indeed, may be more effective than the provisions of COPA. The District Court did not abuse its discretion when it entered the preliminary injunction. The judgment of the Court of Appeals is affirmed, and the case is remanded for proceedings consistent with this opinion.

It is so ordered.

Justice BREYER, with whom THE CHIEF JUSTICE and Justice O'CONNOR join, dissenting.

The Child Online Protection Act seeks to protect children from exposure to commercial pornography placed on the Internet. It does so by requiring commercial providers to place pornographic material behind Internet "screens" readily accessible to adults who produce age verification. The Court recognizes that we should "'proceed ... with care before invalidating the Act,'" while pointing out that the "imperative of according respect to the Congress ... does not permit us to depart from well-established First Amendment principles." I agree with these generalities. Like the Court, I would subject the Act to "the most exacting scrutiny," requiring the Government to show that any restriction of nonobscene expression is "narrowly drawn" to further a "compelling interest" and that the restriction amounts to the "least restrictive means" available to further that interest.

Nonetheless, my examination of (1) the burdens the Act imposes on protected expression, (2) the Act's ability to further a compelling interest, and (3) the proposed "less restrictive alternatives" convinces me that the Court is wrong. I cannot accept its conclusion that Congress could have accomplished its statutory objective—protecting children from commercial pornography on the Internet—in other, less restrictive ways....

The Act's definitions limit the material it regulates to material that does not enjoy First Amendment protection, namely legally obscene material, and very little more. A comparison of this Court's definition of unprotected, "legally obscene," material with the Act's definitions makes this clear....

The Act does not censor the material it covers. Rather, it requires providers of the "harmful to minors" material to restrict minors' access to it by verifying age. They can do so by inserting screens that verify age using a credit card, adult personal identification number, or other similar technology. In this way, the Act requires creation of an Internet screen that minors, but not adults, will find difficult to bypass.

I recognize that the screening requirement imposes some burden on adults who seek access to the regulated material, as well as on its providers. The cost is, in part, monetary. ... According to the trade association for the commercial pornographers who are the statute's target, use of such verification procedures is "standard practice" in their online operations. ...

In sum, the Act at most imposes a modest additional burden on adult access to legally obscene material, perhaps imposing a similar burden on access to some protected borderline obscene material as well.

I turn next to the question of "compelling interest," that of protecting minors from exposure to commercial pornography. ...

The majority refers to the presence of ... software as a "less restrictive alternative." But that is a misnomer—a misnomer that may lead the reader to believe that all we need do is look to see if the blocking and filtering software is less restrictive; and to believe that, because in one sense it is (one can turn off the software), that is the end of the constitutional matter.

But such reasoning has no place here. Conceptually speaking, the presence of filtering software is not an *alternative* legislative approach to the problem of protecting children from exposure to commercial pornography. Rather, it is part of the status quo, *i.e.,* the backdrop against which Congress enacted the present statute. It is always true, by definition, that the status quo is less restrictive than a new regulatory law. It is always less restrictive to do *nothing* than to do *something*. But "doing nothing" does not address the problem Congress sought to address--namely that, despite the availability of filtering software, children were still being exposed to harmful material on the Internet....

My conclusion is that the Act, as properly interpreted, risks imposition of minor burdens on some protected material—burdens that adults wishing to view the material may overcome at modest cost. At the same time, it significantly helps to achieve a compelling congressional goal, protecting children from exposure to commercial pornography. There is no serious, practically available "less restrictive" way similarly to further this compelling interest. Hence the Act is constitutional....

For these reasons, I dissent.

Chapter Twelve
COMMERCIAL SPEECH

The cases in this chapter deal with commercial speech, that is, speech that is primarily intended to generate a business transaction. A common method of commercial speech is product or service advertising, though commercial speech may also be distributed on packaging or in direct-mail literature. The first four cases in this section deal with the constitutionality of government restrictions on truthful commercial speech. The remaining case concerns false advertising.

In *Virginia State Board of Pharmacy v. Virginia Citizens Consumer Council* the U.S. Supreme Court established that pure commercial speech does indeed deserve some degree of First Amendment protection.

In *Central Hudson Gas & Electric v. Public Service Comm'n of New York* the Supreme Court laid down a specific, constitutional test for determining when truthful commercial speech may be subject to regulation. The test makes it clear that such speech is protected against government restrictions, but not to the same degree as political speech.

Bolger v. Youngs Drug Products addressed a difficult issue concerning the classification of commercial speech—an issue that may be important to corporations that publish informational booklets or issues-oriented advertising.

Kasky v. Nike is a highly controversial case in which the California Supreme Court came up with its own test to determine whether a corporation's public efforts to defend itself against allegations in the news media amounted to "commercial" speech.

Greater New Orleans Broadcasting v. United States is the Supreme Court's most recent application of the *Central Hudson* test, and it represents a strict application, with the government facing a considerable burden to justify its restrictions on commercial speech.

FTC v. Colgate-Palmolive Co. is one of the few false-advertising cases to reach the U.S. Supreme Court. Specifically, it illustrates how the Federal Trade Commission can scrutinize "mock-ups" in television commercials and the extent to which the courts will give deference to the FTC's expertise.

VIRGINIA STATE BOARD OF PHARMACY
V. VIRGINIA CITIZENS CONSUMER COUNCIL
Supreme Court of the United States, 1976
425 U.S. 748

Justice BLACKMUN delivered the opinion of the Court.

The plaintiff-appellees in this case attack, as violative of the First and Fourteenth Amendments, that portion of § 54-524.35 of Va.Code Ann. (1974), which provides that a pharmacist licensed in Virginia is guilty of unprofessional conduct if he "(3) publishes, advertises or promotes, directly or indirectly, in any manner whatsoever, any amount, price, fee, premium, discount, rebate, or credit terms ... for any drugs which may be dispensed only by prescription." ...

...

II

The present... attack on the statute is one made not by one directly subject to its prohibition, that is, a pharmacist, but by prescription drug consumers who claim that they would greatly benefit if the prohibition were lifted and advertising freely allowed. The plaintiffs are an individual Virginia resident who suffers from diseases that require her to take prescription drugs on a daily basis, and two nonprofit organizations. Their claim is that the First Amendment entitles the user of prescription drugs to receive information that pharmacists wish to communicate to them through advertising and other promotional means, concerning the prices of such drugs.

Certainly that information may be of value. Drug prices in Virginia, for both prescription and nonprescription items, strikingly vary from outlet to outlet even within the same locality....

III

The question first arises whether, even assuming that First Amendment protection attaches to the flow of drug price information, it is a protection enjoyed by the appellees as recipients of the information, and not solely, if at all, by the advertisers themselves who seek to disseminate that information.

Freedom of speech presupposes a willing speaker. But where a speaker exists, as is the case here, the protection afforded is to the communication, to its source and to its recipients both. This is clear from the decided cases. In *Lamont v. Postmaster General*, 381 U.S. 301 (1965), the Court upheld the First Amendment rights of citizens to receive political publications sent from abroad. More recently, in *Kleindienst v. Mandel*, 408 U.S. 753 (1972), we acknowledged that this Court has referred to a First Amendment right to "receive information and ideas," and that freedom of speech "'necessarily protects the right to receive.'" ... If there is a right to advertise, there is a reciprocal right to receive the advertising, and it may be asserted by these appellees.

IV

The appellants contend that the advertisement of prescription drug prices is outside the protection of the First Amendment because it is "commercial speech." There can be no question that in past decisions the Court has given some indication that commercial speech is unprotected....

Since [1951], however, the Court has never *denied* protection on the ground that the speech in issue was "commercial speech." ...

Last Term, in *Bigelow v. Virginia*, 421 U.S. 809 (1975), the notion of unprotected "commercial speech" all but passed from the scene. We reversed a conviction for violation of a Virginia statute that made the circulation of any publication to encourage or promote the processing of an abortion in Virginia a misdemeanor. The defendant had published in his newspaper the availability of abortions in New York. The advertisement in question, in addition to announcing that abortions were legal in New York, offered the services of a referral agency in that State. We rejected the contention that the publication was unprotected because it was commercial....

Some fragment of hope for the continuing validity of a "commercial speech" exception arguably might have persisted because of the subject matter of the advertisement in *Bigelow*. We noted that in announcing the availability of legal abortions in New York, the advertisement "did more than simply propose a commercial transaction. It contained factual material of clear 'public interest.'" And, of course, the advertisement related to activity with which, at least in some respects, the State could not interfere....

Here, in contrast, the question whether there is a First Amendment exception for "commercial speech" is squarely before us. Our pharmacist does not wish to editorialize on any subject, cultural, philosophical, or political. He does not wish to report any particularly newsworthy fact, or to make generalized observations even about commercial matters. The "idea" he wishes to communicate is simply this: "I will sell you the X prescription drug at the Y price." Our question, then, is whether this communication is wholly outside the protection of the First Amendment.

V

We begin with several propositions that already are settled or beyond serious dispute. It is clear, for example, that speech does not lose its First Amendment protection because money is spent to project it, as in a paid advertisement of one form or another. Speech likewise is protected even though it is carried in a form that is "sold" for profit, and even though it may involve a solicitation to purchase or otherwise pay or contribute money....

Focusing first on the individual parties to the transaction that is proposed in the commercial advertisement, we may assume that the advertiser's interest is a purely economic one. That hardly disqualifies him from protection under the First Amendment....

As to the particular consumer's interest in the free flow of commercial information, that interest may be as keen, if not keener by far, than his interest in the day's most urgent political debate. Appellees' case in this respect is a convincing one. Those whom the suppression of prescription drug price information hits the hardest are the poor, the sick, and particularly the aged. A disproportionate amount of their income tends to be spent on prescription drugs; yet they are the least able to learn, by shopping from pharmacist to pharmacist, where their scarce dollars are best spent. When drug prices vary as strikingly as they do, information as to who is charging what becomes more than a convenience. It could mean the alleviation of physical pain or the enjoyment of basic necessities.

Generalizing, society also may have a strong interest in the free flow of commercial information....

.... Advertising, however tasteless and excessive it sometimes may seem, is nonetheless dissemination of information as to who is producing and selling what products, for what reason, and at what price. So long as we preserve a predominantly free enterprise economy, the allocation of our resources in large measure will be made through numerous private economic decisions. It is a matter of public interest that those decisions, in the aggregate, be intelligent and well informed. To this end, the free flow of commercial information is indispensable....

Arrayed against these substantial individual and societal interests are a number of justifications for the advertising ban. These have to do principally with maintaining a high degree of professionalism on the part of licensed pharmacists....

Price advertising, it is argued, will place in jeopardy the pharmacist's expertise and, with it, the customer's health. It is claimed that the aggressive price competition that will result from unlimited advertising will make it impossible for the pharmacist to supply professional services in the compounding, handling, and dispensing of prescription drugs.... It is also claimed that prices might not necessarily fall as a result of advertising. If one pharmacist advertises, others must, and the resulting expense will inflate the cost of drugs.... Finally, it is argued that damage will be done to the professional image of the pharmacist....

The strength of these proffered justifications is greatly undermined by the fact that high professional standards, to a substantial extent, are guaranteed by the close regulation to which pharmacists in Virginia are subject....

It appears to be feared that if the pharmacist who wishes to provide low cost, and assertedly low quality, services is permitted to advertise, he will be taken up on his offer by too many unwitting customers....

There is, of course, an alternative to this highly paternalistic approach. That alternative is to assume that this information is not in itself harmful, that people will perceive their own best interests if only they are well enough informed, and that the best means to that end is to open the channels of communication rather than to close them. If they are truly open, nothing prevents the "professional" pharmacist from marketing his own assertedly superior product, and contrasting it with that of the low-cost, high-volume prescription drug retailer. But the choice among these alternative approaches is not ours to make or the Virginia General Assembly's. It is precisely this kind of choice, between the dangers of suppressing information, and the dangers of its misuse if it is freely available, that the First Amendment makes for us. Virginia is free to require whatever professional standards it wishes of its pharmacists; it may subsidize them or protect them from competition in other ways. But it may not do so by keeping the public in ignorance of the entirely lawful terms that competing pharmacists are offering. In this sense, the justifications Virginia has offered for suppressing the flow of prescription drug price information, far from persuading us that the flow is not protected by the First Amendment, have reinforced our view that it is. We so hold....

The judgment of the District Court is affirmed.

CENTRAL HUDSON GAS & ELECTRIC V. PUBLIC SERVICE COMM'N OF NEW YORK
Supreme Court of the United States, 1980
447 U.S. 557

Justice POWELL delivered the opinion of the Court.

This case presents the question whether a regulation of the Public Service Commission of the State of New York violates the First and Fourteenth Amendments because it completely bans promotional advertising by an electrical utility.

I

In December 1973, the Commission, appellee here, ordered electric utilities in New York State to cease all advertising that "promot[es] the use of electricity." The order was based on the Commission's finding that "the interconnected utility system in New York State does not have sufficient fuel stocks or sources of supply to continue furnishing all customer demands for the 1973-1974 winter."

Three years later, when the fuel shortage had eased, the Commission requested comments from the public on its proposal to continue the ban on promotional advertising…. After reviewing the public comments, the Commission extended the prohibition in a Policy Statement….

The Policy Statement divided advertising expenses "into two broad categories: promotional—advertising intended to stimulate the purchase of utility services—and institutional and informational, a broad category inclusive of all advertising not clearly intended to promote sales." The Commission declared all promotional advertising contrary to the national policy of conserving energy…. [I]t was recognized that the ban can achieve only "piecemeal conservationism." Still, the Commission adopted the restriction because it was deemed likely to "result in some dampening of unnecessary growth" in energy consumption.

The Commission's order explicitly permitted "informational" advertising designed to encourage "*shifts* of consumption" from peak demand times to periods of low electricity demand….

Appellant challenged the order in state court, arguing that the Commission had restrained commercial speech in violation of the First and Fourteenth Amendments. The Commission's order was upheld by the trial court and at the intermediate appellate level. The New York Court of Appeals affirmed. It found little value to advertising in "the noncompetitive market in which electric corporations operate." …

II

The Commission's order restricts only commercial speech, that is, expression related solely to the economic interests of the speaker and its audience. The First Amendment, as applied to the States through the Fourteenth Amendment, protects commercial speech from unwarranted governmental regulation….

Nevertheless, our decisions have recognized "the 'commonsense' distinction between speech proposing a commercial transaction, which occurs in an area traditionally subject to government regulation, and other varieties of speech." The Constitution therefore accords a lesser protection to commercial speech than to other constitutionally guaranteed expression. The protection available for particular commercial expression turns on the nature both of the expression and of the governmental interests served by its regulation.

The First Amendment's concern for commercial speech is based on the informational function of advertising. Consequently, there can be no constitutional objection to the suppression of commercial messages that do not accurately inform the public about lawful activity. The government may ban forms of communication more likely to deceive the public than to inform it.

If the communication is neither misleading nor related to unlawful activity, the government's power is more circumscribed. The State must assert a substantial interest to be achieved by restrictions on commercial speech. Moreover, the regulatory technique must be in proportion to that interest. The limitation on expression must be designed carefully to achieve the State's goal. Compliance with this requirement may be measured by two criteria. First, the restriction must directly advance the state interest involved; the regulation may not be sustained if it provides only ineffective or remote support for the government's purpose. Second, if the governmental interest could be served as well by a more limited restriction on commercial speech, the excessive restrictions cannot survive....

In commercial speech cases, then, a four-part analysis has developed. At the outset, we must determine whether the expression is protected by the First Amendment. For commercial speech to come within that provision, it at least must concern lawful activity and not be misleading. Next, we ask whether the asserted governmental interest is substantial. If both inquiries yield positive answers, we must determine whether the regulation directly advances the governmental interest asserted, and whether it is not more extensive than is necessary to serve that interest.

III

We now apply this four-step analysis for commercial speech to the Commission's arguments in support of its ban on promotional advertising.

A

The Commission does not claim that the expression at issue either is inaccurate or relates to unlawful activity. Yet the New York Court of Appeals questioned whether Central Hudson's advertising is protected commercial speech. Because appellant holds a monopoly over the sale of electricity in its service area, the state court suggested that the Commission's order restricts no commercial speech of any worth....

This reasoning falls short of establishing that appellant's advertising is not commercial speech protected by the First Amendment. Monopoly over the supply of a product provides no protection from competition with substitutes for that product. Electric utilities compete with suppliers of fuel oil and natural gas in several markets, such as those for home heating and industrial power....

Even in monopoly markets, the suppression of advertising reduces the information available for consumer decisions and thereby defeats the purpose of the First Amendment.... [A]ppellant's monopoly position does not alter the First Amendment's protection for its commercial speech.

B

The Commission offers two state interests as justifications for the ban on promotional advertising. The first concerns energy conservation.... The Commission argues, and the New York court agreed, that the State's interest in conserving energy is sufficient to support suppression of advertising designed to increase consumption of electricity. In view of our country's dependence on energy resources beyond our control, no one can doubt the importance of energy conservation. Plainly, therefore, the state interest asserted is substantial....

C

Next, we focus on the relationship between the State's interests and the advertising ban....

... [T]he State's interest in energy conservation is directly advanced by the Commission order at issue here. There is an immediate connection between advertising and demand for electricity. Central Hudson would not contest the advertising ban unless it believed that promotion would increase its sales. Thus, we find a direct link between the state interest in conservation and the Commission's order.

D

We come finally to the critical inquiry in this case: whether the Commission's complete suppression of speech ordinarily protected by the First Amendment is no more extensive than necessary to further the State's interest in energy conservation. The Commission's order reaches all promotional advertising, regardless of the impact of the touted service on overall energy use. But the energy conservation rationale, as important as it is, cannot justify suppressing information about electric devices or services that would cause no net increase in total energy use. In addition, no showing has been made that a more limited restriction on the content of promotional advertising would not serve adequately the State's interests.

Appellant insists that but for the ban, it would advertise products and services that use energy efficiently. These include the "heat pump," which both parties acknowledge to be a major improvement in electric heating, and the use of electric heat as a "backup" to solar and other heat sources....

The Commission's order prevents appellant from promoting electric services that would reduce energy use by diverting demand from less efficient sources, or that would consume roughly the same amount of energy as do alternative sources. In neither situation would the utility's advertising endanger conservation or mislead the public. To the extent that the Commission's order suppresses speech that in no way impairs the State's interest in energy conservation, the Commission's order violates the First and Fourteenth Amendments and must be invalidated.

The Commission also has not demonstrated that its interest in conservation cannot be protected adequately by more limited regulation of appellant's commercial expression. To further its policy of conservation, the Commission could attempt to restrict the format and content of Central Hudson's advertising. It might, for example, require that the advertisements include information about the relative efficiency and expense of the offered service, both under current conditions and for the foreseeable future. In the absence of a showing that more limited speech regulation would be ineffective, we cannot approve the complete suppression of Central Hudson's advertising....

Accordingly, the judgment of the New York Court of Appeals is

Reversed.

BOLGER V. YOUNGS DRUG PRODUCTS CORP.
Supreme Court of the United States,
463 U.S. 60 (1983)

Justice MARSHALL delivered the opinion of the Court.

Title 39 U.S.C. 3001(e)(2) prohibits the mailing of unsolicited advertisements for contraceptives. The District Court held that, as applied to appellee's mailings, the statute violates the First Amendment. We affirm.

I

Section 3001(e)(2) states that "[a]ny unsolicited advertisement of matter which is designed, adapted, or intended for preventing conception is nonmailable matter, shall not be carried or delivered by mail, and shall be disposed of as the Postal Service directs ."... As interpreted by Postal Service regulations, the statutory provision does not apply to unsolicited advertisements in which the mailer has no commercial interest. In addition to the civil consequences of a violation of 3001(e)(2), 18 U.S.C. 1461 makes it a crime to knowingly use the mails for anything declared by 3001(e) to be nonmailable.

Appellee Youngs Drug Products Corp. (Youngs) is engaged in the manufacture, sale, and distribution of contraceptives. Youngs markets its products primarily through sales to chain warehouses and wholesale distributors, who in turn sell contraceptives to retail pharmacists, who then sell those products to individual customers. Appellee publicizes the availability and desirability of its products by various methods. This litigation resulted from Youngs' decision to undertake a campaign of unsolicited mass mailings to members of the public. In conjunction with its wholesalers and retailers, Youngs seeks to mail to the public on an unsolicited basis three types of materials:

-multi-page, multi-item flyers promoting a large variety of products available at a drugstore, including prophylactics;
-flyers exclusively or substantially devoted to promoting prophylactics;
-informational pamphlets discussing the desirability and availability of prophylactics in general or Youngs' products in particular.

In 1979 the Postal Service traced to a wholesaler of Youngs' products an allegation of an unsolicited mailing of contraceptive advertisements. The Service warned the wholesaler that the mailing violated 39 U.S.C. 3001(e)(2). Subsequently, Youngs contacted the Service and furnished it with copies of Youngs' three types of proposed mailings, stating its view that the statute could not constitutionally restrict the mailings. The Service rejected Youngs' legal argument and notified the company that the proposed mailings would violate 3001(e)(2). Youngs then brought this action for declaratory and injunctive relief in the United States District Court for the District of Columbia. It claimed that the statute, as applied to its proposed mailings, violated the First Amendment ...

II

Beginning with *Bigelow v. Virginia,* 421 U.S. 809 (1975), this Court extended the protection of the First Amendment to commercial speech. Nonetheless, our decisions have recognized "the 'common-sense' distinction between speech proposing a commercial transaction, which occurs in an area traditionally subject to government regulation, and other varieties of speech." Thus, we have held that the Constitution accords less protection to commercial speech than to other constitutionally safeguarded forms of expression....

Because the degree of protection afforded by the First Amendment depends on whether the activity sought to be regulated constitutes commercial or noncommercial speech, we must first determine the proper classification of the mailings at issue here....

Most of appellee's mailings fall within the core notion of commercial speech— "speech which does 'no more than propose a commercial transaction.'" Youngs' informational pamphlets, however, cannot be characterized merely as proposals to engage in commercial transactions. Their proper classification as commercial or noncommercial speech thus presents a closer question. The mere fact that these pamphlets are conceded to be advertisements clearly does not compel the conclusion that they are commercial speech. See *New York Times Co. v. Sullivan,* 376 U.S. 254, 265 -266 (1964). Similarly, the reference to a specific product does not by itself render the pamphlets commercial speech. Finally, the fact that Youngs has an economic motivation for mailing the pamphlets would clearly be insufficient by itself to turn the materials into commercial speech.

The combination of all these characteristics, however, provides strong support for the District Court's conclusion that the informational pamphlets are properly characterized as commercial speech. The mailings constitute commercial speech notwithstanding the fact that they contain discussions of important public issues, such as venereal disease and family planning. We have made clear that advertising which "links a product to a current public debate" is not thereby entitled to the constitutional protection afforded noncommercial speech. *Central Hudson Gas & Electric Corp. v. Public Service Comm'n of New York,* 447 U.S., at 563, n. 5. A company has the full panoply of protections available to its direct comments on public issues, so there is no reason for providing similar constitutional protection when such statements are made in the context of commercial transactions. Advertisers should not be permitted to immunize false or misleading product information from government regulation simply by including references to public issues.

We conclude, therefore, that all of the mailings in this case are entitled to the qualified but nonetheless substantial protection accorded to commercial speech.

III

"The protection available for particular commercial expression turns on the nature both of the expression and of the governmental interests served by its regulation." In *Central Hudson* we adopted a four-part analysis for assessing the validity of restrictions on commercial speech. First, we determine whether the expression is constitutionally protected. For commercial speech to receive such protection, "it at least must concern lawful activity and not be misleading." Second, we ask whether the governmental interest is substantial. If so, we must then determine whether the regulation directly advances the government interest asserted, and whether it is not more extensive than necessary to serve that interest. Applying this analysis, we conclude that 3001(e)(2) is unconstitutional as applied to appellee's mailings.

... The State may deal effectively with false, deceptive, or misleading sales techniques. The State may also prohibit commercial speech related to illegal behavior. In this case, however, appellants have never claimed that Youngs' proposed mailings fall into any of these categories. To the contrary, advertising for contraceptives not only implicates "'substantial individual and societal interests'" in the free flow of commercial information, but also relates to activity which is protected from unwarranted state interference. Youngs' proposed commercial speech is therefore clearly protected by the First Amendment....

We must next determine whether the Government's interest in prohibiting the mailing of unsolicited contraceptive advertisements is a substantial one....

In particular, appellants assert that the statute (1) shields recipients of mail from materials that they are likely to find offensive, and (2) aids parents' efforts to control the manner in which their children become informed about sensitive and important subjects such as birth control. The first of these interests carries little weight. In striking down a state prohibition of contraceptive advertisements in *Carey v. Population Services International*, we stated that offensiveness was "classically not [a] justificatio[n] validating the suppression of expression protected by the First Amendment. At least where obscenity is not involved, we have consistently held that the fact that protected speech may be offensive to some does not justify its suppression."...

The second interest asserted by appellants—aiding parents' efforts to discuss birth control with their children—is undoubtedly substantial. "[P]arents have an important 'guiding role' to play in the upbringing of their children . . . which presumptively includes counseling them on important decisions." As a means of effectuating this interest, however, 3001(e)(2) fails to withstand scrutiny.

To begin with, 3001(e)(2) provides only the most limited incremental support for the interest asserted. We can reasonably assume that parents already exercise substantial control over the disposition of mail once it enters their mailboxes. Under 39 U.S.C. 3008, parents can also exercise control over information that flows into their mailboxes. And parents must already cope with the multitude of external stimuli that color their children's perception of sensitive subjects. Under these circumstances, a ban on unsolicited advertisements serves only to assist those parents who desire to keep their children from confronting such mailings, who are otherwise unable to do so, and whose children have remained relatively free from such stimuli.

This marginal degree of protection is achieved by purging all mailboxes of unsolicited material that is entirely suitable for adults. We have previously made clear that a restriction of this scope is more extensive than the Constitution permits, for the government may not "reduce the adult population . . . to reading only what is fit for children." *Butler v. Michigan*, 352 U.S. 380, 383 (1957). The level of discourse reaching a mailbox simply cannot be limited to that which would be suitable for a sandbox. In *FCC v. Pacifica Foundation* this Court did recognize that the Government's interest in protecting the young justified special treatment of an afternoon broadcast heard by adults as well as children. At the same time, the majority "emphasize[d] the narrowness of our holding," explaining that broadcasting is "uniquely pervasive" and that it is "uniquely accessible to children, even those too young to read." The receipt of mail is far less intrusive and uncontrollable. Our decisions have recognized that the special interest of the Federal Government in regulation of the broadcast media does not readily translate into a justification for regulation of other means of communication.

IV

We thus conclude that the justifications offered by appellants are insufficient to warrant the sweeping prohibition on the mailing of unsolicited contraceptive advertisements. As applied to appellee's mailings, 3001(e)(2) is unconstitutional. The judgment of the District Court is therefore

Affirmed.

KASKY V. NIKE

Supreme Court of California, 2002
27 Cal. 4th 939

KENNARD, J.

Acting on behalf of the public, plaintiff brought this action seeking monetary and injunctive relief under California laws designed to curb false advertising and unfair competition. Plaintiff alleged that defendant corporation, in response to public criticism, and to induce consumers to continue to buy its products, made false statements of fact about its labor practices and about working conditions in factories that make its products....

The issue here is whether defendant corporation's false statements are commercial or noncommercial speech for purposes of constitutional free speech analysis under the state and federal Constitutions. Resolution of this issue is important because commercial speech receives a lesser degree of constitutional protection than many other forms of expression, and because governments may entirely prohibit commercial speech that is false or misleading.

....

I. FACTS

....

Plaintiff Marc Kasky is a California resident suing on behalf of the general public of the State of California under Business and Professions Code sections 17204 and 17535....

Nike manufactures and sells athletic shoes and apparel. In 1997, it reported annual revenues of $ 9.2 billion, with annual expenditures for advertising and marketing of almost $ 1 billion. Most of Nike's products are manufactured by subcontractors in China, Vietnam, and Indonesia. Most of the workers who make Nike products are women under the age of 24. Since March 1993, under a memorandum of understanding with its subcontractors, Nike has assumed responsibility for its subcontractors' compliance with applicable local laws and regulations concerning minimum wage, overtime, occupational health and safety, and environmental protection.

Beginning at least in October 1996 with a report on the television news program 48 Hours, and continuing at least through November and December of 1997 with the publication of articles in the Financial Times, the New York Times, the San Francisco Chronicle, the Buffalo News, the Oregonian, the Kansas City Star, and the Sporting News, various persons and organizations alleged that in the factories where Nike products are made workers were paid less than the applicable local minimum wage; required to work overtime; allowed and encouraged to work more overtime hours than applicable local law allowed; subjected to physical, verbal, and sexual abuse; and exposed to toxic chemicals, noise, heat, and dust without adequate safety equipment, in violation of applicable local occupational health and safety regulations.

In response to this adverse publicity, and for the purpose of maintaining and increasing its sales and profits, Nike and the individual defendants made statements to the California consuming public that plaintiff alleges were false and misleading. Specifically, Nike and the individual defendants said that workers who make Nike products are protected from physical and sexual abuse, that they are paid in accordance with applicable local laws and regulations governing wages and hours, that they are paid on average double the applicable local minimum wage, that they receive a "living wage," that they receive free meals and health care, and that their working conditions are in compliance with applicable local laws and regulations governing occupational health and safety. Nike and the individual defendants made these statements in press releases, in letters to newspapers, in a letter to university presidents and athletic directors, and in other documents distributed for public relations purposes. Nike also bought full-page advertisements in leading newspapers to publicize a report that GoodWorks International, LLC, had prepared under a contract with Nike. The report was based on an investigation by former United States Ambassador Andrew Young, and it found no evidence of illegal or unsafe working conditions at Nike factories in China, Vietnam, and Indonesia.

Plaintiff alleges that Nike and the individual defendants made these false and misleading statements because of their negligence and carelessness and "with knowledge or reckless disregard of the laws of California prohibiting false and misleading statements."

Based on these factual allegations, plaintiff's first amended complaint sought relief in the form of restitution requiring Nike to "disgorge all monies . . . acquired by means of any act found . . . to be an unlawful and/or unfair business practice," and relief in the form of an injunction requiring Nike to "undertake a Court-approved public information campaign" to correct any false or misleading statement, and to cease misrepresenting the working conditions under which Nike products are made. Plaintiff also sought reasonable attorney fees and costs and other relief that the court deemed just and proper.

Nike demurred to the first amended complaint on grounds, among others, that it failed to state facts sufficient to constitute a cause of action against Nike and that the relief plaintiff was seeking "is absolutely barred by the First Amendment to the United States Constitution and Article I, section 2(a) of the California Constitution." ...

. . . .

[L]ike the superior court, the appellate court concluded that Nike's statements were noncommercial speech and therefore subject to the greatest measure of protection under the constitutional free speech provisions. The court stated that this determination "compels the conclusion that the trial court properly sustained the defendants' demurrer without leave to amend." We granted plaintiff's petition for review.

II. CALIFORNIA LAWS PROHIBITING CONSUMER DECEPTION

. . . .

California's false advertising law makes it "unlawful for any person, . . . corporation . . ., or any employee thereof with intent directly or indirectly to dispose of real or personal property or to perform services . . . or to induce the public to enter into any obligation relating thereto, to make or disseminate . . . before the public in this state, . . . in any newspaper or other publication . . . or in any other manner or means whatever . . . any statement, concerning that real or personal property or those services . . . which is untrue or misleading, and which is known, or which by the exercise of reasonable care should be known, to be untrue or misleading . . . ." . . . .

. . . .

III. CONSTITUTIONAL PROTECTIONS FOR SPEECH

. . . .

Although advertising has played an important role in our nation's culture since its early days, and although state regulation of commercial advertising and commercial transactions also has a long history, it was not until the 1970's that the United States Supreme Court extended First Amendment protection to commercial messages. In 1975, the court declared that it was error to assume "that advertising, as such, was entitled to no First Amendment protection." (*Bigelow v. Virginia.*) The next year, the court held that a state's complete ban on advertising prescription drug prices violated the First Amendment. (*Va. Pharmacy Bd. v. Va. Consumer Council.*) The high court observed that "the free flow of commercial information is indispensable" not only "to the proper allocation of resources in a free enterprise system" but also "to the formation of intelligent opinions as to how that system ought to be regulated or altered."

[T]he [federal] Constitution accords less protection to commercial speech than to other constitutionally safeguarded forms of expression." (*Bolger v. Youngs Drug Products Corp.*)

For noncommercial speech entitled to full First Amendment protection, a content-based regulation is valid under the First Amendment only if it can withstand strict scrutiny, which requires that the regulation be narrowly tailored (that is, the least restrictive means) to promote a compelling government interest.

"By contrast, regulation of commercial speech based on content is less problematic." (*Bolger*, supra.) To determine the validity of a content-based regulation of commercial speech, the United States Supreme Court has articulated an intermediate-scrutiny test. The court first articulated this test in *Central Hudson Gas & Elec. v. Public Serv. Comm'n* (1980). . . .

. . . .

The United States Supreme Court has given three reasons for the distinction between commercial and noncommercial speech in general and, more particularly, for withholding First Amendment protection from commercial speech that is false or actually or inherently misleading.

First, "[t]he truth of commercial speech . . . may be more easily verifiable by its disseminator than . . . news reporting or political commentary, in that ordinarily the advertiser seeks to disseminate information about a specific product or service that he himself provides and presumably knows more about than anyone else."

Second, commercial speech is hardier than noncommercial speech in the sense that commercial speakers, because they act from a profit motive, are less likely to experience a chilling effect from speech regulation.

Third, governmental authority to regulate commercial transactions to prevent commercial harms justifies a power to regulate speech that is " 'linked inextricably' to those transactions.".…

The United States Supreme Court has stated that the category of commercial speech consists at its core of "'speech proposing a commercial transaction.'" Although in one case the court said that this description was "the test for identifying commercial speech," in other decisions the court has indicated that the category of commercial speech is not limited to this core segment. For example, the court has accepted as commercial speech a statement of alcohol content on the label of a beer bottle, as well as statements on an attorney's letterhead ….

….

Since its decision in *Bolger*, the United States Supreme Court has acknowledged that "ambiguities may exist at the margins of the category of commercial speech." Justice Stevens in particular has remarked that "the borders of the commercial speech category are not nearly as clear as the Court has assumed." ….

….

IV. ANALYSIS

The United States Supreme Court has not adopted an all-purpose test to distinguish commercial from noncommercial speech under the First Amendment, nor has this court adopted such a test under the state Constitution, nor do we propose to do so here. A close reading of the high court's commercial speech decisions suggests, however, that it is possible to formulate a limited-purpose test. We conclude, therefore, that when a court must decide whether particular speech may be subjected to laws aimed at preventing false advertising or other forms of commercial deception, categorizing a particular statement as commercial or noncommercial speech requires consideration of three elements: the speaker, the intended audience, and the content of the message.

In typical commercial speech cases, the speaker is likely to be someone engaged in commerce--that is, generally, the production, distribution, or sale of goods or services--or someone acting on behalf of a person so engaged, and the intended audience is likely to be actual or potential buyers or customers of the speaker's goods or services, or persons acting for actual or potential buyers or customers, or persons (such as reporters or reviewers) likely to repeat the message to or otherwise influence actual or potential buyers or customers.…

….

Finally, the factual content of the message should be commercial in character. In the context of regulation of false or misleading advertising, this typically means that the speech consists of representations of fact about the business operations, products, or services of the speaker (or the individual or company that the speaker represents), made for the purpose of promoting sales of, or other commercial transactions in, the speaker's products or services....

....

Here, the first element--a commercial speaker--is satisfied because the speakers--Nike and its officers and directors--are engaged in commerce....

The second element--an intended commercial audience--is also satisfied. Nike's letters to university presidents and directors of athletic departments were addressed directly to actual and potential purchasers of Nike's products, because college and university athletic departments are major purchasers of athletic shoes and apparel....

The third element--representations of fact of a commercial nature--is also present. In describing its own labor policies, and the practices and working conditions in factories where its products are made, Nike was making factual representations about its own business operations. In speaking to consumers about working conditions and labor practices in the factories where its products are made, Nike addressed matters within its own knowledge. The wages paid to the factories' employees, the hours they work, the way they are treated, and whether the environmental conditions under which they work violate local health and safety laws, are all matters likely to be within the personal knowledge of Nike executives, employees, or subcontractors. Thus, Nike was in a position to readily verify the truth of any factual assertions it made on these topics.

.... To the extent that application of these laws may make Nike more cautious, and cause it to make greater efforts to verify the truth of its statements, these laws will serve the purpose of commercial speech protection by "insuring that the stream of commercial information flow[s] cleanly as well as freely."

....

Because in the statements at issue here Nike was acting as a commercial speaker, because its intended audience was primarily the buyers of its products, and because the statements consisted of factual representations about its own business operations, we conclude that the statements were commercial speech for purposes of applying state laws designed to prevent false advertising and other forms of commercial deception....

Nike argues that its allegedly false and misleading statements were not commercial speech because they were part of "an international media debate on issues of intense public interest." In a similar vein, our dissenting colleagues argue that the speech at issue here should not be categorized as commercial speech because, when Nike made the statements defending its labor practices, the nature and propriety of those practices had already become a matter of public interest and public debate. This argument falsely assumes that speech cannot properly be categorized as commercial speech if it relates to a matter of significant public interest or controversy....

....

Here, Nike's speech is not removed from the category of commercial speech because it is intermingled with noncommercial speech. To the extent Nike's press releases and letters discuss policy questions such as the degree to which domestic companies should be responsible for working conditions in factories located in other countries, or what standards domestic companies ought to observe in such factories, or the merits and effects of economic "globalization" generally, Nike's statements are noncommercial speech. Any content-based regulation of these noncommercial messages would be subject to the strict scrutiny test for fully protected speech. But Nike may not "immunize false or misleading product information from government regulation simply by including references to public issues."....

....

We also reject Nike's argument that regulating its speech to suppress false and misleading statements is impermissible because it would restrict or disfavor expression of one point of view (Nike's) and not the other point of view (that of the critics of Nike's labor practices). The argument is misdirected because the regulations in question do not suppress points of view but instead suppress false and misleading statements of fact....

....

We conclude, accordingly, that here the trial court and the Court of Appeal erred in characterizing as noncommercial speech, under the First Amendment to the federal Constitution, Nike's allegedly false and misleading statements about labor practices and working conditions in factories where Nike products are made.

V. CONCLUSION

....

In concluding, contrary to the Court of Appeal, that Nike's speech at issue here is commercial speech, we do not decide whether that speech was, as plaintiff has alleged, false or misleading .... Our decision on the narrow issue before us on review does not foreclose those proceedings.

The judgment of the Court of Appeal is reversed, and the matter is remanded to that court for further proceedings consistent with this opinion.

DISSENT

CHIN, J.

I respectfully dissent.

Nike, Inc., is a major international corporation with a multibillion-dollar enterprise. The nature of its labor practices has become a subject of considerable public interest and scrutiny. Various persons and organizations have accused Nike of engaging in despicable practices, which they have described sometimes with such caustic and scathing words as "slavery" and "sweatshop." Nike's critics and these accusations receive full First Amendment protection. And well they should. "The First and Fourteenth Amendments embody our 'profound national commitment to the principle that debate on public issues should be uninhibited, robust, and wide-open . . . .'" . . . .

While Nike's critics have taken full advantage of their right to "'uninhibited, robust, and wide-open'" debate, the same cannot be said of Nike, the object of their ire. When Nike tries to defend itself from these attacks, the majority denies it the same First Amendment protection Nike's critics enjoy. Why is this, according to the majority? Because Nike competes not only in the marketplace of ideas, but also in the marketplace of manufactured goods. And because Nike sells shoes--and its defense against critics may help sell those shoes--the majority asserts that Nike may not freely engage in the debate, but must run the risk of lawsuits under California's unfair competition law and false advertising law, should it ever make a factual claim that turns out to be inaccurate. According to the majority, if Nike utters a factual misstatement, unlike its critics, it may be sued for restitution, civil penalties, and injunctive relief under these sweeping statutes.

Handicapping one side in this important worldwide debate is both ill considered and unconstitutional. Full free speech protection for one side and strict liability for the other will hardly promote vigorous and meaningful debate. . . .

In its pursuit to regulate Nike's speech--in hope of prohibiting false and misleading statements--the majority has unduly trammeled basic constitutional freedoms that form the foundation of this free government. . . .

BROWN, J.

I respectfully dissent.

In 1942, the United States Supreme Court, like a wizard trained at Hogwarts, waved its wand and "plucked the commercial doctrine out of thin air." Unfortunately, the court's doctrinal wizardry has created considerable confusion over the past 60 years as it has struggled to define the difference between commercial and noncommercial speech. The United States Supreme Court has, in recent years, acknowledged "the difficulty of drawing bright lines that will clearly cabin commercial speech in a distinct category." . . . .

Despite this chaos, the majority, ostensibly guided by *Bolger*, has apparently divined a new and simpler test for commercial speech. . . . Unfortunately, the majority has forgotten the teachings of H.L. Mencken: "every human problem" has a "solution" that is "neat, plausible, and wrong." Like the purported discovery of cold fusion over a decade ago, the majority's test for commercial speech promises much, but solves nothing. Instead of clarifying the commercial speech doctrine, the test violates fundamental principles of First Amendment jurisprudence by making the level of protection given speech dependent on the identity of the speaker--and not just the speech's content--and by stifling the ability of certain speakers to participate in the public debate. In doing so, the majority unconstitutionally favors some speakers over others and conflicts with the decisions of other courts.

. . . .

This simple categorization presupposes that commercial speech is wholly distinct from noncommercial speech and that all commercial speech has the same value under the First Amendment. The reality, however, is quite different. With the growth of commercialism, the politicization of commercial interests, and the increasing sophistication of commercial advertising over the past century, the gap between commercial and noncommercial speech is rapidly shrinking. As several commentators have observed, examples of the intersection between commercial speech and various forms of noncommercial speech, including scientific, political and religious speech, abound....

....

Constrained by this rigid dichotomy, I dissent because Nike's statements are more like noncommercial speech than commercial speech. Nike's commercial statements about its labor practices cannot be separated from its noncommercial statements about a public issue, because its labor practices are the public issue. Indeed, under the circumstances presented in this case, Nike could hardly engage in a general discussion on overseas labor exploitation and economic globalization without discussing its own labor practices. Thus, the commercial elements of Nike's statements are "inextricably intertwined" with their noncommercial elements....

....

Constrained by the United States Supreme Court's current formulation of the commercial speech doctrine, I would therefore conclude that Nike's press releases, letters, and other documents defending its overseas labor practices are noncommercial speech. Based on this conclusion, I would find the application of sections 17204 and 17535 to Nike's speech unconstitutional. Accordingly, I would affirm the judgment of the Court of Appeal.

GREATER NEW ORLEANS BROADCASTING ASS'N v. UNITED STATES
Supreme Court of the United States, 1999
527 U.S. 173

Justice STEVENS delivered the opinion of the Court.

Federal law prohibits some, but by no means all, broadcast advertising of lotteries and casino gambling. In *United States v. Edge Broadcasting Co.,* 509 U.S. 418 (1993), we upheld the constitutionality of 18 U.S.C. § 1304 as applied to broadcast advertising of Virginia's lottery by a radio station located in North Carolina, where no such lottery was authorized. Today we hold that § 1304 may not be applied to advertisements of private casino gambling that are broadcast by radio or television stations located in Louisiana, where such gambling is legal.

I

Through most of the 19th and the first half of the 20th centuries, Congress adhered to a policy that not only discouraged the operation of lotteries and similar schemes, but forbade the dissemination of information concerning such enterprises by use of the mails, even when the lottery in question was chartered by a state legislature. Consistent with this Court's earlier view that commercial advertising was unprotected by the First Amendment, see *Valentine v. Chrestensen,* 316 U.S. 52 (1942), we found that the notion that "lotteries . . . are supposed to have a demoralizing influence upon the people" provided sufficient justification for excluding circulars concerning such enterprises from the federal postal system....

Congress extended its restrictions on lottery-related information to broadcasting as communications technology made that practice both possible and profitable. It enacted the statute at issue in this case as § 316 of the Communications Act of 1934. Now codified at 18 U.S.C. § 1304 ("Broadcasting lottery information"), the statute prohibits radio and television broadcasting, by any station for which a license is required, of

> "any advertisement of or information concerning any lottery, gift enterprise, or similar scheme, offering prizes dependent in whole or in part upon lot or chance, or any list of the prizes drawn or awarded by means of any such lottery, gift enterprise, or scheme, whether said list contains any part or all of such prizes."

The statute provides that each day's prohibited broadcasting constitutes a separate offense punishable by a fine, imprisonment for not more than one year, or both. Although § 1304 is a criminal statute, the Solicitor General informs us that, in practice, the provision traditionally has been enforced by the Federal Communications Commission (FCC), which imposes administrative sanctions on radio and television licensees ....

During the second half of this century, Congress dramatically narrowed the scope of the broadcast prohibition in § 1304....

.... Responding to the growing popularity of State-run lotteries, in 1975 Congress enacted the provision that gave rise to our decision in *Edge.* [The statute] now exempts advertisements of State-conducted lotteries from the nationwide postal restrictions in §§ 1301 and 1302, and from the broadcast restriction in § 1304, when "broadcast by a radio or television station licensed to a location in . . . a State which conducts such a lottery." The § 1304 broadcast restriction remained in place, however, for stations licensed in States that do not conduct lotteries. In *Edge,* we held that this remaining restriction on broadcasts from nonlottery States, such as North Carolina, supported the "laws against gambling" in those jurisdictions and properly advanced the "congressional policy of balancing the interests of lottery and nonlottery States."

In 1988, Congress enacted two additional statutes that significantly curtailed the coverage of § 1304. First, the Indian Gaming Regulatory Act authorized Native American tribes to conduct various forms of gambling—including casino gambling—pursuant to tribal-State compacts if the State permits such gambling "for any purpose by any person, organization, or entity." ... Second, the Charity Games Advertising Clarification Act of 1988, extended the exemption from §§ 1301-1304 for state-run lotteries to include any other lottery, gift enterprise, or similar scheme—not prohibited by the law of the State in which it operates— when conducted by: (i) any governmental organization; (ii) any not-for-profit organization;

or (iii) a commercial organization as a promotional activity "clearly occasional and ancillary to the primary business of that organization." There is no dispute that the exemption ... applies to casinos conducted by State and local governments. And, unlike the 1975 broadcast exemption for advertisements of and information concerning State-conducted lotteries, the exemptions in both of these 1988 statutes are not geographically limited; they shield messages from § 1304's reach in States that do not authorize such gambling as well as those that do....

Thus, unlike the uniform federal antigambling policy that prevailed in 1934 when 18 U.S.C. § 1304 was enacted, federal statutes now accommodate both pro-gambling and antigambling segments of the national polity.

II

Petitioners are an association of Louisiana broadcasters and its members who operate FCC-licensed radio and television stations in the New Orleans metropolitan area. But for the threat of sanctions pursuant to § 1304 ... petitioners would broadcast promotional advertisements for gaming available at private, for-profit casinos that are lawful and regulated in both Louisiana and neighboring Mississippi. According to an FCC official, however, "under appropriate conditions, some broadcast signals from Louisiana broadcasting stations may be heard in neighboring states including Texas and Arkansas," where private casino gambling is unlawful.

Petitioners brought this action against the United States and the FCC in the District Court for the Eastern District of Louisiana, praying for a declaration that § 1304 ... violate[s] the First Amendment as applied to them, and for an injunction preventing enforcement of the statute.... [T]heDistrict Court ruled in favor of the Government. The Court applied the standard for assessing commercial speech restrictions set out in *Central Hudson Gas & Elec. Corp. v. Public Serv. Comm'n of N. Y.* (1980), and concluded that the restrictions at issue adequately advanced the Government's "substantial interest (1) in protecting the interest of nonlottery states, and (2) in reducing participation in gambling and thereby minimizing the social costs associated therewith." ....

A divided panel of the Court of Appeals for the Fifth Circuit agreed with the District Court's application of *Central Hudson,* and affirmed the grant of summary judgment to the Government....

The majority relied heavily on our decision in *Posadas de Puerto Rico Associates v. Tourism Co. of P. R.,* 478 U.S. 328 (1986), and endorsed the theory that, because gambling is in a category of "vice activity" that can be banned altogether, "advertising of gambling can lay no greater claim on constitutional protection than the underlying activity." ....

While the broadcasters' petition for certiorari was pending in this Court, we decided *44 Liquormart, Inc. v. Rhode Island,* 517 U.S. 484 (1996). Because the opinions in that case concluded that our precedent both preceding and following *Posadas* had applied the *Central Hudson* test more strictly—and because we had rejected the argument that the power to restrict speech about certain socially harmful activities was as broad as the power to prohibit such conduct—we granted the broadcasters' petition ....

III

In a number of cases involving restrictions on speech that is "commercial" in nature, we have employed *Central Hudson's* four-part test to resolve First Amendment challenges:

"At the outset, we must determine whether the expression is protected by the First Amendment. For commercial speech to come within that provision, it at least must concern lawful activity and not be misleading. Next, we ask whether the asserted governmental interest is substantial. If both inquiries yield positive answers, we must determine whether the regulation directly advances the governmental interest asserted, and whether it is not more extensive than is necessary to serve that interest." 447 U.S. at 566.

In this analysis, the Government bears the burden of identifying a substantial interest and justifying the challenged restriction....

IV

All parties to this case agree that the messages petitioners wish to broadcast constitute commercial speech, and that these broadcasts would satisfy the first part of the *Central Hudson* test: Their content is not misleading and concerns lawful activities, i.e., private casino gambling in Louisiana and Mississippi....

The second part of the *Central Hudson* test asks whether the asserted governmental interest served by the speech restriction is substantial. The Solicitor General identifies two such interests: (1) reducing the social costs associated with "gambling" or "casino gambling," and (2) assisting States that "restrict gambling" or "prohibit casino gambling" within their own borders. Underlying Congress' statutory scheme, the Solicitor General contends, is the judgment that gambling contributes to corruption and organized crime; underwrites bribery, narcotics trafficking, and other illegal conduct; imposes a regressive tax on the poor; and "offers a false but sometimes irresistible hope of financial advancement." With respect to casino gambling, the Solicitor General states that many of the associated social costs stem from "pathological" or "compulsive" gambling by approximately three million Americans, whose behavior is primarily associated with "continuous play" games, such as slot machines. ...

We can accept the characterization of these two interests as "substantial," but that conclusion is by no means self-evident. No one seriously doubts that the Federal Government may assert a legitimate and substantial interest in alleviating the societal ills recited above, or in assisting like-minded States to do the same. But in the judgment of both the Congress and many state legislatures, the social costs that support the suppression of gambling are offset, and sometimes outweighed, by countervailing policy considerations, primarily in the form of economic benefits. Despite its awareness of the potential social costs, Congress has not only sanctioned casino gambling for Indian tribes through tribal-state compacts, but has enacted other statutes that reflect approval of state legislation that authorizes a host of public and private gambling activities.... Whatever its character in 1934 when § 1304 was adopted, the federal policy of discouraging gambling in general, and casino gambling in particular, is now decidedly equivocal.

Of course, it is not our function to weigh the policy arguments on either side of the nationwide debate over whether and to what extent casino and other forms of gambling should be legalized.... But we cannot ignore Congress' unwillingness to adopt a single national policy that consistently endorses either interest asserted by the Solicitor General. Even though the Government has identified substantial interests, when we consider both their quality and the information sought to be suppressed, the crosscurrents in the scope and application of § 1304 become more difficult for the Government to defend.

V

The third part of the *Central Hudson* test asks whether the speech restriction directly and materially advances the asserted governmental interest. "This burden is not satisfied by mere speculation or conjecture; rather, a governmental body seeking to sustain a restriction on commercial speech must demonstrate that the harms it recites are real and that its restriction will in fact alleviate them to a material degree." ....

The fourth part of the test complements the direct-advancement inquiry of the third, asking whether the speech restriction is not more extensive than necessary to serve the interests that support it. The Government is not required to employ the least restrictive means conceivable, but it must demonstrate narrow tailoring of the challenged regulation to the asserted interest—"a fit that is not necessarily perfect, but reasonable; that represents not necessarily the single best disposition but one whose scope is in proportion to the interest served." On the whole, then, the challenged regulation should indicate that its proponent "'carefully calculated' the costs and benefits associated with the burden on speech imposed by its prohibition."

As applied to petitioners' case, § 1304 cannot satisfy these standards. With regard to the first asserted interest—alleviating the social costs of casino gambling by limiting demand—the Government contends that its broadcasting restrictions directly advance that interest because "promotional" broadcast advertising concerning casino gambling increases demand for such gambling, which in turn increases the amount of casino gambling that produces those social costs. Additionally, the Government believes that compulsive gamblers are especially susceptible to the pervasiveness and potency of broadcast advertising. Assuming the accuracy of this causal chain, it does not necessarily follow that the Government's speech ban has directly and materially furthered the asserted interest. While it is no doubt fair to assume that more advertising would have some impact on overall demand for gambling, it is also reasonable to assume that much of that advertising would merely channel gamblers to one casino rather than another. More important, any measure of the effectiveness of the Government's attempt to minimize the social costs of gambling cannot ignore Congress' simultaneous encouragement of tribal casino gambling, which may well be growing at a rate exceeding any increase in gambling or compulsive gambling that private casino advertising could produce.

We need not resolve the question whether any lack of evidence in the record fails to satisfy the standard of proof under *Central Hudson,* however, because the flaw in the Government's case is more fundamental: The operation of § 1304 and its attendant regulatory regime is so pierced by exemptions and inconsistencies that the Government cannot hope to exonerate it. Under current law, a broadcaster may not carry advertising about privately operated commercial casino gambling, regardless of the location of the station or the casino. On the other hand, advertisements for tribal casino gambling authorized by state compacts—whether operated by the tribe or by a private party pursuant to a management contract—are subject to no such broadcast ban, even if the broadcaster is located in or broadcasts to a jurisdiction with the strictest of antigambling policies. Government-operated, nonprofit, and "occasional and ancillary" commercial casinos are likewise exempt....

From what we can gather, the Government is committed to prohibiting accurate product information, not commercial enticements of all kinds, and then only when conveyed over certain forms of media and for certain types of gambling—indeed, for only certain brands of casino gambling—and despite the fact that messages about the availability of such gambling are being conveyed over the airwaves by other speakers....

.... There surely are practical and nonspeech-related forms of regulation—including a prohibition or supervision of gambling on credit; limitations on the use of cash machines on casino premises; controls on admissions; pot or betting limits; location restrictions; and licensing requirements—that could more directly and effectively alleviate some of the social costs of casino gambling....

The second interest asserted by the Government—the derivative goal of "assisting" States with policies that disfavor private casinos—adds little to its case. We cannot see how this broadcast restraint, ambivalent as it is, might directly and adequately further any state interest in dampening consumer demand for casino gambling if it cannot achieve the same goal with respect to the similar federal interest. Furthermore, even assuming that the state policies on which the Federal Government seeks to embellish are more coherent and pressing than their federal counterpart, § 1304 sacrifices an intolerable amount of truthful speech about lawful conduct when compared to all of the policies at stake and the social ills that one could reasonably hope such a ban to eliminate. The Government argues that petitioners' speech about private casino gambling should be prohibited in Louisiana because, "under appropriate conditions," citizens in neighboring States like Arkansas and Texas (which host tribal but not private commercial casino gambling) might hear it and make rash or costly decisions. To be sure, in order to achieve a broader objective such regulations may incidentally, even deliberately, restrict a certain amount of speech not thought to contribute significantly to the dangers with which the Government is concerned. But Congress' choice here was neither a rough approximation of efficacy, nor a reasonable accommodation of competing State and private interests. Rather, the regulation distinguishes among the indistinct, permitting a variety of speech that poses the same risks the Government purports to fear, while banning messages unlikely to cause any harm at all. Considering the manner in which § 1304 and its exceptions operate and the scope of the speech it proscribes, the Government's second asserted interest provides no more convincing basis for upholding the regulation than the first.

.... The judgment of the Court of Appeals is therefore

Reversed.

Justice THOMAS, concurring in the judgment.

I continue to adhere to my view that "in cases such as this, in which the government's asserted interest is to keep legal users of a product or service ignorant in order to manipulate their choices in the marketplace," the *Central Hudson* test should not be applied because "such an 'interest' is per se illegitimate and can no more justify regulation of 'commercial speech' than it can justify regulation of 'noncommercial' speech." *44 Liquormart, Inc. v. Rhode Island,* 517 U.S. 484, 518 (1996) (concurring in part and concurring in the judgment). Accordingly, I concur only in the judgment.

FTC v. Colgate-Palmolive Co.
Supreme Court of the United States, 1965
380 U.S. 374

Chief Justice WARREN delivered the opinion of the Court.

The basic question before us is whether it is a deceptive trade practice, prohibited by § 5 of the Federal Trade Commission Act, to represent falsely that a televised test, experiment, or demonstration provides a viewer with visual proof of a product claim, regardless of whether the product claim is itself true.

The case arises out of an attempt by respondent Colgate-Palmolive Company to prove to the television public that its shaving cream, "Rapid Shave," out-shaves them all. Respondent Ted Bates & Company, Inc., an advertising agency, prepared for Colgate three one-minute commercials designed to show that Rapid Shave could soften even the toughness of sandpaper. Each of the commercials contained the same "sandpaper test." The announcer informed the audience that, "To prove RAPID SHAVE'S super-moisturizing power, we put it right from the can onto this tough, dry sandpaper. It was apply * * * soak * * * and off in a stroke." While the announcer was speaking, Rapid Shave was applied to a substance that appeared to be sandpaper, and immediately thereafter a razor was shown shaving the substance clean.

The Federal Trade Commission issued a complaint against respondents Colgate and Bates charging that the commercials were false and deceptive. The evidence before the hearing examiner disclosed that sandpaper of the type depicted in the commercials could not be shaved immediately following the application of Rapid Shave, but required a substantial soaking period of approximately eighty minutes. The evidence also showed that the substance resembling sandpaper was in fact a simulated prop, or "mock-up," made of plexiglass to which sand had been applied. However, the examiner found that Rapid Shave could shave sandpaper, even though not in the short time represented by the commercials, and that if real sandpaper had been used in the commercials the inadequacies of television transmission would have made it appear to viewers to be nothing more than plain, colored paper. The examiner dismissed the complaint because neither misrepresentation—concerning the actual moistening time or the identity of the shaved substance—was in his opinion a material one that would mislead the public.

The Commission, in an opinion dated December 29, 1961, reversed the hearing examiner. It found that since Rapid Shave could not shave sandpaper within the time depicted in the commercials, respondents had misrepresented the product's moisturizing power. Moreover, the Commission found that the undisclosed use of a plexiglass substitute for sandpaper was an additional material misrepresentation that was a deceptive act separate and distinct from the misrepresentation concerning Rapid Shave's underlying qualities. Even if the sandpaper could be shaved just as depicted in the commercials, the Commission found that viewers had been misled into believing they had seen it done with their own eyes. As a result of these findings the Commission entered a cease-and-desist order against the respondents.

An appeal was taken to the Court of Appeals for the First Circuit.... That court sustained the Commission's conclusion that respondents had misrepresented the qualities of Rapid Shave, but it would not accept the Commission's order forbidding the future use of undisclosed simulations in television commercials.... We granted certiorari to consider this aspect of the case and do not have before us any question concerning the misrepresentation that Rapid Shave could shave sandpaper immediately after application, that being conceded.

....

II

In reviewing the substantive issues in the case, it is well to remember the respective roles of the Commission and the courts in the administration of the Federal Trade Commission Act. When the Commission was created by Congress in 1914, it was directed by § 5 to prevent "[u]nfair methods of competition in commerce." Congress amended the Act in 1938 to extend the Commission's jurisdiction to include "unfair or deceptive acts or practices in commerce"—a significant amendment showing Congress' concern for consumers as well as for competitors....

This statutory scheme necessarily gives the Commission an influential role in interpreting § 5 and in applying it to the facts of particular cases arising out of unprecedented situations. Moreover, as an administrative agency that deals continually with cases in the area, the Commission is often in a better position than are courts to determine when a practice is "deceptive" within the meaning of the Act. This Court has frequently stated that the Commission's judgment is to be given great weight by reviewing courts.... Nevertheless, while informed judicial determination is dependent upon enlightenment gained from administrative experience, in the last analysis the words "deceptive practices" set forth a legal standard and they must get their final meaning from judicial construction.

... We granted certiorari to consider the Commission's conclusion that even if an advertiser has himself conducted a test, experiment, or demonstration which he honestly believes will prove a certain product claim, he may not convey to television viewers the false impression that they are seeing the test, experiment, or demonstration for themselves, when they are not because of the undisclosed use of mock-ups.

We accept the Commission's determination that the commercials involved in this case contained three representations to the public: (1) that sandpaper could be shaved by Rapid Shave; (2) that an experiment had been conducted which verified this claim; and (3) that the viewer was seeing this experiment for himself. Respondents admit that the first two representations were made, but deny the third was.... The parties agree that § 5 prohibits the intentional misrepresentation of any fact that would constitute a material factor in a purchaser's decision to buy. Respondents submit, in effect, that the only material facts are those that deal with the substantive qualities of a product. The Commission, on the other hand, submits that the misrepresentation of *any* fact so long as it materially induces a purchaser's decision to buy is a deception prohibited by § 5.

The Commission's interpretation of what is a deceptive practice seems more in line with the decided cases than that of respondents. It has long been considered a deceptive practice to state falsely that a product ordinarily sells for an inflated price but that it is being offered at a special reduced price, even if the offered price represents the actual value of the product and the purchaser is receiving his money's worth....

It has also been held a violation of § 5 for a seller to misrepresent to the public that he is in a certain line of business, even though the misstatement in no way affects the qualities of the product. As was said in *Federal Trade Comm. v. Royal Milling Co.:*

> If consumers or dealers prefer to purchase a given article because it was made by a particular manufacturer or class of manufacturers, they have a right to do so, and this right cannot be satisfied by imposing upon them an exactly similar article, or one equally as good, but having a different origin.

The courts of appeals have applied this reasoning to the merchandising of reprocessed products that are as good as new, without a disclosure that they are in fact reprocessed. And it has also been held that it is a deceptive practice to misappropriate the trade name of another.

Respondents claim that all these cases are irrelevant to our discussion because they involve misrepresentation related to the product itself and not merely to the manner in which an advertising message is communicated. This distinction misses the mark for two reasons. In the first place, the present case is not concerned with a mode of communication, but with a misrepresentation that viewers have objective proof of a seller's word. Secondly, all of the above cases, like the present case, deal with methods designed to get a consumer to purchase a product, not with whether the product, when purchased, will perform up to expectations. We find an especially strong similarity between the present case and those cases in which a seller induces the public to purchase an arguably good product by misrepresenting his line of business, by concealing the fact that the product is reprocessed, or by misappropriating another's trademark. In each the seller has used a misrepresentation to break down what he regards to be an annoying or irrational habit of the buying public—the preference for particular manufacturers or known brands regardless of a product's actual qualities, the prejudice against reprocessed goods, and the desire for verification of a product claim. In each case the seller reasons that when the habit is broken the buyer will be satisfied with the performance of the product he receives. Yet, a misrepresentation has been used to break the habit and a misrepresentation for such an end is not permitted.

… [T]here are other situations which also illustrate the correctness of the Commission's finding in the present case. It is generally accepted that it is a deceptive practice to state falsely that a product has received a testimonial from a respected source. In addition, the Commission has consistently acted to prevent sellers from falsely stating that their product claims have been "certified." We find these situations to be indistinguishable from the present case. We can assume that in each the underlying product claim is true and in each the seller actually conducted an experiment sufficient to prove to himself the truth of the claim. But in each the seller has told the public that it could rely on something other than his word concerning both the truth of the claim and the validity of his experiment. We find it an immaterial difference that in one case the viewer is told to rely on the word of a celebrity or authority he respects, in another on the word of a testing agency, and in the present case on his own perception of an undisclosed simulation.

Respondents again insist that the present case is not like any of the above, but is more like a case in which a celebrity or independent testing agency has in fact submitted a written verification of an experiment actually observed, but, because of the inability of the camera to transmit accurately an impression of the paper on which the testimonial is written, the seller reproduces it on another substance so that it can be seen by the viewing audience. This analogy ignores the finding of the Commission that in the present case the seller misrepresented to the public that it was being given objective proof of a product claim. In respondents' hypothetical the objective proof of the product claim that is offered, the word of the celebrity or agency that the experiment was actually conducted, does exist; while in the case before us the objective proof offered, the viewer's own perception of an actual experiment, does not exist....

We agree with the Commission, therefore, that the undisclosed use of plexiglass in the present commercials was a material deceptive practice, independent and separate from the other misrepresentation found.... Respondents claim that it will be impractical to inform the viewing public that it is not seeing an actual test, experiment, or demonstration, but we think it inconceivable that the ingenious advertising world will be unable, if it so desires, to conform to the Commission's insistence that the public be not misinformed....

III

We turn our attention now to the order issued by the Commission....

The Court of Appeals has criticized the reference in the Commission's order to "test, experiment, or demonstration" as not capable of practical interpretation. It could find no difference between the Rapid Shave commercial and a commercial which extolled the goodness of ice cream while giving viewers a picture of a scoop of mashed potatoes appearing to be ice cream. We do not understand this difficulty. In the ice cream case the mashed potato prop is not being used for additional proof of the product claim, while the purpose of the Rapid Shave commercial is to give the viewer objective proof of the claims made. If in the ice cream hypothetical the focus of the commercial becomes the undisclosed potato prop and the viewer is invited, explicitly or by implication, to see for himself the truth of the claims about the ice cream's rich texture and full color, and perhaps compare it to a "rival product," then the commercial has become similar to the one now before us. Clearly, however, a commercial which depicts happy actors delightedly eating ice cream that is in fact mashed potatoes or drinking a product appearing to be coffee but which is in fact some other substance is not covered by the present order.

... We believe that respondents will have no difficulty applying the Commission's order to the vast majority of their contemplated future commercials....

Reversed and remanded.

GLOSSARY OF LEGAL TERMS

Following are some common legal terms relevant to the substance or procedural aspects of communications law:

Absolutist. One who interprets the First Amendment of the Constitution to provide absolute protection for speech, subject to no exceptions.

Action. A lawsuit.

Affirm. To uphold the decision of a lower court.

Answer. A defendant's formal legal response to a civil complaint. The answer might deny facts alleged by the plaintiff, or it might claim certain legal defenses or privileges.

Appellant. The party that appeals a court judgment to a higher court; sometimes also called the *petitioner.*

Appellate court. A review court that determines whether the court below made any errors in its application of the law and whether those errors warrant a different result.

Appropriation. The commercial use of a person's name or likeness without consent. One of the commonly recognized forms of invasion of privacy.

Arraignment. A proceeding in which an accused is brought before the court to hear the charge against him and to enter a plea of "guilty" or "not guilty."

Bench trial. A trial in which all factual and legal determinations are made by a judge, without the presence of a jury.

Brief. A persuasive document prepared by the lawyer arguing a case in court. It sets forth the factual and legal arguments being made on the client's behalf.

Cause of action. A particular factual occurrence or circumstance that entitles a person to sue.

Certiorari. A discretionary order commonly used by the U.S. Supreme Court to indicate which cases the Court will hear on appeal. This is also referred to as granting "cert."

Common law. Legal rules and principles that originate solely from court decisions, as distinguished from the laws enacted by legislative bodies.

Complaint. The initial court document filed by a plaintiff. It identifies the alleged legal violation and formally requests a legal remedy, such as monetary compensation.

Continuance. A court order postponing a trial or other proceeding to a later time or day.

Damages. Monetary compensation that may be recovered in court by a person who was unlawfully harmed by another.

Defendant. The party against whom a legal remedy is sought in a civil lawsuit, or against whom punishment is sought in a criminal case.

Demurrer. A challenge to the legal sufficiency of an opposing party's pleading. Usually filed by a civil defendant, alleging that the plaintiff's complaint fails to state grounds for a valid legal claim.

Dictum. A superfluous comment in a judicial opinion; a statement that is not necessary to the court's decision and therefore does not carry the force of precedent.

Discovery. The ascertainment of relevant facts, prior to trial, by the parties to a lawsuit. Formal discovery tools used by lawyers include oral depositions, requests to produce documents, and mental examinations.

Diversity action. A lawsuit that comes within the jurisdiction of the federal courtsbecause the parties are citizens of different states.

Equal time rule. A statutory requirement that whenever one candidate for public office uses broadcast time, the radio or TV station must afford equal opportunity to all other candidates in the race.

Fair use doctrine. A limited privilege to use copyrighted material for productive purposes without the owner's consent.

Fairness doctrine. A Federal Communications Commission rule requiring, among other things, that broadcasters provide contrasting viewpoints on public issues. The main provisions of the doctrine were abandoned by the FCC in 1987, but some in Congress have since vowed to enact the doctrine as a statute.

False light. A wrongful representation of an individual in a false and highly offensive manner before the public. Recognized in many states as a form of invasion of privacy.

Freedom of Information Act (FOIA). An act of Congress requiring that most documents of federal agencies be open to public inspection.

Gag order. A court order directing attorneys, witnesses, or other trial participants not to discuss the case with the media. Sometimes a gag order is aimed at news reporters, directing them not to report on legal proceedings until the proceedings are concluded. Also called a *restrictive order.*

Grand jury. A body of citizens whose duty is to determine whether probable cause exists to formally charge someone with a crime.

Holding. The central legal principle to be drawn from a court decision.

Indictment. The formal accusation issued by a grand jury against a person charged with a crime.

Injunction. A court order that a defendant act, or refrain from acting, in a particular manner.

Intellectual property. Products of the mind, including copyrights, trademarks, and patents, that have legal status apart from any physical property in which they may be embodied.

Intrusion. A tort consisting of a highly offensive invasion of a person's physical seclusion or private affairs. One of the legally compensable forms of invasion of privacy.

Judgment of the court. The final decree of a court—the disposition of the case, the determination of which side "wins." At the appellate level, the judgment usually is to *affirm* or *reverse* the judgment of the court below.

Liable. Legally responsible; obliged to pay compensation.

Libel. A false communication that wrongfully injures the reputation of another. In many jurisdictions *libel* refers only to defamation that occurs in writing; oral defamation is called *slander*.

Litigant. A party to a lawsuit; a plaintiff or defendant.

Motion. A formal request that a judge make some kind of ruling in favor of the applicant. Examples: motion for a continuance, motion for summary judgment.

Opinion of the court. An official, written explanation of the reasons behind a court's judgment. Opinions are generally issued for publication only by appellate courts, though some trial courts also issue written opinions.

Per curiam. "By the court." A *per curiam* appellate opinion is an unsigned opinion that represents the court as a whole, as distinguished from an opinion signed by a particular judge.

Plaintiff. The party who initiates a civil lawsuit.

Pleadings. Court documents which contain the parties' formal allegations of their respective claims or defenses. Examples include the plaintiff's *complaint* and the defendant's *answer*.

Preliminary hearing. In criminal cases, a hearing to determine whether the government truly has enough evidence against the accused to warrant a full-blown trial.

Prior restraint. A government restraint on expression that is imposed prior to publication or other dissemination to the public, as distinguished from sanctions imposed following publication.

Probable cause. Reasonable ground to believe that a person has committed a crime.

Punitive damages. A monetary sum awarded to a plaintiff, over and above the amount needed to compensate the plaintiff for his property loss or injury. Punitive damages, also called *exemplary damages*, are awarded in order to punish a defendant for malicious conduct.

Respondent. The party against whom an appeal is made.

Restraining order. An interim court order forbidding the defendant from engaging in allegedly harmful behavior. Typically it is effective until a full proceeding can be conducted on the plaintiff's application for a permanent injunction.

Scarcity rationale. The primary legal justification for broadcast regulation, based on the fact that the radio spectrum is limited and cannot accommodate all who might wish to be broadcasters.

Standing. A direct, tangible, legally protectable stake in a legal controversy. It is a basic principle of law that a party must have standing to sue.

Stay. A court order that stops or temporarily suspends a judicial proceeding or the enforcement of a law or judgment.

Strict scrutiny. In constitutional law, the strictest level of judicial review for statutes and other actions of government. Under strict scrutiny, government action that impedes freedom of speech can be valid only if the action is found to serve a compelling public interest.

Subpoena. A command, backed by legal authority, to appear at a designated time and place to give testimony.

Subpoena *duces tecum.* A command to turn over stipulated notes, photographs, videotape, or other documentary evidence that is deemed relevant to a legal proceeding.

Summary judgment. A common procedure for ending a lawsuit prior to trial. A party to a lawsuit is entitled to summary judgment in his favor if there is no disputable issue of fact and established legal rules clearly dictate that he would prevail at trial.

Sunshine Act. The federal open-meetings law. It requires public access to the meetings of about fifty federal agencies, including the Federal Trade Commission and the Federal Communications Commission.

Time, place, and manner restriction. A government limitation on speech that is not based on the content of expression. Such a restriction is more likely to be constitutionally valid than an outright ban or a content-based limitation.

Tort. A wrongful act, other than breach of contract, for which the law gives the injured party some legal remedy against the wrongdoer in civil court. Examples include invasion of privacy, trespass, libel, infliction of mental distress, and negligence.

Trial court. The first court to handle a legal dispute. In this court evidence is presented to determine the facts of the case, and the trial judge applies the law to those facts.

U.S. Court of Appeals. The main appellate court in the federal judicial system—the next step up from district court.

U.S. District Court. The main trial court in the federal judicial system.

U.S. Supreme Court. The top court in the federal judicial system and the final authority on the meaning of the U.S. Constitution.

Venue. The county or district in which a criminal or civil case may properly be filed and adjudicated.

Voir dire. The questioning of prospective jurors to determine if they should sit on the jury in a particular case.